THE
WESTERN'S HYDRAULICS

J.K. Lewis

Book Law Publications
Nottingham

Bathed in the early morning light of 7 January 1977, D1048 *Western Lady* pauses to change crews at Westbury with a heavy stone train from Merehead Quarry. *(David Birt)*

THE
WESTERN'S
HYDRAULICS

J.K. Lewis

Book Law Publications

Nottingham

First published by Atlantic Transport Publishers, 1977
Published 2006 by Book Law Publications

© J.K. Lewis 1977

ISBN 1-901945-54-5

Printed by The Amadeus Press, Cleckheaton, BD19 4TQ

CONTENTS

INTRODUCTION

IT is now little more than a matter of record that the mainline diesel-hydraulic locomotives placed in service by the Western Region of British Railways between 1958 and 1965 proved controversial from the very outset. In the midst of a huge national modernisation scheme largely intended to emulate the dieselisation policies which had swept steam traction from North America's railroads in something less than a decade, the Western Region argued for and eventually gained grudging approval to focus its own plans around the sort of lightweight diesel-hydraulics then entering service in West Germany. The stage was thus set for the introduction of a fleet of technically-advanced units of motive power that would lay the foundations of the high-speed railway of the future, yet bring the WR into direct conflict both with its political masters and the remainder of BR. What is remarkable is the degree of interest in and argument about the merits of the WR's diesel-hydraulics which persists some forty years after these events were set in motion.

The present volume is by no means the first to chart this intriguing chapter of Britain's railway history, nor is it likely to prove the last, such is the continuing vigour of the debate. Some historians have concluded the WR's independent traction policy to be an inspired piece of foresight, whilst others see it as merely another attempt by a haughty and aloof regional administration to be different. Most agree that the Western Region experienced considerable difficulties in adjusting to the reality of no longer being the master in its own house, but opinions are still divided as to exactly why what once promised to be the most significant episode in locomotive engineering since the days of Churchward in fact developed into one of the costliest and most notorious *debàcles* of British Railways' whole existence.

It is the duty of this author to declare a personal interest in and affection for what may well be regarded as the final flowering of the Great Western's independent outlook, though it is to be hoped that this has not unduly prejudiced the maintenance of an objective stance in the preparation of this volume. One element of this objectivity is the frequent reference to events on railway systems overseas, especially in West Germany and the United States, and whilst it is appreciated that these may be of limited interest to readers approaching the subject from a British perspective, their inclusion is an important part of the text. As one of the cradles of practical large-scale railway dieselisation, the United States provided a model which British Railways was to follow with some considerable vigour, even though time and experience would eventually show it not only to be imperfect but also incompatible with many of the conditions under which BR was forced to labour. Nevertheless, American influences remained prevalent on BR well into the nineteen-sixties and themselves served to militate against the British adoption of the rather different technologies espoused by the railways of many other countries, none more so than

the West German diesel-hydraulics favoured by the WR. Worthy of particular attention are the levels of service performance obtained by the Deutsche Bundesbahn from its V200s, the machines which provided the inspiration for the separatist WR policy, and these are examined in detail in order to provide perspective for the story of mainline diesel-hydraulics on British Railways. Also of interest is the challenge posed by diesel-hydraulics of similar lineage to the strong diesel-electric school in the United States during the 1960s, if only due to the essential similarities with the political and operational factors affecting the WR, and a brief summary of this episode is included along with the detailed description of the parent V200s.

Obviously, within the parameters of any book of this kind it would be impossible to record every item of available information, and accordingly there are necessary limitations of which the reader should be aware. Operational history has had to be limited to a 'broad brush' approach concentrating upon the more salient points of the WR fleet's career, as has the coverage of diesel-hydraulic traction abroad. Likewise, the author has elected to forgo a blow-by-blow account of the events behind the design and construction of each individual locomotive type in order to allow more space in which to analyse the reasoning behind and practical impact of the opposing WR and BTC-Central policies. By contrast, some previous commentators have chosen to exclude the D9500 0-6-0s from their examinations of the WR's diesel-hydraulic fleet, on the basis that they did not feature in the original 1955 motive power strategy. Whilst a valid point, neither did the two North British designs nor, for that matter, the Beyer-Peacock 'Hymeks' and yet all three types are vital components of the story as a whole. As the D9500s originated from the same expansion of the Pilot Scheme as the 'Hymeks', and were constructed at Swindon exclusively for WR use, the author has chosen to include them in this survey. It is up to the reader to draw his or her own conclusions about the impact of each on WR dieselisation.

Without a doubt, the WR's diesel-hydraulics were for much of their lives very much less successful than had been hoped for. Despite this, they still managed to produce some of the most outstanding examples of locomotive performance of their time, and one cannot help but wonder what could have been achieved if only the original proposals had not been so drastically reshaped by political and economic forces. If, some twenty years on, this work merely succeeds in helping to set a sometimes obscure record straight, the author for one will consider it to have served its purpose well.

J.K. Lewis
November 1996

Right: In the company of Brush Type 4s, 'Hymek' No.7017 takes fuel at Ranelagh Bridge, just outside Paddington Station, on 25 April 1973 *(Brian Morrison)*

ACKNOWLEDGEMENTS

Without the assistance of the following organisations this book could not have been, and sincere gratitude is expressed for their invaluable help.

Krauss-Maffei AG, Munich, Germany
Motoren und Turbinen Union Gmbh, Friedrichshafen, Germany
JM Voith Gmbh, Heidenheim, Germany
MAN-GHH (Great Britain) Ltd, London
British Brown-Boveri Ltd, Telford, Shropshire
GEC-Paxman Diesels Ltd, Colchester, Essex
Brush Electrical Machines Ltd, Loughborough, Leicestershire
The National Railway Museum, York
The Public Record Office, Kew
The History & Glasgow Room, The Mitchell Library, Glasgow

Sincere thanks are also due to the following individuals for their help and patience during the course of this project:

C.P Atkins, Robert Baker, Hugh Ballantyne, David Birt, C.G. Bulman, Gunter Burr, Elizabeth Carmichael, Tim Edmonds, D.J. Everson, G.F. Gillham, Tom Heavyside, Margit Heil, J.C. Hillmer, P.J. Horton, David Joy, W.A. Kelsey, Nigel Kendall, Kevin Lane, Colin G. Maggs, Colin J. Marsden, J.N. Mays, Brian J. Miller, Brian Morrison, Peter Nicholson, B.J. Nicolle, Dr L.A. Nixon, Norman E. Preedy, Peter J. Robinson, D. Trevor Rowe, G. Scott-Lowe, Paul Shannon, R.H.G. Simpson, Roger Siviter, Mrs G. Steinert, D.H. Tompkins, J. Watson, J.S. Whiteley, Graham B. Wise, E.W. Youldon, A.V. Zahler.

Chapter 1

MODERNISATION AND THE WESTERN REGION

GIVEN its penchant for publicity over much of its 109-year life, the Great Western Railway was allowed to slip away very quietly indeed on the night of 31 December 1947, the last Great Western train from London departing for Penzance behind No.5037 *Monmouth Castle* without any hint of celebration. Indeed, it can now be argued that, for the Great Western at least, there was very little to celebrate about, as the placing of the four mainline railway companies under Government control through the auspices of the British Transport Commission would do much to foster a bureaucracy largely unmoved by the sort of enterprise and individual initiative that many thought to epitomise the GWR.

This, however, all lay in the future, and overnight the Great Western simply became the Western Region of the BTC's Railway Executive, headquartered in the former Hotel Great Central at 222 Marylebone Road, London. For the important post of Chairman, the BTC had originally chosen the Great Western's last General Manager, Sir James Milne, whose experience in the field of railway administration by far exceeded that of any other candidate. To its displeasure, though, the Commission found Sir James unwilling to postpone his retirement or abandon his opposition to the basic concept of a nationalised railway, and when it became apparent that he was unable to agree terms of reference with the BTC, the task of heading the Executive fell to Sir Eustace Missenden, latterly General Manager of the Southern Railway. Milne's reluctance to preside over the running of the infant British Railways was blamed for encouraging an intransigent attitude amongst Great Western senior management as a whole and, whether this was fair criticism or not, it is true that several of his former colleagues also declined to serve on the Railway Executive at that time. As a result, Great Western representation on the RE was distinctly marginal, consisting of former Chief Goods Manager David Blee, who took up the post of Commercial Member. Several contemporary observers noted that Blee seemed to be uncomfortable in his new position, and it is certainly indisputable that the presentation of Western Region concerns at an executive level proved somewhat less than effective for the first few years of the new regime.

In addition to Missenden and Blee, the RE included five other full-time members dealing with the various aspects of running a railway, two of whom (V.M. Barrington-Ward, in charge of operations, and J.C.L. Train, responsible for civil engineering) came from LNER backgrounds, the staff member, W.P. Allen, from the trades-union movement, and the Deputy Chairman, General Sir William Slim, from the armed forces. By far the most difficult position to fill had been that of Member for Mechanical & Electrical Engineering, whose responsibilities would include not only the formulation of many of the most important policies of the new nationalised railway but also the unification of the disparate practices of the old 'Big Four' companies. The task would require foresight, resolve and tact in equal measure, and the appointment was complicated by the need to have a figure able to build a rapport with all parts of the railway network, each of which would retain its own hierarchy

of engineering designers. The Minister of Transport's eventual choice was Robert A. Riddles, latterly the Vice-President for Engineering of the London, Midland and Scottish Railway and before that Director of Transportation Equipment for the Ministry of Supply. Already familiar with the difficult task of binding rival concerns together in the pursuit of a common objective, to Riddles would fall many of the responsibilities for modernising a system wearied both by war and by worsening economic fortunes.

On the motive power side, all new construction excepting that already underway was cancelled upon nationalisation, making an entirely fresh start at least theoretically possible, and thus confronting Riddles with the dilemma of whether to invest in steam, diesel or electric motive power. Although Britain's railways were still largely reliant upon steam traction, increasing demands for speed and operating economy, coupled with demonstrations of successful mainline electrification both in Europe and the United States, did much to commend the latter as the logical choice for future construction. Mainline electrification in Britain, however, already had a sporadic history, with different initiatives at different times using largely incompatible equipment. Of the four pre-nationalisation companies, it was the Southern Railway that had the greatest mileage of electrified trackage, a 600V dc third-rail system radiating out of London into the Home Counties to handle the very considerable commuter traffic. The Southern had intended eventually to electrify its entire network, but the combined effects of the Depression and World War II meant that, by the time of nationalisation, there were still large tracts of its system reliant upon steam. Electrified suburban railways were also to be found on both the London, Midland and Scottish and the London and North Eastern Railways, but the only true mainline electrification scheme existed on the LNER, starting with the former North Eastern Railway's coal-hauling Newport-Shildon line which had been electrified since 1916. The NER had been hoping to expand the network to cover passenger traffic between Newcastle and York but work had been delayed, first by World War I and then the 1923 Grouping. The success of the Newport-Shildon line undoubtedly contributed to the 1927 Weir Report's recommendation that mainline railways across the British Isles should be electrified, but the LNER had not the capital necessary to expand the scheme, and by the mid-1930s rising costs and falling traffic would mandate a return to steam working. Nowhere else was there the money required to implement the scale of change advocated by the Weir Report, but in 1936 the LNER did commence work on electrifying the former Great Central Manchester-Sheffield line on a 1500V dc overhead catenary system. Work was well advanced by the outbreak of war in 1939 and when work resumed in the late 1940s, it was confidently expected in many quarters that the Woodhead Electrification would provide a blueprint for future modernisation.

As always, the undeniable advantages of an electric railway had to be balanced against its enormous initial cost, and this was the argument that would be echoed by the powerful and vociferous lobby in favour of the diesel. Diesels had been used extensively in the United States since the mid-1930s and, by the end of World War II, steam locomotive production in that country had ceased almost entirely. Advocates of the diesel pointed out its greater cleanliness, operating economy, capacity for work and availability, and found its stark modernity no hindrance in a country hungry for change. The main disadvantage from the railways' point of view was an initial cost about three times greater than that of comparable steam traction, largely due to the diesel's requirement for a costly transmission system capable of matching engine speed to track speed. This was a direct result of the diesel engine's characteristics of torque developed over a relatively limited speed range, below which the engine would stall, whereas maximum horsepower would be developed near to or at the engine's maximum rotational speed. Early attempts to reconcile these demands to railway traction use had seen such machines as the Sulzer-Börsig and Kitson-Still locomotives where large cylinders directly connected to the driving wheels operated on compressed air or steam at low track speeds, changing to diesel operation as velocity increased. The abject failure of these creations to rival the performance of contemporary steam locomotives confirmed the suspicions of many that the diesel would only be harnessed as a viable railway prime mover when allied to a transmission unit capable of coupling it to the driven wheels through gearing appropriate to the prevailing conditions. The simplest solution would have been the sort of multiple-speed constant-mesh gearbox then used on road vehicles, but this was unsuitable for large high-powered locomotives due to the lack of suitable clutch materials, let alone the problems that would be encountered by the driver in manually selecting gears of the requisite size. Accordingly, the development of the mainline diesel locomotive in Britain, as elsewhere, focused upon two specific transmission modes; electric and hydraulic. The only exception to this rule was the outlandish 'Fell' diesel-mechanical 2-D-2, which quickly proved itself too complex to be a viable proposition.

From his perspective, Riddles was diametrically opposed to the mass purchase of mainline diesel locomotives, seeing it as an unnecessary expense that would succeed only in delaying his ultimate goal of widespread electrification. Although in favour of diesel shunters - influenced, no doubt, by his experiences on the LMS - and diesel railcars for local trains, Riddles wanted the principal services electrified. Under the terms of Government instructions on capital spending, however, he was unable to proceed in this direction. The simple reality of the situation was that, after six years of war, the railways needed every penny they could get in order to carry out long-overdue repair work and, in view of the extensive need for postwar reconstruction in all areas of the country, the Government was unwilling to commit significant sums of money to railway modernisation. As a result, and in the face of considerable opposition, Riddles took the controversial yet ineluctable decision to retain steam for the time being, meeting immediate demands for additional motive power through the creation of a new range of standard designs for use on all regions of British Railways. Recognising that the time taken to implement even this measure would exceed the railways' ability to manage with existing locomotive stocks, Riddles sanctioned the continuance of pre-nationalisation building programmes until 1951. For four years, therefore, railway workshops continued to manufacture new engines to pre-war designs, along with a small number of diesel shunters and prototype mainline diesels, after which locomotives to the new BR Standard designs would at last begin to enter traffic. The deployment of these would occupy the affairs of BR's mechanical engineers to the exclusion of all else, certainly until October 1953 when the Railway Executive was abolished and Riddles retired in protest against the new order.

Against all expectations, this policy allowed Swindon to produce locomotives of unashamedly Great Western parentage into the early nineteen-fifties. A criticism commonly levelled at the GWR was that through the 1920s and especially the 1930s the company had not evolved the sort of large new designs being unveiled by its competitors, though even its most ardent detractors conceded the unquestionable advantages of a range of effective, highly standardised locomotives, few of which were more than forty years of age. The magnitude of the improvements brought by Churchward's Franco-American-inspired engineering revolution at the turn of the century had been such that, for more than thirty years, Swindon had not needed to tread anything than an innately conservative path but, under Charles Collett, a production engineer who lacked much of Churchward's pioneering spirit, stagnation had begun to set in. Coupled with the various tensions brought about first by the Grouping of 1923 and then the Depression of the 1930s, this promoted an atmosphere at Swindon whereby there was a very real fear of making any alterations to standard practice, regardless of how inappropriate to current conditions it might be. Often referred to by scornful and perhaps envious outsiders as 'Wiltshire Wisdom', this self-imposed isolation inevitably brought about a dangerous state of complacency that would prove itself to be one of the company's worst enemies as the Great Western fell behind in the fields of internal streamlining and high superheat. Rudely awakened by the pressures of World War II and under the stewardship of the Great Western's last CME, F.W. Hawksworth, Swindon had at last embarked upon making good the lost ground of the Collett era, but was ultimately hampered by wartime restrictions and constrained even further by post-1948 bureaucracy.

Nevertheless, by 1951 the Western Region possessed a range of steam locomotives that were comparatively undated in design terms and which could, and indeed were to be brought up to full effectiveness through the application of cheap and simple modifications. That these constituted the vast bulk of the WR's motive power did not reflect any lack of enterprise within the company itself so much as the absence of a spur to do anything to the contrary. The Great Western had been well aware of the evolution of forms of locomotion other than steam and had pursued these developments with interest and enthusiasm where it was felt that some benefit might accrue through their adoption. As early as 1892, discussions had been held at a high level regarding the possible electrification of the Severn Tunnel and were only abandoned when Churchward's new range of steam locomotives proved able to match the performance standards of the proposed electrics, and at a lower capital cost. This would not be the end of the Great Western's interest in electric traction, however, and in 1936 it had been suggested that the entire system west of Taunton should be electrified, though the possibility remains of this being a ruse with which to force a halt in the steady rise of coal prices.

More far-reaching was a Board decision in early 1929 to investigate the possibilities of mainline diesel-electric traction, primarily for the London suburban services but with longer-haul routes in mind also. Once again, the idea did not progress beyond a theoretical examination due to the high initial cost and relatively restricted use of available equipment, though the study was almost certainly responsible for initiating the gradual acquisition of diesel shunters for yard work. Starting in 1933, a number of locomotives to various designs was acquired for evaluation and, by the time of nationalisation in 1948, the GWR had in service or under construction at Swindon a total of eight 350bhp diesel-electric 0-6-0s. These were essentially to the same English Electric design developed in conjunction with and used by the LMS, all but one using EE's 6K diesel engine, but the Great Western's programme was always restricted in scope and in no way whatsoever comparable with that instituted by its northern rival.

Above: Although Great Western locomotive design had undoubtedly stagnated during the 1930s, it did provide the infant British Railways with a large fleet of efficient and basically modern steam locomotives, which were further improved by the judicious application of minor improvements throughout the 1950s. Rebuilt with a double chimney and new front end only the year before, No.6004 *King George III* is assisted on the climb to Dainton with the 11.05 Paddington-Penzance by D808 *Centaur* on 8 August 1959. *(Hugh Ballantyne)*

Below: The Great Western's principal experience of diesel traction had been with its fleet of diesel railcars placed in service from 1934 onwards. Although the first examples were intended for use on lightly-patronised express services, later production was aimed at branchline and suburban workings. This included a number of twin sets, such as No.s W33/38 seen sandwiching a trailer coach in 1954. *(M.W. Earley Collection, National Railway Museum)*

The Great Western had been more pioneering in the field of diesel railcars, firstly for light express services and latterly to provide an alternative to steam push-and-pull trains on rural branchlines, but although the concept was new and exciting, the engineering of the vehicles was quite conservative, utilising a 121bhp AEC engine and Wilson preselective epicyclic gearbox originally designed for motor bus applications. With these railcars, the GWR became the largest British user of the diesel engine for rail passenger traction and, in conjunction with the limited number of diesel shunters being put into service, projected a strategy for dieselisation which broadly paralleled Riddles' own ideas on the subject. That, however, was as far as the Great Western's interest in diesel traction at that time went, Swindon's plans

for a future generation of mainline locomotives being focused in a quite different direction.

Although a protagonist neither of mainline dieselisation nor electrification, Hawksworth was conscious of the need to increase the efficiency and versatility of railway motive power. Mindful of the Great Western's increasing difficulty in obtaining good quality coal under wartime conditions, Hawksworth had been particularly interested by the introduction of the world's first gas-turbine locomotive, placed in service by the Swiss Federal Railways as Class Am 4/6 No.1101 during September 1941. Encouraged by a personal inspection of the locomotive made whilst participating in the 1946 International Railway Congress at Lucerne, he had persuaded the Great Western Board to purchase a single machine for evaluation as a possible replacement for the 'King' 4-6-0's on the steeply-graded mainline west of Newton Abbot. The early post-war years would see no relaxation of the difficulty in acquiring marine steam coal at reasonable cost, this time due to the Government's export drive, and the provision of an oil-fuelled gas-turbine would augment GWR plans to convert a sizeable number of steam locomotives to oil firing. A specification was duly agreed between the Great Western, the Brown-Boveri Company and the Swiss Locomotive Works of Winterthur, calling for a 2500bhp locomotive with an A1A-A1A wheel arrangement and a 90mph top speed. A single-stage turbine with an integral axial-flow compressor was to be incorporated, burning heavy oil and transmitting power to the rails through a direct-current electrical transmission. Although the plans for widespread oil-firing would soon be scuppered by the lack of available foreign exchange with which to buy the required quantities of oil, the gas-turbine project remained active and the BBC-SLM locomotive, after preliminary trials in Switzerland, was delivered to the Western Region of British Railways on 5 February 1950, entering revenue-earning service on 10 May as No.18000. A second locomotive had already been ordered from Metropolitan-Vickers of Manchester, initially as a joint GWR-MetroVick project, but nationalisation and various technical problems conspired to delay its debut until January 1952 when it entered service as No.18100. Unlike its Swiss counterpart, No.18100 was of a Co-Co wheel arrangement and nominally rated at 3000bhp with an effective tractive effort of 60,000lb, which caused it to be hailed as the most powerful locomotive in the British Isles.

Both locomotives were to amass considerable mileages on regular passenger workings and, although suffering various teething troubles, would impress footplatemen, officials

and observers alike with their strength and versatility. Despite this, by the end of 1953 BR had decided that the gas-turbine did not provide the immediate replacement for steam that was sought. Repeated problems with turbine blade, combustion chamber and traction motor failures might have been overcome with further development, but not the turbines' habit of consuming fuel at a near-constant rate whilst in operation, regardless of trailing load. This was due to the fact that around two-thirds of the turbine's total power output was re-absorbed by its own compressor, leaving the remaining third available for tractive purposes, which meant that a very large amount of energy had to be consumed just to keep the turbine ticking over. Although overall efficiency under maximum load conditions comfortably exceeded that of any comparable steam or diesel locomotive, the two gas-turbine locomotives only achieved full economy when being operated at full power, something which was not viable over much of the WR mainline and which was betrayed by fuel consumption on a cost basis more than twice that of a 'King' 4-6-0 or the LMS diesel twins 10000/10001. In the light of these incontrovertible if unpalatable facts, plans to modify the locomotives to burn pulverised coal were dropped and in January 1958 No.18100, already out of traffic pending a major refit, was withdrawn for conversion into a prototype 25kV ac locomotive for the West Coast electrification. Towards the end of 1959 No.18000 too was taken out of service and, after a period of storage, returned to Switzerland for use as a mobile testbed under the auspices of the International Union of Railways (UIC).

BR's experiences with the gas-turbine locomotive were not unique; nowhere in Europe did it live up to early expectations. The original Swiss locomotive No.1101 ran some quarter of a million miles but was eventually converted to a straight electric in the early 1950s, the project not being considered sufficient a success to justify costly repair work on the turbine. In the Soviet Union, four gas-turbine locomotives were constructed and tested between 1959 and 1965 but were never taken into railway stock, development being

Above: In the immediate post-war years, the GWR gave serious consideration to the gas-turbine locomotive as an eventual replacement for steam traction, going so far as to order a pair of prototype locomotives. The first, No.18000 came from Brown-Boveri in Switzerland, and is seen passing through Moreton Cutting at the head of the 07.00 service from Weston-super-Mare to Paddington on 16 April 1955. *(T.E. Williams Collection, National Railway Museum)*

suspended when available diesel technology began to outstrip foreseeable traction requirements. Quantities of intercity multiple units utilising gas-turbine propulsion were placed in regular service on both the French and German state railways, though neither programme would be expanded to encompass the series production of gas-turbine locomotives. Only in the United States did the breed see any widespread use, where the Union Pacific Railroad built up a fleet of twenty-five 4500bhp locomotives followed by thirty 8500bhp twin-units from Alco-GE. Fuelled on traditionally cheap residue oil and used to haul massive tonnages over the Wasatch mountains between Ogden, Utah and Cheyenne, Wyoming, the Union Pacific found its 'Big Blows' both powerful and reliable, but costly to maintain and operationally inflexible if reasonable economy was to be assured. The soaring oil prices of the late 1960s finally rendered the turbines uneconomic, and they all disappeared with almost indecent haste over the winter of 1969/70, ousted by less powerful but more frugal diesels. Had the WR experiments continued, British gas-turbines would almost certainly met a similar fate at that time.

With the curtailment of the gas-turbine programme, the WR had very little experience that it could draw upon in the field of non-steam mainline traction, and this would provide a constant source of comment in the events of 1955 and beyond. As early as 1948 the Railway Executive, acting on a request from Lord Hurcomb, the first Chairman of the BTC, had created the Harrington Committee with the aim of generating a long-term traction policy for the infant British Railways. Although Riddles was reputedly one of

11

Above: Pictured heading the down 'Merchant Venturer' through Ruscombe in 1954, No.18100 was the Western Region's second gas-turbine, built by Metropolitan-Vickers of Manchester. Although more powerful than its Swiss counterpart, the locomotive suffered numerous problems and saw only sporadic use in revenue-earning service. *(Russell-Smith Collection, National Railway Museum)*

the prime movers behind the idea of such a committee, he in fact chose to avoid direct participation, shrewdly forecasting that the best choice for the railways from an operational viewpoint would doubtless prove beyond the bounds of available economic resources. The Committee's deliberations were long and extensive, and when it eventually made its report in 1951 to the new BTC Chairman, Sir John Elliot, it had broadly echoed Riddles's own views on the subject, recommending that given BR's ties with the coal industry, coal should continue to provide the railways' staple fuel, with electrification gradually replacing steam. By this time, however, economic conditions were beginning to change unfavourably for the steam locomotive. There was evidence of a growing shortage of suitable steam coal on the home market, whilst foreign exchange for oil purchases became increasingly plentiful. Postwar industrial expansion was contributing to the steady stream of labour leaving the railways, with dire effects upon locomotive maintenance in particular. Lastly, public opinion was demanding a faster, cleaner railway with enhanced amenities and standards of service. Faced with the need to recast the nation's railways or otherwise lose traffic to rival carriers, Elliot's successor, General Sir Brian Robertson, organised a committee of senior BTC and BR officers entrusted with the task of formulating ideas for the modernisation and re-equipment of the railway system, based on the premise that their recommendations could be implemented within five years and completed within fifteen. Their deliberations would have to take account of the limited funds available for any such scheme, as well as the need to ensure that actual spending was spread throughout the course of the work. It was also

expected that the result would be a more efficient and profitable network. Reconciling such a mandate with other areas of Government policy, such as those pertaining to heavy industry and employment, would prove to be no easy task. Six months of intensive work on the committee's part produced the Modernisation Plan which, after acceptance by the BTC, was published as a report on *The Modernisation and Re-equipment of British Railways* in January 1955. The plan envisaged the equipping of all freight stock with continuous brakes (although vacuum rather than air, the cost of the latter having scuppered similar proposals put before the Ideal Stocks Committee back in 1948), reconstruction and replacement of railway infrastructure and the replacement of steam traction by diesels and selective electrification. Projected costs amounted to some £1240 million, and Parliamentary approval was given some months later.

On the motive power front, it was proposed to direct initial investment towards diesel traction in order to eradicate steam haulage, eventually progressing to full electrification wherever practical. Estimated expenditure of £125 million over fifteen years would provide about 2500 line service locomotives by 1970, accompanied by some 1200 shunting and transfer locomotives at a cost of £25 million: it is worth noting that few of the former were to be of high power output as such locomotives were no longer seen as being cost-effective. Further large sums were allotted to the purchase of 4600 diesel railcars, of which some 300 were already on order. Construction of steam locomotives for passenger trains was to cease by 1956, and that of other types as soon as traffic demands were satisfied, with elderly, numerically small and inefficient classes to be condemned as soon as possible.

The problem with all this was the exact form which the new traction should take, and here Riddles' successor, R.C. Bond was placed in a position that very nearly proved untenable. Himself a member of the committee which had formulated the Modernisation Plan, Bond was torn between his own personal faith in the steam locomotive as an efficient unit of railway motive power, and the recognition that political and economic circumstances were inexorably forcing the widespread introduction of the diesel locomotive on to British Railways, quite possibly before it reached maturity. Along with some similar machines being constructed for export markets, the British railway industry's experience of modern mainline diesel traction, was largely restricted to the sort of heavy diesel-electrics typified by the five locomotives then in regular front-rank service with BR. These, the LMS Co-Cos 10000/10001 and the SR 1Co-Co1s 10201-3, despite their considerable differences in design and appearance, were all diesel-electrics based around a common powerplant in the form of the English Electric 16SVT engine mated to that company's Model 822 generator. This combination, though unwieldy and particularly so in 10201-3, had proved itself successful as a tractive unit and was heavily promoted by the industry's lobbyists as a natural choice for further development.

Under the terms of the BTC's proposals, the Western Region would be totally dieselised west of Newton Abbot by 1970, with a large fleet of diesel-electric locomotives working passenger and freight traffic to London and back. The WR management, however, whose independence had survived nationalisation to be re-kindled by the decentralising policies of the 1953 Transport Act, was motivated both by its lack of confidence in the BTC's existing motive power policies and by its restricted experience of modern mainline traction to approach the problems posed by modernisation in a wholly fresh light. Given its conclusions, the heavy-weight diesel-electric as a subject for future construction was a concept that the WR would prove reluctant to accept.

Chapter 2
THE DIESEL-HYDRAULIC CONCEPT

HAVING created its Modernisation Plan and intertwined it with the ascendancy of the diesel locomotive, the BTC was faced with the task of determining exactly what quantities and types of equipment would be required to turn its strategies into reality. Late in 1954, the Commission approved Bond's proposal to place in service some 171 mainline diesels for a trial period of three years - what was to become known as the Pilot Scheme - during which time the varying costs and performances of each type under service conditions would be closely studied preparatory to placing any large orders. To this end, invitations to tender in accordance with specifications set down by Bond and his Chief Electrical Engineer, S.B. Warder, were circulated to all British locomotive manufacturers, one in Australia, one in Canada and three in the United States. The decision to do this rather than to develop those designs which had already proved themselves in service (few though they were) was made not so much for operational reasons as political ones. The BTC's investment in new forms of traction was quite obviously going to be a heavy one, and large portions of British industry felt that they were entitled to a share of the pickings. Very few, however, were prepared to alter established engineering and design procedures to do so, and this would ultimately shape the modernisation of Britain's railways.

Since the responsibility for funding new motive power lay solely with the BTC, many of BR's regional officers were resigned to having to make do with whatever they were given. From the very beginning, however, it was evident any further move towards a centralised locomotive policy would meet stiff resistance on the Western Region, where there still was widespread resentment of the Standard steam designs' lack of traditional Great Western features in favour of a marked bias towards LMS precepts. Fundamental icons such as the precision machining and erection of components were felt to have been discarded by a faceless corporate anonymity and there were a few small grains of truth in the boast that Swindon scrapped bearings with closer tolerances than those that Derby outshopped. The WR's early experience of the 'Britannia' Pacifics in particular was unhappy to say the least and led the majority of operating staff to condemn the new Standards as inferior to the locomotives which they were intended to replace, an opinion which was to harden when the BTC summarily dismissed their complaints as chauvinistic and unsupported by facts. The already-fragile relationship between Paddington and Marylebone Road deteriorated further when, in the very year of the Modernisation Plan's creation, the WR was coerced into taking an allocation of the new 9F 2-10-0s, only to find them prey to braking deficiencies and bouts of uncontrollable slipping under load. Although problems were only to be expected with a whole range of new designs, the many months which elapsed before corrections were made to locomotives already in traffic left WR enginemen with a hearty dislike of anything that smelt even faintly of 'LMS'. To many, that which the BTC was now contemplating fairly stank of it.

In actual fact, the WR's antipathy towards the fruits of British Railways' initial motive power policy had largely paralleled that of the BTC itself, hard to appreciate though this might have been at Swindon. The original aim of the British Transport Commission had been to integrate all forms of publicly-owned transport but, from an early stage, the Railway Executive had proved reluctant to subordinate specific railway concerns to the wider objectives of the BTC as a whole. Symptomatic of this had been the Executive's decision, largely on the initiative of Riddles, to proceed with the design and construction of the Standard steam classes against the recommendations of the Commission itself. Although Riddles' decision had been justified by the inadequacy of available funds to support more progressive strategies, the BTC's misgivings multiplied as the passage of time saw an increasingly powerful Railway Executive become ever less ready to acknowledge the control of the Commission. The schism that inevitably resulted from this impasse persisted until the re-organisation of 1953, when the BTC finally abolished the Railway Executive and took direct control of British Railways for itself. It was confidently expected that the work of integration and reconstruction which had been embarked upon at the time of nationalisation could now be resumed, reinvigorated and unencumbered by the various conflicting demands so far placed upon the system by economic and political considerations.

Although often unwilling to conform to the will of the BTC, the Executive had been scrupulous in preserving the

Below: The first tangible result of British Railways' new motive power policies as they applied to the Western Region was the allocation of BR Standards to a number of WR sheds, such as Class 7 Pacific No.70018 *Flying Dutchman* seen skimming the troughs at Goring at the head of the up 'Bristolian' soon after its entry to service in 1951. Although they would perform some sterling work prior to being transferred off the WR at the end of the decade, protracted teething problems both with the 'Britannias' and several other of the Standard classes would do much to alienate Swindon's locomotive engineers from their counterparts at the BTC. *(M.W. Earley Collection, National Railway Museum)*

subservience of the various regional administrations, something which the expanded BTC would find increasingly hard to manage in the coming years. Taken as a whole, the Chief Regional Officers were better-educated, more experienced and more highly-paid than their counterparts on the RE and when under the ramifications of the 1953 Transport Act they had been elevated to regional General Managers, each sitting on an Area Board, they had quickly set out to assume many of the responsibilities formerly conferred upon the Railway Executive. Their new-found autonomy, however, in no way prepared them to deal with the increasing numbers of financial, operational and technical specialists that were being recruited to form the so-called Central Staff of the BTC, answerable in turn to the General Staff which supervised all areas of BTC activity on behalf of the Commission itself. Having regained control of its own territory, the Western Region in particular proved reluctant to accept orders from above whilst, in contrast, many BTC-Central staff saw it as their prerogative and responsibility to oversee the actual implementation of the Modernisation Plan, with or without the co-operation of the various regions. In particular, the Central Staff was anxious to ensure that motive power policy did not become subverted in the way that many considered it had been by the Railway Executive in 1948, and the more vigorously either side argued for its own way, the more fierce became the opposition. It was in this unhappy atmosphere of mutual suspicion that the details of the full-scale dieselisation of British Railways would be first worked-out.

Independent to the' last, and acutely conscious of the magnitude of change which the Modernisation Plan proposed, the Western Region management had itself made a comprehensive study of the Plan's implications, some of the conclusions of which proved to be at serious variance with the Central Staff's own position. In particular, the WR had formulated a list of prime economic and operational elements needing consideration, among the most critical of which was the total integration of motive power policy with the other aspects of railway modernisation. Equally important in the eyes of the WR's chief officers was expediting the fitment of automatic continuous brakes to the greater part of the wagon fleet in order to maximise the use of motive power as well as to narrow the gap between the speeds of fast passenger and slow freight trains. Any such increase in speed would demand high power:weight ratios from the new motive power, so as to provide rapid acceleration to the summit of the permissible speed range, to maintain pace up long inclines, and to allow the recovery of time lost through unexpected delays. The fact that the vast majority of BR's wagon stock was composed of four-wheel, short-wheelbase vehicles with an effective maximum speed of 40mph or so served to make the ability of a locomotive to accelerate smartly and maintain speed on an incline even more important in freight service than in passenger traffic.

Although the desirability of high power:weight ratios had long since been expounded by the distinguished Russian locomotive engineer, Professor Georgei Lomonosov, himself an architect of early Soviet dieselisation, the WR's appetite had already been whetted by the performance of the two gas-turbine locomotives with their exceptionally high specific outputs. Obtaining similar power:weight ratios from the less powerful diesel locomotives then available would necessitate weight savings of around a third, a move that made sense given the expected impact of the continuous-braking programme in eliminating reliance upon adhesion-related locomotive braking force when working heavy loose-coupled trains. Locomotives of the lowest possible weight would also help facilitate the 20-ton axle loading desired by the BTC's Chief Civil Engineer so as to bring the weight concentration of a diesel locomotive into line with that of a steam engine of comparable power. It was this last consideration, coupled with fear of track damage under heavy braking loads, that was to prolong the use of the 1Co-Co1 arrangement long after it had become obsolescent.

This layout had originated on the three mainline diesel-electrics built for the Southern Region, whose experience of axle-hung traction motors on multiple-units had led it to specify an 18-ton axle load for the new diesels. At the time of the WR's first deliberations on its future, controlled road tests were being carried out on the latest of these machines, the 2000bhp No.10203. Completed the year before, this was now viewed in some quarters as a possible candidate for quantity construction and use across British Railways as a whole, including the Western Region. Far from being a lightweight, high-output machine in the mould of the two gas-turbines, 10203 was an extremely large and heavy beast which, in comparative tests with one of the Bulleid 'Merchant Navy' Pacifics on the Waterloo-Exeter route, had shown itself inferior to the steam locomotive at any speed above 30mph on level track. The results of these tests had also been extrapolated to provide estimated running times for the locomotive in express service over several of BR's other principal routes, including Paddington-Penzance. Although the computed timings for the diesel were marginally quicker than those of a 'King'-class 4-cylinder 4-6-0 east of Exeter, the WR was horrified to discover that the design to which the BTC might well entrust the running of the 'Cornish Riviera' was in fact incapable of surmounting unassisted the gradients west of Newton Abbot with the consists then envisioned. If diesel-electrics of this sort were to replace the 'Kings', the WR would be

faced with the choice of reducing train loads considerably, continuing the practice of routine piloting west of Newton Abbot, or reducing the gearing of the traction motors and thus impairing the locomotives' ability to run fast on the level. To an administration wedded to ongoing service accelerations, further gains in operating efficiency and continued high levels of passenger comfort, none of these alternatives would provide a palatable option.

The identification of a possible solution to this conundrum is generally credited to H.H. Phillips, Assistant Regional General Manager of the WR who, as the late Brian Reed noted in his excellent *Diesel-Hydraulic Locomotives of the Western Region* (David & Charles, 1975), was endowed with an understanding of railway logistics exceptional even for a man of his position. Phillips could hardly have failed to notice the reconstruction and modernisation of the various European railway networks and to have contrasted this to the situation in the United States where the railroads were losing custom hand-over-fist to air and road transport. He was certainly astute enough to recognise the Modernisation Plan as a unique opportunity to restructure Britain's railways in order to ensure their future prosperity, and perceived the questions of continuous braking and of the high power:weight ratio as being the twin keystones of future development. Seeking a diesel of an output sufficient to give performance comparable with that of a 'King', Phillips produced some simple calculations which showed that a starting tractive effort of 44,000lb would be sufficient to meet all of the WR's foreseeable requirements. Further investigations revealed that the even torque provided by modern transmission systems would allow the weight of a

fully-laden locomotive to be cut to 80 tons without sacrificing adhesion. The need was thus for a diesel locomotive able to offer a more closely optimal adhesive weight, lower axle load and better hill-climbing abilities than any suitable diesel-electric then available, yet still be able out-accelerate an express steam locomotive. Phillips saw an answer in the shape of five 80-ton 2100bhp diesel-hydraulic locomotives of the B-B wheel arrangement placed in service by the German Federal Railways or Deutsche Bundesbahn during the course of 1954 and which, within the space of twelve months, were achieving an average of 10,000 miles/month/locomotive in express train haulage. These V200-class locomotives appealed to Phillips not only by their minimal weight and excellent performance, but also the fact that their hydraulic transmission design conferred excellent tractive effort characteristics throughout the speed range. One ostensible drawback was their use of lightweight, quick-running engines which, professed the commonly-held wisdom of the time, could not equal the reliability of their slow-speed equivalents, and experience of mainline dieselisation in the United States had indeed implied an inverse relationship between locomotive availability and the profusion of moving and wearing parts in the powerplant. On the strength of this alone, the high-speed engines and hydraulic transmissions of the German locomotives should not have compared favourably with domestic offerings, and the very idea of their use on BR would encounter opposition from the start, both inside and outside the BTC. Phillips, however, had established a sound foundation for his recommendations in the shape of the V200s' enviable service record to date, largely a function of depot repair facilities which exploited the traction units' low weight to effect rapid replacement of failed components with freshly-overhauled replacements, and he was sufficiently persuasive in his arguments to secure the backing of the WR's Regional General Manager, Keith Grand.

More significantly, Phillips' ideas were also supported by the Chairman of the Western Region Area Board of the BTC, Reginald Hanks, who had trained at Swindon but left the Great Western in 1922 to join the fledgling motor industry, rising up the corporate ladder at Morris Motors' Oxford plant during one of that concern's most fruitful and innovative periods. Vice-Chairman since 1948 of the Nuffield

Organisation, Morris' parent, Hanks would undoubtedly have assumed eventual control of the group had it not been for Nuffield's merger with the rival Austin concern in 1952. The new British Motor Corporation that resulted would soon be controlled almost entirely by former Austin executives and Hanks, always an opponent of the merger, rejoined the railway in 1955. Undeniably, BMC's loss was very much the WR's gain as Hanks brought with him not only vast managerial experience but also a valuable and independent outlook on both commercial and engineering issues. In particular, his years of experience at Nuffield, spanning the motor car's progress from a plaything of the rich to a practical and economical form of personal transport for the masses, had created within him the firm belief that Swindon's apparent preoccupation with high power:weight ratios was indeed justified. Hanks' evaluation of the issue was quite simple; if BR's forthcoming diesel locomotives were to offer an acceptable blend of economy and performance in operational service, they would have to join virtually every other modern form of transport in using lightweight, quick-running engines allied to non-electric transmissions. Whilst the LMS and SR diesel-electric designs then being considered formed an effective antithesis to this ideal, the German diesel-hydraulics fitted the bill in nearly every way. Hanks' arguments, backed by his broad experience and record of achievement, would prove vital in securing official approval for Phillips' proposals.

Fired with enthusiasm, the WR Board began to campaign for a fleet of diesel-hydraulic rather than diesel-electric locomotives under the following premises:

1) The WR had only limited experience of heavy electrical equipment and did not wish to have to organise its frequent maintenance and repair, reasoning that steam locomotive fitters could be more easily retrained to deal with hydraulic transmissions; furthermore, as they were physically lighter than heavy electrical units, hydraulic transmissions would need less specialised handling facilities, allowing the utilisation of existing plant.

2) Diesel-hydraulic locomotives could produce a higher sustained tractive effort at lower speeds than any comparable diesel-electric, a capability which could be put to good use on the steeply-graded mainline west of Newton Abbot as well as between there and London.

3) The use of diesel-electrics weighing 125 tons or more was extravagant if equal performance could be delivered by a diesel-hydraulic of 80 tons. Not only would such machines be cheaper to operate and maintain, but were also currently (1955) cheaper to buy as well.

4) Minimal overall weight, combined with the relatively low unsprung mass inherent in the diesel-hydraulic concept would allow locomotives of greater route availability, reduce wear on track and avoid the necessity for the costly uprating of underline structures.

5) The lightweight construction and simple driveline arrangements of contemporary diesel-hydraulics would allow such locomotives to be constructed without additional carrying axles. The locomotives' total weight would thus be available for adhesive purposes, a critical consideration in the successful everyday working of trains over the steep gradients west of Newton Abbot.

6) Not only could a diesel-hydraulic manage two coaches more on an exacting schedule than a comparable diesel-electric and still keep time, but in overall concept seemed to be much more in accord with the principal aims of the Modernisation Plan.

So cogent was this reasoning that the proposals soon had the full support of the Regional Chief Mechanical Engineer, R.A. Smeddle, allowing the WR to bring pressure to bear on the BTC for the inclusion of some high-power diesel-hydraulics in the Pilot Scheme orders. Despite the opposition of technical specialists on the Central Staff, Phillips' proposals gained a sympathetic hearing from General Sir Brian Robertson (whose primary concern, suggested some of the industry's less charitable observers, was to avoid any crossing of swords with the WR management so early in his Chairmanship of the BTC) and, after much debate, limited approval was given for the Region to pursue its objective.

Below: The WR's continuing pursuit of high specific outputs from its motive power found a suitable model for dieselisation in the West German V200-class diesel-hydraulic. Technically a generation ahead of virtually any other contemporary mainline diesel, production of locomotives to the same basic design would continue for more than a decade. V200 107, one of a later series revised and uprated with more powerful engines, poses in the snow when new. *(Krauss-Maffei)*

Above: A major attraction of the lightweight diesel-hydraulics as far as the WR was concerned was the ease with which existing facilities could be adapted in order to deal with them. An example was Newton Abbot Works, originally built by the Great Western Railway in 1893, extended and modernised in 1924, then finally refurbished as a diesel repair centre in the late 1950s, in which guise it is seen playing host to a trio of D800 'Warships' and a D6300 Type 2. *(Colin J. Marsden Collection)*

Even so, fundamental problems between the WR and the BTC still remained to be overcome before any definite action could be taken.

The WR's intended model for its own locomotives, the DB V200 B-B, was a radically different creation to that which the BTC envisaged. Indeed, of the various problems that would dog the mainline diesel-hydraulic throughout its career on British Railways, the most pervasive was always the sheer breadth of the gulf separating the different philosophies of British and German traction design. All of the mainline diesel locomotives so far produced in Britain had been of heavyweight construction, dependent for rigidity upon a heavy load-bearing frame supporting an unstressed body structure. Mechanically, only two of the seven locomotives then in service had been equipped with quick-running engines, both of which had given considerable maintenance problems. Although these difficulties were undoubtedly due to the detail design of the chosen units rather than a function of their basic format, the result had been to influence the BTC against any high-speed diesels for traction use.

Much more to its liking were the LMS twins No.s 10000/1 and the Southern trio No.s 10201-3, all of which used the same design of heavy, slow-running engine coupled to a complex direct-current electrical transmission, a concept that had been proven on numerous mainline units in use on major US railroads since the late 1930s. Having had experience of mainline electrification since the turn of the century, many American railroaders looked favourably upon the diesel-electric as a locomotive having all the advantages of a straight electric but, by embodying an integral generating plant, without the financial burdens imposed by the need for electrical supply and distribution installations. Indeed, at the time of the BTC's interest, so great were the monetary savings to be made by American railroads in opting for diesel power over electrification that several (namely Cleveland Union Terminal, Great Northern, New Haven, Norfolk & Western and, eventually, the Milwaukee Road) chose not to replace life-expired equipment on electrified lines but rather to de-energise the overhead wires and run the trains behind new diesel-electrics instead! The comparatively great weight of such locomotives was of less importance than in Europe due to the considerable length of most American trains and the concomitant high horsepower demands; by the late 1940s, at least three builders were offering four-unit diesel-electric combinations producing up to 8000bhp. Such considerations tended to outweigh the triple disadvantages of cost, complexity and the inability to generate high powers at low track speeds, the last being a shortcoming that the WR quickly discovered with its gas-turbines.

Several concerns were looking to supply the BTC's demands for rail traction diesel engines, and the Commission's eventual choice would be complicated by political as well as engineering considerations. The road vehicle industry was already involved in the supply of low-output units, with Gardners of Patricroft furnishing engines for the 204bhp shunters and BUT (British United Traction, a consortium representing the trolleybus and railcar interests of commercial vehicle builders AEC, Albion and Leyland) smaller engines for the diesel railcars then entering service. For use in high-power line service locomotives, however, the choice lay between a number of designs, not all proven, pre-eminent amongst which was English Electric's 16SVT, a sixteen-cylinder vee-formation design already favoured by the BTC through its successful use in the LMS and SR diesel pioneers. Developed out of its 'K' range during the late 1930s, EE had eschewed the two-stroke arrangement for the new engine because of the additional compli-

cations involved, despite the layout's espousal by American rivals such as General Motors and Fairbanks-Morse. Deprived of the higher specific outputs per unit of cylinder volume promised by the two-stroke cycle, the four-stroke 16SVT was a sound and reliable unit that nevertheless owed its power principally to its sheer size; in Mark II form, it would develop some 2000bhp at 850rpm from a swept capacity of 247 litres, with an attendant engine weight of 40,760lb. Another handicap was imposed by EE's accounting methods, which dictated the retention of outdated design features long after designers wanted to replace them and rivals actually had. Ironically, the 16SVT would soon be eclipsed in the high-power stakes by a rival EE group product which did employ the two-stroke cycle, namely the immortal Napier 'Deltic', but, despite their undoubted advantages (aided in the 'Deltic's case by its aero-engine lineage), two-stoke diesels would never be regarded with any great favour by British Railways and their use was always limited, both spatially and in number.

Although virtually guaranteed BTC patronage, which eventually came in the shape of orders for the 16SVT, the related eight-cylinder 8SVT and two models of 'Deltic' engine (T9-29 and D18-25), EE would not secure a monopoly over the Pilot Scheme business. Given the sheer scope of the Modernisation Plan's proposals, BR's demand for engines would in fact exceed EE's capacity to deliver, whilst the BTC had also begun to baulk at the idea of putting all its eggs into one basket. Therefore, smaller orders were placed with Crossleys, Mirrlees and Paxmans, along with one which would prove very significant in the years to come. Several British constructors had been fulfilling export orders for diesel-electric locomotives using heavyweight, slow-running engines manufactured by the Swiss concern of Sulzer Brothers, whilst two Sulzer-engined locomotives placed in service by the CIE in Ireland during 1951 had performed well enough to justify the purchase of a dozen more in 1956. Offering significantly more power than equivalent EE units, the design had attracted the attention of the London Midland Region's Chief Mechanical & Electrical Engineer, J.F. Harrison, whose advocacy proved vital to Sulzer's inclusion in the Pilot Scheme orders. Three related four-stroke units were on offer, the in-line 6LDA28 of 1160bhp and 8LDA28 of 1550bhp being complemented by an engine which Sulzers heralded as the most powerful of its kind in Western Europe. This was the 12LDA28, a twin-bank twelve-cylinder design which could not only deliver some 2300bhp at 750rpm, but also weighed less and incorporated fewer moving parts than its English Electric rival. The engines from Winterthur had accrued an enviable record in service worldwide, and facili-

ties for UK production already already existed through a licensing agreement between Sulzers and Vickers of Barrow-in-Furness, almost all BR's demands being met by the output from the Cumberland plant.

By contrast with the 120-ton behemoths being drawn-up in British factories, the German V200 locomotives were almost sylph-like, fundamentally due to their stressed-steel construction. This technique was pioneered by the American civil engineer Stepan Timoshenko but soon adopted by the aircraft industry, being based upon the realisation that thin metal sheet, if appropriately shaped and stiffened, could be made to serve the load-bearing function normally fulfilled by heavy girderwork. Its use in British railway vehicles was virtually unknown, a source of considerable intrigue when one considers that English Electric's diverse contemporary product range included the highly successful *Canberra* bomber and *Lightning* fighter aircraft, during the development of which much work had been done in the fields of stressed-skin construction and stress-testing. Despite this, EE blindly persevered with the 'strength frame' style of construction, apparently oblivious of its origins in the need for detachable and therefore unstressed bodysides on the LMS diesel twins in order to facilitate engine installation in the low-roofed workshops at Derby. (Even in the United States, most manufacturers had by then adopted a bridge-truss style of construction whereby the supporting members for the bodysides were arranged so as to carry a component of any loading imposed upon the mainframe itself.) Although the continued use of this technique on many of the Pilot Scheme diesels achieved little but to raise their weight to a point where extra carrying axles were required, EE for one seemed to lack the ability, or at least the will, to translate its knowledge of stressed skin construction from one aspect of its operation to another.

The German locomotives were also significantly different in respect of their power equipment. During the early postwar period, German manufacturers had concentrated on developing compact, high-speed lightweight diesels which, although of a significantly lower output than the English product, were small enough for two engine-transmission assemblies to be fitted in one locomotive to produce a unit of comparable capabilities but at a lower all-up weight and cost. The V200 concept made use of engines made by Maybach, MAN and Daimler-Benz, coupled to hydraulic transmissions of Maybach-Mekydro or Voith manufacture. Although these components differed in many respects, standardisation of mountings, connections and the like insisted upon by the DB enabled a V200 to run with any permutation of units, such as a MAN engine coupled to a Mekydro transmission at one end and a Daimler-Benz unit coupled to a Voith transmission at the other. Not only were these components sufficiently light to permit engine power:weight ratios of about 250bhp/ton as compared to the 110bhp/ton of the EE 16SVT unit, but were complemented by the hydraulic transmissions' ability to withstand prolonged high power outputs at low speeds, ideal for starting a very heavy train on an incline. Similar prolonged outputs by a diesel-electric near to standstill would almost invariably result in the gross overheating and consequent virtual destruction of the electrical conductors.

There were no insurmountable technical problems involved in coupling hydraulic transmission units to conventional slow-speed diesels, in mating high-speed engines to electric transmission or, for that matter, in utilising prime movers and transmission units of either type in strength-frame or stressed-skin structures. However, as was to be demonstrated by later developments, none of these hybrids could equal the overall performance and high power:weight ratio of the original V200 design and, in its initial proceedings, the WR remained adamant in rejecting any such compromise of its technical ideal. Yet just such a beast, in the form of a heavyweight diesel-electric design converted to hydraulic transmission, was precisely what the BTC proposed as an initial try-out, regardless of the WR's reasoning behind the use of diesel-hydraulics in the first place. Committed to its own agenda, the WR was set on a course which would end in direct conflict both with the BTC and the remainder of BR.

Chapter 3
A CONFLICT OF OPINIONS

THE spring of 1955 saw an increasing expectancy within British Railways that the Western Region would indeed get its own way over the matter of future traction policy. At the beginning of the year, Bond, Smeddle and various others had visited Germany for the purpose of evaluating diesel-hydraulics at first hand, on behalf of both the WR and the BTC. Smeddle retained faith in what had become a conviction whilst Bond was sufficiently impressed not just by the validity of the WR's case but also by what he had himself seen to agree that some mainline diesel-hydraulics should definitely constitute part of the Pilot Scheme. Bond undoubtedly had a subsidiary motive in mind; at the time, electrification schemes were being proposed for both the London Midland mainline as far north as Manchester, and the Eastern Region mainline south of Leeds. Nothing similar was intended for the Western Region and Bond's interest must have been excited by the potential of the diesel-hydraulics as a long-term substitute for full-scale electrification. Nevertheless, diesel-electric designs, of which BR as a whole and British industry had most experience, would answer for the majority of orders.

Thus encouraged, Paddington began to indulge itself in some more concrete proposals, involving not only a fleet of diesel-hydraulic mainline locomotives but also a substantial number of diesel-multiple units for secondary services, utilising engines and transmissions fully-interchangeable with those of the new locomotives. There was, however, a problem over the supply of the equipment, the BTC being put under intense pressure to ensure that all material required under the terms of the Modernisation Plan was procured from British concerns. Although the Commission had invited tenders from selected foreign manufacturers and had gone so far as to arrange a visit by Sir Brian Robertson to General Motors' Electromotive locomotive factory at La Grange, near Chicago, the chances of BR investing in EMD or any other foreign-made locomotives were slim. Whilst GM was willing to supply, possibly on a spread-payment basis, backlogged orders from diesel-hungry US railroads meant that BR's requirements could not be met for some time to come. In any case, the Government was unwilling to sanction the level of dollar spending necessary to import large numbers of ready-built locomotives, GM not being happy to expand its EMD operation into the UK despite having operated a British subsidiary (Vauxhall Motors) since 1925. Subsequently, a UK licensing agreement would be concluded between EMD and Lancashire lorry-maker Leyland Motors in 1958, but by then the BTC was already committed to other sources of supply, and no orders would be forthcoming. British constructors represented by the Locomotive Manufacturers' Association (LMA) had objected to the American giant's involvement in any way whatsoever, apparently subscribing to the view that state-owned industries had a duty to support indigenous commerce under virtually any circumstances. Pressure not to buy from German concerns was stronger still, with lingering feelings of hostility left over from the war years reinforced by the fact that the West Germans' rapidly expanding diesel engine producers were now threatening the position of British engineering concerns in a number of vital and hither-to-secure world markets.

Under such circumstances, any possibility of a quantity purchase of German traction equipment by a nationalised industry such as the BTC was perceived as being a potential embarrassment to the very highest levels of government itself, and collapse of the entire diesel-hydraulic project for the want of suitable home-built equipment seemed inevitable. Assistance, however, was to come from the most unlikely quarter when the LMA itself, on behalf of one of its most vocal constituents, pointed out that the licenses necessary to build the required equipment in the United Kingdom were in fact already held by a British company. This was the North British Locomotive Company of Springburn, Glasgow which, seeking an opening into the expanding diesel locomotive business and intent on facilitating the assembly of complete locomotives in its two Glasgow factories without undue reliance upon possible rivals for the supply of electrical equipment, in 1951 had acquired the British rights to the manufacture of Voith hydraulic transmissions. Although first taken out as early as 1937, the franchise had effectively lapsed at the start of the war and was still largely dormant when, in 1953, NBL concluded a second agreement, this time with Maschinenfabrik Augsburg-Nürnberg AG, allowing the manufacture under license of the complete range of MAN medium- and high-speed compression-ignition oil engines of between 100 and 2000bhp. At the time that the Modernisation Plan was made public, although having produced a number of Voith-equipped diesel-hydraulic shunting locomotives, NBL had yet to assemble a single MAN engine. Nevertheless, such was the WR's enthusiasm for diesel-hydraulic traction that NBL engineers worked-up outline proposals for 1000 and 2000bhp locomotives with MAN engines and Voith transmissions, broadly conforming to BR specifications. Given the company's apparent readiness to fulfil the WR's requirements, allied to the fact that Glasgow was one of the economically-depressed areas which the Government was eager to assist, the LMA had little difficulty in persuading the Scottish Board of Industry to lobby the BTC on NBL's behalf, and before long formal channels of discussion had been opened between Marylebone Road and Queen's Park.

The engine which NBL felt best suited WR requirements was the MAN L12V18/21A, a twelve-cylinder four-stroke vee-formation unit of conventional construction and inspiration used in a number of German locomotive and multiple-unit designs and thus a feature of the V200 concept, though at the time of the NBL-BTC negotiations no MAN-engined V200s had yet been constructed. Crankcase and cylinder block assemblies were of mild steel, welded-up with cast steel stretchers and an additional flat bracing piece across the top of the vee, giving a one-piece assembly with an included angle of 60° between cylinder banks. Cylinders were of 180mm bore by 210mm stroke, giving a total swept capacity of 64.13 litres, the cylinder liners themselves being of cast iron. Pistons were one-piece castings in aluminium alloy, each having four compression rings (of which the topmost was chrome-plated for longer life) and two oil control rings, the latter intended to prevent excess crankcase oil from being drawn into the combustion chambers and thus burnt off. There was, however, no provision for oil to be

cast balance weights bolted to crankweb extensions to counteract the out-of-balance forces that would otherwise be generated by the reciprocating action of pistons and rods.

Twelve separate cast iron cylinder heads were used, one for each cylinder, with each head housing two inlet and two exhaust valves along with a fuel injector and a decompression valve, the latter to allow the engine to be more easily turned-over during maintenance as well as facilitating priming prior to start-up after any lengthy period of idleness. A single camshaft low down in the neck of the vee, gear-driven off the crankshaft, actuated the valves through pushrods featuring roller followers at their lower ends. These pushrods were actually located in sealed tubes outside the main mass of the cylinder blocks themselves. A light cover on top of each cylinder head was secured by four setscrews and was easily removed for adjustment of the valves' rockergear and screw-type tappets. Exhaust gas were ducted through two exhaust manifolds per side to a MAN L12/629 centrifugal turbocharger located between the rocker boxes at the engine's flywheel end. At full throttle, turbocharger speeds could be as high as 18,000rpm but, with peak boost pressure not exceeding 10.4psi, the provision of an exhaust wastegate to prevent overboosting was not deemed necessary. Also located between the cylinder banks was a pair of Bosch fuel injection pumps, each resembling a tiny six-cylinder engine with individual spring-loaded plungers arranged in-line to distribute fuel to the injectors. Injection timing was determined by a miniature camshaft in each unit, driven from the engine's timing gear and provided with its own dedicated lubrication system, whilst the actual amount of fuel delivered depended upon engine speed, control being via pneumatically-operated helices in the plungers.

Complete, each engine weighed-in at 8500lb, with a rated speed of 1400/1445rpm maintained by a hydraulic governor. At 1445rpm, it was considered to have a railway rating of 1000bhp, with 1100bhp at 1500rpm for one hour's duration, a surprisingly high output for a push-rod diesel of such conventional design and relatively modest dimensions. The engines were built to exacting standards however, and although a cold start was permissible, the very fine tolerances made it at least desirable to preheat the units via their cooling systems prior to start-up. Whilst this did entail a certain loss of operational flexibility combined with additional mechanical complication, the BTC was not too distressed since the inclusion of preheaters would allow the locomotives to be kept warm whilst standing, so avoiding the need for expensive antifreeze solutions.

The concept of the Voith transmission was directly derived from the work of the German engineer Hermann Föttinger in the early years of the century. In 1903, whilst employed by the Vulcan Shipbuilding Company of Stettin, he was given the task of designing and perfecting an electric transmission for turbine-powered steamships where the high rotational speeds of the turbines exceeded the capacity of geared transmissions then available. After a year's experimentation and research, Föttinger had reached the conclusion that electric power was too complex and expensive to be a viable solution, and so instead had combined a centrifugal pump and hydraulic turbine in a common casing to produce the world's first torque converter. By rotating the centrifugal pump, the power source forced oil contained within the casing onto the blades of the hydraulic turbine, causing it to turn and so drive the output shaft. The transmission oil was then redirected through guide vanes to the pump or impeller. As the oil transmitted energy rather than any specific rotational motion, the design allowed the input shaft to differ in speed from the output shaft in an infinitely variable ratio between fixed limits, thus allowing the engine of a vehicle to run at its most efficient speed regardless of the actual velocity of the vehicle. Given a constant input, the characteristic of the Föttinger transmission is that torque increases in inverse proportion to output speed,

Above: At the time of the BTC's first serious enquiries into the availability of mainline diesel-hydraulic locomotives, the only suitable high-speed engine offered by a British concern was the 12-cylinder MAN L12V18/21, imported by the North British Locomotive Company of Glasgow. This is a later B-series unit, seen here installed on a D6300 underframe along with transmission, dynastarter and vacuum exhausters prior to the erection of the body sides. *(Mitchell Library)*

Below: Cross-sectional view of the MAN L12V18/21 engine, showing the low-level camshaft operating the valves through pushrods and rockers. *(MAN)*

directed against the underside of the piston as a precaution against overheating. Each piston drove through a plain connecting rod onto a seven-bearing crankshaft, in order to simplify the design of which, rods from opposing pistons were arranged to sit side-by-side on a common crankpin, requiring bore spacings of the two cylinder banks to be slightly staggered. Another benefit of this arrangement was that by greatly reducing the number of crankwebs required, the six-throw crank made a far greater bearing surface available without any increase in crankshaft length. Conversely, however, the side-by-side location of paired rods on the same journal did have the effect of introducing a bending moment at the centrepoint of each crankpin, thus imposing greater working stresses upon the shaft as a whole. As originally produced, the L12V18/21's crankshaft was dynamically balanced as an entity in its own right and did not feature a torsional vibration damper, though it did make use of

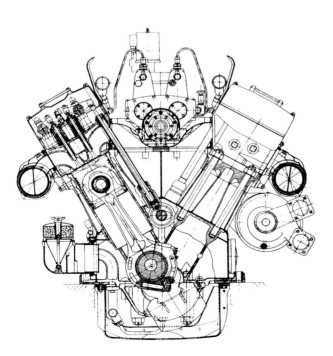

22

making it ideally suited to the needs of both rail and road traction. Inevitably, some power is lost in the form of heat generated, but not unduly so, and the greatest drawback of the system is the size of converter needed to deal with large power outputs. Where space was restricted, as in a railway locomotive, step-up gears were used between engine and converter to increase the rotational speed of the converter, and so its capacity and efficiency.

Föttinger undoubtedly made a major technological breakthrough in inventing his torque converter but actually developing it as a practical proposition for commercial use was quite another thing, and it was not until the 1930s that the first hydraulic transmissions suitable for heavy rail traction were created by the J.M. Voith concern. The Voith transmission as developed for use in the V200s featured a series of three fluid-filled circuits to cover the track speed range, each being of a different size, oil capacity and blade formation in order to suit the requirements of the sub-range for which it was intended. Whilst more complex, this layout was reckoned to offer considerable gains in efficiency over a single large converter. Under normal running conditions, only one circuit of the three was full of transmission oil at any particular time, changes between them being effected automatically by emptying one coincident with the filling of the next. As well as producing a seamless change with no break in tractive effort, albeit with a reduction in output power during the course of the change, this also allowed all three converters to be located upon a common primary shaft, there being no need to physically disengage those impellers running in the two 'dry' converters. The actual changeover process was co-ordinated by a centrifugal governer measuring road speed and a hydraulic cylinder used to monitor engine output, allowing the precise moment of change to vary according to operating conditions. An additional link to the driver's controls drained all three converters whenever the throttle was returned to the 'idle' position, so preventing any unintentional movement taking place. Reversing gears were contained within the transmission block and, as a result, axledrives needed only to be of a simple bevel variety. As the changeover points between converters were set to suit the torque curve of the engine(s) used, the ultimate speed and tractive effort capabilities of the locomotive as a whole were determined by the ratio of these final drive units. Hence, in theory at least, an express passenger locomotive could use power equipment identical to that of a heavy freight unit, the two differing only in terms of axledrive specification.

Orders were placed with NBL in the summer of 1955 for five 2000bhp and six 1000bhp diesel-hydraulic locomotives, all based around the MAN L12V18/21A engine and Voith L306r transmission. Given not only that the MAN and Voith units were the heaviest of all the powertrain assemblies used in the V200 locomotives, but also the fact that NBL had little or no experience of stressed-skin construction, the chances of the WR's parameters of 2000bhp on four axles and 80 tons all-up weight ever being fulfilled looked slim from the start. In the event the BTC CME's department, which had taken charge of the technical aspects of the BR/NBL negotiations, refused to accept responsibility for a four-wheel bogie carrying 40 tons with a 450bhp drive on each axle. Citing fears of poor riding at speed, excessive track loadings and insufficient low-speed adhesion, it therefore forced through a six-axle design of heavyweight construction which defeated most of the WR's aims in specifying a diesel-hydraulic to begin with. By doing so, the Commission sacrificed any chance of success these machines might have had, and thus both the 2000bhp Type 4s and their smaller 1000bhp Type 2 half-sisters ended up as underpowered, awkward contrivances that no-one, least of all the BTC, really wanted.

As it appeared certain that these unfortunate machines were all that would be readily forthcoming from the home

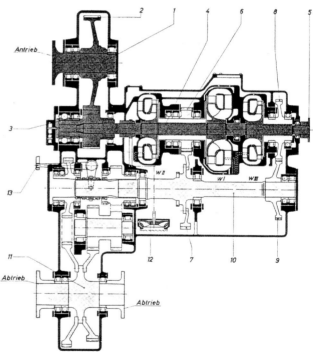

Top: The Voith L306r triple-converter transmission used by NBL in the D600 and initial D6300 locomotives. The output shaft is at the bottom of the block. The first four units were imported complete from Germany, with the remainder being assembled by NBL at Glasgow. *(Voith)*

Bottom: Schematic longitudinal section of the Voith L306r transmission; primary parts are shaded dark and secondary parts light. Components are identified as follows: 1, input shaft; 2 & 3, step-up gears; 4, primary shaft; 5, auxiliary power take-off; 6 & 7, Stage 1/Stage 2 transfer gears; 8 & 9, Stage 3 transfer gears; 10, intermediate shaft; 11, output shaft; 12, converter filling pump; 13, reversing gear actuating lever; WI, first stage converter; WII, second stage converter; WIII, third stage converter. *(Voith)*

Above: The BTC wanted to ensure that evaluation of the diesel-hydraulic concept was performed within the framework of a heavyweight locomotive, an opinion not shared by the WR. One of the results of this policy, Type 2 B-B D6321 pilots Churchward 2-8-0 No.4705 over Dainton Bank with the 07.43 Nottingham-Plymouth on 5 August 1961. *(Hugh Ballantyne)*

Below: What the WR wanted, and eventually got, was a version of the German V200 lightweight B-B adapted for British conditions. The result is exemplified here by D862 *Viking*, seen climbing Dainton from the opposite direction with the 09.20 Falmouth-Paddington on 5 September 1963. *(John S. Whiteley)*

industry, with or without the BTC's co-operation, the WR made the first moves towards establishing direct contact with the German manufacturers of the V200. There were, it must be said, some considerable doubts at Swindon regarding the sagicity of purchasing large numbers of diesels which would not only be built by outside contractors, but would also be reliant upon these same firms for the supply of spare parts. Since the turn of the century, Swindon had acted as a kingpin in the supply and maintenance of the GWR's locomotive stocks and although orders for new locomotives had been placed with outside suppliers both before and after nationalisation (including one with North British for fifty pannier tanks in 1928), there remained a real

antipathy towards the idea of devolving any more work than necessary from the ambit of the railway workshops.

Whilst it was recognised that much of the componentry required for the new locomotives, not least of all the engines and transmissions themselves, would have to be acquired from commercial manufacturers, it was desired that final construction and erection should take place at Swindon, possibly under the sort of licensing arrangement used by many companies in the fulfilment of large export orders. Given that a major attraction of diesel-hydraulic traction had been the ease with which existing facilities and personnel could be deployed in order to service and maintain it, there can then have seemed little point in seeing expensive plant at Swindon lying idle whilst the machines were bought-in from outside. The importance of the Works to the WR as a whole remained as great as ever, and the prospect of redundancies amongst the workforce or any scaling-down of operations there would not have been welcomed by the Western Area Board.

A liaison was soon established between the WR and the Maybach Motorenbau of Friedrichshafen and, through the agencies of that concern, the WR was formally introduced not only to Krauss-Maffei of München-Allach who were responsible for the overall design and construction of the V200s, but also to the Engineering Department of the Deutsche Bundesbahn. The WR was still drawn towards the power:weight ratio of 26bhp/ton offered by the V200 design as compared to the 15bhp/ton offered by the Southern 1Co-Co1 or the 17bhp/ton promised by the forthcoming North British A1A-A1As and, in an intriguing reprise of Churchward's purchase of the three French compound Atlantics half a century before, consideration was given to purchasing a standard V200 from Germany for in-service evaluation on the WR. This, however, was doomed to failure, for though the generous Great Western loading gauge would accomodate the German machine, the V200's underside clearances were to prove insufficient for British use. Moreover, the BTC was insisting (not unreasonably) that all locomotives should conform to the national L1 loading gauge and, less defensibly, frowned upon the acquisition of

a foreign-built locomotive even for experimental purposes.

This disappointment was tempered somewhat when Maybach assured the WR that there was nothing to prevent a production line being set up in the UK to produce a version of the V200 to comply with BR specifications. Evidence was cited of growing monthly mileages on the part of the V200s and details given of a complete range of locomotives of between 800 and 3000bhp, all sharing common mechanical components. Furthermore, Maybach were willing to supply six complete engine-transmission sets, along with cardan shafts, axledrives and control equipment at an attractive price, whilst Krauss-Maffei would be happy to grant a license for the construction of V200-type locomotives in BTC workshops, backing this up with engineering drawings and expert advice. If the trial units proved satisfactory, then Maybach and K-M would allow expansion of the fleet by finding suitable UK licensees for the mechanical units. License fees payable to K-M in respect of the superstructure and bogies would be arranged on a sliding scale, the payment per locomotive being decreased as production quantities rose, and reduced further still if the BTC sub-contracted any aspect of the work to Krauss-Maffei themselves. In view of the eagerness of the WR for the V200, and the fact that such an arrangement would permit construction of new motive power whilst offsetting the effects of declining steam-derived work in BR workshops, these terms were accepted by the BTC. At around the same time, the WR dropped its proposal for diesel-hydraulic multiple-units, although this was later resurrected at BTC behest in diesel-electric form for the 'Blue Pullman' trains.

The enthusiasm for the licensing arrangement was by no means restricted to the WR. Krauss-Maffei were quick to recognise both the WR's perceived requirements and the fact that the V200 fitted these specifications like a glove. Even under the terms of a licensing agreement with the BTC and British sub-contractors, successful performance by V200-type locomotives on the WR could well mean a steady stream of very lucrative business from a dieselising British Railways. Furthermore, the operation of such locomotives by BR could constitute a prominent and prestigious 'shop window' for K-M products in general, an important consideration at a time when US diesel manufacturers were wresting export custom away from European builders on a regular basis. Once an agreement had been reached, WR and BTC staff participated in visits to Germany so as to gain practical experience with equipment of the type on order and in January 1956, formal instructions were given to Swindon Works by the BTC with regard to the construction of three B-B locomotives of the K-M design to absorb the forthcoming machinery. This additional order was thereby officially incorporated into the Pilot Scheme.

Whereas the MAN units used in the NBL products represented in many ways the zenith of conventional compression-ignition oil engine development, the MD650 engine which Maybach would supply to the BTC was an altogether more advanced beast. Established in 1909 by Dr Karl Maybach and the airship pioneer Count Ferdinand von Zeppelin, the Maybach Motorenbau had from its inception specialised in the construction of high-quality internal combustion engines for aircraft, marine and automotive applications. During the 1930s the firm had diversified into the fast-growing field of diesel engines for railway traction and had amassed considerable experience with the development of the G-Type, a four-stroke twelve-cylinder vee-formation engine in both normally-aspirated and supercharged forms, with power outputs up to 800bhp. Although these relatively limited outputs restricted their use to railcars, including the famed 'Flying Hamburger' consists, the G-Types not only proved the concept of high-speed diesel engines for rail traction but also the use of components such as roller bearings for crankshafts and connecting rods. Development

continued throughout the war years with the related HL-series petrol engine, eventually reaching maturity in the form of the twelve-cylinder HL230-P45, a 700bhp unit that powered the redoubtable Tiger tank and which introduced several of the most important features to be seen in postwar construction. After a series of heavily-revised G-Types (classified GTO) had been constructed to assess the value of these modifications, Maybach pressed ahead with the development of a fresh design incorporating the best features of all the engines built up until then. The result would be an integrated family of engines which sought to combine maximum performance with strength, lightness and economy. The MD-series, as it was christened, included units of both in-line and vee configurations, ranging between 22 and 86 litres swept capacity, all of which contained a high proportion of interchangeable components. For railway applications, however, two were of especial interest: the twelve-cylinder MD650 as used in the V200s and the sixteen-cylinder MD865.

The MD650 incorporated a cast iron crankcase and engine frame structure, with cylinder banks facing each other at a 60° angle. Cylinders had a bore of 185mm and a stroke of 200mm, giving a total swept capacity of 64.51 litres. Pistons were of a two-piece bi-metal design, a conventional alloy skirt being surmounted by a detachable steel crown designed to withstand high combustion temperatures. (These steel crowns, by the way, could be removed for routine examination or replacement of the piston rings without the need to withdraw the entire piston and connecting rod assembly.) A further safeguard was the provision of flexible oil pipes on the connecting rods to cool the underside of the pistons, the latter being arranged so that this cooling oil could flow through a channel in the piston crown below the combustion surface. Returning oil then served to lubricate the conrod gudgeon pin bearings. Cast iron cylinder liners were individually replaceable and were a loose fit into the block, being sealed by rubber rings top and bottom. A channel was run in the liner periphery between each pair of sealing rings, vented to the outside through an open inspection port in the outer face of each cylinder block, leakage of oil or coolant through the port signifying failure of the lower or upper sealing ring respectively. A further soft iron ring at the top of the bore provided a gas-tight seal between cylinder liner and head. The crankcase was of the 'Tunnel' design, derived from the Maybach HL; the crankshaft it contained had circular webs enclosed in roller bearings forming the main shaft supports, their outer races being located in the transverse crankcase stiffeners. The resulting ensemble lent great rigidity both to the rotating components and to the engine structure, the double function of these discs as both crankwebs and main bearings giving more space for the crankpins, so enabling load to be well spread over the lead-bronze big-end bearings of the connecting rods. The rods themselves were of fork-and-blade configuration, those on the right-hand bank having bifurcated big-ends, each shell spanning the two halves of the fork. Each left-hand connecting rod located within the forked end of the corresponding right-hand rod, its bearing shell sliding over the outer surface of that on the forked rod. As the blade big-end had twice the bearing surface of each half of the forked rod, working loads were divided equally between cylinder banks.

As with the MAN engine, twelve individual cylinder heads were used, though manufactured from mild steel. The similarity, however, ended there as the Maybach units were very much more sophisticated, with three inlet and three outlet valves per cylinder. Each set of valves was actuated by rocker arms driven from overhead camshafts, individual shafts being provided for the inlet and exhaust functions on each cylinder bank. All rockers were of the roller type with integral hydraulic tappets to reduce wear and so ensure minimal maintenance requirements. The camshafts, four in all,

 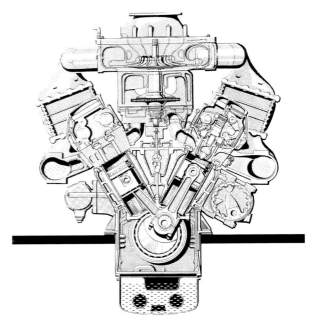

Above Left: The first Swindon-built diesel-hydraulics were equipped with Maybach power equipment, initially supplied direct from Germany and subsequently assembled under license in Britain. This is the 12-cylinder Maybach MD650 engine used in the early D800s, showing off such details of its construction as the vertically-mounted centrifugal turbocharger. *(MTU)*

Above Right: Cross-sectional view of a Maybach MD-series diesel, illustrating the tunnel crankcase with its roller-bearing crankshaft, twin overhead camshafts on each cylinder bank, and vertically-mounted centrifugal turbocharger. *(MTU)*

were gear-driven from the crankshaft, a layout which, despite its complexity, promised more accurate valve events and therefore a greater output than with a pushrod mechanism. In order to conserve space, each cylinder head had a one-piece L'Orange fuel injector and pump assembly actuated by the cam gear, with a separate regulating shaft determining the quantity of fuel delivered via a helix in each injector. The Maybach AGL123 turbocharger was of vertical-shaft form, intended to occupy otherwise unused roofspace, with an exhaust-driven axial-flow turbine located below (and concentric with) a centrifugal blower operating at speeds of up to 13,000rpm. Feed air entering the turbocharger casing at the top was directed down onto the hub of the blower, the action of which caused it to be flung outwards under centrifugal force. Diffuser vanes on the inner surface of the casing itself then acted to collect the displaced air, the extreme velocity of which provided a boost in pressure of 10.4psi at the engine's inlet manifolds. Quite apart from its space-saving attributes, the AGL123's design promised a high degree of efficiency and reliability over a long service life. The technologically-advanced specification of the engine as a whole enabled it to produce some 1135bhp at 1530rpm with an attendant weight of 10,250lb, despite the cast iron basis of its construction. In order to achieve this, many components were both highly-stressed and produced to very close tolerances, so demanding preheating to around 40°C prior to use, a process which took about 45 minutes but greatly abated wear during the starting cycle.

Also covered by the agreement was the Maybach Mekydro K104 transmission. Like its Voith counterpart, the Mekydro was a development of the basic Föttinger principle, but with one important difference. During the late 1920s, Maybach had recognised two major failings in the

Föttinger transmission as it then stood, the greatest of which was the need to fill the converter every time that power was applied and empty it whenever power was removed or applied to a different converter in the sequence. This inevitably brought about a significant decrease in responsiveness, a situation which was compounded by the fairly rapid decomposition of the transmission oil resulting from the high temperatures encountered within the converters. Furthermore, restriction to two or three hydraulic stages meant that the two extremes of the speed-tractive effort curve, i.e. starting and continuous high-speed running, were to be found within the areas of lowest converter efficiency. Dr Maybach envisaged a solution to this in the form of a single large torque converter, permanently filled and coupled to a variable-ratio mechanical transmission so as to provide the required flexibility. This latter took the form of a self-changing four-speed gearbox with a series of permanently meshed gears, the majority of which rotated freely on layshafts but could be engaged with one another as and when required by means of over-running claw clutches. These, developed to facilitate the use of semi-automatic overdrive units on Maybach's motor cars, avoided the need to synchronise rotating gearclusters under high load conditions, and allowed the concept of the Mekydro transmission to be made a reality.

The first Mekydro units were built in 1938 but activities were interrupted by the outbreak of war and, despite their intended use in a new generation of armoured fighting vehicles, development eventually ceased altogether. After the close of hostilities, Maybach undertook a redesign of the concept and by the early 1950s had two variants in commercial production, the KL64 for engines up to 600bhp, and the K104 for engines up to 1000bhp. Like its smaller sister, the K104 used a conventional step-up gear attached to the input flange, driving a permanently-filled single-stage torque converter, the output from which led directly to the gearbox. Whilst the converter provided a variable relationship between engine speed and track speed, the overall gearing was determined by the status of the gearbox, gear stages being changed automatically dependent upon track speed and power output as measured by a centrifugal governor.

At the moment of change, movement of a distribution valve in a complex hydraulic control block located above the gearbox would admit pressurised oil to the operating cylinders for the appropriate claw clutches as well as to a further small cylinder located within the converter itself.

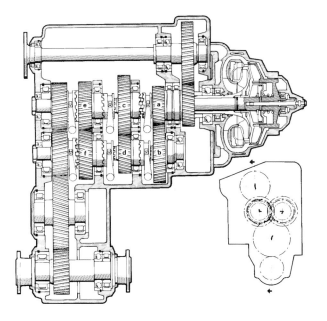

This provided sufficient axial movement of the turbine runner to move the turbine assembly out of the flow of oil from the pump wheel, which now impinged upon a secondary rotor not normally part of the circuit. This created a weak reverse torque which, by decelerating the driven gearwheels, allowed the inclined teeth on the over-running clutches to engage and establish a rigid link between the chosen gears. Only with this process completed would the converter be re-engaged in order to prevent the possibility of driveline shunt, engine speed having remained constant throughout the gearchange operation. The unidirectional nature of the claw clutches meant that the rotation of the change speed gears had to be fixed also, necessitating the provision of a pair of separate reversing gears at the output end of the casing, also operated through the main control block. Under emergency conditions, such as failure of the control system between cab and transmission, gear changes could be performed through the use of manual controls acting directly upon the hydraulic valving. This feature, however, was not a viable means of operating a locomotive other than for getting it off the running lines and out of the way. Input capacity was 966bhp as compared with the 950bhp of the Voith unit, about 50bhp being absorbed from each engine by the demands of auxillary pumps, generators and the like. Unlike the Voith unit, however, stage changes involved a complete break in tractive effort at the wheels, albeit of extremely short duration.

As the ordering of non-steam mainline traction began to accelerate, the BTC began to devote itself towards some of the secondary aspects of railway modernisation. One of its first steps in this regard was the evolution of a power classification system for the latest generation of motive power, and in July 1956 the Commission unveiled a new code whereby locomotives of between 600 and 1000bhp were classified as Type A, 1000 to 1250bhp as Type B and 2000bhp or over as Type C. Whilst simple to use, these proposals had a fundamental flaw insofar that they failed to cater for the whole range of locomotive capacities, most notably those of similar capability to a Class 5MT steam locomotive. A further serious omission was of any category for machines boasting significantly more than 2000bhp, which the BTC was just beginning to appreciate as necessary, if not cost-effective. In November 1957, therefore,

Above Left: Schematic longitudinal section through a Maybach Mekydro transmission unit. The input is at top left, driving through a pair of step-up gears to the torque converter at top right, which in turn transmits power to the integral four-speed self-changing gearbox. Change-speed gear wheels are labelled a-f, with the over-running claw clutches readily visible between them. Reversing gears are situated at the left-hand end of the casing above the output shaft. *(MTU)*

Above Right: Mated to the MD650 was the Maybach Mekydro K104 transmission. Of single-converter construction, the design achieved the required flexibility of operation through the use of an integral self-changing gearbox. The output flange can be seen at the bottom of the unit, with the torque converter behind the dome-like casing at the near end of the block. *(MTU)*

they were replaced by a new classification system whereby locomotives of 650 to 1000bhp were known as Type 1, 1000 to 1250bhp as Type 2, 1500 to 1750bhp as Type 3, 2000 to 2500bhp as Type 4 and 2500 to 3000bhp as Type 5. It was under these terms that the Pilot Scheme diesel-hydraulics appeared, and to many it was apparent that the importance of regional individuality so often stressed by the BTC Chairman had, in fact, over-ridden the need for standardisation expressed in the Modernisation Plan. The decision of the WR to maintain its diesel-hydraulic policy contrary to the inclinations of a predominantly pro-diesel-electric BTC might well have been a valid one in terms of the applicability of traction types to regional needs, but the situation that emerged from this was one where the existence of two diametrically opposed schools of thought, coupled with the needless meddling of some higher BTC officers, succeeded only in introducing locomotive designs that would contravene all the terms of the WR's dieselisation scheme. Moreover, their creation would mark the end of a carefully planned policy of standardisation that dated back to the early days of Churchward and which, if left alone, would have continued for the full lifespan of the hydraulics. As a result, the criteria for dieselisation so carefully evolved by the WR were compromised before they could be put into effect, and the direction to be taken in the years ahead was thus subjected to a change which was both important and irrevocable.

Chapter 4

THE D600 'WARSHIPS'

THE first tangible move towards implementation of the WR's diesel-hydraulic traction policy was taken, somewhat reluctantly, by the BTC itself. During the summer of 1955, a preliminary order for five 2000bhp locomotives (to be numbered D600-4) and six 1000bhp locomotives (to be numbered D6300-5) was placed with the North British Locomotive Company of Glasgow, and was ratified that November. As the only British manufacturer having the commercial arrangements required for the supply and installation of the German traction equipment, the BTC at that stage had no choice of supplier other than NBL if the new locomotives were to be built in private workshops. Although the WR was still primarily interested in adapting the German V200 to suit UK conditions, the acquisition of such locomotives would mean either buying them complete from Krauss-Maffei in Munich, something to which the BTC could not accede for political reasons, or alternatively concluding the necessary arrangements to build them under license in Britain. At the time that negotiations were being finalised between the BTC and NBL, discussions between the WR and Maybach were at a very early and essentially still-informal stage, and the eventual license-building agreement was still some way off. Another consideration was the BTC's undoubted fear of the consequences, both political and economic, of allowing foreign suppliers access to a home market where domestic constructors were ill-equipped to meet the demands of a massive state-financed railway modernisation programme. Although still diesel-hydraulics, it was felt that the forthcoming D600s and D6300s would at least be designed and made in Britain, and that any future large orders for such machines would not imperil the position of domestic suppliers either in home or in export markets. From the WR's viewpoint, acceptance of NBL's proposals was regarded primarily as an expedient means of paving the way for further developments, rather than implicit approval of the designs themselves.

The BTC, meanwhile, having yielded to WR demands for high-power diesel-hydraulics, was determined to impose its own conditions. As recounted in Chapter 3, the engineers of the BTC's Central Staff had an innate distrust of the lightweight construction adopted by Krauss-Maffei, and eventually mandated a heavyweight six-axle design displaying a mix of Anglo-American and German practices which experience would prove to be often uneasy bedfellows. Justifying its decision, the BTC professed itself reluctant to sanction outputs at the rail as high as 450bhp per axle, and to this coupled a requirement for braking force sufficient to allow the working of heavy unbraked trains until such time as the Modernisation Plan had been fully implemented in all aspects. The resulting quintet of 'heavy duty' locomotives was, in the BTC's opinion, directly equivalent to the 2000bhp 1Co-Co1 diesel-electrics then being ordered from English Electric though, in reality, the chosen method of construction served to negate the inherently better power:weight ratios offered by the diesel-hydraulic format, producing machines with most of the diesel-electric's vices but few of its virtues.

NBL's initial quote for the five 2000bhp locomotives placed them at £86,000 each, an attractive price for units of

that output which, to the untrained eye, reflected the lower initial costs of diesel-hydraulic as opposed to diesel-electric traction. In reality, for an order of only five units, it was something of a bargain which waived many overheads such as drawing office costs in the hope of gaining repeat orders. These costs, of course, had to be absorbed by NBL and would have been higher still had the BTC not been willing to accept a machine broadly based upon the LMS diesel twins 10000/10001, the already-proven structural aspects of which allowed NBL to reproduce certain items and reduce costs accordingly. The fact that fundamentally experimental units were produced at prices akin to those of mass-produced service locomotives is indicative of NBL's desperation to gain much-needed follow-up orders from the BTC in order to compensate for the falling volume of home- and export-market steam traction work. Also required was a level of cheese-paring in manufacture, and so a locomotive already the result of compromise between the WR and the BTC's Central Staff became compromised further whilst under construction.

The underframes of the locomotives were formed from a welded and rivetted ensemble of large steel I-sections, surmounted by thick floor plates. As the frame height was above the level of the buffers, the ends deepened in section and met with cast steel dragboxes, the tapering form of the dropends bringing buffing loads gradually up to floor height and so resisting local deformation. Notably, in order to reduce superfluous weight, given the massive underframe, the superstructure was manufactured almost entirely from aluminium with only localised steel reinforcements. Another 'first' was the employment of specialist industrial designers by a BTC presumably convinced that mere railway staff were incapable of imparting a proper finish to the new machines! More seriously, the Commission had noted with some trepidation the huge multiplicity of bodystyles and even livery variations which commercial locomotive builders in North America had thrust upon the dieselising railroads, and for its own part wished to ensure at least an element of visual continuity between the offerings of different suppliers. Some overall guidelines were drawn-up in conjunction with the BTC's own design office, outside consultants then being engaged to liaise with the builders during construction with the aim of overseeing the detailed

Top: D600, BR's first Type 4 locomotive under the Modernisation Plan and the Western Region's first diesel-hydraulic, seen on test in Scotland in December 1957, prior to delivery from NBL. The locomotive is still in undercoat, with numbering and nameplates yet to be applied. *(Voith)*

Middle: Construction of Type 4 diesel-hydraulics proceeds apace at the Queen's Park Works of the North British Locomotive Company late in 1957. Dominating proceedings are a pair of underframes, that in the centre of the shot showing-off the boxed apertures for the transmission units and the adjacent longitudinal engine bearers. An assortment of components including a Spanner train-heating boiler, a D600 bogie frame and its associated cast bolster, is visible to the fore. *(Mitchell Library)*

Bottom: Weight diagram for D600-4 *(National Railway Museum)*

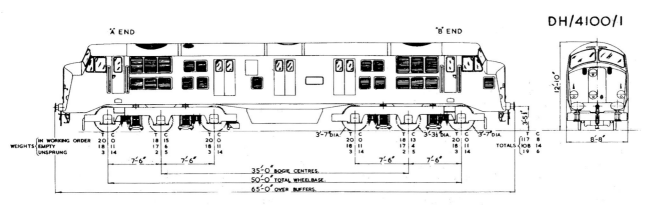

DH/4100/1

'A' END   'B' END

12'-0"

3-5½"

3'-7" DIA.   3'-3½" DIA.   3'-7" DIA.

		T	C		T	C		T	C		T	C		T	C		T	C			T	C
WEIGHTS	IN WORKING ORDER	20	0		18	15		20	0		20	0		18	13		20	0	TOTALS	117	8
	EMPTY	18	11		17	6		18	11		18	11		17	4		18	11		108	14
	UNSPRUNG	3	14		2	5		3	14		3	14		2	5		3	14		19	6

7'-6"   7'-6"   7'-6"   7'-6"

35'-0" BOGIE CENTRES.
50'-0" TOTAL WHEELBASE.
65'-0" OVER BUFFERS.

8'-8"

Top: D600 about halfway to completion at Queen's Park, with engines, transmissions, radiator blocks and Alpax cab assemblies installed on the underframe. The small size of the engine units in relation to the bulk of the locomotive as a whole is noticeable, especially when compared to the West German V200s. *(Mitchell Library)*

Bottom: The installed engine and transmission assembly of the D600, pictured prior to the fitment of bodyside cladding. The partial recession of the Voith transmission in the underframe is apparent, as are the cardan shafts for the final drive protruding from the hollow bogie pivot. The engine is a German-built L12V18/21A, indicated by the use of a MAN turbocharger rather than the Napier unit later specified. *(Mitchell Library)*

application of these basic groundrules. In the case of the NBL hydraulics, the work was supervised by Professor J.B.McCrum and although the basic form followed that of the earlier LMS locomotives, certain changes were made in the interests of appearance. The slab sides of the previous machines gave way to a tumblehome contour, albeit in the form of two flat sections with a sharp dividing line at waist level, the bottom of the panelling curving away below the underframe. The cabs were of two-window rather than three-window construction in the interests of aesthetics and ergonomics alike, with stainless-steel handrails being set into recesses on either side of the cab doorways. Like the rest of the body panelling, the cab assembly was of aluminium construction so as to save weight, though in the shape of numerous castings welded together on a jig. Combining steel and aluminium in this manner to create a single structure presented some considerable danger of galvanic corrosion, and preventative measures were taken through the application of a zinc-chromate primer to all aluminium-steel contact points vulnerable to attack. Ahead of the windscreens, the rather blunt nose of the LMS machines gave way to a clean-cut profile featuring a slightly tapering front surface, the bulbousness typical of American designs such as EMD's E7 or Fairbanks-Morse's C-Liner being avoided through the use of small-radius curves separating gently-rounded horizontal and vertical panels. The central part of each nose end had to be upright in order to accomodate the somewhat stunted gangway connections required to allow communication between two locomotives working in multiple. When not in use, these were concealed by flush-fitting light alloy doors, flanked on each side by grilles protecting the 'Desilux' airhorns.

With dieselisation still in its infancy, there had not yet been any moves to modify coaching stock from the traditional system of heat supplied by low pressure steam from the locomotive to some form more appropriate to modern traction, such as electrically-powered heating units. Accordingly, the D600s needed to be equipped with oil-fired steam generators of the sort then used on American passenger diesels and, of the three British-made units best-suited to rail traction use, the Spanner Mark 1a would be selected as that with which BR already had most experience. Taking the form of an automatically-controlled vertical boiler, administered as required from the driver's cab by the fireman, this piece of apparatus was mounted laterally slightly off-centre in the D600 in order to permit a cross-passageway from one side of the locomotive to the other. Using this as a centrepoint, the remainder of the internal equipment was arranged in a roughly symmetrical fashion on each side. Mounted equidistant between the train-heating boiler and the rear bulkhead of each cab was a MAN L12V18/21A engine, driving through step-up gears to a Voith L306r main transmission block situated tight against each cab so as to position its output end directly over the bogie centre. On the first two units to be constructed the driveline components were something of a bone of contention as, despite its licensing arrangements and promises to the BTC of all-British manufacture, NBL had bought them ready-assembled from MAN's Augsburg and Voith's Heidenheim works in Germany. The engines were, after all, the first of their kind that NBL had dealt with, and the move was understandable both from the point of view of gaining initial installation experience and in speeding construction of the first locomotives whilst production arrangements for Glasgow-built engines and transmissions were in hand. Engines were set at 1000bhp at 1445rpm whilst transmission change-up points were 29 and 57mph. Interestingly, the transition points between the various converters under deceleration were slightly lower, at 53 and 27mph.

Due to the generic inability of internal combustion engines to start themselves, the need for an initial cranking action was fulfilled through the provision of a dynastarter for each engine. These acted first as starter motors driven off the locomotive batteries then, when the engine was running of its own accord, as generators supplying current to the batteries and thence the rest of the electrical system. On D600-1 the dynastarters were Brown-Boveri 33kW units, situated between the engines and the train-heating boiler and connected to the former through a flexible coupling, integral voltage regulators ensuring a 100V supply when generating, regardless of running speed. Above each was mounted a light alloy fuel tank, one of 475 and the other of 375 gallons capacity. Engine exhaust was ducted out through the roof above the transmission end of each engine, the space above the transmission itself being used to accomodate the cooling groups. Each radiator bank was distanced from the locomotive sides and located in an individual compartment, air flow being maintained at the required level by a cooling fan in the roof space, driven by a thermostatically-controlled electric motor. Although the radiators handled only engine coolant, separate heat exchangers were plumbed into the water circuit to dissipate excess heat from the engine and transmission oils, an arrangement which also had the desirable characteristic of bringing these fluids up to working temperature much more quickly than would otherwise have been so. The same layout of cooling equipment was duplicated at both ends of the locomotive, the only difference being that the groupings were staggered by equal distances from the locomotive centreline in order to permit a walk-through gangway, yet retain correct weight distribution.

The cabs themselves, along with the nose ends, made extensive use of blown glassfibre for insulation and noise reduction purposes, concealed behind melamine lining panels, but reflected the lack of any formal agreement between the BTC and the footplatemen's association on cab design. As a result, North British had been left to do the job with little in the way of precedents or guidelines and so the unfortunate driver was confronted by a rather idiosyncratic control layout, inspired in part by then-current American practice. On each side of the nose access doors in the middle of the cab's front bulkhead was located an instrument panel, that on the left containing the driver's main gauges (speedometer, engine rev-counter and brake pressure) and that on the right the lighting controls and control equipment for the train-heating boiler, this being the responsibility of the fireman. Both crew members benefitted from the provision of upholstered chairs, in stark contrast to the simple tip-up wooden seats of the steam engines that the locomotives were intended to replace; enginemen suddenly found that it was at last more comfortable to sit than to stand! Brake controls for both locomotive and train were situated on a shelf to the driver's left whilst a pedestal to his right, between him and the nose access, contained various warning lights, the engine starting controls and the power and reversing levers for the main control system. The latter, supplied by British Thompson-Houston, was of the electro-pneumatic variety with seven power notches, interlocked so as to prevent reversal of the transmissions except when the locomotive was stationary, or the selection of any engine power setting above minimum with the reversing lever in the 'Engines Only' position. Another safeguard isolated the controls of the unoccupied cab as well as those of any locomotive coupled in multiple.

Provision had been made from the start for the multiple working of locomotives with another 2000bhp D600 or up to two 1000bhp D6300s, one driver being responsible for the working of all locomotives coupled in multiple and being able to exercise control from the leading cab. Here a distinction should be drawn between the concepts of working in multiple and double-heading, for the former relied upon all locomotives concerned sharing the same type of control system; if this was not the case, and it frequently was not, or steam/diesel combinations were required, oper-

ations had to be performed in the accepted way with a crew in each locomotive. Air for the control system as well as for the locomotive brakes, sanding gear and windscreen wipers was provided by a pair of electrically-driven Westinghouse compressors, one in each nose end, whilst an exhauster of the same manufacture for the vacuum train brakes was located alongside each engine. The two brake systems were interconnected so that whilst application of the locomotive's straight air brake by the driver was always independent of the train vacuum brake, service operation of the latter would incur a corresponding application of the locomotive's own brakes via a proportional valve. Also incorporated was a Driver's Safety Device consisting of a treadle which had to be depressed by the driver's foot whilst the locomotive was under power. The releasing of this treadle, or the operation under emergency conditions of a push button located on the fireman's side, would initiate a process culminating in the shutting-down of the engines and full application of the brakes.

By and large, the North British Type 4 changed little between conception and construction, with one critical exception. Given the record of the Ivatt-designed Co bogie (itself largely inspired by GM's Electromotive passenger bogie) as a good rider in high-speed service, it was initially adopted almost unchanged for the new machines. This should have done much to facilitate an early delivery, something for which the BTC continued to press despite the obvious magnitude of the task facing NBL but, in the event, the Glasgow firm's inexperience with mainline diesel traction proved an insurmountable obstacle given the constraints of the timescale involved. Quite simply unable to devise a suitable bogie allowing all axles to be driven, and under pressure from the BTC to finalise the detail specification, NBL took the existing Ivatt design, reduced its length somewhat and altered it to an A1A arrangement, in effect returning it to the condition in which it was first proposed for use under 10000/10001. The inclusion of idling axles emasculated one of the basic arguments behind the BTC's 'heavy duty' specification, namely its refusal to accept 450bhp drives on four driven axles, as well as decreasing available adhesive weight by a third, though the locomotive's total weight ensured that this factor remained relatively high by diesel-hydraulic standards. In the final assessment, culpability for this contrivance must lie not so much with NBL as with the BTC (and especially that body's Technical Development & Research Committee) for allowing prejudice and dogma to dominate design work in the first place. Similar interference on its part, in the name of reducing track loadings, would be responsible for the use of the Bulleid/Bollen 1Co bogie under English Electric's rival Type 4, and thus the proliferation of the clumsy and heavy D200s rather than the desired expedient of uprating the more compact and workmanlike Ivatt design.

Apart from the compromised driving configuration, most original details of the Ivatt design were retained, such as bogie side members fabricated from two deep plates joined by welded ties and ribs to form box members with integral extensions for the axlebox guides. These side members were then married up with rivetted transverse stretchers and headstocks to form the bogie mainframe assembly. The superstructure was supported in the manner patented by Ivatt on the LMS locomotives, using a large cast steel double bolster connected to the bogie frame by pairs of swing links and with rubbing pads at each corner to carry the locomotive's weight. A large circular opening in the centre of the bolster, above the idling axle, accepted a turret protruding from below the superstructure which was responsible for carrying braking, traction and side thrusts as well as providing a bogie pivot. Each turret was of sufficiently large diameter to accomodate the transmission output and from there, cardan shafts led to the outer axles on each bogie. As no arrangement had been made with Voith

Top: On 17 February 1958, an interested crowd survey D600, by now named *Active,* preparing to leave Paddington with the inaugural press trip to Bristol. The return leg of this ill-fated journey would be completed on one engine following mechanical failure of the second unit. *(Colin J. Marsden Collection)*

Bottom: By the time that the second batch of D600s began to arrive on the WR, the first pair had already entered revenue-earning service. On 5 October 1959, D600 departs Paddington light engine for Old Oak Common; the disfiguring effect of the various route indicators and other accoutrements on NBL's clean nose design is clearly visible. *(B Webb/B.J. Miller Collection)*

regarding the provision of axledrive assemblies, David Brown units of the spiral bevel and helical gear double-reduction variety were utilised. Both driving wheels of 43" diameter and carrying wheels of 39" diameter were of spoked design running in Timken roller-bearing axleboxes. These bore on H-section equalising beams carried within the bogie side members, the purpose of which was to facilitate load transfer between adjacent wheelsets. This in turn allowed the primary coil springs located between the equalising beams and the frame itself to be of a reduced rate, so giving a better ride. Secondary suspension between bogie and bolster was through four pairs of full-elliptic leaf springs, sandwiched between the bolster and the swing-link spring plank. Clasp brakes on all wheels were applied by four Westinghouse compressed-air cylinders mounted on each bogie, as were the sandboxes.

Delivery had been projected for fifteen months from the time of the order, but completion of the first locomotive would not in fact take place until November 1957. In retrospect, the failure to meet the agreed schedule reflected not only NBL's own difficulties but also BR's insistence on specifying extras after the original contract had been signed. As an example, when testing of the Yarrow wheelsets revealed slight inequalities capable of producing noticeable vibration at high speeds, dynamic balancing was ordered for all five locomotives, although D600 was largely complete and D601 well advanced. Other items fitted at extra cost included various controls and ancillaries, end footsteps, brackets for route indicator stencils and WR ATC (automatic train control) apparatus. Representing a cost to the BTC of some £87,500, D600 was handed over to its new owners in December, hauling several test trains in Scotland before finally leaving Queen's Park Works for Swindon. It had been outshopped in BR green with black bogies and underframe equipment, a 4"-wide light grey bodyside stripe and the customary red bufferbeams and

stocks. Below the BR emblem near the centre of the body-side was carried a large nameplate that identified D600 as *Active*, the type being officially considered as the 'Warship' class. The decision that D600 should perpetuate the tradition of named locomotives was largely taken at the request of the Western Region Area Board, and this was reflected in the style of the plate. Of oblong shape, the nameplates featured a 'Clarendon' script similar to that used by the old GWR, with the 'Warship Class' identification below the name in a small sans-serif font. Unlike the old Great Western plates which had been fabricated from brass and steel, the new design was a one-piece casting in light alloy, but nevertheless succeeded in providing an accomplished finishing touch to the locomotive as a whole. As well as having the honour of being the first named diesel on BR, to D600 would fall the unassailable distinction of being the first Type 4 to be delivered.

D600 spent its first few weeks on the WR engaged in testing and driver training, its first public duty being to head a 340-ton train from Paddington to Bristol and back on 17 February 1958, carrying representatives of the press and a party of VIPs including the Minister of Transport. Stops were made at Reading, Didcot and Swindon and whilst no spectacular feats were achieved on the westbound trip via Bath (indeed, it was the sheer lack of spectacle that made the 95mph ascent of Dauntsey bank so impressive) the return to London was to provide rather more of a talking point. Shortly after leaving Bristol on the direct line through Chipping Sodbury, a sudden drop in oil pressure thought to have been induced by a faulty bearing caused one of the engines to shut down, necessitating that the rest of the journey be made on half-power at reduced speed. This simultaneously proved the arguments of both the protagonists and opponents of the WR traction policy; the high-speed, light-weight German engines were not 100% reliable (perhaps less so than than a single large slow-speed unit with fewer wearing parts) but the twin-engine installation did allow the locomotive to keep running, despite its infirmity, and thus make such failures less of a hindrance to traffic.

Fortunately for the WR, the press did not make any great issue of the incident, and once D600 was repaired its capabilities were assessed by means of running-in trips and dynamometer car tests, in which it was joined by sister locomotive D601 *Ark Royal* in March. The principal aim of this was to establish the maximum load which the new locomotives could reliably handle, especially over the formidable grades of the South Devon banks. Although the answer of ten coaches or 375 tons meant that piloting would still be necessary for the heavy summer holiday trains, the D600s could maintain existing schedules with such loads whilst returning a considerable fuel saving compared to the outgoing 'King'-class 4-6-0s. Work levels were gradually increased and experience gained until, on 16 June 1958, the WR felt sufficiently confident in its new acquisitions to roster D601 for the 'Cornish Riviera'. This was the first time that this train had been diesel-hauled non-stop between London and Plymouth and once again the D600s eclipsed the rival D200 diesel-electrics on the Eastern Region, the 'Flying Scotsman' not being converted to diesel haulage for nearly a week longer. Fuel capacity of the new locomotives was sufficient to allow a round trip without refuelling, even with the train-heating boiler in operation, and for the time being the pair continued to work these trains turn and turn about with their steam counterparts. In that same month, D601 spent some time running trial trips between Plymouth

33

Above: For a number of years, the big 'Six Hundreds' could be numbered amongst the backbone of the WR's motive power fleet, working in conjunction not only with the Swindon D800s but also the 'Castles' and 'Kings'. On a sunny 4 July 1961, D603 *Conquest* awaits time at Plymouth North Road with the chocolate and cream coaching stock of the up 'Cornish Riviera'. *(Norman E. Preedy)*

Left: With the arrival of the lighter, faster and more reliable D800 'Warships', the D600s were displaced from many of the top passenger workings, but D601 *Ark Royal* was still needed to pilot D832 *Onslaught* on an up train heading past West London Junction and under Mitre Bridge on 8 June 1962. *(R.H.G. Simpson)*

Below: As time progressed, various alterations were made to the type. Outside Swindon Works in 1963, D604 *Cossack* displays the obligatory yellow warning panel, electrification flashes and the substitution of mesh for louvres in the upper row of radiator grilles. *(B.J. Miller Collection)*

and Newton Abbot with loads of up to 490 tons including the Churchward dynamometer car, in conjunction with 'Castle', 'Hall' and 'Manor' 4-6-0s in order to determine the abilities of various steam and diesel combinations, insufficient diesels being available for regular multiple-working.

It was not until that November that D602 was to arrive on the WR and, although nominally identical to D600-1 and delivering the same 49,460lb of tractive effort, there were important differences. Engines and transmissions, whilst of the same design as before, were now built by NBL themselves in order to come within the terms of their agreement with the BTC. Whilst the transmission units were basically identical to their German counterparts, the Glasgow-built engines made use of British ancillary components so as to reduce dependence upon imported parts, NBL internal correspondence dated as early as December 1957 noting that British electrical equipment was not only cheaper but also lighter than German equivalents. Therefore, dynastarters were now of English Electric rather than Brown-Boveri manufacture, CAV fuel injection pumps supplanted the Bosch variety and MAN turbochargers gave way to Napier units, certain of these modifications subsequently being applied to the original engines. At the same time the engine coding became L12V18/21S, S for 'Supercharged' superceding the German A for 'Aufladung', an unnecessary change that would cause innumerable difficulties in years to come. As in the first two locomotives, no interchange of engine or transmission units was foreseen by the BTC and so connections and mountings were made to suit individual components, rather than facilitating standardisation in the way envisaged by the WR. It was NBL's difficulties in assembling these initial Glasgow-built engines and transmissions that delayed this second series of locomotives, the last, D604, not emerging from Queen's Park Works until January 1959. The trio carried the names *Bulldog*, *Conquest* and *Cossack* respectively and were sent to join their elder sisters at Plymouth Laira, handling the premier West Country and Bristol expresses.

With the arrival of the first three K-M/Swindon D800 B-Bs at the same time, the WR had all eight of its prototype Type 4s in service on top link trains between London and the South West. In some ways, the very arrival of the Swindon-built locomotives rendered the A1A-A1As instantly obsolete, for their delivery marked the culmination of a long and bitter struggle on the WR's part to realise its ambitions, now more than vindicated by the early success of the lightweight D800s in traffic. When editorial comment in the June 1958 edition of *Trains Illustrated* noted that the D600s weighed some 45 tons more than the K-M V200, the inference was that specification of hydraulic transmission for a heavyweight locomotive was simply an extravagance, and although the tone was generally one of acclamation for English Electric's rival Type 4, its unspoken assessment of the D600 echoed feelings within both the BTC and the WR. Furthermore, despite encouraging initial performances from D600-1, both in terms of availability and their capabilities at the head of a train, the arrival of the Swindon D800s saw a palpable decline in the willingness of depot staff to diagram the NBL machines for the most important duties. Accordingly, it came as no surprise that a D800 should be subjected to controlled road testing before its Glaswegian counterpart, and a logical progression when the BTC's option on a further thirty-three D600s was cancelled in favour of a similar number of D800s to be built by NBL with MAN/Voith engine-transmission groups.

Admittedly, the D600s were the brainchild of the BTC rather than the WR and so neither Swindon nor Paddington had any great affection for the beasts, but by the end of their first year of service, problems were beginning to emerge which ran deeper than simple dislike. Whilst the D600s were solid machines well capable of running hard when occasion demanded, as several early instances of 100mph speeds on the 'Cornish Riviera' had proved, the many compromises inherent in their design always lurked close to the surface. With some 50% more deadweight than the WR's competing D800 design, the North British Type 4s had to concede a small but decisive advantage to the Swindon machine in terms of high-speed performance under load. Though the extra rolling resistance imposed by the D600's bulk was equivalent to no more than 400lbs of drawbar force, when applied to the NBL machine's lower overall engine output it proved sufficient to be noticeable on long gradients or when accelerating away from a speed restriction, the effects of which could be to accrue quite a few minutes of downtime on a long journey. Furthermore, certain mechanical components were quickly identified as weak links in the design, needing regular inspection and maintenance if consistent operation was to be ensured. Nevertheless, the aggregate performance of D600/1 in their first eighteen months of service had been sufficient to raise high expectations, implying an achievable mileage of about 90,000 miles per locomotive per year. Sadly, this would represent the sum-

mit of their achievements, and within a relatively short time these large and impressive machines would begin to show the strain of regular express passenger duties upon both engines and transmissions, culminating in an inexorable decline in availability. The performance of D602-4 was less encouraging from the very start and, even allowing for their later entry to service, mileage returns to the end of 1959 remained at a level nearly 40% lower than those of the first two locomotives.

The consistently higher mileages and availability of the first two locomotives compared with their later sisters is notable, and some senior BR officers later admitted that NBL might have done better to have sourced all the MAN engines required for the diesel-hydraulic orders direct from Augsburg, but the demands of the BTC itself made this impossible. What did happen was that poor reliability exerted its own effects upon both usage and availability, with NBL's confusing reclassification of components serving to keep locomotives out of traffic for longer than need have been, especially after North British ceased trading and parts had to be ordered direct from MAN in Germany. Inevitably, this served to force the extension of service intervals for locomotives in traffic, with predictably ill effects upon mechanical components. In the original form fitted to the D600s, the MAN engine's bottom end was its weakest aspect and bearing life, although initially acceptable, could never be described as remarkable. Excessive crankshaft vibration could also pose a problem and some considerable experimentation had to be done before the correct specification of joints in the cardans linking engine and transmission was arrived at. Undamped forces at this point were also the cause of a series of premature transmission bearing failures. Neither were the engines completely free of top-end difficulties, with relatively high rates of piston-ring wear and valve seat erosion, though once again these were not totally beyond what the WR was prepared to regard as an acceptable limit for its first high-power diesels.

The Glasgow-built L12V18/21S units from the outset suffered from additional problems due to the use of often sub-standard components in their construction and as NBL-supplied spare parts began to be applied to the original L12V18/21A engines, failure rates increased on these as well. The real deterioration in MAN engine performance in general would come as serious difficulties with an uprated and more numerous variant began to overload

Below: Looking rather forlorn, a snow-shrouded D603 *Conquest* awaits attention outside Swindon Works in the company of a pair of D800 'Warships' on 6 December 1964. As time went by, the D600s were to become increasingly regular visitors to Swindon for the rectification of engine and transmission maladies. *(R.H.G. Simpson)*

maintenance facilities both at Swindon Works and at the running depots. Under such conditions, these early units with their limited applicability and restricted parts compatibility often assumed a very low priority for the completion of routine maintenance and overhaul work, resulting in amplified failure rates and longer periods out of service. Usual practice would have been to have replaced the engines with new units to the revised design, but the extensive re-equipment of five non-standard locomotives could not be economically justified, whilst the rebuilding of A- and S-series engines to the later 'B' specification was neither practicable nor, given the later engine's service record on the WR, desirable. By 1965, individual mileage returns for the type had fallen below 70,000 miles per annum, D600/1 still managing to outperform the later trio though the differential between the distances covered by the best and worst locomotives was now down to some 25%. This deterioration would continue to accelerate for the remainder of their service life.

However, it must also be pointed out that a large proportion of those faults keeping locomotives out of traffic were not concerned with the major units at all, but rather with supporting auxilliaries. As the locomotives aged, some of the David Brown final drive units became a regular service problem, as did parts of the electrical system. Difficulties here included the deterioration of insulation leading to short-circuits and fires, faulty wiring terminals resulting in lack of continuity, and the ingress of damp which could result in either! The multiple-working apparatus suffered considerably in this regard and eventually, since the locomotives were allowed to work in-multiple only with 'Orange Star'-coded units, namely other D600s and D6300-5, the equipment was at first isolated and subsequently removed altogether. Some of the electrical

Below: The second half of the 1960s saw the North British 'Warships' ever more frequently employed on freight trains. At the head of a Penzance-Paddington parcels train, D602 *Bulldog* heads into the gathering gloom at Cambourne on the evening of 3 July 1966. *(G.B. Wise)*

machines used such as dynastarters and cooling fan drives were major culprits in their own right, and frequently resulted in damage to the locomotives' mechanical parts or electrical systems.

A further frequent cause of locomotives being removed from traffic was failure of the train-heating boiler, which could suddenly cease working for no apparent reason, or refuse to start working at all. Once again, many of the problems revolved around the boilers' control circuits and the electrical system in particular, with many components seemingly of insufficiently high specification to remain reliable within the traction environment. With all its coaching stock equipped for steam heating, British Railways had no choice but to incorporate these devices in its early diesels if they were to be used on passenger duties and despite prolonged testing with different designs and manufactures, found that virtually every steam boiler available had its own set of problems. As a necessary evil, the horrendous failure rates sustained by train-heating boilers were something that BR and its passengers had to tolerate for many years and in this respect, the D600s suffered in common with virtually every other WR, and indeed BR first-generation diesel.

One way in which the original North British Type 4s remained superior to the D800 fleet was in terms of their high adhesive weight and braking force. As a result, by the mid-1960s they were spending most of their time on heavy freight movements, especially block oil tanker workings and the Cornish china clay traffic. In this respect, some drivers considered the North British locomotives inferior only to a D1000 'Western', especially where high levels of tractive effort and braking power were preferred to outright speed, but there was little doubt that the D600s were rather too large to be deployed comfortably on many of the Cornish secondary lines. When occasion demanded, passenger turns did arise from time to time but the general consensus of opinion amongst both enginemen and maintenance staff was that the D600s were no longer fit to be entrusted with the protracted periods of full-throttle working necessary in express passenger duties. Accordingly, any relief from freight traffic tended to be on workings where schedules were relatively relaxed, principally parcels duties interspersed by the occasional off-peak passenger train during the summer months. Even then, the big 'Six Hundreds' usually got no further east than Plymouth before being relieved, the most frequent exceptions to this rule being locomotives deputising for a failure in traffic or those scheduled for routine overhaul working their own way to Swindon.

Physically, there were comparatively few alterations to the type, one of the first being the fitment of additional heating units after crews complained of the cabs' tendency to become unduly cold during the winter months. Demisting of the cab windows proved similarly poor, and in October 1959 oil-damaged heater hoses beneath D604's cab floor were replaced by units of an uprated specification, a modification which was progressively applied to the other members of the class. D603 would end up more extensively modified than its classmates, however, the legacy of an accident suffered after a year or so's service on the WR. Although the actual degree of damage sustained was not particularly severe, it was quite widespread in extent and included derangement of both transmission units, a problem which North British engineers felt could not be rectified at Swindon. As a result, in June 1960 the locomotive was sent to Glasgow for the necessary remedial work, in the course of which NBL were apparently embarrassed to find that many components for this expensive and almost-new machine had already become unavailable. Notably, these included the 'Alpax' castings for the cab structures, items held in stock being sufficient only for the remaining D6300s, and the repaired D603 is reputed to have been returned to the WR with new cab assemblies

Above: The odd passenger working still arose on occasions, especially summer Saturdays, and on 13 August 1966 D601 *Ark Royal* was to be found in charge of the 13.05 Penzance-York, seen here at Bodmin Road. Note that the locomotive has lost its folding headcode discs in favour of split indicator boxes. *(G.B. Wise)*

fabricated from sheet steel in addition to a number of non-standard mechanical components. Paradoxically, photographs published a few years ago demonstrate that at least one spare alloy cab assembly existed, which by the late 1960s had been dumped outside Swindon Works, and why it was not used in the repair of D603 can only be guessed at.

Other alterations were slight. Late in 1962, after concerns were expressed for the safety of track workers given the relatively silent approach of diesels, all five D600s received yellow warning panels above the bufferbeams at each end. At about the same time, the louvres in the upper row of bodyside radiator grilles were replaced by wire mesh in order to increase the air flow over the elements themselves, with the aim of increasing the total cooling capacity. A few years later, in line with similar modification programmes carried out on those D6300s and D800 'Warships' so equipped, the headcode discs were removed and replaced by two hideous route indicator boxes at each end, one either side of the nose gangway. Other than for the addition of yellow warning panels, livery stayed constant until the repainting of D600/2 in the new Rail Blue livery, D602 being turned out with small yellow panels and a single logo above each nameplate late in 1966. D600 stayed green for a few months more and therefore received the definitive version of the new identity with full yellow ends and BR logos on each cabside. There would be no further change to either of these schemes, nor to the standard green still carried by D601/3/4.

Increasingly confined to Cornwall where their idiosyncracies were well-known by maintenance staff, the swan-song for the type came in August 1967 when, in view of the large numbers of English Electric Type 3 Co-Cos being transferred from South Wales to the Eastern Region, D601/2/4 were reallocated to Landore depot in Swansea. In doing this, the WR hoped to exploit the D600s'

undoubted capabilities for working heavy unfitted or partially-fitted freight trains, and, outstationed at Pantyfynnon, the three 'Warships' were tried on mineral trains in the Swansea and Llanelly areas as well as on general goods traffic over the southern end of the Central Wales line. Such a move augured well for the future of the type by placing it in full-time service on the sort of work to which it was well-suited and, further to improve the D600s' low-speed tractive effort characteristics, a scheme to replace their existing 2.84:1 final drives with lower-geared units was informally hatched-out by some maintenance staff and might well have seen use.

In retrospect, however, the experiment was doomed from the very outset. Not only were the three North British Type 4s once again plagued with clearance problems arising from their sheer bulk, but were also the first NBL-built or MAN-powered diesels of any description allocated to South Wales sheds. Availability plummetted as the effects of unfamiliarity amongst both operating and maintenance staff took their toll, a situation not helped by the fact that nearly all spares had to be requisitioned and sent from either Swindon or Laira. After a few months of relative inactivity, they were returned to Laira at the end of November 1967 and officially withdrawn just a month later, thus being deprived of their new TOPS identity of Class 41. It is regrettable but undoubtedly true that if the D600s had been built as slow-speed diesel-electrics, as the BTC would have liked, their numbers would have been very much greater and their service lives considerably longer.

Chapter 5
THE D6300s

THE six locomotives specified by the second part of the initial order for diesel-hydraulics in many ways typified the BTC's failure to maximise its opportunities under the terms of the Pilot Scheme. Intended as a mixed traffic design, their proposed deployment was the ousting of steam traction on those local services still to be loco-hauled, working the lighter and slower duties of the freight traffic spectrum and providing banking assistance where required, especially in Devon and Cornwall. As with American practice, it was intended that more demanding duties should be handled by coupling two or three of these 1000bhp locomotives together and operating them in multiple under the control of a single crew, though such utilisation would be primarily restricted to freight traffic as a function of the locomotives' relatively low maximum speed. It is worth noting that as early as 1956, whilst outline design work on the North British diesel-hydraulics was still underway, British Railways had only reluctantly given approval for the continued production of steam locomotives, in the form of 9F 2-10-0s for the Western Region, in view of their short (though still twenty years or more) expected lifespans. The irresistable argument had been that the locomotives were required for heavy freight duties beyond the capacity of current single-unit diesel designs, the regular deployment on heavier trains of diesels working in multiple being deemed uneconomic. Remarkably, that message had obviously failed to reach those members of the BTC's Central Staff busily engaged in formulating BR's future traction policies.

Rated as a Type 2, the D6300 B-B design was an obvious derivative of the larger D600 'Warship', sharing the same type of engine and transmission as well as much in the way of detail. Theoretically, the lower initial cost of each D6300 should have provided a better way of assessing the practical aspects of diesel-hydraulic traction, the same financial out-

Below: Weight diagram for D6300-5. Subsequent NBL Type 2 diesel-hydraulics differed in a number of ways, as described in the text. *(National Railway Museum)*

lay allowing the total conversion of a restricted geographical area as opposed to the provision of diesels on a few isolated express passenger services. In addition, their use on duties where sustained high outputs at speed were not so much a requisite as the ability to produce high levels of adhesion and tractive effort encouraged examination of the potential of a light diesel-hydraulic to perform the same tasks as a diesel-electric with a larger and more powerful engine. Should this be the case, and experience with the diesel-hydraulic layout elsewhere suggested that it might well be, then the use of hydraulics could offer significant savings both in terms of capital and of operating expenditure. An especially good opportunity for an enlightening comparison between diesel-electric and diesel-hydraulic traction at work under British conditions would be afforded by North British's construction at the same time of ten similar machines with identical engines but GEC electrical transmissions. However, it was an opportunity that would be left untaken.

As subsequent events were to prove, the D6300s shared not only mechanical components with their Type 4 sisters but also the same confused genealogy for which the BTC was wholly responsible and this, coupled with the inadequate analysis of their intended role, would exert a damaging effect upon their operational potential. At the time that the order was placed, along with those for the five D600s and ten D6100 diesel-electrics, the price quoted for the D6300s was some £53,000 per locomotive, a figure which was once again kept low in the hope of gaining further orders. As it was, due to ambiguity in the original agreement and a general apathy on the part of the BTC, various modifications would have to be specified before completion of the locomotives, succeeding not only in doubling the quoted delivery period but also in raising the final cost to £55,000 per locomotive. Similar cost increases and delivery delays were suffered with the diesel-electrics for much the same reason.

For operational purposes, two D6300s were regarded as being equivalent to a single D600, and this philosophy was reflected in their construction. With their common roots

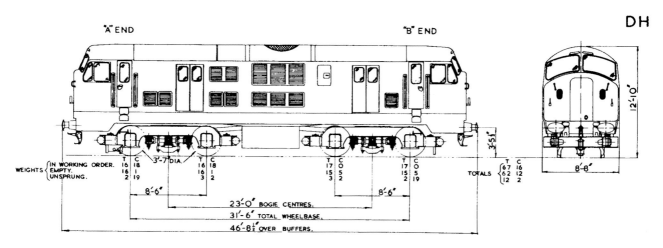

Above: D6300, British Railways' first Type 2 diesel-hydraulic, pictured outside North British's Queen's Park Works upon completion in January 1959. Although the basic proportions leave something to be desired aesthetically, the general standard of finish is commendably neat. *(Mitchell Library)*

and shared use of major mechanical components, it was only natural to expect certain structural similarities between NBL's Type 2s and Type 4s, but the degree to which the finished Type 2 was to copy the larger locomotive would reflect the pressures imposed on NBL by the locomotives' ultra-competitive pricing. In order to allow at least some measure of profit in the finished result, economies had needed to be made wherever possible, including drawing office and production costs, and it showed. Underframes were of similar conception to those used in the Type 4s, with heavy steel sections rivetted and welded to produce the traditional strength frame favoured by the BTC. Once again, tapering dropends were provided to mate up to cast steel dragboxes and so resist damage under normal end loadings, but use of a single transmission unit necessitated the provision of an aperture in the centre of the frame, rather than the system of driving through hollow bogie pivots used in the D600s. Given the great size and strength of this assembly, there was little requirement for load-bearing members of any size in the superstructure and so the locomotives once again featured a very high proportion of aluminium in their composition. In fact, part of NBL's reasoning behind the use of this material in the Type 2s was to permit the manufacture of those aluminium components required for the D600s in greater, and thus more economical quantities. To a great extent this consideration determined the outward appearance of the locomotives, especially in the cab area where the requirement for a gangway to allow multiple-working suggested the use of the structure originally designed for the D600s, with its extensive use of specially-cast and fabricated components. In the Type 4s, the resulting assembly had been one of the most attractive used on any diesel locomotive to date; on the D6300s the same cab frame but with the nose end truncated to a mere six inches or so gave an overly-arcuate impression when seen from ahead and a most unattractive spectacle of tight curves and sharp edges when viewed in profile.

The engine was a NBL-assembled MAN L12V18/21S as used in D602-4 and set at the same rating of 1000bhp at 1445 rpm. Situated over one of the bogies, the engine was cradled in a subframe mounted on semi-resilient pads to minimise vibration, the whole assembly being offset from the loco-

motive's longitudinal centreline with the output end of the engine facing away from the nearest cab. From this point, a short cardan shaft drove a step-up gearbox located on top of the Voith L306r main transmission block, once again assembled by NBL in Glasgow, which projected downwards through the floor into a space between the two water tanks feeding the train-heating boiler. From here, angled cardan shafts led to the inner axle on each bogie, from where a separate shaft relayed drive to the outer axle. As on the D600s, all cardan shafts were of German Gelenkwellenbau (GWB) design, license-built by Hardy-Spicer, whilst axledrives were by David Brown. At the end of the transmission block furthest from the engine, another cardan shaft connected the step-up gearbox to a 50kW dynastarter mounted on a welded steel carrier. A 450-gallon alloy fuel tank was provided in the roof space above the dynastarter, slightly offset so as to provide a walk-through gangway whilst finally, furthest away from the engine and next to the second cab was the train-heating boiler, a Spanner Mark 1a of 1000lb/hour steaming capacity. The space around the transmission formed a separate cooling compartment, with bodyside radiator blocks through which cool air was drawn by an electric fan in the roof space. The cabs themselves would quickly be designated 'A' and 'B', 'A' cab being that nearest the engine, and were furnished in a manner similar to that of the D600s, with extensive use of plastic laminates and the same idiosyncratic control layout. Given the absence of a nose end, entrance to the flexible gangway intended to connect locomotives working in multiple was effected directly from the cab. Although all related fittings were provided by NBL, installation of the gangways themselves was not undertaken at Glasgow, BR preferring to do the job for itself upon receipt of the machines.

The bogies, although twin-axled units of 8'6" wheelbase, were also closely related to those of the D600s and inspired

by the Ivatt design for the LMS Co-Cos. Like those of the Type 4s they were built up out of heavy box sections with a load-free pivot, traction and braking thrusts being taken by bearers mounted on the single swing-link bolster. Dynamically-balanced spoked wheels of 43" diameter identical to those of the D600s were carried in the same Timken roller-bearing axleboxes whilst the final drive units were also of a similar spiral bevel and helical gear variety, though with a higher reduction ratio to compensate for the Type 2's lower designed speed. Although this measure of standardisation with the D600s was useful, the central transmission output driving through cardan shafts rendered the hollow pivot offered by the D600 design superfluous, and the question remains as to why NBL failed to arrange for the cast steel Commonwealth design used under the D6100s to be adapted to suit the D6300s as well, thus making a further contribution towards reduced design costs. As with NBL's two other Pilot Scheme designs, Westinghouse straight air brakes were specified on D6300-5, interlocked with train vacuum brakes for normal use but capable of independent operation. Four compressed-air cylinders were provided on each bogie to apply clasp brakes, being charged by a single Westinghouse compressor located adjacent to the control cubicle on 'A'-cab bulkhead, whilst a motor-driven exhauster of the same manufacture was floor-mounted beside the engine to service the train vacuum brakes. External detail was similar to that of the larger locomotives with louvred bodyside grilles, polished aluminium window surrounds, end marker lights beneath headcode discs and a rather complex arrangement of combined airhorn and air-intake grilles. The Type 2s also carried the same livery of standard green with grey roof panels and bodyside stripe, underframe details once again being in black. The number was carried in white seriffed characters under each cab side window along with the distinctive diamond-shaped NBL Queen's Park worksplate. Such details, however, were not sufficient to disguise the basic inelegance of the design.

By the time that the first locomotives were delivered in early 1959, circumstances had changed dramatically in a way that would affect the entire course taken by British Railways in its quest for improvement. The 1955 Modernisation Plan had hinged upon the concept of increasing overall efficiency through the introduction of modern traction, so enhancing the railways' ability to compete with rival forms of transport. Very soon, however, the proposals would be made obsolete by the practical effects of the 1953 Transport Act, which had not only allowed traditional railway customers to switch their freight traffic to road haulage in ever-increasing quantities but had also put in motion plans for an integrated network of motorways, nullifying at a stroke the Plan's promised efficiencies. The reaction of both Government and the BTC was predictable and amendments to the original strategy were announced with the aim of regaining profitability for the system as a whole within a five-year span. In July 1957, in response to the BTC's recommendation that full-scale dieselisation on

an immediate basis would be the best way to extricate British Railways from its worsening financial problems, the BTC CM&EE published the paper *Main Line Diesel Locomotives: Limitation of Variety*, in which the immediate acceleration of dieselisation using a limited number of locomotive types was advocated. However well-intentioned this may have been, its actual effect (given the lack of any firm guidance from the BTC as to which locomotive designs it wished to perpetuate) was to constitute implicit approval for the quantity purchase of any mainline diesel that appeared to suit BR's requirements. The terms of the Pilot Scheme were thus cast to the winds and since the NBL Type 2 diesel-hydraulic came within the parameters of BR's new traction policy, an order was placed in November 1957 for a further fifty-two examples of the type. Constituting part of the BTC's 1958 Western Region Supplementary Programme, these were intended to expedite the replacement of steam west of Newton Abbot.

Although essentially similar, the design of the production batch varied in several important ways from that of the first six, of which the principal difference concerned the engine. Throughout 1956 and 1957, MAN had been mounting a concerted development programme aimed at increasing the output of its engines, and NBL production was revised to incorporate the various improvements current on German-made units. Chief of these was a revised crankshaft with larger diameter crankpin journals and a vibration damper at the nose end, both measures helping to counter the tendency towards torsional vibration at high crankshaft speeds. Other changes made in the pursuit of enhanced power included stronger forged aluminium pistons, redesigned connecting rods, single-piece exhaust manifolds with branches tuned for optimum turbocharger performance, and resituated fuel injection pumps. Wherever possible, British-made ancillary equipment was retained on the new engines, the output of which was boosted to 1100bhp at 1530rpm. In addition, NBL incorporated electric priming pumps controlled by the starting circuit to improve engine oil circulation during start-up. Activated by the operation of the driver's starting switch, the pump supplied lubricating oil at 25psi until the engine reached a steady idling speed, at which point its own inbuilt mechanical pumps would become effective, causing a pressure-sensitive switch to isolate the electric pump. The revised unit was classified L12V18/21B, and on this occasion North British resisted tampering with the nomenclature, perhaps because no logical alternative presented itself. By this time, the WR had established direct contact with Glasgow and its specifying of interchangeability of engine and transmission components caused these engines to be mounted in revised sub-frames resting on four bonded-rubber feet, part of the agreement being that MAN/Voith equipment should be fully-interchangeable with the Maybach equivalents then being fitted to the first D800s. Although the BTC sanctioned this requirement at an additional cost of £1500 per locomotive, the opportunity to outshop a D6300 with Maybach equipment would never be taken, even when spares shortages were keeping MAN/Voith locomotives sidelined for weeks at a time.

Also revised was the transmission which was now of Voith's latest LT306r model. Although lighter and more compact than the L306r it superceded, the LT306r had a higher input capacity of 1036bhp, matching the more muscular characteristics of the new engine. In order to achieve this, the step-up ratio of the new unit differed from that of the old and so did the settings for the converter change-up points, at a nominal value of 25mph and 50mph representing an approximate 8% increase over the older transmission. This, coupled with the higher rated speed of the new engines, required that the output shaft gear ratios be increased by a factor of 30% in order to preserve the same 75mph top speed in the third converter stage with the engine

Top: Part of the BTC's reasoning behind the order for the North British Type 2 B-Bs was that they could work mainline trains in pairs, or alternatively perform pilot and branch line duties singly. Fulfilling the latter role, D6303 pilots No.4914 Cranmore Hall over Dainton with the 12.20 Cardiff-Newquay on 30 July 1960. *(Hugh Ballantyne)*

Bottom: The second series of D6300s differed quite considerably from the first, principally in terms of transmission and cooling arrangements. On 28 September 1963, only days before the closure of the Exe Valley branch between Dulverton and Stoke Canon, D6318 waits to leave Bampton with the 15.20 service to Exeter. NBL Type 2s had replaced the long-standing 14xx 0-4-2Ts for the last few weeks of operation on the branch, as signified by the Hawksworth autotrailer immediately behind the locomotive. *(Hugh Ballantyne)*

running at maximum power. The different proportions of the new block necessitated a longer, angled cardan shaft between engine and transmission, whilst the need to accomodate both Voith and Mekydro units led to the dynastarter being relocated to the locomotive floor, where it was driven off the end of the main shaft. This at least eliminated the steel carrier of D6300-5 which would prove excessively resonant in service. Quantity production of the LT306r would take place at Queen's Park, though the first ten units would be assembled at Heidenheim, NBL supplying those items specific to the D6300 order. Delivery of the first two units was expected for December 1958, with the remainder following at the rate of two per month thereafter.

To afford the greatest possible compatibility with the Type 4 diesel-hydraulics then being built at Swindon, the decision was taken to equip this second series of North British Type 2s with Behr-Serck cooling equipment, the main feature of which was the replacement of the electric fan motor by a hydrostatic unit under automatic control. This, in conjunction with the use of hydraulically-operated radiator shutters controlling the flow of air over the radiator elements, made the cooling process a rather more exact one than hitherto. Normally, with the engine at idle the fan was stationary and the shutters were in the closed position. As power was applied, the fan would begin to rotate and the shutters open slightly, both attributes increasing with load. Ultimately, the system was under thermostatic control and should coolant temperature rise or fall beyond predetermined limits, the normal relationship between engine speed and cooling airflow would be overridden. Externally, the twin bodyside radiator grilles were replaced by a single large meshed aperture which, whilst tidying-up the locomotives' appearance, seemed rather out of character with the other grilles which remained louvred. Also omitted from D6306 onwards were the small 'eyebrow' air intakes in the roof dome over the cab windows. A further difference was the installation of a marine-style oil-fired engine preheater which, not being specified by the BTC until late 1959, was fitted to earlier locomotives retrospectively.

These were the major changes, but not the only ones. In view of the intention to order MAN-engined D800s, the

Below: A nostalgic reminder of the 'Southern' west of Exeter, savagely pruned by the WR during the 1960s. On 31 August 1964, station staff busy themselves as D6321 arrives at Torrington with the 13.15 train from Barnstaple Junction. Passenger services here ceased during October 1965, but the branch to Meeth remained open for goods traffic until 1982. *(P.J. Horton)*

electro-pneumatic control system of the first six Type 2s gave way to a fully-electric Brown-Boveri set-up in D6306-57, albeit using an Ardleigh 302/IG/3 engine governer rather than the MAN unit of the Type 4s, the batch being identified for multiple working compatibility by a 'White Diamond' coding. In conjunction with this, a minor redesign of the driver's controls was undertaken to bring the D6300s into line with the standards evolved for BR's standard Type 2 diesel-electric locomotives. All, incidentally, were equipped with WR ATC, and had the highest power setting on their controllers locked-out during the initial running-in period. Roller-bearing axleboxes at first continued to be of Timken manufacture but from D6332 onwards were changed to those of Skefko pattern. Locomotive air brakes were now of Oerlikon design (license-built by Davies & Metcalfe) with enlarged bogie cylinders giving an 11% increase in braking force and twin Reavell exhausters for the continuous brakes. D6306-25 received Clayton RO-100 train-heating boilers manufactured under license by English Electric, giving way to Stone-Vapor OK4610 units on D6326-57. Both types of boiler could be operated with the engine turned off, additional battery capacity being provided to suit, for which the BTC had to pay extra. Subsequently, the WR would limit this requirement to one hour only, having decided that its expensive new diesels would not be best employed pre-heating coaching stock.

D6326 was also the first locomotive to be equipped with a recalibrated overspeed relay, the unit being set to trip at 80mph rather than the previous setting of 90mph; earlier locomotives were progressively modified to the new standard. From D6334 the headcode discs were replaced by twin headcode panels flanking the gangway doors, whilst revised anti-overheating safeguards were fitted from D6335. In due course NBL provided similar equipment in kit-form for the earlier locomotives which was fitted at Swindon in the course of routine maintenance. The original arrangement shut off the engine completely once coolant temperature rose above a pre-set level whereas the revised system, benefitting from operational experience, merely returned the unit to idle, allowing the coolant to be circulated through the radiators and back to the engine's water jacket. This obviated the possibility of latent heat trapped within a stationary engine raising coolant temperatures to the point where damage might result.

These modernised machines had a continuous tractive effort of 30,000lb as opposed to the 23,900lb of the original batch, but paid for this improvement in other ways. The 61-ton weight of D6300 was cut to 60 tons in D6306-25 but at an attendant cost of £64,500, whilst D6326 onwards had their flexible gangways installed by NBL, weighed half a ton more and cost the BTC an extra £250 for the privilege. D6300 did not enter service until January 1959 and although delivery of D6306 was promised for February of that year, it did not arrive until October. The last, D6357 was scheduled for June 1960 but in the event, construction was postponed to give NBL-produced D800s priority and the final Type 2 did not reach Swindon until February 1962. The delays were in part due to the need to accomodate design modifications mandated by the BTC, but there is also evidence that North British was becoming overwhelmed by the sheer scale of its commitments. For example, NBL spent much of 1959 engaged in arguments with British Brown-Boveri regarding the considerable difficulties being experienced in Glasgow with the assembly and setting-up of the locomotives' electrical systems. North British regarded the German equipment with little favour, suspecting that the WR had specified it on its D800s solely to reduce the amount of design work needing to be done at Swindon, and although enquiries had been made as early as November 1957 regarding the possible supply of GEC equipment instead, a suitable interface could not be devised to allow multiple-working with BBC-controlled D800s.

Above: From December 1960 onwards, North British amended the D6300 specification to include train headcode indicators at either end. On 12 September 1962 the penultimate Type 2, D6356, pauses with a test train at Dumfries on the erstwhile Glasgow & South Western Railway's mainline to Carlisle. All the NBL-built diesel-hydraulics were tested on BR metals in the Glasgow area before being dispatched south to the WR. *(Norman E. Preedy)*

Some suppliers were equally frustrated with NBL, notification being received in December 1958 that some of the transmission parts sent to Voith in Germany had been found to have been incorrectly machined, thus necessitating remedial work at Heidenheim. Similarly, a May 1959 letter from Serck complained that final assembly of the complex cooling units was being delayed by NBL's failure to provide proper installation drawings.

The first D6300s entered service in equal numbers from Swindon (82C) and Plymouth Laira (83D) sheds, their pronounced physical resemblance to the D600s earning them the soubriquet of 'Baby Warships'. Immediate modifications included the provision of an extra exhauster and a different Driver's Safety Device to that originally fitted, D6305 having these and certain other modifications performed at North British where it had been returned for remedial work following the failure of its acceptance tests. Before long, minor underframe modifications were made after damage had resulted to poorly-situated components, and in 1960 the WR began to fit ATC gear to the batch. As the production series of locomotives started to arrive on the WR they too were allocated to Laira, with the exception of D6336-7 which were sent to Newton Abbot and D6347/55-7 which were dispatched to work out of the new diesel depot at Bristol Bath Road. Some locomotives from both batches were fitted with Zwicky automatic fuel-filling shut-off valves which permitted refuelling from a high-volume supply without risk of blow-back or overfilling.

Although the D6300s had been ordered with branchline work in mind, by the time that they were delivered the Beeching proposals had succeeded the Modernisation Plan and many of their intended services no longer ran. Concurrent with this, the pace of BR dieselisation as a whole was steadily accelerating so it was no surprise that the class should be put to work over the entire Western Region south of Birmingham, although remaining a relatively uncommon sight north of Worcester and in South Wales. Their usual *mode d'emploi* was on light freight trains, banking turns and as pilot engines although from late 1963 onwards some

twenty-three locomotives, all equipped with Stone-Vapor boilers, were transferred to Old Oak Common where they became a regular sight on empty stock trains to and from Paddington. They also assisted with light freight trains across the London Division, ranging from the Oxford-Abingdon car trains to block tanker workings between the oil terminals at Ripple Lane and Staines West. By contrast, due to their restricted multiple-working possibilities and parts commonality with the D600s, the first sextet were confined to Devon and Cornwall, principally on the mainline west of Exeter although seeing use on light passenger and freight trains on the network of secondary lines around Barnstaple. Initially, mileage returns were encouraging at about 35,000 miles per annum, but gradually fell as the type was displaced to lesser duties in later years, principally the cement, china clay and milk traffic west of the River Tamar.

As with the other MAN-powered classes, the D6300s were scourged by chronic engine problems which blighted their record from an early date. Early in 1960, with half the class still to enter service, reports were received from the Eastern Region of MAN engines suffering complete piston failure following the breakage of the fuel injector insert in the cylinder head, and similar instances soon occurred on the WR. The root of the problem was the inserts' tendency to flutter in their mountings at high outputs, giving rise to an eventual stress fracture, and whilst the early failures were restricted to the L12V18/21B engines, similar breakages began to be reported on both A- and S-series engines as their mileage increased. After a change from austenitic to nimonic steel inserts proved ineffective, NBL decided to

modify the cylinder head design itself in order to give the insert more support and so prevent fluttering in the first place. Whilst this was quickly applied to new production, existing heads had to be redrilled and retapped and, as breakages continued, a shortage of serviceable spares soon resulted. Accordingly, a modification programme was instituted at Laira depot, with Engines Division staff revising MAN heads to the new standard as locomotives came in for maintenance. Whilst this was still underway, another problem began to make itself felt, namely that of broken big-end securing bolts. An alternative design of bolt was prepared and applied to engines from June 1960, the original type being withdrawn from use that December. Unlike the injector inserts, however, this effort met with rather less than total success, and the new big-end bolts continued to break as before.

Even bearing in mind the known shorter service lives of high-speed diesels compared with their slow-running counterparts, the maintenance demands of the WR's MAN engines proved to be excessive, the broken big-end bolts being accompanied by a generally high rate of attrition of sspiston rings and crankshaft bearings. In part, this may have been exacerbated by the engine's capability to start cold and, of the three classes of MAN-engined locomotive deployed on the WR, it was the D6300s that were most likely to be outstationed in yards or branchline termini overnight. Provided that ambient temperatures were not unduly low, crews would most probably not bother to preheat before starting a locomotive in such a situation, and whilst starts of this sort were not unduly damaging in absolute terms, the cumulative effects over several months of service did nothing to prolong engine life. Piston and valve defects were also rife, the majority apparently due to overheating, whilst the units proved to be anything but oil-tight. Lastly, there were many problems involving the Napier turbochargers, some of which had been experienced on other parts of BR, though the majority of failures on the WR could be traced back to exhaust system leaks. Once again, this difficulty was never really overcome, though a similar problem with airbox fractures on D6300s had been solved by changing to pressings of a different section, which proved less prone to vibration.

The D6300s' problems were not restricted to their engines, however. Like the D600 'Warships', D6300-5 were troubled in their early years by a series of transmission bearing failures, a malady eventually traced to cardan shaft vibration which may well have contributed to some of the early crankshaft failures as well. The revised componentry used in subsequent locomotives overcame this problem, but introduced another in the form of the complex Behr-Serck cooling units. Early locomotives suffered from excessive coolant loss, though this was soon remedied by resiting the

Top: The type also found work on freight duties, both in the London Division and elsewhere. On 14 March 1966 D6353 brings a pair of carflats into Abingdon, near Oxford, terminus of the short branch from Radley. The line was largely sustained by the traffic to and from the adjacent British Motor Corporation works, exemplified by the Austin-Healey and MG sportscars seen in the background, awaiting dispatch by rail. *(R.H.G. Simpson)*

Middle: Far from the sleepy rural branches of North Devon, the D6300s were employed working empty stock trains between Old Oak Common and Paddington. On 23 May 1967, the final member of the class, D6357, is seen entering Paddington with the stock for the 11.45 service to Bristol. *(R.H.G. Simpson)*

Bottom: An interesting variation is displayed by D6327 at Old Oak Common depot during November 1966, in that the locomotive sports a 'shaped' warning panel of the sort more usually applied to the larger D600 and D800 types. Evidently, an unknown painter felt that the D6300's nickname of 'Baby Warship' justified the adornment. *(D.J. Everson)*

overflow pipe from the header tank. More problematic was the failure of the moveable radiator shutters, the first recorded instance of this being in August 1959 when a unit on test at NBL suffered breakage of the brazed joint between the shutter actuating arm and spindle. The following month, Serck reinforced the joint by adding a grub screw, but by June 1960 these too were beginning to break, rendering the shutters inoperable. The WR suggested that the failures were due to balljoints elsewhere in the linkage running dry and seizing but Serck refuted this, claiming that the balljoints were functioning satisfactorily, having been lubricated for life during the course of assembly. A change was then made to welded actuating arm assemblies, with apparently positive results, and quantities of these were in due course delivered direct from Serck to Laira for fitment to locomotives already in traffic. The WR had also been concerned to discover that NBL had delivered at least two locomotives (D6314/5) to Swindon containing only negligible amounts of corrosion inhibition oil in their cooling systems. Since the solution (Esso Kutwell) was only partially effective in preventing the degradation of copper-based components to begin with, maintenance of the correct concentration was vital if corrosion was to be avoided, and orders were given that all other locomotives in service be checked accordingly.

As with most of BR's other early diesels, the electrical and other ancillary systems created their own particular difficulties. NBL's dislike of the BBC all-electric control could hardly have been diminished when, during an April 1960 field visit to Laira, WR maintenance staff took the opportunity to query the operation of the standstill relay. Intended to prevent reversal of the transmission taking place whilst the locomotive was moving, this relay was apparently impossible to reset unless the engine was first shut-down and, to their embarrassment, NBL's representatives found the design of the apparatus to be such that no modification could be made other than to revise the WR's operating manual for the class accordingly... Another query involved the premature failure of English Electric dynastarters, many of which had suffered fouling of their internal surfaces. This was diagnosed as being due to oil contamination from the engines, which in turn increased the probability of electrical malfunction or even fire. Another source of dynastarter failures had been the burn-

ing-out of the reverse current relays, caused by the tendency of some MAN engines to 'hunt' at tickover for the first few minutes after starting, and had been overcome by a combination of heavier relays and careful adjustment of the engine controls. In later years, there were a lot of problems resulting from circuit faults in the complex wiring looms, and these were not so easily overcome.

All this, combined with the failings inherent in the uprated engine design, helped to ensure that few locomotives from the later batch returned much in excess of 40,000 miles

Above: Although never particularly reliable, the North British Type 2s continued to be popular with traffic operators for light branchline and trip workings. On 8 August 1971 D6334 heads a short train of milk tankers into Exeter St Davids, probably a consignment off the Hemyock branch which would become part of a train forwarded to London later that day. Note the retention of the old seriffed numerals despite the blue livery. *(Norman E. Preedy)*

Below: Eventually, most surviving D6300s, by then termed Class 22s, received the standard blue livery with all-over yellow ends, something which did nothing to compliment their already-uneasy lines. So garbed, though impressively clean, D6332 heads a vans train off the Morris Cowley branch at Kennington Junction sometime in July 1967. Given that the two leading vehicles are both Italian State Railways ferry vans, the train is most likely laden with components destined for BMC's Innocenti car factory in Milan. *(R.H.G. Simpson)*

per annum. In fairness, BR Type 2 averages as a whole were not that much higher, reflecting the sort of work for which small locomotives tended to be rostered, but the D6300s' generally poor reliability did tend to ensure their continued use on less arduous and therefore less productive duties. As time went by, the class as a whole became increasingly associated with the West Country, the locomotives' low power and relatively compact dimensions making them well-suited for services over the numerous lightly-laid branchlines of the region, as well as for trip freights in the Bristol, Exeter and Plymouth areas. Conversely, their limited capabilities could sometimes prove a hindrance on faster or heavier trains and whilst the D6300s put in some very good work on the former LSWR lines west of Exeter, as well as on the

heavy summer Saturday workings to Exmouth and Sidmouth, they remained an uncommon sight on the mainline between Exeter and Salisbury where the extra power of the D800 and D7000 types was preferred. More suitably, D6300s were found employment on the Taunton-Barnstaple route, the connecting Exe Valley and Culm Valley lines, the Heathfield, Launceston and Moretonhampstead branches and, west of Plymouth, the Fowey, Helston, Newquay and Perranporth lines. Long distance duties over the WR mainline were always rare, although examples of the type did occasionally operate in tandem to work passenger trains in Cornwall, especially the heavily-laden summer services to and from Newquay. Summer Saturdays of this period also saw D6300 activity on the St Ives branch, through coaches being detached from the 'Cornish Riviera' at St Erth and worked up the branch by a pair of Type 2s. In 1966, however, the removal of the run-round loop at St Ives put paid to such manoeuvres, through passengers then having to change between mainline trains and the branch's DMU shuttle at St Erth.

D6300s also continued to provide pilot assistance to trains on the gradients west of Newton Abbot, though less and less frequently as both diesel-hydraulic and diesel-electric designs in excess of 2500bhp began to take charge of heavier duties. Like several other of the Type 1 and Type 2 diesels delivered under the auspices of the Modernisation Plan, changes in traffic patterns meant that the D6300s were continually chasing a decreasing workload. For a while they proved indispensible for those duties where a Type 2 locomotive of minimum dimensions and axleloading was required, such as the ammunition trains to the US Air Force supply dump at Welford Park on the former Lambourne Valley Tramway, or milk traffic from the United Dairies plant at Hemyock, terminus of the seven-mile branch from Tiverton Junction. Under Beeching, such services were largely doomed by their high operating costs relative to the level of traffic carried and as the closure notices were posted, so the need for lightweight locomotives like the D6300s declined. Indeed, for the first few years following the final demise of Western Region steam, members of the class would be more frequently employed working demolition trains over closed sections of railway, notably the Somerset & Dorset line which proved very unfamiliar territory indeed, the S&D having succeeded in retaining steam haulage to the very end. Deployment on transitory workings of this kind did not constitute an acceptable substitute for regular duties, however, and it was this diminution of suitable work, as much as any mechanical failing, that saw a large proportion of the class spending long periods in store

at various locations during the later 1960s. Eventually, a number of the London allocation would make their way west once more, although most of the Old Oak Common machines would be taken out of traffic during the course of 1968 and withdrawn shortly after.

Modifications to the type, excepting those made during and immediately after construction were slight and mainly cosmetic in nature. The mandatory yellow warning panels and overhead electrification flashes became a common sight from 1962 onwards, whilst on many locomotives the original twin gangway doors were replaced by a pair of folding 'jack-knife' units. Furthermore, during heavy repairs some locomotives originally provided with folding headcode discs were rebuilt with split headcode panels, mounted higher than those on locomotives so equipped by NBL, and in the form of a pair of cumbersome protruding boxes rather than being flush with the end panels. Not until later would Swindon adopt the NBL pattern for further rebuilds, with a much better final result. Not all disc-equipped machines received this modification, and neither would all be garbed in the blue livery introduced in 1966. Originally

Above: Modified with flush-fitting headcode boxes and a four-piece folding gangway door assembly, D6331 prepares to take a Bristol-bound mixed freight out of Gloucester New Yard on 15 July 1969. D6320, seen in the background, has also been rebuilt with headcode boxes but, unlike D6331, retains its original design of gangway doors. *(Norman E. Preedy)*

with small end warning panels and a centrally-placed 'arrow' motif, the livery would undergo gradual change until the final version sported a logo on each cabsheet and full yellow warning ends which did nothing to enhance the locomotives' already curious lines. At the same time, the final demise of BR steam traction saw the D-prefixes removed from the running numbers. An enduring weakness seemed to be the side valence panels which became easily detached and so, in conjunction with the weathered paintwork worn by many presented a rather debauched appearance. Under the 1972 TOPS renumbering scheme the type received the designation Class 22, but none would survive long enough to take up their new five-digit computerised numbers.

Chapter 6
THE D800 'WARSHIPS'

WHILST the BTC was negotiating with North British over the construction of that concern's eleven Pilot Scheme diesel-hydraulics, work was quietly but surely progressing at Swindon on the design and construction of the WR's own concept of modern motive power. After much lobbying and badgering on the part of the WR, an agreement had been concluded between the BTC and the German concerns of Krauss-Maffei and Maybach for the construction of a revised version of the V200 in BR workshops, using German mechanical components. The eventual result of this, the realisation of the WR's ambitions, was a trio of 2000bhp B-B locomotives numbered D800-2 which emerged from Swindon Works from August 1958 onwards as indubitably the most advanced Type 4 to be put into traffic by British Railways under the auspices of the Modernisation Plan.

There was a price to be paid for such gratification, however, and it quickly manifested itself in the form of a deluge of work for the Swindon Works Drawing Office. Technical drawings began to reach Swindon from Krauss-Maffei at München-Allach in the spring of 1956 and before any design work as such could progress every one of these drawings, which eventually numbered over two hundred in quantity, needed not only to be converted into Imperial measurements but also translated from difficult technical German into comprehensible English. Once this time-consuming and laborious task was completed the Swindon draughtsmen were faced with the problem of compressing the V200 design to fit the national BR L1 loading gauge. Not only did this entail a 10" reduction in height and a narrowing of the body by 16", but also an increase in ground clearance, without any adverse affect upon the completed package's ability to accept the established V200 mechanical units.

Below: The culmination of a huge amount of effort, the WR's first D800 finally takes shape at Swindon on 15 September 1957. The all-welded construction of the Krauss-Maffei bodyshell is readily apparent, as is the 'speed whisker' proposed for the nose and actually chalked on the first locomotive prior to painting. *(B. Webb/B.J. Miller Collection)*

Given the complexity of the V200's superstructure, the reduction in physical dimensions that had to be made and the need to perform vital stress calculations at every stage of the design process, much credit is reflected upon the Swindon design staff by the fact that the plans for the first D800 locomotive had been completed by the end of August 1957. Not unnaturally, Swindon mounted a jealous guard over these, the WR CME, R.A. Smeddle instructing that they were to be released to no outside party, including other parts of BR, until further notice. All involved were aware of the huge contribution afforded by stressed-skin construction towards the unusually favourable power:weight ratios of the German diesel-hydraulics, and that upon Swindon's ability to reproduce the V200 monocoque rested not only the success of the new D800s but also the credibility of the WR's entire traction policy. The finished D800 superstructure would be required to support all equipment other than the bogies (and these too in a crane-lift), to be capable of withstanding an end-loading of up to 200 tons, and yet be of smaller overall dimensions than the German original. For a first essay in stressed-skin construction, it was indeed a tall order.

The matter had not been concluded without a measure of boardroom conflict over the appearance of the finished locomotive. Smeddle at first proposed to replicate in most respects the V200s' external design for the forthcoming Swindon machines, but the BTC's Design Panel had different ideas. The restrictions imposed by the BR loading gauge would mean reducing the amount of soundproofing material incorporated within the bodyshell in order to allow sidewalls and bulkheads to be reduced in thickness and, as a result, some concern had been expressed over possible sound levels within the cabs. To alleviate any problem that might occur, as well as to allow a little more space within the engine room, outside consultants retained by the BTC proposed moving the cabs outboard, thus eliminating the bulbous nose characteristic of the V200. This suggestion was met with enthusiastic approval by the BTC Design Panel, which had misgivings about the possible appearance of the V200 profile when compressed to British dimensions. The flat-front proposal also allowed the fitment of the communicating gangways made a mandatory requirement by the BTC for locomotives of mainline capability. A small-scale model was produced to illustrate the proposals and, having received a favourable reception at Swindon, in March 1956 was inspected by E.S. Cox for the BTC and Christian Barman for the WR. However, the scheme was not welcomed by the WR Board, and it was eventually decided that the Design Panel should limit its interest in the D800s to minor matters of detailing and livery. Many viewed with regret the rejection of the flat-front proposal, but it is the considered opinion of this author at least that the slab-sided construction of the D800s needed the counterpoint provided by the rounded nose, and that the alternative style was put to better use in a subsequent project.

The structure that eventually resulted was built up out of ordinary mild steel, stainless having been considered but rejected due to it being not only more costly but also difficult to work and to weld. Even so, the minutes of the

Swindon Locomotive Committee record that some considerable difficulty was had in sourcing all the material from British suppliers, some gauges and specifications not being widely available on the home market at that time. Foundation of the whole assembly was a pair of $6^{1}/2$" diameter tubes running from end to end, supplemented by deep but light-gauge longitudinal members between the bogies and box sections running along the outer length of the locomotive at solebar level. The tubes passed through a number of transverse stretchers, themselves extended downwards between the central longitudinal members, the whole being welded up to form a light but strong honeycomb structure. This was capped by steel deckplate with apertures for the transmission units, these being supported at their lower extremities by frame extensions which also provided a location point for the bogies. The underframe was completed with the addition of built-up dragboxes and bufferbeams at the ends, the latter being integrated with platework recessed below deck level to form a rigid perimeter frame. In fact, this was made all the more vital by the impracticality of placing the steel tubes at buffer height, as on the V200s, due to British loading gauge restrictions. As with the D600s therefore, the bufferbeams were slightly below the level of the principal chassis members and additional reinforcement had to be provided in order to ensure the proper distribution of end forces into the bodyshell.

The next stage was the welding of the bodyside uprights and bulkheads to the frame, upon which the body structure itself would be erected. To these sections, which were chiefly of folded steel angle, were fixed the side sheets which were then cut to provide window and grille openings before being tensioned by the application of numerous tiny spot-heatings, each at intervals of about an inch. To preserve body strength, the size of these openings was kept to a minimum and the heavily-loaded centre section was initially unpierced. The sidesheets extended upwards, curving in above strong double cantrails to form the load-bearing component of the roof which, incidentally, had a three-arc profile strongly reminiscent of previous Swindon products. Cabs were of twin-screen design, superficially similar to the NBL arrangement at the front, but with the side windows spanning the two cantrails and so slightly recessed from the bodyside except at their extremities. In the V200 with its less steeply-aligned cantrails, these windows were flush with the body and the height reduction that dictated this compression on the Swindon locomotive also necessitated a squatter nose contour in order to maintain good forward visibility. Nonetheless, the revised shape was quite successful in emulating the charismatic and almost arrogant looks of the original, and besides which took up very little more space than the abortive flat-fronted cab would have done. The roof consisted of light-alloy detachable panels from end to end, allowing complete mechanical units to be lifted in and out during maintenance. Weight of the basic structure was a little over eleven tons, substantially less than a comparable strength frame unit, but more remarkable still was that where such constructional methods required standards of accuracy that could normally be achieved only with the use of purpose-made jigs, D800 was virtually built by hand and from painstaking measurement of the completed assembly, the jigs for future construction were created. Clearly, Swindon had not forgotten the lessons relating to high-precision engineering learned in earlier years!

Despite the reduction in overall dimensions, packaging of components within the D800 bodyshell largely followed the example of the parent design. Slightly off-centre in order to permit a walk-through cross-passage was a Spanner Mark 1a train-heating boiler with a maximum steaming capacity of 2000lb/hour. On each side of this were Behr-Serck cooling units, one for each engine, both of which could be lifted in and out of the locomotive as a complete unit for overhaul or replacement. Each unit came complete with radiator shutters and hydrostatic pump-driven fan, thermostatically controlled to maintain temperatures at around the optimum 80°C, fan speed and shutter opening increasing proportionate to engine speed. Should coolant temperatures fall below 75°C fan action would cease whilst, conversely, temperatures in excess of 90°C would cause the engine to shut down. A further switch prevented the engines from being started should their temperature be below 40°C, when damage might be caused, although this latter could be bypassed in case of emergency. Engine pre-heating on D800 and D801 was facilitated by the train-heating boiler, but on D802 a change was made to dedicated pre-heating units within the cooling system.

Flanking the cooling groups were the twin Maybach MD650 engines, located in flexibly-mounted subframes for interchangeability and situated over the inner bogie axles, with the output ends facing towards the cabs. Each engine drove through a cardan shaft, supplied by Maybach as part of the deal, to the Mekydro K104 main transmission block, body-mounted with its output end protruding down through the floor over the bogie centreline. The comparatively great height of the cab floor from rail level allowed the transmission machinery to sit below the access passageway behind the driver's position, with a further cardan shaft going forward under the floor to the 16.5kW dynastarter located in each nose end. As with the V200, the D800 design carried its fuel supply below floor level in order to conserve space. Four welded steel fuel cells located in the honeycomb between the two central frame members carried some 800 gallons of diesel oil between them, simultaneously allowing the more accessible areas outboard of the locomotive's centreline to house the electric starting batteries.

The size restrictions imposed on the D800 did tell, however, in the adverse effect that they had upon accessibility to the locomotive's inner parts. Whereas the V200 had a full-height passageway down each side of the engine room, its more stunted English counterpart could only accomodate a rather cramped gangway with a central crossover, the negotiation of which was made difficult, despite good lighting, by the presence of low-level cardan shafts. Furthermore, a certain amount of juggling had been necessary in order to fit everything in, with the result that some quite important components were hidden away in corners and under obscure access traps. Even so, if the D800 could be a mechanic's nightmare in some respects, it more than redeemed itself in the matter of cab design. Retention of the curved nose had made the installation of a communicating gangway well-nigh impossible without an unsightly projection in which to house it and so, for the first time on a BR high-power diesel, the requirement was dropped. This of course made more room within the cab itself, as well as helping to render it commendably draught-free, a process which was aided by the generous use of glassfibre insulation pads behind perforated alloy lining panels. The driving position was redolent of the layout used on the Deutsche Bundesbahn V200s and, rather than the pedestals adopted by North British, the driver's controls were set-out on a sloping desk with gauges and switches on a panel below the windscreen. Nearer the driver were operating handles for the Laycock-Knorr locomotive air brake and the vacuum train brake, the two being connected by a proportional valve, whilst an additional control valve could be set to give a more progressive braking action in order to prevent bunching on loose-coupled freight trains.

Control equipment consisted of an all-electric system supplied by Brown-Boveri and imported direct from their Mannheim plant. Of six-notch variety with an additional position for engine idling, the main controller had controlling and reversing handles mechanically interlocked to prevent the direction of travel being changed whilst under power, or engine speed being raised above idle with the transmission out of gear. During normal running engine oil temperature and pressure, coolant level and temperature, transmission oil temperature and pressure, and engine speed were all monitored by electrical sensors, and if any fluctuated outside preset limits the engine in question would be shut down automatically. Similar safeguards applied to engine start-up, along with an additional relay that isolated the dynastarter if the engine failed to fire within a given time from first being turned-over, as well as imposing a minimum time delay between starts in order to protect the locomotive batteries from overloading. Provision was also made for multiple working of up to three locomotives in all via 36-point connectors, and for the control of auxiliaries and lighting circuits. An interface between control and braking systems was provided through the WR's own ATC set-up and a Driver's Safety Device which, once activated, first brought the engines to idle and then made a progressive brake application. Additionally, upon start-up the transmissions remained locked-out until working levels of air pressure and brake vacuum were achieved. The WR appears to have been rather daunted by the complexity of the BBC electrical system and, since few of Swindon's electricians had any direct experience with equipment of this kind, D800 was fitted-out by Brown-Boveri personnel who simultaneously trained BR employees to take over on subsequent locomotives.

If the body structure was judged to be radical, and it certainly was, then the bogies were nothing short of revolutionary. Built to a patented K-M design, the rationale behind which had been to eliminate as many points of wear as possible, the basis of each was a welded frame with a dropped centre. No provision was made for the traditional hornplates as the axles were carried in pivoted radius arms cantilevered out from a rubber-bushed bearing on the centre transom. These shared a common alignment with plate steel torque reaction arms, bolted at one end to the axle's final drive casing. The other end was suspended from the bogie frame by a rubber damper, the function of which was to minimise axle-lift under torque loading without interfering with the action of the suspension, thus optimising both adhesion and ride. Primary suspension between the wheels and bogie frame was via a leaf spring situated above each radius arm over the axle centreline whilst secondary suspension, between the bogie and superstructure, was catered for by a larger inverted leaf spring on each side of the bogie frame. Accomodated within a cleft between each pair of axlebox arms was a Maybach C33 axledrive, consisting of a

crownwheel-and-pinion set mounted on the axle by taper roller bearings. These were fed oil under pressure by a double-acting gear-type pump to ensure positive lubrication regardless of the direction of travel. Driving wheels were plain discs, of cast construction and restricted to 39'" diameter so as to reduce overall height. This in itself prompted objections from within the BTC, motivated by American research which had suggested the possibility of track damage being caused under braking by vehicles with a high load concentration per inch of tyre tread. Although the D800 made rather a poor showing in this respect, with a coefficient of 0.153 compared to the 0.148 of English Electric's D200 1Co-Co1 or 0.141 of the Derby/Sulzer D1 of the same arrangement, let alone the 0.078 of a 'Castle'-class 4-6-0, UK operating conditions were such that the expected problems did not in fact arise.

K-M's policy of eliminating as many wearing components as possible was also reflected by the bogie's lack of any physical pivot, locomotive weight being taken through the secondary leaf springs at their centre point. This was then transmitted to the outer ends of each spring where it acted upon links, the upper ends of which bore upon coil springs housed in pans on the bogie frame. This arrangement only dealt with vertical loads, traction and braking forces being taken by manganese rubbing faces located in the well of the bogie, which also housed an arrangement of rods and bell-cranks. The rods were linked to brackets hanging from the locomotive superstructure, the mechanism as a whole providing a geometrical axis around which the bogie rotated. In addition, it was intended to provide the small amount of sideplay calculated to be necessary. The only other physical connections were the cardan shafts running from the axledrives to the output flanges of the transmission block projecting down between the bogie transoms, and the flexible hoses for the brakes and sanding gear. Sanding action, from boxes in the locomotive superstructure, was by compressed air and arranged through the locomotive's control system so that only the leading wheels of each bogie received sand, regardless of the direction of

Below: The K-M pivotless bogie, seen here in the form fitted to the German V200 locomotives but identical in all but detail to the original D800 version. Note particularly the complex location mechanism in the central well and the axles cantilevered out in pivoted radius arms. *(Krauss-Maffei)*

travel. Four compressed-air cylinders on each bogie were responsible for actuating the clasp brakes, each wheel being flanked by a pair of shoes.

D800 was completed towards the end of June 1958, being finished in the green livery with grey relief and polished metal trim already chosen for the D600s. Nevertheless, the contrast in appearance between the products of the Swindon and Glasgow factories was immediately apparent, D800's strong but harmonious lines imbuing the machine with a dynamic yet graceful quality quite lacking in any of its diesel contemporaries. This was further enhanced by the centrally-placed cast nameplate, relieved in the customary red, bearing the title *Sir Brian Robertson*, a gesture to the BTC's Chairman who, against the counsel of his advisors, had permitted the WR to turn its vision into reality. The only marring features were the clumsy and incongruous headcode discs and stencil holder placed on the nose ends, the last item attached to the louvred access door for the dynastarter. Fortunately, a proposal to adorn the finished locomotive with the already-anachronistic 'speed whiskers', DMU-style, had come to nought some time previously.

Vanguard, displaced from D800 at the last minute, instead made its bow that November on D801 and thus made the type part of the 'Warship' class, with the inevitable result that colloquial references led to confusion between the radically different D600 and D800 designs. (To add to the WR's difficulties, a sizeable number of ex-LMS 'Jubilee' 4-6-0s already carried the names of Royal Navy fighting ships and although no duplication would actually occur, in a few cases, such as that of No.45712 *Victory* and D860 *Victorious*, things came perilously close!) It had been intended that the last of the trio should carry raised stainless steel numerals and a matching bodyside stripe, but problems were experienced in attaching these items to the outer skin and, after the use of aluminium extrusions was also discounted, D802 *Formidable* entered service that December in exactly the same garb as her two elder sisters. Protagonists of the 'Buy British at all costs' philosophy did not take long to point out that Swindon had taken nearly a year longer than NBL to evolve its Type 4s, albeit with a 30% weight saving, and more importantly that the D800s with their absorption of drawing office, tooling and license fees cost a hefty £145,000 apiece. NBL's decision to undercut costs so as to attract repeat business was conveniently forgotten.

Given the terms of the Modernisation Plan under which they were acquired, the three new locomotives should have been submitted to exhaustive type tests in service before any decision was made regarding future purchases. As it was the WR, eager not to lose the position of strength which the D800 lent to its beleaguered case for diesel-hydraulic power and perhaps anticipating the BTC's decision to accelerate the programme of railway modernisation, began to think in terms of a whole operational fleet. As early as 1956, with many aspects of the diesel-hydraulic programme still to be finalised, WR management had elected to advance the deadline for total dieselisation from the 1985 then envisaged by the BTC to a much more ambitious (and prophetic) 1968, a goal which the Commission was soon to adopt as its own. This in turn implied a quickening of new diesel deliveries, and in February 1957 permission was sought and granted for a further a further thirty 2000bhp B-Bs of K-M design to be built at Swindon as part of the 1958 WR Supplementary Programme. It was conceded that, in view of the urgent need for new motive power, the WR could not wait for British production lines to be set up and that another series of parts would have to be imported from Maybach's German plants. Nevertheless, the BTC was still firm in its desire to see the British manufacture of as many components as possible in line with the original BTC-Maybach-KM agreement of January 1956 and, in April 1958, Maybach concluded agreements for the licensed production in the UK of both MD-series diesels and Mekydro transmissions. The diesel contract went to Armstrong-Siddeley Motors of Coventry, a well-respected company perhaps best known for its bespoke motor cars which, sadly, were already in a state of terminal decline. Although Armstrongs had another mainstay in the design and construction of aero engines, various models of its 'Sapphire' turbojet figuring in a wide variety of contemporary military aircraft, orders were insufficient to sustain A-S's extensive production facilities. Having been forced to lay-off skilled men on several occasions during the course of 1957 and with the spectre of lucrative assembly and development work for other concerns expiring in the near future, the company welcomed the Maybach contract as an opening into an expanding and vibrant business.

Although having little prior experience with diesel engines of any kind, Armstrong-Siddeley had high hopes of selling powerplants for marine and stationary generator applications in addition to satisfying the requirements of the BTC, and accordingly assumed British rights to the entire range of MD-series diesels from 200 to 2000bhp. Despite the need to create a dedicated assembly operation in a new factory at Ansty, on Coventry's north-eastern outskirts, the start-up costs of the diesel venture were relatively low, the company producing many of the smaller components required through the use of the machinery and labour already employed in its Parkside plant. Armstrongs' remit would not extend to the British production of Mekydro transmission units, however, for reasons which ranged from the company's involvement with the rival SRM torque-converter transmission to the BTC's desire to achieve the widest practicable distribution of work amongst domestic suppliers. Instead, Maybach's chosen partner would be Stone-Platt Industries of London which, unlike Armstrong-Siddeley, was already an established supplier to the railway industry through one of its subsidiaries, J. Stone & Company. Besides supplying large quantities of electrical equipment to their own designs for use on locomotives and carriages, from the late 1940s onwards Stones had sought to expand their activities by means of licensing agreements allowing them to manufacture designs patented by foreign suppliers, notably the American Vapor-Clarkson steam-heating boiler for which Stones acted as UK agents. Given the company's depth of experience in the engineering field, not least with the minature steam turbines used to drive some locomotive generators, Stones' Deptford factory was seen as an ideal site in which to initiate the British production of Mekydro equipment and in due course the plant would go on to produce Maybach-designed axledrives, intermediate gearboxes and cardan shafts.

With the conclusion of these two contracts, the final arguments against the series production of D800s largely collapsed. Although the first D800 had yet to enter service, the BTC had already decided that future Type 4 orders for the WR should favour the Swindon design over its North British counterpart, and options on a further thirty-three D600s for 1958/9 delivery were relinquished accordingly. In their place would come an equal number of NBL-built D800s, using MAN/Voith power equipment similar to that in D6306-57 and compatible with those machines for parts interchange, this substitution being formalised in an official

BTC order lodged with North British at the start of July 1958. The idea of Springburn building D800s in parallel with Swindon surprised many contemporary observers, though the logic behind the BTC's decision was in fact three-fold. Firstly, the WR's requirements for new Type 4 diesel-hydraulics remained undiminished, regardless of whether they were answered by deliveries of D600s or D800s, and Swindon's construction capacity was insufficient to meet demand within an acceptable timescale. Secondly, having invested heavily in the MAN and Voith agencies in preparation for the series construction of diesel-hydraulics, NBL had staked its hopes on further D600 orders, instead of which it was now having to confront the prospect of making men redundant in an area already beset by high rates of unemployment. Thirdly, since the WR was already committed to delivery of some sixty-three MAN/Voith-powered hydraulics under the terms of existing orders, the purchase of similarly-equipped D800s would facilitate the use of service spares already kept in stock by the WR, thus allowing time for the two Maybach/Mekydro assembly operations in the UK to become established. NBL at that time had no rights to use the patented K-M body structure and so an alteration had to be made to the original agreement, licensing the company to participate in the manufacture of K-M-type locomotives of 2000bhp and over for the British market whilst at the same time protecting K-M's interests in overseas markets. In fact, most of the technical advice which NBL duly received was to emanate from Swindon rather than München-Allach, and a consultation fee was correspondingly deducted by the BTC from the price of every Glasgow-built D800.

The result of all this bargaining was that virtually overnight, on paper at least, the WR had amassed a fleet of some sixty-six D800s as opposed to the three originally sanctioned. The first of Swindon's new batch, D803 Albion emerged from the erecting shops in March 1959 and thereafter the production line set up where 'Castles' and 'Kings' had once been made turned out 'Warships' at the rate of one a month. Experience gained not only with the three D800s but also with other K-M locomotives in service across Europe had suggested that benefit might be derived from certain changes and so, whilst outwardly identical to their predecessors, the locomotives of Lot 437 incorporated a number of important technical modifications. All sixty engines required for the batch, along with three spares, were of the same MD650 variety and supplied direct from Maybach's German factory so as to permit unhindered construction, although ten would first be shipped completely knocked-down (CKD) to Armstrong-Siddeley in order to initiate assembly at the new Ansty plant. Prior to their arrival in Coventry, however, A-S's parent company, Hawker-Siddeley, decided to merge its engine-building interests with those of the rival Bristol Aeroplane Company, with the express intention of developing and producing a suitable powerplant for the RAF's much-vaunted but eventually ill-fated TSR2 tactical strike aircraft. Accordingly,

Below: Weight diagram for Maybach/Mekydro-equipped D800s from D802 onwards. (*National Railway Museum*)

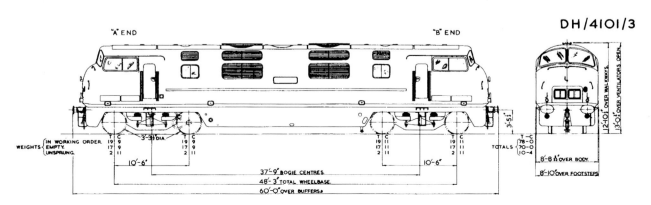

not only the aero engine but also the diesel and motor car interests of both Armstrong-Siddeley and Bristol would be combined under the banner of the new Bristol Siddeley Engines concern (BSE), the Industrial & Marine Division of which assumed responsibility for the Ansty factory under the management of W.H. 'Pat' Lindsey. As a partial result of the upheavals which inevitably followed, production of MD-series engines at Ansty took some time to become established and the ten knocked-down units were eventually incorporated in the last locomotives built under Lot 437.

To accompany these engines, Maybach also supplied some sixty-three Mekydro K104 transmission units, a proportion of which were shipped CKD for assembly by Stones. Although unchanged in principal, this particular batch marked the start of a new series incorporating the many improvements which Maybach engineers had developed through service experience gained with the design to date. Most important of these was the replacement of the original design of torque-converter housing, made from light alloy and incorporating a water jacket for cooling purposes fed from the main radiator block. This casing had proved a frequent source of trouble, especially through leakage and cross-contamination of coolant and oil, and was now superceded by a new cast-iron housing of solid construction to match the main transmission block itself. The need for a water jacket was overcome by the simple expedient of circulating transmission oil through a remote heat exchanger plumbed-in to the cooling system. Other changes included a minor redesign of the gearwheels and the claw-clutch mechanism, whilst the smaller blade rings in the converter were pressed from brass rather than steel as hitherto, so as to reduce the incidence of fissures and extend their service life. The overall effect of these modifications was not only to improve the operation and reliability of the design but also to increase its input capacity, therefore allowing the engines to be uprated to 1135bhp at 1530rpm. Gear change-up points remained unaltered at 24, 40 and 67mph under full power; where less than full power was being used, proportionately lower change-up points were applied.

Furthermore, experience in Germany had shown that the six widely-spaced power notches of the Brown-Boveri control system were resulting in operational difficulties, so the opportunity was taken to install a derivative system revised to offer seven power notches. Unlike that of D800-2 which could only be worked in multiple amongst themselves, the new unit offered full compatibility with D6306-57 and therefore locomotives so equipped were identified with the same 'White Diamond' branding on the bufferbeam. In retrospect it would have been desirable for these improvements to be incorporated in the D800 design from the outset, but opinion at the time had been that BR had enough difficulties to overcome without having to deal with equipment as yet unproven. The first three locomotives were therefore fitted with proven but essentially obsolete equipment, and would not be modified to the new standard. In fact, had more operational experience been gained with this first trio prior to finalising the specification of the second Swindon and North British batches, an even more flexible system might have been chosen. By the time that the desirability of this became evident, sufficient work had been undertaken on D803 and its successors to make any such alteration uneconomic.

There was also a host of lesser modifications. The Maybach engines, themselves revised with pistons of improved design, were cradled in new four-point subframes devised with component interchange in mind, whilst the dynastarters were rewired in order to give a constant voltage when operating, and the starting batteries revised accordingly. The Beclawat patent cab side windows were revised with a heavier frame section to overcome the rapid distortion experienced in the first three locomotives, whilst a thicker

Above: Equipped with both headcode blinds and the new yellow warning panels, D822 *Hercules* awaits departure from Platform 1 at Exeter St Davids with the down 'Torbay Express' on 28 May 1962. *(Tom Heavyside)*

Below: Eventually, most if not all of the early D800s would receive the yellow warning panels before being rebuilt with headcode boxes. Its route indicator frame already redundant, D802 *Formidable* accelerates past Wormwood Scrubs at the head of a down express train. *(R.H.G. Simpson)*

layer of insulation was applied to the cab bulkheads so as to reduce the transmission of noise from the engine rooms. In February 1959 it was also decided that tyres for this batch should be turned to the standard BR profile rather than the GWR pattern specified for D800-2. Commencing with D813, the Spanner Mark 1a boiler was replaced by a Stone-Vapor unit, presumably in the interests of standardisation with D6326-57, though in 1961 D818 became the sole recipient of a horizontal-barrel Spanner Mark IIIa boiler which it retained for the rest of its working life.

D813 also introduced end footsteps hung from the bufferstocks for better access to lamp brackets and the like, along with twin 'letterbox' access doors in each side below cab floor level. The hinged doors replaced screwed traps in the same location, the intention being to ease maintenance of the transmission. In terms of appearance, the most striking change was the removal of the clumsy disc indicators from the nose ends in favour of a pair of adjacent route-indicator panes which opened outwards to give access to the dynastarter. This was applied from D814 onwards and did more than any other modification to enhance the locomotives' appearance, unlike the makeshift installations on the D600s. Along with the bufferstock footsteps and transmission access doors, the revised route indicators were progressively applied to earlier members of the class as they came into Swindon for repair. Other retrospective modifications concerned the provision of ribbed metal kick plates below the cab doors and the use of a revised pressure reducing valve to achieve a slight diminution of the peak locomotive braking force. This latter was first applied to D822 in May 1960, the intention being to reduce the incidence of over-heating brake blocks which, in turn, were thought to be responsible for thermal cracking of the tyres.

The first major departure from the precedents set by D800 itself came with the twenty-eighth locomotive of the Swindon batch, D830 *Majestic*. Although initially ordered with standard Maybach/Mekydro power equipment, construction of D830 was not very far advanced when it was chosen for the trial installation of a pair of high-speed diesel engines manufactured by Paxmans of Colchester, which had attracted the BTC's interest as a possible means of reconciling the purchase of diesel-hydraulics with its policy of supporting domestic suppliers. Indeed, the manufacturers claim that the engines were specifically built as a domestic alternative to the German units, with full BTC co-operation, and that the experiment was thus instigated by Paxmans rather than the BTC itself. Officially known as the 12YJXL, though sometimes billed as the 'Ventura', the engine was a twelve-cylinder four-stroke design of 60° vee-formation, the frame of which was fabricated from high-grade steel plate, welded-up with cast stretchers and stress-relieved prior to machining. Cylinder bore was 197mm with a stroke of 216mm, giving an overall swept volume of nearly 79 litres. Valvegear was of the pushrod type and aspiration effected through a single Napier turbocharger. The finished unit fitted neatly between its MAN and Maybach competitors in terms of weight at some 9930lbs and was more powerful than either, producing some 1200bhp at 1500rpm. In order to gain service experience with the design, a single pair of engines was purchased for use in D830 although much of their advantage was negated through being set to 1135bhp at 1530rpm so as to conform with the standard Maybach-Mekydro transmission units. Moreover, the extra length of the Paxman engines necessitated special subframes and prevented their use in other locomotives of the same type, or of standard MD650s in *Majestic*. The pair of Ansty-assembled Maybach engines displaced by this development became part of the spares pool.

The Paxman engines delivered pleasing results both on test and in general service, and in November 1961 the WR became involved in discussions regarding the uprating of the 12YJXL to 1350bhp by means of increased boost pressure, so as to make it suitable for use in the new D1000s. The suggestion of the BTC was that the units in D830 should be so treated as a preliminary trial, but the scheme was rendered impractical by the limited input capacity of the Mekydro transmissions, along with the pre-production nature of some components within the engines themselves. Despite its early promise, however, the 12YJXL was not to replace either the MAN or Maybach engines as major components of the WR's diesel-hydraulic formula. The early cessation of D800 orders, strained relations between BR and Paxmans as a result of serious problems encountered by Paxman engines used in two classes of Type 1 diesel-electric and, more significantly, the BTC's general dislike of high-speed diesel engines all conspired to influence BR against broadening the scope of the experiment, and so D830 remained unique in terms of its equipment. Although the pair of 12YJXL units would be maintained in service up until D830's eventual withdrawal, the type would never see use in any other front-line WR diesel-hydraulic.

Production of D800s at North British would take longer to be established than at Swindon and the first of the NBL locomotives, D833, would not be handed-over to BR until June 1960. Whilst NBL had received a full set of D800 drawings from Swindon, a large amount of detail redesign would prove necessary to accomodate not only the different power equipment but also NBL's own working practices. In particular, construction of the D800 bodyshells involved a greater use of welding than anything yet built at Queen's Park, and a large number of early problems revolved around distortion of the structure caused by excess heat. Creating some of the complex sheet metal shapes needed for the nose area in particular presented another challenge to NBL staff, and in January 1959 Swindon offered to supply ten pairs of finished cab structures in order to minimise delay, though the offer was not taken up. Despite the various difficulties, the resulting locomotives were built to a generally high standard and were far better machines than their predecessors which, after all, had been compromised from the outset. Even so, not all of NBL's modifications would meet with the WR's approval, a February 1960 memorandum from Swindon rather tersely noting that the construction of D833's cab floor bore little resemblence to current Swindon production and bemoaning the need to alter the drawings accordingly!

The most significant difference between the NBL D800s and their Swindon counterparts concerned the choice of power equipment. Whilst accepting the principle of Glasgow-built D800s, the WR had wanted them to feature Maybach engines compatible with its own series. The BTC

Top: The pair of Paxman 12YJXLs fitted to D830 represented a brave attempt by the manufacturers to break into the lucrative market for high-speed diesel engines. More highly developed than the MAN whilst eschewing most of the Maybach's more complex features, the design might well have proved an ideal prime mover for future WR hydraulics had not D800 construction been terminated so prematurely. *(GEC-Paxman Diesels Ltd.)*

Bottom: Although there would be a large number of technical differences between the two types, North British's run of D800 'Warships' would, to the untrained eye, prove largely indistinguishable from the equivalent Swindon product. Still factory-fresh after less than a month in traffic, D834 *Pathfinder* pauses between duties at Old Oak Common depot on 21 August 1960. *(G.B. Wise)*

55

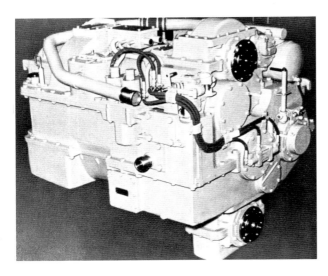

Above: As with the production run of Type 2s being built by NBL at the same time, D833-65 adopted a revised transmission unit, the Voith LT306r, which allowed the rating of the engines to be set at the full 1100bhp. Despite its greater input capacity, the new transmission was both lighter and more compact than the L306r it replaced. *(Voith)*

Below: Even with the gradual encroachment of 'Westerns' and diesel-electrics onto express services, until the late 1960s 'Warships' still dominated haulage of all but the heaviest and most prestigious trains to and from the West Country. At the head of the 11.30 service from Paddington, North British-built D841 *Roebuck* departs Par en route for Penzance on 13 August 1966. *(G.B. Wise)*

opposed this, however, principally to distribute work as widely as possible among its established suppliers, but also to ensure that NBL's D800 order should not be worth significantly less to its manufacturers than that for the cancelled series of D600s. D833-65 were therefore specified with MAN engines and Voith transmissions on condition that basic interchangeability should be maintained, but this was not to be realised. In March 1960, NBL informed Swindon that the physical constraints imposed by the BR loading gauge had reduced to an unacceptable degree the

clearance between the top of the bogie and the bottom of the transmission. The problem could be rectified by relieving the underframe section above the bogies to allow a slight relocation of the transmission block and, with thirteen underframes already completed, North British was anxious that the WR should sanction the alteration as soon as possible. This Smeddle did but with the proviso that, with a score of Mekydro-equipped D800s already in traffic, Swindon-built 'Warships' would not be modified in this fashion until the requirement to fit Voith transmissions actually arose.

The MAN engines were of the same L12V18/21B variety used in D6306-57, though mounted in a similar manner to the Maybach engines in D803-32. Five spares were included in the contract, to be shared between the NBL-built D800s and the second batch of D6300s, although they were not strictly interchangeable between classes without alterations to various connections - another compromise of the original criteria. NBL did rather better with the transmissions, which *were* compatible with the LT306r units fitted to the later Type 2s. As before, cardan shafts were of German GWB design supplied through Hardy-Spicer, though now of a similar pattern to the Stones-made GWB shafts fitted to Mekydro-equipped locomotives. Control was by a BBC seven-notch all-electric system standard with those of D803-32, although the engine speed settings in each of the notches had been revised to give a better spread of power throughout the speed range, as well as avoiding vibration periods. Earlier D800s were quickly modified to suit although, once again, D800-2 would differ due to their older six-position controllers. In fact, the exact specification of controllers varied slightly even between Swindon's later D800s and the NBL batch, and the need to reset this equipment accordingly acted to deter the use of Maybach engines in D833-65, as it did with D6306-57. A further difference was that the NBL locomotives featured an interface between their fire detection and control systems which acted to cut off the supply of fuel to the engines in the case of fire, a worthwhile modification which was subsequently applied to the Swindon batch.

Paradoxically, the choice of train-heating boiler would revert to Spanner Mark 1a, but with one vital modification. Those D800s already in traffic had been plagued by a series of inexplicable boiler failures whilst running, and eventual-

Above: From the summer of 1962, D800s would begin to work trains bound for LMR destinations north of Bristol, albeit those running via Newport and Shrewsbury. Emerging from under the road bridge at the east end of Hereford station on 14 July 1962 is D868 *Zephyr* at the head of a Plymouth-Manchester express. *(Norman E. Preedy)*

ly it had been deduced that this was due to intermittent air starvation. As the engines drew their air supply from within the engine room, particularly heavy engine loadings would drag air into the diesels faster than it could be replenished from outside the locomotive, resulting in the boiler flame being extinguished. After some heart-searching and fears of structural weakness, it was decided to cure the problem by cutting ventilating louvres between the double cantrails on one side of the boiler compartment. This provided the desired solution without any ill effects and was standardised on all new locomotives from D833 onwards as well as being applied to those already in service during the course of routine overhauls. External appearance was as for D814 *et sequr* with the twin-panel headcode box, BR green livery and warship names in alphabetical order, beginning at D833 with *Panther*. From D852, the revised engine temperature control fitted to the later D6300s was specified following problems with the earlier system, whilst locomotives from D856 also received bulk-loading fuel valves as extra-cost items. In each case, NBL provided Swindon with kits of parts for the preceding locomotives, and in due course BR applied these modifications to the Swindon-built units as well. Also improved during the production run were the standards of finish applied to the body panels after some of the first locomotives began to suffer premature deterioration of their Prestolith coating, a combined sealing paste and primer used as a protective layer on all K-M-type structures. From June 1960 onwards, therefore, NBL-built D800s had their outer surfaces phosphated prior to painting. Not applied to the Glasgow-built locomotives was the sprayed asbestos coating on the engine room walls, omitted on instructions from Swindon which had ceased applying the material to its own D800s from March 1960 onwards.

Less easy to remedy were matters relating to weight, cost and delayed delivery. Regardless of everyone's best efforts, the particular mix of equipment specified on the NBL locomotives ensured that each weighed-in at an all-up figure in excess of 80 tons, compared to 78 tons for D830 and 78´ tons for the Maybach-engined locomotives. More seriously, despite the expense to NBL of all the additional work involved, and the fact that increased production helped to spread the licensing costs payable by the BTC to K-M, the D833-65 series was limited in cost to £115,000 per locomotive compared with the £119,000 for Swindon production. The net result was that North British suffered a heavy finan-

cial loss on the order, matters being further complicated when production difficulties conspired to delay the locomotives' completion. Whilst some of these, such as the need to modify the underframes, originated at NBL, many were due to the failure of suppliers to meet their own deadlines. One example concerned the late delivery of cardan shafts, and whilst Swindon was able to loan a number of units from its own stocks to facilitate fitting-up, NBL had no choice but to await the proper components from Hardy-Spicer before the locomotives could be outshopped. Delivery of D865 did not take place until June 1962 and only then after construction of the later D6300s had been postponed, culminating in the BTC threatening to pursue a claim for some £300,000 worth of compensation through the courts. North British, although having developed ties with GEC for the supply of heavy electrical equipment used in the 'Blue Pullmans', the D6100 and D8400 diesel-electrics and in the ten Class AL4 25kV electrics built for the West Coast electrification in 1960/1, never established any permanent relationship with a diesel engine builder other than MAN. The company did not, therefore, get the sort of large orders from the BTC that had been hoped for, and the financial losses encountered in the construction of D833-65 were particularly grievous. With the delayed completion of the last few Type 2s for the WR in 1962, NBL would neither seek nor be offered the task of building any further locomotives, diesel-hydraulic or otherwise for British Railways, and within a relatively short time would cease locomotive construction altogether.

As dieselisation gathered pace, the BTC placed a further D800 order with Swindon in May 1959. The five locomotives for which it called were to have Maybach-Mekydro power equipment and follow the overall design of D803-32, albeit embracing those improvements applied to the NBL batch. The use of British Steel Corporation cast-steel bogie frames had been considered, but there were both cost and weight penalties, and Smeddle elected to retain the existing

Above: The final 'Warship' was always unique in its carrying of a cowl above the cab windscreens to conceal the warning horns, resituated there during an abortive scheme to provide electric train heating. D870 *Zulu* is seen passing through Southall in the late afternoon of 19 October 1963 with a train of milk empties bound for Cornwall. *(R.H.G. Simpson)*

design. Although allocated its own lot number, the series emerged from Swindon hot on the heels of the first production batch, between March 1961 for D866 *Zebra* and June 1961 for D869 *Zest*, being products of the same production line. The exception was D870 which did not appear until September, following sister locomotive D830 in becoming the subject of a mechanical trial. The question this time was one of train heating, no attempt having been made so far to replace the traditional low-pressure steam system. This however, was increasingly unsatisfactory, particularly in terms of steam-generator failures which contributed to a large proportion of locomotives being unavailable for service, and prompted the BTC to look for something more appropriate. That something very quickly proved to be electrically-powered carriage heaters, which had the attraction of being compatible with both diesel and electric traction, in the case of a diesel being supplied by an auxiliary generator located within the locomotive itself. Although requiring modifications to the D800's existing electrical sys-

tem, the fitting of one of these posed no great difficulty other than the amount of energy which it would itself consume. Proposing to raise the power output through a higher degree of turbocharging, the WR's engineers soon found themselves dealing with a more complex problem.

The advantage to be had from pressure-charging the MD650, as with any other engine, was reliant upon two factors, the first of which was the improvement in cylinder filling gained in the early part of the combustion cycle when the inlet manifold velocity tends to be at its lowest. The second was that the greater density of air in the cylinders allowed the introduction of a correspondingly greater fuel charge, therefore producing a stronger combustion action. Both of these apply regardless of the means used to achieve forced-air induction, though the turbocharger, being dependent upon exhaust gas flow for its impetus, tends to be less effective at low engine speeds than the mechanically-driven supercharger. The actual extent to which any engine can be pressure-charged is governed by three basic criteria, the first of which is the ability of the engine structure to handle the extra power unleashed; with its robust build, this presented few problems for the MD650. The second restriction concerns the pressure-chargers themselves and their effects upon the charge air. Regardless of the type of blower used, be it of axial-flow, centrifugal or volumetric design, the price to be paid for any mechanically-induced increase in the rate of flow is inevitably the rise in temperature resulting from the compression of air fed into the engine. Beyond a certain point, this warm air will begin to expand during the journey from the blower to the cylinders and, although the magnitude of the resulting pressure drop within the inlet tract is relatively small, it can still prove sufficient to bring about a serious reduction in the density of the charge. Lastly, charge-air temperature exerts a quantifiable effect upon the heat of combustion and of the resulting exhaust gases, which in turn have to be limited if the manufacturer is to avoid the need to make many of the top-end components from costly heat-resistant metals.

With the existing turbocharging levels already near their permitted maximum, it soon became apparent that any increase in the output of the MD650 could only be achieved through the use of charge air aftercoolers or intercoolers. These took the form of airboxes situated between blower and engine, containing dedicated low-temperature water matrices through which all charge air was passed on its way to the inlet valves. Since the charge air temperature was typically rather higher than that of the water matrix, the intercooler acted as a heat exchanger transferring heat from the charge air to the water and thence to the outside atmosphere. By raising the effective upper limit of turbocharger efficiency, this allowed a corresponding increase to be made in turbocharger size and/or speed. MD650s so equipped could be uprated to the degree required to handle the load of an auxiliary generator, and the WR decided to establish a

trial installation on D870. As well as the modifications to the engines and electrical system, it was also intended to alter the transmissions so as to eliminate converter drag whilst idling, this being achieved by a small readjustment of that part of the hydraulic circuit normally used to disengage the turbine wheel during gearchanges.

All the necessary components for the scheme were ordered and final assembly of the locomotive had actually commenced when an abrupt policy change saw the experiment abandoned, D870 entering traffic some two months late sans generators, intercoolers and modified transmissions. The only clue was the fitment of ETH jumper cables below the bufferbeam, which meant that the airhorns had to be moved from their normal position in the lower front valance to a new one on the roof dome above the windscreens, where they were protected by a fibreglass cowl. Even when the redundant cables were removed, this modification remained as a tangible reminder of BR's continuing failure to tackle the ever-more important issues of train heating and power supply to rolling stock. It also formed a recognition point for the last 'Warship' to be built as, by late 1961, it had long been recognised that something of rather larger capacity was needed for future front-line work. The first fruits of that project, the D1000 series, were already under erection at Swindon and would provide some of the greatest successes and the deepest despair of the whole WR diesel-hydraulic era.

Chapter 7
THE D800S IN SERVICE

D800's entry to revenue-earning service on the Western Region came in a fanfare of publicity on 14 July 1958, when it was named *Sir Brian Robertson* in a ceremony at Paddington Station. After a brief stay at Swindon running shed (82C) it left in August for Plymouth Laira, where it joined the first two NBL D600s in working the up 'Cornish Riviera' and returning via an evening service to Bristol. After a short period of running-in at Swindon, D801-2 joined their classmate at Laira in the November and December of that year. Initial turns on the 'Limited' by D800 were undertaken with a mixture of pride and trepidation because the capability of the locomotive could only be judged by careful analyses of V200 performance in Germany. This was far from being a satisfactory state of affairs and the WR was eager to carry out controlled road tests at the earliest opportunity. Between its initial running-in and entry to general service, therefore, D801 was submitted to a series of intensive on-line trials between Didcot and Bristol. As with generations of preceding Great Western steam power these were performed in conjunction with the 1901 Swindon dynamometer car (W7W), which could indicate drawbar pull, track speed and mileage to a high degree of accuracy. These readings were integrated to produce a rolling record of locomotive drawbar horsepower, analysis of the performance being deepened by the additional recording of throttle openings, fuel consumption rates, engine and transmission temperature levels, and even climatic conditions. The result was a complete picture of the ability of a locomotive to perform under actual operating conditions. For the testing of D801, loadings varied between 105 tons and 525 tons, all of which required to be started from a stand on the 1:74 upgrade to Filton Junction.

Much to the relief of the WR, the 'Warship' came through with flying colours and a remit to work trains of up to 400 tons unassisted south of Bristol. Given the generally higher line speeds then in force, loadings on the Birmingham expresses would be limited to just under 370 tons. Both figures represented an increase equivalent to two coaches over any comparable diesel-electric, even though during the testing process the overall efficiency of the D800's hydraulic transmission was shown to be slightly less. Limits for freight trains were slightly lower than those for passenger workings, partly due to load limitations imposed by the three-link couplings then in use, and partly for reasons of braking power. Indeed, from an early stage it was recognised that the D800's relatively low all-up weight would be a handicap on freight work and operations were restricted to consists where at least a portion of the train was continuously-braked.

With all eight of its prototype Type 4s in service, the WR began to look towards a programme of schedule-cutting and so pressed for further deliveries, a prayer which was answered when the first Swindon production batch began to take to the rails in March 1959. With all the D600s in service and steam haulage virtually eradicated from the 'Cornish Riviera', attention began to turn towards the equally prestigious 'Bristolian'. Only in 1954 had the pre-war timing of 105 minutes been restored and now, with sufficient D800s available to implement diesel haulage for the

summer season, the WR pulled off a publicity coup by paring down the timing to a record 100 minutes. Not only did this boost custom but also regained the title of 'Britain's Fastest Train' for the WR. On a less comforting note, it also revealed a major shortcoming in the locomotives' design. Although officially limited to 90mph, the tight schedule was soon resulting in speeds peaking at 100mph or more and, fearful for the welfare of his trackwork under those small, heavily-loaded driving wheels, in August 1959 the Chief Civil Engineer abruptly placed a 90mph speed maximum over all lines for all locomotives. This in turn called for sustained periods of hard working uphill so as not to lose time, something of which the D800s fortunately proved capable.

As events were to show, the CCE's action was prescient, though not in the manner intended. Despite the tremendous respect in which most held the new locomotives, by the summer of 1959 the enthusiasm of WR enginemen for working the D800s up to the 'ton' and beyond was waning rapidly. For reasons that seemed unfathomable, the 'Warships' had developed a tendency towards wild riding over track irregularities, a trait that worsened as mileage increased. Many diesels had a pronounced fore-and-aft motion when coasting that was uncomfortable and no more, but the behaviour of the D800s was uncivilised enough to become alarming. Indeed, it is fortunate that no 'Warship' was involved in a serious accident at this time, though the prudence of footplate staff coupled with the rapid imposition of an 80mph speed limit to the design were undoubtedly deciding factors.

Although a major mishap was thus avoided, the whole affair caused great embarrassment to the WR, not just because the 'Bristolian' was forced to revert ingloriously to its former 105-minute timing but also because some commentators took the opportunity to criticise the whole D800 concept as a foolish misadventure, lacking the sagicity of proven engineering principles. There was little that the WR could do save order a full investigation, place faith in its decision and ride out the storm, but it was an unpleasant time for all concerned. Matters were not helped by the fact that whilst the overall timing of the 'Bristolian' had been relaxed, an additional stop had also been scheduled, thus keeping most of the point-to-point average speed requirements just as high as before! As further 'Warships' entered service, they were allocated to Laira for services between London and the West Country, and one sparkle of sunshine amidst the gloom was their rostering on the 'Torbay Express'. Here as elsewhere, however, dieselisation was only gradual and the 'Warships' remained disabled by their newly-imposed speed restriction.

Not unnaturally, the rough-riding problems caused great consternation amongst Swindon's engineers, and a lengthy investigation was undertaken as soon as the full extent of the problem became apparent. As soon as the possibilities of track defects or some manufacturing fault had been eliminated, the WR sought assistance from the originators of the bogie design, Krauss-Maffei in Munich, whose engineers were quick to confirm that no similar troubles had been encountered with the DB V200s in the same type of service.

TO PLYMOUTH & LONDON

Above: The 'Warships' were first put to work on the crack 'Cornish Riviera' alongside their D600 namesakes. D807 *Caradoc* pulls into Par with the down 'Limited' on 28 May 1961. *(Tom Heavyside)*

Below: On 15 June 1959, D804 *Avenger* recorded the shortest time ever between Bristol and London, on the inaugural run of the 'Bristolian' to its new 100-minute schedule, when speeds exceeding 100mph were achieved at three separate locations. Such exploits were rapidly outlawed when serious riding deficiencies became apparent in the type. *(R.H.G. Simpson)*

However, further investigations by BR, K-M and the DB soon proceeded to reveal that, due to prevailing conditions in postwar Germany, only limited experience had been gained of operating the V200s at speeds much in excess of 80mph. The possibility was thus implied that the K-M bogie might be unfit for the sort of high-speed work expected on the WR and, if this were indeed the case, then the entire D800 fleet would have to be re-equipped with bogies of a different design. Krauss-Maffei, just as alarmed by this prospect as the WR, suggested that the choice of wheel profile might be causing excessive oscillation, and D803 duly had its tyres recut to a 1:50 cone. At the same time, a 50,000-mile limit between tyre turnings was imposed upon the remainder of the class.

Before long, however, Swindon established the crucial factor to be the bogie's movement relative to the locomotive body rather than to the track. As explained in the preceding chapter, the K-M bogie was of pivotless design, providing both rotary and lateral movement through an arrangement of bell-cranks and links, a mechanism to which WR engineers proceeded to devote considerable attention. Within a commendably short time they discovered that, whilst the pivoting gear was doing an excellent job in terms of rotation, lateral play was almost wholly afforded by the deflection of the various rubber-bushed joints both there and in the radius arms when subjected to sideways load. The WR's investigators had been alerted to the implications of this when a comparison of V200 and D800 bushes showed the latter to have a far lower degree of compliance,

Above: Despite the bogie problems, dieselisation of services proceeded but at a rate slower than planned. During the first week that the train was diesel-hauled, D801 *Vanguard* leaves Churston with the up 'Torbay Express' on 5 August 1959. In the bay platform, 0-4-2T No.1470 waits to proceed with the 11.40 service to Brixham. *(Hugh Ballantyne)*

Below: Sectional and plan views of the K-M bogie, illustrating not only the details of its construction but also the mechanism by which the bogie is pivoted around a central geometrical axis. Note that the transmission is located rigidly against the locomotive body, all movement between bogie and super-structure being taken up by splined and jointed cardan shafts. *(Krauss-Maffei)*

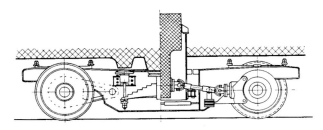

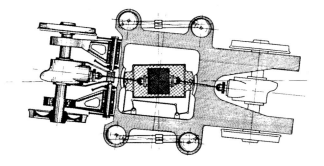

further examination revealing their deflection to be so slight and the inertia factor sufficient that, at high speeds, a virtually solid connection existed between bogie and under-frame. As the locomotives aged and the bushes wore, the effective sideplay increased but at the expense of a deterioration in lateral control, hence the wild riding. Use of softer bushes would have a similar effect and, since such behaviour was obviously inappropriate to express passenger locomotives, an alternative remedy was devised. Early in 1960, the pivoting gear was removed from D813, the existing secondary suspension arrangement being modified to create a conventional swing-link arrangement not unlike that used by the MetroVick gas-turbine No.18100. Telescopic dampers and rubber bump-stops were added to control lateral movement of the bogie, the increased translation of which required reprofiled rubbing faces for the longitudinal thrust plates, whilst Molykote was applied to the coil spring guides to alleviate wear.

Coincidentally, an all-rubber suspension arrangement suitable for the D800s had been designed by the Metalastik concern, and in June 1961 D804 was fitted with bogies featuring a large rubber spring. Initial results were promising and in July 1962 it was proposed that ten further 'Warships' should be so modified, but the WR CME elected to defer the scheme due to its high cost and doubts over the service life of the rubber springs. Furthermore, testing of the swing link arrangement under D813 had so far shown it to meet all requirements without any change to the tyre profile and in late 1963, having been cleared for 90mph working, the design was standardised for use under all D800s. The rubber suspension experiment was therefore terminated. By this time, however, the WR already had in service large numbers of D1000 C-Cs employing a three-axle version of the K-M bogie and, with priority for modification being accorded to these, the last D800 was not altered until well into 1964. To the WR's chagrin, therefore, anticipated timetable changes were thwarted once again. (The efficacy of Swindon's redesign would be graphically if tragically demonstrated in September 1967, when a Paddington-Bristol express train in the charge of D853 *Thruster* was derailed at Foxhall Junction, just west of Didcot. The official enquiry which ensued found that, due to driver error, the train had negotiated the crossover between relief and main lines at something close to 70mph rather than the 25mph prescribed, the inevitable result of which was that the last four coaches were derailed. Had the riding and tracking qualities of the revised K-M bogie then fitted to the D800 class been anything less than exemplary, there can be no doubt that the locomotive itself would have left the rails and taken the entire train with it, causing casualties very much more severe than the single death and 23 injuries actually suffered.)

Whilst all this was going on, the WR remained steadfast in its intention to dieselise 100% that territory west of Newton Abbot, even if it was unable to immediately improve on steam timings in doing so. As the NBL series of D800s began to arrive from July 1960 onwards, timetables were progressively recast to benefit diesel traction and elbow steam off-stage. By the end of that year, all but two of Laira's celebrated allocation of 'King'-class engines had been dispersed to other sheds, some to begin a short new life in South Wales, whilst the D600s also began to be relegated to more mundane duties. At the same time, arrival of the first D7000 and D1000 locomotives allowed the full implementation of dieselisation on the Paddington-Birmingham services, concentrating the D800s in the West Country. The appearance of the first D1000s on London-Plymouth workings, however, did mean that 'Warships' began to work into South Wales and on the west-to-north services between Newport and Crewe instead of handing over to steam traction at Bristol Temple Meads. Even so, the D800s remained visitors to rather than inhabitants of the Principality, most workings being as part of the cyclic Plymouth-Shrewsbury diagrams which entailed some local work before returning to Devon. Initially, the 'Warships' were all allocated to Laira but from early 1961 a large percentage of the class was transferred to Newton Abbot, each depot maintaining both MAN- and Maybach-engined examples, though in the fullness of time most of Newton Abbot's D800s would come to be NBL-built machines. Locomotives from both depots would be instrumental in sealing the fate of steam west of Newton Abbot, with very little being seen after December 1962. With the D1000s operating away from their Laira base, the task of heading the heavy summer trains fell to the D800s, sometimes piloted by a D6300 or otherwise working in multiple with another D800 to cope with the 500-ton loads. East of Exeter, severe gradients were no longer a major consideration, and loads considerably in excess of this were often handled by a single 'Warship', albeit at full throttle for much of the time. Despite this, for both economic and operational reasons, the WR tried to keep train loads at around the 350-400 ton level, particularly as point-to-point speeds began to rise in the mid-1960s.

This, however, was very much the Indian Summer of the 'Warships' and, as the Western Region's requirements turned inexorably towards more powerful locomotives, their star began to wane. The discontinuation of the D1000s' use on complex cyclic diagrams after maintenance problems became evident came at a time when changes within the WR management hierarchy would see opinion already turning against diesel-hydraulic power. With the allocation of the WR's first Brush Type 4 diesel-electric Co-Cos to Old Oak Common in December, which would be followed by further D1500 allocations to Canton and Landore over the next two years, there was an increasing desire to confine the hydraulics to simple 'out and home' workings. This manifested itself in the D800s being largely superseded on the more demanding West of England trains

by D1000s, many of which had themselves been displaced from the Birmingham-Paddington service, and instead deployed in a new theatre of operations. The transfer to the WR of the former LSWR lines west of Salisbury had brought with it a plethora of steam workings right into the heart of the WR's diesel empire and, as a result, from August 1964 'Warships' began to displace the Bulleid Pacifics from their Plymouth-Waterloo stamping grounds, though sentimental considerations would dictate that the last runs of the 'Atlantic Coast Express' be made under 'Merchant Navy' power. Southern Region crews at South Western Division depots such as Basingstoke, Eastleigh, Salisbury, Waterloo and Woking were rapidly trained on the D800s, this being restricted to the Maybach/Mekydro locomotives in order to simplify the task in hand. In later years, however, an increasing number of the NBL-built MAN/Voith machines would also be employed on the Waterloo services.

By deploying its 'Warships' in this way , the WR hoped to prepare for the new semi-fast Waterloo-Exeter service to be introduced that September, though crew unfamiliarity and motive power shortages would at first conspire to produce the frequent substitution of diesels by steam. Once these problems were overcome, 'Warships' became a familiar sight not only here and on freight workings to Southampton Docks, but also on Waterloo-Weymouth trains diverted via the switchback Mid-Hants line in order to permit the undertaking of work connected with the Bournemouth electrification scheme. Originally a steam turn, the arduous gradients of the 'Alps' were not best-suited to the light-footed Bulleid Pacifics, and their replacement by D800s was effected as quickly as possible. The 'Warships' had already become occasional performers on the Exeter-Plymouth portion of the former LSWR mainline, but the decline of this as a through route saw them restricted to just one Brighton-Plymouth passenger working via Okehampton from September 1964. Whilst this was terminated at Exeter after a few years, the class continued to haul freight over the route until its demise in 1968, although to D827/65 would fall the unusual distinction of hauling the last revenue-earning train over the route, a freight train

Below: After a period of intense activity, Swindon Works came up with a revised design of bogie which was at first tested under D813 *Diadem*, seen here passing through Starcross with an up express on 1 September 1960. Note that the locomotive carries both the new bufferstock footsteps and the hinged access doors at the base of the cab but not, as yet, the four-digit route indicators. *(B.J. Miller Collection)*

diverted after severe storm damage had blocked the WR mainline at Dawlish. This took place in February 1969, some nine months after official closure!

This victory for WR motive power utilisation was in many ways a somewhat pyrrhic one, gained at the cost of the virtual disappearance of the D800 type from top-link WR passenger duties. Although no longer used on the Birmingham services, however, many of the WR's D1000 'Westerns' were engaged in working the accelerated South Wales trains, resulting in many services of a secondary nature (though still designated as Class One in the timetable) being rostered for 'Warship' haulage on an every-day basis. This applied especially to stopping trains on the long stretch of mainline west of Plymouth which, along with local freight traffic, provided a regular diet of balancing workings for D800s between long-distance duties. These were chiefly in the form of inter-regional workings where a hand-over to diesel-electric traction would take place at Bristol or Birmingham, supplemented for the period of the summer timetable by additional trains intended to cater for the holiday traffic to popular West Country resorts such as Weston-super-Mare, Ilfracombe and Newquay.

By the late 1960s, a steadily increasing number of these inter-regional trains would be worked all the way to WR destinations by diesel-electrics and, to cope with this, Laira crews began training on the ubiquitous Brush Type 4s from June 1967 onwards. A surplus of D800s was thus created west of Bristol and between August 1967 and January 1968 twenty-one NBL-built D800s were transferred to Old Oak Common to work the semi-fast Birmingham-Paddington service via Banbury and Princes Risborough. These replaced WR-allocated D1500s which, since the resumption of express services over the now-electrified London Midland mainline, were felt excessive for the demands of those relatively light stopping trains which remained to serve the old Great Western route. The diesel-electrics were in turn transferred to fill power shortages on the LMR, some going to the North-West to displace steam traction whilst others were put to work on coal trains in the Nottingham Division. Late in 1967, however, the commencement of long-overdue resignalling and track re-mod-

Above: By the winter of 1962/3, 'Warships' were handling the majority of passenger workings between Paddington and the West Country. In the almost-arctic snows of February 1963, D805 *Benbow* heads under clear signals into Taplow with the up 'Mayflower'. *(Colin J. Marsden Collection)*

elling work at Paddington necessitated the temporary diversion of many WR passenger services in and out of London. For their part, the Birmingham trains were re-routed to run into Marylebone and, given the London Midland Region's known dislike of hosting regular diesel-hydraulic workings on its territory, it was not long before responsibility for the services was restored to Brush Type 4s. Whilst completion of the work at Paddington soon allowed the return of the WR's Birmingham trains to that station, the D1500s had displaced the 'Warships' for good and many of the latter quickly went into storage at Old Oak Common. Those left in service at that depot were redeployed on Hereford trains via Oxford and Worcester, but their reign here was a short one and at no time did they succeed in displacing the D7000s more familiar to the route.

Comparatively few modifications were made to the D800s during their career other than those instituted during the course of production. One point of dissatisfaction was the gearing of the Voith LT306r transmissions used in the NBL batch, which were ordered to duplicate those in D6306-57. As they only had three stages rather than the four of the Mekydro unit, and had been set with the 75mph top speed of the Type 2s in mind, the converter change points on D833-65 proved undesirably high at 34mph and 65mph. NBL had been aware of this and had suggested the use of a revised axle drive ratio in October 1958, but this had been rejected by the WR CME who noted his concern not only with regard to reduced maximum speed but also to the increased criticality of ground clearance beneath the larger drive casing, especially once the tyres were worn. Smeddle gave his opinion that the effect on performance would not be particularly injurious anyway, but in this he was proved wrong, and subsequently a number of spare LT306r units had their gearing sets modified to give not

Top: 'Warships' appeared on freight workings from quite an early stage, although for reasons of braking power usually restricted to light duties or those where at least part of the consist was continuously braked. On 16 July 1966, D851 *Temeraire* waits to leave Redruth Goods Yard with that afternoon's pick-up freight for Truro. *(G.B. Wise)*

Bottom: From mid-1964, 'Warships' began to be used in strength on Waterloo-Exeter trains over the old LSWR route. On 19 October 1965 a travel-stained D819 *Goliath* passes through Basingstoke with the 13.00 departure from Waterloo. *(Norman E. Preedy)*

Above: Although never branchline locomotives, for years the 'Warships' were regular visitors to the single line section between Par and Newquay, especially with trains of holiday makers during the summer months. On 13 August 1966, D850 *Swift* pulls into Par with the 11.45 Newquay-York service. *(G.B. Wise)*

only more favourable change points but also enhanced performance at low speeds. One drawback of this modification was that the altered transmissions were no longer operationally compatible with the original LT306r specification, and both transmissions in a locomotive had to be of exactly the same variety if some very odd performance characteristics were to be avoided. Neither did it succeed in curing the Voith's habit of running hot, betrayed by the penetration of heat and fumes into the cabs, necessitating the cutting of ventilation holes in the noses of most Voith-equipped D800s.

Another problem to afflict the NBL locomotives concerned their cardan shafts, Swindon experiencing great difficulty in withdrawing those linking engine and transmission on the just-delivered D833. Apparently, with all the locomotive's internal equipment in position, only four of the eight securing bolts were accessible, and the method of fixing the cardans was subsequently revised. Some premature deterioration of the integral rubber couplings was also experienced, though this was something which afflicted MAN/Voith and Maybach/Mekydro locomotives equally, and was eventually overcome by the redesign of the offending components. Major changes to the Swindon-built 'Warships' were relatively uncommon, though D821 *Greyhound* was modified in the mid-1960s with a revised Driver's Safety Device having pneumatic rather than vacuum actuation and in 1968 became the last of a numerical sequence from D803 to be fitted with BR AWS to supplement the ATC apparatus already fitted. Smeddle proposed the outshopping of a Mekydro-equipped D800 with MAN engines as a comparative experiment in June 1961, and gave instructions for the engine/transmission couple's torsional vibration characteristics to be assessed, but a month later the idea was dropped. Although the Swindon Locomotive Committee minutes note that it was intended to resurrect the scheme the following year, no Swindon-built D800 would ever receive MAN power, largely due to the need to revise the controller settings to suit.

Interchangeability was also limited between the prototype and production Swindon batches, though the old-pattern MD650 engines fitted to D800-2 were eventually rebuilt to the then-current production standard. Due to their six-notch control systems and lower transmission input capacity, however, engines fitted to this trio were always set to the original output of 1035bhp at 1500rpm. The original sextet of German-built MD650s proved to be money particularly well-spent, with a few exceeding some three-quarters of a million miles of service prior to overhaul. Similarly, when in line with German practise BR engineers opened up the first Mekydro K104 transmission

Top: Another ex-LSWR route to see the 'Warships' was the late-lamented line between Barnstaple and Ilfracombe. D806 *Cambrian*, its maroon livery by now overpainted with yellow ends, prepares to leave the North Devon resort sometime in 1968. Note also the replacement of the original indicator discs with headcode panels. *(B.J. Miller Collection)*

Middle: From late 1964 onwards, Swindon Works would begin to outshop D800 'Warships' in the maroon livery hitherto reserved for the larger 'Westerns'. On 2 June 1966, an immaculate D839 *Relentless* passes southwards through Kennington Junction with Hawksworth inspection saloon W80943W in tow. Note that the multiple-working apparatus has already been removed from this 'Warship', betrayed by the empty plinth adjacent to the nearest front buffer. *(R.H.G. Simpson)*

Bottom: D831 *Monarch*, seen shunting a milk train at Yeovil Junction on 15 April 1967, was the first of its kind to be repainted in blue and largely succeeded in complying with the initial recommendations of the BR Design Panel, carrying small yellow warning panels, double-arrow logos on the cabsheets and numbers (albeit of the obsolescent seriffed style) situated below the engine-room windows. *(C.G. Maggs)*

Above: The standard style evolved for the 'Warships' utilised full yellow ends with logos and numbers on each cabsheet. Co-opted from Salisbury for SR engineering duties, D813 *Diadem* approaches Dunbridge station during track relaying on 13 April 1969. *(G.F. Gillham)*

for a routine inspection at around the 250,000-mile mark, they found relatively little wear. From then on, transmissions tended to be left in place until they failed or alternatively had accumulated such a high mileage that a precautionary overhaul was considered advisable, usually at around 375,000 miles. Sad to say, a time would come when Mekydros would have to be taken out of traffic at much lower mileages due to the premature failure of bearings within the gearbox. After reaching a climax during the mid-1960s, the problem was partly overcome through imposing higher standards of quality control during overhaul work, though never eradicated completely. Both Mekydro and Voith transmissions remained susceptible to damage arising from overheating, itself usually a result of engine cooling system malfunction.

The greatest overall alterations in the appearance of the 'Warships' concerned matters of livery. Initially all were painted in the standard green with grey relief and red bufferbeams, but increasing concern for the safety of track gangers due to the rapid and near-silent approach of diesels soon saw this amended. In August 1960 the adoption of an oscillating 'Mars' light of the sort popular in the United States was discussed at Swindon, but the idea was not proceeded with, D845 and D858 instead being modified in 1961 by the addition of yellow nose access doors and a white roof dome above the cab windows. The white roof was soon abandoned but the yellow panel was extended in size, shaped to conform with the style of the locomotive front and applied to all members of the class from mid-1962 onwards, along with the mandatory electrification flashes. This as a standard was not to last for long, and from the end of 1964 it was decided to extend the maroon livery applied to the D1000 locomotives to the D800s as well. The basic style was similar to the earlier green, except that the grey stripe disappeared and the BR locomotive emblem was replaced by a coaching-stock cypher. Cabside numerals were repositioned slightly and nameplate backgrounds changed from red to black. This period of individualism would be equally short-lived as the new standard blue liv-

ery was imposed from the end of 1966 and not all D800s, therefore, received the maroon. Confusion reigned at first, with some of the early repaints being garbed in an almost turquoise shade bearing little resemblance to the correct Monastral or Rail Blue. Subsequent repaints adopted the prescribed colour, albeit with small yellow ends and the obsolescent seriffed numbers; some of these early Rail Blue locomotives had a completely matt finish, designed to reduce time in painting as well as dirt collection in service. In reality, it looked awful and was quickly replaced by a 75% matt or 'eggshell' finish which retained most of the advantages but was considerably more pleasing to the eye.

Some time elapsed before a definite style was evolved, with a full-length bright yellow end wrapped-round to follow the windscreen rake, numbers below the engine room windows and a double-arrow logo on each cabsheet. Early repaints had their running gear rendered in umber to disguise the effects of brake dust and road dirt and, whilst these parts soon reverted to black, D864 *Zambesi* ran for some while in a unique scheme whereby umber was applied to the entire locomotive from the beltline down! The full yellow ends were also applied to non-blue locomotives as they passed through works in the interests of safety. Not all of the class would survive long enough to receive the new blue colour scheme, and at least eight 'Warships' would be withdrawn in either the standard maroon or hybrid maroon with yellow ends. Some 'Warships' also persisted in carrying seriffed numbers and/or wrong-sized logos although most eventually conformed to the standard style which, from about 1969, was itself revised to dictate numbers on each cabsheet with a single logo located below the nameplate. Although less pleasing than the preceding green and maroon liveries, the blue could look attractive if kept clean but

unfortunately, at the combined mercies both of the elements and powerful cleaning chemicals, many locomotives left much to be desired in this regard. Under the TOPS scheme, Maybach-engined locomotives became Class 42 and MAN-engined examples Class 43, although none were allocated five-digit computerised numbers. The solitary Paxman-engined D830 was included in Class 42 by virtue of its Mekydro transmissions and Swindon build.

In many ways, the 'Warships' relegation to second-string duties from the mid-1960s onwards was, operationally speaking, a logical one. Less powerful than either a D1500 or a 'Western', the D800s were not always compatible with the faster schedules then coming into force, and furthermore were beginning to suffer from failing availability figures compared with those of their early years. As mentioned, there was a crop of troubles with Mekydro transmissions at one point and although the Maybach-manufactured MD650 engines never experienced the magnitude of failings endemic in their license-built MD655 and MD870 cousins, they inevitably suffered from a maintenance point of view as workshop facilities became overloaded with remedial work. The MAN engines, however, were plagued by serious mechanical shortcomings and, like their D600 and D6300 predecessors, NBL-built D800s spent weeks at a time out of traffic awaiting repair. Problems common to both groups concerned engine cooling systems, chiefly arising from thermostat failure, loss of coolant and leakage from the hydrostatic circuit, and continuity failures in the complex all-electric control system. Between them, the cooling and control systems accounted for nearly 70% of all D800 casualties in service. Train-heating boilers were also a regular source of trouble, again largely due to control failures, and several locomotives spent lengthy periods restricted to freight traffic due to unserviceable boilers. As the 1960s drew to an end, the 'Warship' class as a whole was increasingly to be found employed on freight traffic, although always at a disadvantage on really heavy movements due to the locomotives' restricted brake force. Around the time that the D1000s were dual-braked, a feasibility study was done on the D800s with a view to the possible fitment of train air brakes, but concluded that problems would arise in locating the additional brake reservoirs required. As a result, the scheme was abandoned at a very early stage and the 'Warships' retained train vacuum braking only, further restricting their use.

The swansong of the D800s came in late 1968 when a desire to accelerate train timings on the West of England services called for a unit of motive power stronger than either a D1000 or a D1500. Having calculated that 4500bhp was sufficient to handle the forecast loadings on the tightest schedule compatible with the line speeds then in force, the WR decided to use D800s operating in tandem, only to find that the little-used multiple-working equipment had been disconnected or removed on most locomotives as a regular source of electrical faults. This necessitated the refitment of the equipment to fifteen Class 42s which were then deployed in pairs on the principal London-Plymouth services, along with some of the more heavily-patronised services to Newton Abbot and Penzance. Although the reduced timings increased passenger loadings the exercise was not a success, due not least to the plummeting availability figures of the D800s, and when in 1969 new timetables ended the tradition of dividing Down trains into separate Kingswear and Plymouth sections at Exeter or Newton Abbot, it was decided to run trains to each destination at alternate hours, all being rostered for D1000 haulage. That, effectively, was the end of the 'Warships' short reign over the WR's top-link passenger traffic.

Chapter 8
THE **D7000 'HYMEKS'**

OF all the faults that characterised the original policies of the BTC with regard to the acquisition of diesel power, one of the most serious must have been the initial failure to invite tenders for Type 3 locomotives. These, defined in the motive power table as units of between 1500 and 1750bhp, would be of similar capability to the various Class 5 mixed-traffic 4-6-0s which had demonstrated themselves to be one of the key elements of the modern railway, equally capable of standing in for a failed express passenger locomotive on a crack train or working a heavy unfitted freight. The fact that early orders called for no Type 3 locomotives of any kind testified not only to the influencing of the Pilot Scheme orders by the incomplete power classification of 1956 but also the BTC's delusion that a small range of diesel units could be multiple-worked in various combinations to produce whatever unit of traction was required. In the United States, where trainloads often exceeded the capacity of the diesel-electrics then available, this was an excellent way of procuring the sort of power needed for the most demanding workings whilst, by operating the units individually rather than in groups, still retaining small locomotives suitable for lighter duties. British operating conditions did not require the 6000 and 8000bhp outputs that the Americans deployed and whilst the 'multiple unit' policy provided an excellent vehicle for achieving standardisation, from an operational viewpoint it was at best impractical and at worst downright wasteful, especially when the pairing of Type 2s saw potential Type 4 power being used to do a Type 3 job.

As a result, it did not take long for requests from all over British Railways for Type 3 locomotives to be forwarded to the BTC. For its part, the Western Region was particularly unhappy at the prospect of having to use the NBL Type 2 design as a replacement for some four hundred or so 4-6-0s of the 'Hall', 'Grange' and 'Manor' classes, along with another two hundred 2-6-0s of similar capacity, and yearned for a diesel-hydraulic that would fill the void left by their eventual withdrawal. In this it was not alone, with both the Eastern and Southern Regions aware of the lack of potential replacements for their own Class 5 locomotives, and in July 1957 the BTC paper *Mainline Diesel Locomotives:*

Limitation of Variety, recognising that the problem could not be addressed through further diversification of motive power constructed around existing guidelines, had contained strong indications of a more favourable attitude towards Type 3 diesel power. A detailed set of specifications had already been issued to interested parties, calling for a mixed-traffic locomotive of 1500-1750bhp output with wide route availability, a 90mph service ceiling and a 19-ton axleload. It was generally accepted that the design(s) chosen for the ER and SR would be diesel-electrics and that for the WR a diesel-hydraulic, but no specific conditions to this end were imposed at first. Accordingly, a variety of tenders was received from various manufacturers covering both diesel-electric and diesel-hydraulic formats as well as a multiplicity of engine designs.

In June 1959, the results of the tendering became known in the shape of three orders for Type 3 locomotives placed by the BTC with private contractors. English Electric was given the go-ahead to produce forty-two diesel-electric Co-Cos of 1750bhp for the ER, whilst the Birmingham Carriage & Wagon Company received an order for ninety-eight 1550bhp Sulzer-engined diesel-electric Bo-Bos for the SR. The BTC had wished to standardise upon English Electric's design only, but the Co-Co could offer neither the electric train heating nor the wide route availability demanded by the Southern Region, hence the decision to order two separate designs. Both were built in quantity without prototypes, confirming the now-urgent need for Type 3 power, as was the third, an order for forty-five 1740bhp diesel-hydraulic B-Bs for the Western Region. This was won by Beyer-Peacock (Hymek) Ltd of Manchester, a consortium consisting of Beyer-Peacock, Bristol-Siddeley Engines and Stone-Platt Industries which had been formed specifically to tender for the Type 3 order. All three met each others', and the WR's needs in a unique way. BSE and Stones held licenses for the UK manufacture of Maybach railway traction equipment but were unable to

Below: Weight diagram for the first batch of Beyer-Peacock Type 3s, D7000-44. *(National Railway Museum)*

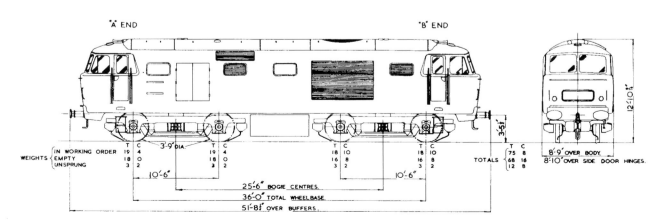

realise the full sales potential of their products so long as the WR's intake of diesel-hydraulics was governed by Swindon Works' restricted capacity for new construction. Beyer-Peacock, on the other hand, was an old-established and well-respected locomotive builder whose fortunes had waxed and waned with the rise and fall of the Beyer-Garratt locomotive. Pursuing new markets, first in the form of a collaborative venture with Metropolitan-Vickers, then in the manufacture of light diesel-hydraulic shunters for sale abroad, it had met with little success in either and saw the WR's diesel-hydraulic policy as a lifeline leading to restored prosperity.

As Beyer-Peacock (Hymek) Ltd was only a trading company, the actual construction of the forty-five locomotives was subcontracted, BSE and Stones producing the power equipment whilst Beyer-Peacock (Gorton) Ltd erected the locomotives at its Manchester works. Although there were many detail differences between the two designs, the finished product was conceptually similar to the Deutsche Bundesbahn's V160 class, a medium-duty B-B fashioned around a single engine-transmission set of 1900bhp output. By following this lead, B-P's design gained sufficient a weight reduction over its competitors to allow a locomotive of optimal adhesive weight to be produced on a conventional load-bearing chassis. This had the welcome effect of saving Beyer-Peacock the trouble of concluding yet another license agreement with Krauss-Maffei, as well as the task of making its staff conversant with the skills of stressed-skin construction. B-P's chosen layout shared certain similarities with that of the NBL Type 2s, the frame consisting of a welded structure of mild steel girders surmounted by thick floorplates, with a central aperture for the transmission block. Once again, the chosen wheel diameter did not allow the frame to lie at buffer height and so a dragbox and buffer-beam assembly had to be built up at each end in order to resist buffing forces. As this strength frame constituted the main load-bearing structure of the locomotive, the body framing was welded-up out of lighter angle iron and clad with thin steel panels.

The body design itself was the result of collaboration between B-P, the BTC's Design Office and the industrial consultants Wilkes & Ashmore of Horsham, Sussex, and was without doubt one of the better efforts to be seen on BR metals. Despite the comparatively short body length of 51 feet, the designers managed to impart a contour that was at once both distinctive and attractive. Each cab had a reverse-angle profile, surmounted by a fibreglass roof dome which was itself absorbed into the higher roof contour between the cabs. Beneath the large double windscreens at each end was a one-piece, four-digit route indicator whilst the bufferbeams were skirted by a lip which not only integrated them into the cab outline but also served as a side-to-side walkway, being capped with a strip of aluminium chequerplate. Similar attention to detail was found in the specification of the bodyside windows, twin-pane sliding Widney units with smart aluminium frames. Two ventilation grilles on each side were of similar proportions, with matching brightwork around their edges. The real quality of the design can be gauged not only by the fact that it remained little altered until final withdrawal, but also that it was adopted with few changes for the BRCW prototype *Lion* in 1963. Softened somewhat, and made less distinctive if no less attractive, it was used on the Brush D1500 Co-Cos of the same year, in which form it is still readily to be seen on Britain's railways today.

Mechanically, the heart of the B-P design was the Maybach MD870 diesel engine. Although not hitherto used on BR, the MD870 was a direct development from the MD865 and thus had a similar line of descent to the MD650 used in the D800s. Essentially a sixteen-cylinder version of the smaller engine, the MD865 had incorporated a fabricated crankcase, the greater rigidity of which suited the vee-

Above: The pioneer 'Hymek', D7000, was exhibited when new at the Institution of Locomotive Engineers' Exhibition at Marylebone in May 1961 and is seen on display there, sandwiched between Standard Pacific No.71000 *Duke of Gloucester* and English Electric's ill-starred 'GT3' gas-turbine 4-6-0. *(R.H.G. Simpson)*

Below: Basis of the 'Hymek' design was the Maybach MD870 diesel engine. A 16-cylinder unit, it followed the MD650 in most respects but incorporated from the outset such refinements as intercooling and fabricated construction. An incidental benefit of having twin blowers instead of the MD650's single large unit was that the resulting short exhaust pipes suited the pulse turbocharging concept then in vogue. *(MTU)*

sixteen's additional length, yet saved weight and cost compared to a cast iron equivalent. As noted in Chapter 3, many smaller parts were shared in common with the MD650 and eventually even the fabricated crankcase design would be applied to the twelve-cylinder engines. The transition from MD865 to MD870 came with the application of a higher degree of turbocharger pressure so as to increase output to 2000bhp, which in turn required the addition of intercoolers to the existing manifold system. These took the form of small radiator matrices within airboxes mounted at the free

Above: To deal with the greater power output of the MD870, a stronger transmission unit was specified in the form of the Mekydro K184. Essentially an enlarged and strengthened K104, it nevertheless shared few components in common with its smaller counterpart. *(MTU)*

end of the engine, through which all charge air passed on its way from the twin turbochargers to the inlet tract. By connecting these matrices to a specific low-temperature water circuit, turbocharger boost could be increased significantly without any undesirable heating of the charge air, allowing a gain in power of up to 15% from the same swept volume.

Despite the considerable increase in power so achieved, the MD870 otherwise deviated remarkably little from the proven design, even the cylinder heads remaining unchanged with their twin overhead camshafts and mechanically-actuated Bryce-Berger L'Orange injection system. Most of the differences between the new Type 3's engine and those of its predecessors on the WR related to the actual installation, most notably the fact that the subframe (in the form of two separate steel rails) was welded directly to the locomotive chassis itself rather than being removable as before. The breakable joint between engine and underframe thus became the eight 'Cushyfoot' high-deflection resilient pads supporting the crankcase itself, each of which was angle-mounted by the dynafocal principle. As a result, the pads were best-placed so as to absorb both engine weight and dynamic forces. At the time of its introduction, the MD870 figured amongst the most powerful traction diesels of its size anywhere in the world, and although B-P would in fact downrate the unit to 1740bhp at 1500rpm in order to meet BTC specifications, its availability proved to be the deciding factor in making a single-engined Type 3 diesel-hydraulic design an economic proposition. All of the engine units supplied to B-P were built by BSE at Ansty, although the initial twenty contained a higher proportion of German-made components than the rest.

As in the NBL Type 2s, the engine was mounted with its centre point above the inner axle of one of the bogies, driving via a short cardan shaft the Mekydro K184 transmission block mounted on the floor in the centre of the locomotive. Basically a larger and stronger version of the revised K104 unit fitted to D803-32, the K184 had few parts in common with the smaller unit but was sufficiently similar in concept and general arrangement to be introduced without the need for a major staff familiarisation programme. One important difference was that each claw clutch was operated by an individual fork, necessitating a revised control block with twice the number of operating pistons. This did, however, have the advantage of reducing the gear masses moved during each individual change. Gear

change-up points were set slightly higher than on the K104 at 26mph, 42mph and 70mph, although once again this was variable dependent upon load. Like the engine, it was the transmission's similarity to the units used in the D800s rather than its having been proved in service in Germany that led to its large-scale adoption without UK trials. Capable of handling some 1800bhp at the input, the K184 was of such a size that B-P had no small difficulty locating it in the locomotive, and eventually had to settle for an arrangement where virtually every cardan above floor level lay at an angle.

Various auxiliaries were located around the engine and transmission; between the engine itself and the 'A' cab bulkhead was the braking frame, containing the Kunz-Knorr air brake, its associated Laycock-Knorr compressor and a pair of Northey Model 125PE exhausters for the train vacuum brakes. Also located here was the control system and multiple-working equipment. With initial experience of the D800s' multi-stage BBC control systems demonstrating a certain level of operational inflexibility under some conditions, in October 1958 the WR had decided that a stepless engine control system should form part of the forthcoming Type 3 order. B-P and BSE therefore elected to use an electro-pneumatic system of Brush manufacture, with an air-driven control link between driver and power unit. Engine speed was determined by the position of the driver's main controller, a cam at the base of which acted upon a pilot air valve which in turn regulated the pressure of air supplied to the R32gp pendulum governor on the engine itself. Electric actuation was retained for the transmission control and auxiliary systems, as well as for some of the multiple-working controls. Locomotives coupled in multiple were nevertheless joined by an air line, the pressure contained in which determined the degree of throttle opening on the trailing locomotive, a 10% excess being allowed for leakage. Although similar to those used in several contemporary diesel-electric designs, the B-P Type 3 installation was compatible neither with the standard BR system nor with those of the WR's existing diesel-hydraulics. Coded as 'Yellow Triangle', the class was therefore able to work in multiple only within itself, and even then to a limit of two locomotives.

Other engine room equipment included Vokes paper air filters located in the roof coving, which supplied the engine turbochargers with inlet air via flexible trunking. These fulfilled the valuable function of keeping charge air as cool as possible prior to reaching the turbochargers as well as avoiding the problems of boiler air starvation experienced on the early D800s. The remaining space was largely occupied by an 800-gallon boiler water tank located above the transmission block and above that, in the roof space, was a small gravity tank to keep the injectors 'drowned', fed by pumps from the main fuel tanks between the bogies. As with the other Maybach engines, the MD870's injectors derived their actuation from the engine valvegear and so needed no separate pressure pump, injection being facilitated via an integral plunger within each injector body. The amount of fuel injected was determined by the rotation of the plunger within the injector, a helix machined on the plunger itself meeting with a return port in the body, relieving fuel pressure and so ceasing injection. The further the plunger was rotated, the later the helix would meet the return port on each stroke, so increasing the level of fuel delivered.

Next to the transmission block, in its own compartment and offset so as to permit a walk-through gangway between cabs, was the Behr-Serck cooling unit. Angled cardans led from the transmission block and also to the dynastarter which, for lack of anywhere else to put it, was mounted on the floor beneath the cooler unit. Lack of interior space was always a problem with the type, and negotiation of the walkway was complicated by the angled cardans and the fact that at its narrowest point, between the radiator shutters and the bodyside, the gangway only measured some 18" across. Lightweight doors separated the cooler group from the engine room and from the third compartment, located next to the 'B'-end cab. This was home to a Stone-Vapor OK4616 train-heating boiler, capable of a steaming rate of 1750 lbs/hour and fed from the main fuel supply. Also incorporated was a Stone's 'Vapor Watchman' engine pre-heater. Oil-fired, the unit was used prior to start-up but additionally could be set to maintain engine temperature during short lay-overs, so reducing the need for excessive engine idling.

Given the lack of an agreement with K-M or any other builder, Beyer-Peacock had a free hand with respect to the design of running gear and specified 10'6" wheelbase bogies to the well-tried Commonwealth pattern. A product of the American General Steel Castings Corporation but marketed in Britain by English Steel Castings, the Commonwealth was derived from the standard passenger coach bogie design of the Pennsylvania Railroad. Its foundation was a heavy one-piece cast steel frame from which was hung, on swing links, a single bolster pivoted from the locomotive underframe and bearing on the bogie frame through triple full-elliptic leaf springs constituting the secondary suspension. Axleboxes were of the Timken taper-roller variety and although riding in vertical guides cast into the bogie frame, did not bear directly upon it. Instead, they were suspended by the raised extremities of a long dropped-centre compensating beam joining the two axles on either side of the bogie. Primary suspension between each beam and the bogie frame itself was provided by a pair of helical springs bearing on the cast frame at their upper ends and resting in pressed steel pans at their lowers, these pans in turn being pivoted from the compensating beam. The design facilitated load transfer by carrying a proportion of any excess load on one axle of a bogie along the compensating beam to its mate, allowing for softer primary springs and therefore a better standard of riding over a wide speed range. Ride quality as a whole was tailored to meet the characteristics of the locomotive design by careful attention to the strength of springs and the length of the swing links.

Plain disc wheels were used, though of a non-standard 45"-diameter dictated by the BTC's obsession with tyre loadings. Not only did this raise the level of the mainframe and so require the built-up dragboxes, but also necessitated that the cardan shafts from the transmission block's output flanges be angled upwards to meet the Maybach C33v spur-and-bevel axledrives on the inner axles. From that point, horizontal shafts drove the C33 drives on the outer axles. All drives had horizontal torque reaction members bearing on rubber dampers, as with the K-M bogies, in order to improve adhesion and reduce transmission wear under heavy load conditions. Since the transmission output protruded down through the locomotive frame, twin fuel tanks had to be fitted on either side of the frame to leave room for the transmission and cardans, total fuel capacity amounting to some 800 gallons. Braking arrangements consisted of a quartet of compressed air cylinders on each bogie, operating one pair of clasp brakes per wheel, whilst bogie-mounted sandboxes fed pneumatic sanding gear.

The layout of the cab interior was completely unlike those of any of the WR's existing diesel-hydraulics, though similarities with some diesel-electrics reflected the consultations that had by now taken place between the BTC and the enginemens' Trade Unions. A desk ran across the entire width of the locomotive below cab window level, extended backwards to form pedestals on each side of the driver's footwell. Above this desk ran an angled panel carrying various switches and speedometer, engine rev-counter and vacuum gauges, as well as the straight air brake control. The pedestal to the driver's left carried the vacuum brake handle whilst that to his right mounted the power and reversing

Above: The Beyer-Peacock Type 3 was unique amongst WR diesel-hydraulics in its use of the Commonwealth bogie. The design's essentials are seen to advantage in this detail shot of D7018's running gear, notably the cast manganese steel bogie frame and equalising beam, the primary coil springs and the secondary leaf springs affixed to the swing-bolster. *(Author's Collection)*

controllers, the handbrake wheel and a switch panel. Directly in front of him on the desk lay the horn button, sanding control and air brake pressure gauges, one for each bogie. An additional panel at the edge of the driver's windscreen contained various warning lights whilst a number of auxiliary controls were provided on the fireman's side. Additional gauges placed within the engine room also required periodic checking and, along with the supervision of the train-heating boiler as required, these too were the responsibility of the fireman. Amongst the Western Region's diesel-hydraulics, the B-P Type 3 was unique in having windscreens made out of Triplex gold-film laminated glass, which had a thin layer of gold sandwiched between two sheets of glass during the production process. Although expensive, this technique served to minimise the effects of glare as well as facilitating demisting by the simple expedient of passing a small electrical current through the gold film. Also new to the WR was the livery chosen for the new locomotives, which, like the bodystyle, had been decided by Wilkes & Ashmore. In fact, the consultants had elected to repeat the scheme that they had created for the Eastern Region's 'Deltics', with the BR standard green being relieved by a wide green-yellow skirt and a grey roof. The cab window area was picked-out in off-white whilst running numbers were in raised alloy figures on each cabsheet.

As direct competitors for a large proportion of BR's future Type 3 orders, it is interesting to compare the Beyer-Peacock design with the rival D6700 Co-Co, the first of which entered service late in 1960. Most obvious was the English Electric design's additional bulk, with an overall length of 62' and an all-up weight of 102 tons compared with the 51' and 75 tons of the D7000, though both could

Above: D7006 is bathed in the watery sunshine of 4 November 1961 as it stands in Bath Spa station awaiting the departure of the 08.10 service from Bristol to Salisbury. The locomotive's pleasingly clean appearance reflects the fact that it had been in BR service for less than a month when this photograph was taken. *(Hugh Ballantyne)*

Below: The 'Hymek' was intended primarily as a replacement for the WR's various mixed-traffic 4-6-0s, and so an especially apposite comparison is afforded by this view of D7039 piloting No.6907 *Davenham Hall* on the 16.25 Cardiff-Portsmouth service. The date is 22 June 1963 and the train is seen approaching Twerton Tunnel, between Bristol and Bath. *(C.G. Maggs)*

negotiate a four-chain curve. Also shared was approximate gross engine output, which meant that the B-P locomotive could claim a power:weight ratio of 23bhp per ton as opposed to the 17bhp per ton of the D6700. Unusually, it was the diesel-electric design which returned marginally better tractive effort figures, with a starting effort of 55,000lbs and continuous effort of 35,000lbs at 13.6mph exceeding the diesel-hydraulic's 50,200lbs and 33,950lbs respectively, though the D7000 did develop its continuous rating at the slightly lower speed of 12.3mph. In fact, the D6700's slight advantage on paper had been secured by the use of electrical machines which favoured high outputs at low speed at the expense of high-speed performance. Whereas the D7000 would prove a true all-rounder, equally at home on an express passenger train or a heavy goods working, EE's Type 3 was very much a low-speed slogger, and it was no coincidence that many examples of the design would be used to replace Class 8 2-8-0s on freight duties in various parts of the country. Through its use of three-axle bogies, however, the D6700 could claim significantly lower axle loadings despite its greater overall weight, which also contributed to a higher braking force, some 50 tons as compared with only 33 tons for the diesel-hydraulic. Bearing in mind the avowed intention of British Railways to equip the entire wagon fleet with continuous brakes, a premise around which the WR's entire dieselisation policy had been based, this was a limitation which the region's operators were happy to accept.

Having adapted the old foundry and boiler shops at Gorton to deal with diesel production, B-P could handle up to twenty units at once and rapid progress was made. Indeed, such was the headway that the first member of the class, D7000 was handed over to the WR on 16 May 1961, some three months ahead of schedule, with D7001 following just over a month later. By the middle of August 1962 the entire batch was in service working out of Bristol Bath

Road, with the exception of D7022/4/5/28-39 which were allocated to Cardiff Canton. The first change of any note occurred when D7003 was delivered with its warning horns relocated from behind the bufferbeam to a new position atop the cab roof in an attempt to make them more audible. All subsequent production was equipped in a similar manner and the first three locomotives were modified similarly soon after. The second was the bestowal of their distinctive nickname, this being derived from the name of the company responsible for their design. Itself a contraction of the 'hydro-mechanical' tag sometimes applied to the Mekydro transmission, 'Hymek' was a soubriquet which the D7000s were to keep until the end of their career on BR.

The obvious need which the WR had for these locomotives was demonstrated by the placing of an order for an additional fifty units in July 1960, prior to the completion of D7000 itself. Details were as for the first forty-five except for the specifying of Westinghouse locomotive air brakes and that company's Model 2E38/B compressor, along with a Spanner Mark III train-heating boiler. Delivery commenced hot on the heels of the first batch in August 1962 and had been completed by December 1963. The receipt of this order not unnaturally heightened B-P's hopes of securing even more custom, and at one time total 'Hymek' orders were expected to amount to some three hundred locomotives. In reality, however, one of the first nails in the diesel-hydraulic's coffin would prove to be the last in that of the Gorton concern. Soon after the abandonment of the Pilot Scheme, it became obvious that the continuous-braking programme for the wagon fleet was not proceeding with the expected alacrity. This put the diesel-hydraulics at a distinct disadvantage and none more so than the 'Hymeks', working heavy unbraked coal trains on the steep grades of the South Wales valleys with less than 70% of the brake force of comparable diesel-electrics. A 1960 BTC survey of future motive power requirements had recommended the adoption

Above: In early 1962, 'Hymeks' began to replace 'Castles' on trains between South Wales and Paddington, a duty which they would continue to perform until the arrival in force of the larger D1000s. On 3 July 1963, D7037 joins the line from Bristol Temple Meads at Stoke Gifford Junction, having just come through the Severn Tunnel with a train from Pembroke Docks. *(John S. Whiteley)*

Below: Another early deployment of 'Hymeks' was on the Cheltenham trains, including the prestigious 'Cheltenham Spa Express'. Less celebrated but still an important part of the timetable were stopping trains such as the 14.59 Cheltenham-Swindon service, seen emerging from the east end of Sapperton Tunnel behind D7018 on 31 May 1962. The 'Hymek' will have had plenty of opportunity to show its mettle on the climb from Brimscombe and, for some years, members of the class were employed as banking engines at this location. *(C.G. Maggs)*

Above: Except for a few years in the late 1960s, the type was a regular sight on trains between South Wales and the South Coast, as well as other inter-regional workings to SR destinations. Looking smart in its original paint scheme of two-tone green with small yellow warning panels, D7068 leaves Winchester at the head of a Bournemouth-Manchester express in August 1966. *(Dr L.A. Nixon)*

of diesel-electric traction as a national standard, and the slowing-down of the wagon braking programme lent additional weight to the BTC's prejudices. The 1960 recommendations thus became official policy, and whilst existing orders for diesel-hydraulics would be honoured, no more were to be placed. Therefore, BR's final 'Hymek' order, lodged with B-P in December 1961, called for only six locomotives to the amended specification, whilst at the same time orders were placed for 140 EE Type 3s to help displace 'Hymeks' from the South Wales coal traffic. The last 'Hymek', D7100 was delivered in February 1964 and shortly after, B-P took a contract for 54 Derby/Sulzer Type 2s at a wholly unremunerative rate in order to keep the works ticking-over until new orders could be secured. In the event, none were forthcoming and the thirty-sixth locomotive was the last, the rest being re-directed to BR's Derby Works as Beyer-Peacock entered voluntary liquidation. With each example costing an average £87,950 and orders for fifteen spare engines and transmissions to boot, the total value of the 'Hymek' programme to B-P had been close to £9 million.

Although initial deliveries of the class were to the new diesel depot at Bristol Bath Road (82A) in order to allow dieselisation of the South Wales-South Coast services between Bristol and Salisbury, the rapid progression of crew training soon saw the 'Hymeks' sphere of operations broadened with fitted freight and passenger workings to Cardiff, Plymouth, Taunton, Portsmouth, Weymouth and London. In the October of 1961 a number of 'Hymeks' were sub-shedded at Westbury (82D), first for freight trials and subsequently turns on the heavy stone trains from Merehead, a task with which they would be strongly associated in later life, though a briefer but more glamorous assignment was the working of Swindon-York and York-Bristol passenger trains over the former Great Central mainline south of Leicester. By the end of the year, clear-

ance and load tests had begun with a view to operating the type in the South Wales valleys and, from January 1962, Cardiff and Radyr crews began training on a 'Hymek' sent up each day from Westbury and returning in the evening so as to facilitate maintenance. This bore fruit in the first allocations of 'Hymeks' to Cardiff Canton from February 1962 onwards and, with the completion of the first driver training programmes in the London Division, 'Hymeks' began to be rostered on South Wales-Paddington expresses from March. These were formerly the responsibility of 'Castles', 'Britannia' Pacifics and, after their displacement from the West of England trains, 'King'-class engines, and it had been intended to dieselise them using D1000 locomotives. In the event, however, the opening of the M4 motorway dictated immediate service accelerations before the larger locomotives were available, and so 'Hymeks' were diverted from lighter duties. Fortunately, schedules were still relatively slow and so what were essentially mixed traffic locomotives were not overtaxed by the 450-ton loadings on what had once been the preserve of Class 7 and Class 8 steam power. One probable effect of this deployment was a minor amendment to the then-current build specification, locomotives delivered from May onwards being equipped with securing clips on the cab ends with the carrying of train headboards in mind.

Slower but no less demanding was the working of some of the WR's second-line express and fast stopping services, notably over the north-to-west route west of Shrewsbury, which included various Penzance-Manchester, Liverpool-Cardiff and Cardiff-Newcastle turns, the latter via Gloucester. These were chiefly the province of Canton-shedded locomotives, Cardiff and Bristol sharing between them assorted London-area duties ranging from the 'Cheltenham Spa Express' to Didcot-Paddington parcels trains. 'Hymeks' became a regular sight in Devon from September onwards when they assumed responsibility for a number of secondary services to and from London, also regularly being rostered for the Newton Abbot-Rogerstone goods workings, for which Newton Abbot received its first allocation of the type in the shape of D7075/98-100. The use of 'Hymeks' on virtually all goods traffic within South Wales had long been the WR's intention and the Newton Abbot-Rogerstone workings were only part of this strategy, a further long-distance duty being the heavy Radyr-Salisbury coal trains. To service these, as well as the large number of coal and steel workings in the valleys and along the South Wales mainline itself, the WR had intended to allocate some forty-five 'Hymeks' to the new diesel depot at Swansea Landore. By the time that work was complete, however, the decision to foreshorten the diesel-hydraulic programme had already been taken, and the redistribution of work necessary to accomodate the WR's allocation of standard diesel-electrics meant that Landore's involvement with 'Hymeks' would be limited to thirty-three of Cardiff's allocation for maintenance only. Many goods services within South Wales still handled by steam would thus be converted direct to English Electric Type 3 haulage, with the majority of those duties already handled by 'Hymeks' rapidly following suit.

Experience to date had shown that the diesel-hydraulics were not at their best on heavy unbraked coal trains, and the BTC's decision to suspend the continuous-braking programme for the wagon fleet inevitably meant that the 'Hymeks' days in South Wales were numbered. Furthermore, enormous changes were occurring in terms of the volume and pattern of freight work west of Newport, with the result that by 1964 local Type 3 requirements had slumped to a level only half that of the three hundred locomotives forecasted in 1959. Accordingly, given the number of EE D6700s allocated to the WR and their preferred status for mineral traffic, it made sense to standardise upon that design for all Type 3 diagrams within South Wales, to the virtual exclusion of the 'Hymeks'. Canton, however, would continue to boast a small stud of D7000s for services to London and Portsmouth until the latter became the responsibility of diesel multiple-units in 1965. Subsequently, with the redeployment of much of the WR's cross-country DMU fleet, 'Hymeks' would once again become a common sight on the Cardiff-Portsmouth service, finally relinquishing the duty in the spring of 1973. Another working which took 'Hymeks' deep into Southern Region territory was the Exeter-Waterloo service and although it was never officially booked as a D7000 turn, 'Hymeks' made spasmodic but persistent appearances at Waterloo for years, deputising for D800 'Warships'.

It was at this time that a number of failings in the D7000 design were to make themselves keenly felt with a corresponding fall in availability, all the more so since the depot heavy maintenance programme was not yet running at full capacity and all major unit failures had thus to be referred to Swindon Works. Two major problems were prevalent, the first of which was the inordinately high rate of failures in the cardan shafts either side of the transmission block, and the second concerning difficulties with correct gear selection in the block itself. During attempts to find the root cause of these problems some forty locomotives had their engines downrated from the normal output of 1740bhp at 1500rpm to 1350bhp, whilst a trio of newly-delivered locomotives were uprated to 1920bhp, this figure representing the maximum input capacity of Swindon Works' engine dynamometer. By going to each of these extremes, the WR hoped to see whether or not the output of the engine had any effect upon the regularity or seriousness of the problem and, in the case of the downrated locomotives, hopefully avoid trouble for some time to come. Contemporaneously, another forty locomotives had the first gear stage in the transmission locked out of use, a move which temporarily assuaged the difficulty at the cost of reducing both transmission efficiency and low-speed tractive effort. For its part, Beyer-Peacock retained four newly-built 'Hymeks' for technical analysis, these eventually entering service some six months after completion.

After nearly a year's investigation, the transmission defect was deemed to be due to changed tolerances, instituted so as to simplify production, which were resulting in temperamental operation of the reverse-torque mechanism and claw clutch responsible for changing gear. Often the difficulties had been compounded by consequential damage to the gears themselves; operating under conditions of full load with over 1700bhp on tap, incorrect gear selection was bound to lead to damage sooner or later. The solution was simple enough, involving the imposition of the correct tolerances and, as a precautionary measure, the strengthening of certain gearbox components including the hubs of the gearwheels themselves. Contrary to some subsequent claims, blame in this instance did not rest with the British licensees. Similar problems occurred shortly afterwards with K184 units in service in Germany and the problem was eventually traced to Maybach's works in Friedrichshafen, where corrective action was quickly taken.

The cardan shaft problem was one that did not succumb to rectification quite so easily, some of the worst occur-

Top: 'Hymeks' were also to be seen on former Southern Region metals between Exeter and Salisbury. On 24 July 1965, D7095 reverses onto the Sidmouth portion of the 12.00 from Waterloo at Sidmouth Junction. In the distance, D6324 can be seen waiting in the goods yard to work the Exmouth portion of the same train. *(P.J. Horton)*

Bottom: One working with which the 'Hymeks' would become particularly strongly associated was the handling of trains between Paddington, Worcester and Hereford. On 2 August 1964, D7067 heads west out of Worcester Shrub Hill on the final leg of its journey to Hereford. *(R.H.G. Simpson)*

Top: With the demise of steam, the versatile Type 3s quickly came to dominate the minor freight lines of the Mendips. On 29 December 1967, D7007 passes Frome on the Radstock branch with a train from North Somerset Quarry Sidings. D7007 was one of the first 'Hymeks' to receive the BR blue livery, a rather unpleasant scheme which did away with all relief other than for the small yellow warning panel. *(Hugh Ballantyne)*

Bottom: Other than in South Wales and East Somerset, the comparatively heavy 'Hymeks' were not a common sight on country branches but there were exceptions, such as the line from Taunton to Minehead. On 18 July 1970, a still-green D7026 pulls into a bucolic and unspoilt Williton with the 06.20 Oxford-Minehead service. *(Hugh Ballantyne)*

rences involving dynastarters being torn from their mountings and flailed around the engine room. As a first step, softer couplings in the form of bonded rubber sections between yoke and shaft were applied to the cardans spanning engine and transmission, as well as to the auxiliary shaft from transmission to dynastarter. By doing this, it was hoped to eliminate transmission shunt under changing load conditions with a consequent extension of shaft life, but the problem did not in fact abate until an additional flexible coupling was fitted to the primary input shaft which, in conjunction with those modifications already implemented, succeeded in balancing the system and so reduced shaft failure rates to more acceptable levels. All this would take some considerable time to arrange, and it would not be until 1965 that the programme of corrective modification would be completed and the last locomotives returned to their original specification of 1740bhp and four transmission stages.

Other frequent sources of trouble were big-end bearings and turbochargers, mostly arising from the use of cheaper, non-original components by BSE, and regular overheating damage to cylinder heads occasioned by cooling system failures. The first such instances had involved the same sort of coolant loss problems as had afflicted some of the NBL Type 2s, and a cursory investigation found the cause to be the same as well, namely that coolant was being ejected from the radiator header tank under braking surge. The overflow pipe was duly repositioned, and a general recall of the type to Swindon Works saw this particular shortcoming very quickly eliminated. Cooling system defects continued to be reported, however, the most usual complaints citing incorrect operation or failure of the moving radiator shutters, and oil leakage from the high-pressure lines connecting hydrostatic pump and fan motor. Engine water pumps too gave serious trouble with persistent leaks, the same fault having been experienced in some diesel-electric designs where it had been cured by a revised design of sealing gland. From 1963, Bristol-Siddeley began to fit this improved seal to all new Maybach engine production, but application to engines already in WR service did not commence until 1966, by which time the problem had assumed epidemic proportions.

Yet another headache concerned the early appearance of fatigue cracks in the crankcases of BSE-built units, a fault hitherto virtually unknown on MD-series engines, and which was found to be due to sub-standard welding during manufacture. In other cases, the same welding deficiencies led to the eventual corrosion of the engine structure, which in turn resulted in internal leakage and the cross-contamination of coolant and lubricating oil. For a time, some difficulty was experienced with the soft iron rings used to provide a seal between the upper end of the cylinder liner and the cylinder head, whilst the liners themselves proved prone to premature failure; on a few occasions, sufficient coolant was released into the cylinders to precipitate hydraulic locking, resulting in serious engine damage. Cylinder liner failures had been experienced with some MD-series units in service with other undertakings and was deemed to be due to cavitation by the cooling water, but in the WR's case this was exacerbated by unsuitable coolant additives that chemically attacked both the liners and their rubber sealing rings.

Outside the engines, train-heating boilers proved to be a perennial nuisance on the D7000s as on virtually every other BR diesel so equipped, and for a multitude of reasons did not settle down to give the sort of good service achieved on other railways. Despite the best efforts of all concerned, they could never be made truly reliable and in later years developed a worrying proclivity for setting themselves alight. For this reason a number of 'Hymeks' ended up with this equipment isolated, and were thus confined to freight workings for most of the year. Although only a few of these problems could be attributed directly to the 'Hymek's design, many being shared with a variety of other

Top: A contrast in liveries as D7047 and D7088 take a rest from their labours at Newport Ebbw Junction in June 1971. D7047 displays an early blue livery with small yellow panels but with the grey window relief reinstated, whilst D7088 carries the final scheme with a full yellow end extended to wrap round the window area. *([The other] Peter J. Robinson)*

Bottom: For some years, a quintet of 'Hymeks' was used to provide banking assistance on the Lickey Incline. In their last year of use on this duty, D7022/3 assist 'Peak' 1Co-Co1 D109 on a heavy mineral train bound for the Eastern Region, seen approaching the summit of the 3½-mile climb at Blackwell on 1 May 1971. *(W.A. Kelsey)*

BR motive power, their early occurrence did prove a significant embarrassment both to the WR and to Beyer-Peacock, especially since the Type 3 diesel-electrics had provided largely trouble-free service from the outset. Indeed, it is recorded that Roland Bond, by then Technical Advisor to the British Railways Board, was so unhappy with the 'Hymeks' early service record that he originated the plan to fulfil future WR Type 3 requirements with English Electric D6700s though, if the truth be told, the writing on the wall was already legible for the diesel-hydraulic genre as a whole on British Railways.

Despite these troubles, the 'Hymeks' continued to deliver a generally high standard of service, though often in pastures new. From the summer of 1963 the WR had sufficient of the new D1000 locomotives for them to replace the Type 3s on the Paddington-South Wales trains, so permitting service accelerations. This, along with the ever-greater quantities of English Electric Type 3s assigned to the WR, eventually allowed the redistribution of Canton's entire 'Hymek'

allocation, sixteen of which moved to Plymouth Laira where they joined the quartet newly reallocated from Newton Abbot. The remainder found a new home at Old Oak Common alongside D7076/8 which had been allocated there from new, being used to supplement the D6300s on empty stock workings and local freights, and to replace Worcester's stud of 'Castles' on the Paddington-Hereford services. Here one might say that the D7000s found their true vocation, with light trains and (at that time) superlative track making speeds of 90mph and more the rule rather than

the exception. The 'Hymeks' work on the Hereford trains impressed many observers and, with the D1000s suffering from a spate of chronic maintenance problems, the sight of a D7000 back at the head of a South Wales express became by no means uncommon. Even with the faster schedules then in force, the 'Hymeks' could still keep time under favourable conditions provided that drivers took full advantage of their performance potential.

Shortly after the delivery of the last 'Hymek' in February 1964, the handing-over of the Birmingham-Paddington ser-

Above: On 24 February 1973, No.7001 stands at Stratford, East London, after working an Acton-Temple Mills freight. Cross-London transfers of this sort made 'Hymeks' regular visitors to Eastern Region metals for some years. Note that the air horns have been moved from their original position behind the bufferbeam to the standard location on the cab roof. *(B.J. Nicolle)*

Left: On 31 March 1973, six weeks before the end of 'Hymek' workings on the Cardiff-Portsmouth trains, No.7093 heads south beneath a stormy sky, passing Wylye with the 09.09 service from Cardiff. *(G.F. Gillham)*

vices to D1500 Co-Cos saw the D1000s concentrated at Laira, so displacing that shed's allocation of 'Hymeks'. Some returned north to Cardiff whilst the others were split between Bristol Bath Road and Old Oak Common, a pattern that was to remain unchanged for some time other than for the return of D7068-72/4 to Newton Abbot to cover a number of West Country duties. Within a short while, however, they would be dispersed again when it was found to be more effective to cover 'Hymek' duties in Devon and Somerset with locomotives diagrammed from Bristol Bath Road. As well as traffic on the mainline between Bristol and Plymouth, 'Hymeks' would be rostered for duties on the Taunton-Minehead branch, Bristol-Bath services over the old Midland Railway line, and on the former LSWR lines west of Exeter, especially on the Barnstaple-Ilfracombe section where traffic, although declining, could still be quite heavy in the summer months. They also continued to work many of the stopping passenger and most of the freight movements over the Southern mainline between Salisbury and Exeter. Less obviously, D7000s were beginning to dominate freight traffic on the network of secondary lines in East Somerset, initially coal trains between Radstock and Frome, creosote tankers between Cheddar and Cranmore and, slightly further afield, milk traffic between Highbridge and the creamery at Bason Bridge. There was also a measure of stone traffic from the quarries of the area, laying a small but vital foundation for the huge increase in aggregates traffic that would take place after 1970 and which would provide the WR with much-needed traffic at a time when business across all sectors was slow. 'Hymeks' would continue

to work this expanded traffic into the early 1970s, after which volumes became so great that the WR had no choice but to substitute more powerful locomotives in the shape of D1000s and D1500s.

The distribution of 'Hymeks' in this manner would remain until 1967 when, under the terms of the National Traction Plan, the wholesale slaughter of small, non-standard diesel types would create a serious motive power shortage on the Eastern Region, compensated for by transferring large numbers of EE Type 3s out of South Wales to ER sheds. From the October of that year, all freight traffic west of Swansea was therefore handled by 'Hymeks' once more. Doubts had been expressed about their suitability for this given their restricted braking force, but in practice the ever-declining amount of traffic meant that trains were often only a few wagons long. Although almost never seen west of Plymouth, the D7000s continued to range far and wide over the Western Region and even beyond it. As well as their routine visits to the Southern Region, 'Hymeks' would be observed working goods trains on to London Midland Region metals both in the London area and in the West Midlands. Many of their visits to LMR locations around the capital were at the head of cross-London freight transfers which frequently took 'Hymeks' into Eastern Region territory at Stratford, where they provided an intriguing contrast with some of the ER's own more esoteric examples of motive power!

Another effect of the transfer of WR D6700s to the Eastern Region was that 'Hymeks' took over the task of assisting north-bound trains over the infamous $3^1/2$ miles of the Lickey Incline, on the former Midland mainline southwest of Birmingham. With the transfer of this territory to the Western Region, provision of one or more banking engines at Bromsgrove had become a WR responsibility and although most passenger trains no longer required banking, there were a number of heavy freight consists that regularly did. Steam traction had been replaced in 1964 by a quartet of EE Type 3s, but now these too were to leave for the ER. After a number of trials, Bath Road's D7021-5 were based at Worcester from late 1967 onwards specifically for this duty, three locomotives being outstationed at Bromsgrove at any one time. Since uphill speeds often fluc-

tuated about the 26mph gearchange point, it was felt desirable to obviate any possibility of the locomotives' transmissions 'hunting' between the first and second stages whilst engaged on banking duties. Accordingly, D7021-5 had first gear once again locked-out for the rest of their stay at Worcester. As before, this move adversely affected the locomotives' low-speed tractive effort in a duty where it was needed most, and 'Hymeks' used as bankers at locations such as Sapperton and Upwey were not modified in this way, conditions not being judged sufficiently extreme. Things on the Lickey were somewhat different and in this regard, the 'Hymeks' low braking force also had to be taken into consideration. In the event of a heavy unbraked freight train stalling or becoming divided on the bank, there were very real fears that a single D7000 on the rear might not be able to prevent the consist from running away down the incline. Two 'Hymeks' could be worked in multiple but as train weights were often sufficient to dictate three bankers for braking purposes, another driver was required to take charge of the third locomotive, which then usually led the other two. The same five locomotives performed this vital role for some years, even continuing for a while after the London Midland Region regained control of the line north of Bromsgrove, but during the course of 1971 were replaced by LMR-allocated D6700s.

Engine and transmission corrections excepted, subsequent modifications to the class were slight and mainly cosmetic. All were delivered in the livery described for D7000, the only difference being that the black-painted bufferbeam sill was finished in green-yellow to match the bodywork on D7001 and all subsequent examples. Yellow end warning panels and electrification flashes were applied to the 'Hymeks' from mid-1962 in company with other BR diesels, but none would gain the maroon livery applied to the larger WR diesel-hydraulics, nor their coaching-stock cyphers. The first of the type to be turned out in the standard blue livery with the double-arrow logo was D7004 in December 1966 but quite apart from its blue being of the wrong shade, all relief was eliminated other than the warning panel. This scheme quite spoiled the locomotive's looks,

and it was fortunately not long before the white cab window surrounds were reinstated. This was made standard for the entire class until the advent of full yellow ends in mid-1968 which, being extended around the windows in place of the grey, did not have the harmful effects upon the locomotives' appearance that it did upon some of their less fortunate brethren.

Not all locomotives received the new blue livery but the full yellow ends were applied during works visits to locomotives still in green. Nevertheless, one of the first 'Hymek' withdrawals in 1971 retained its green livery and small warning panels until the very end and in all, around a quarter of the class would be withdrawn in either the green or early blue liveries. Under the TOPS scheme the 'Hymeks' became Class 35 but due to their short expected lifespan, their new five-digit numbers were not applied, allowing the locomotives to retain their distinctive raised metal numerals. These however, had a tendency to disappear, especially in the locomotives' declining years and it was not at all uncommon to see Class 35s with missing numerals replaced by standard adhesive figures. Not replaced were the redundant 'D'-prefixes which were often removed altogether, or at least overpainted in Rail Blue. Upon withdrawal, a particular effort was made by shed staff to remove these numerals, a policy which had a noteworthy if freakish result in the shape of No.7017, withdrawn from Old Oak Common early in May 1973. Reinstated to service less than a week later, the locomotive was found already to have lost all four sets of numerals, a situation that was corrected by the application of adhesive numbers to the driver's cabsides only, and which persisted until the 'Hymek's second and final withdrawal two years later.

Chapter 9
THE D1000 'WESTERNS'

IT is a sad but nonetheless inescapable fact that the Western Region's ultimate development of mainline diesel-hydraulic traction, the D1000 'Western', was in many ways a late developer and failed to show of what it was really capable until too late. This is not to say that there was anything fundamentally wrong with the design, as from a technical viewpoint it was no less accomplished than its best diesel-electric counterparts. Rather, the D1000s were afflicted with a multitude of small problems already seen in other classes which came to a head in the new design, and which marred their formative years with a catalogue of mechanical failures which were not overcome until their fate was sealed. Indeed, with the aid of hindsight it is almost possible to say that the eventual fate of the 1955 Western Region traction policy had been decided before the first D1000 turned a wheel in traffic.

The inspiration behind the type was the desire for a locomotive that could not only replace a 'King' 4-6-0 or a D800 'Warship', but significantly improve upon the performance of either. The direction in which Great Western, and subsequently WR, service patterns should proceed had been recognised as early as 1945, when the possibility of longer and heavier trains had been discounted due to the likelihood of operational problems over the south-western section and the prohibitive expense of lengthening station platforms to suit. Therefore, the preferred policy was one of a greater number of accelerated services, and by the mid-1950s speed itself had become a selling-point, especially with the emergence of a national motorway network in sight. Not wishing to have to reduce train complements further, the WR wanted a locomotive capable of handling rather more demanding schedules than would the forthcoming D800s, and in August 1957 preliminary discussions were held regarding the design of a so-called 'Type 5' diesel-hydraulic.

First thoughts revolved around a six-axle version of the V200, originally built by Krauss-Maffei as a demonstrator to secure orders where low axleloadings were an essential prerequisite. Although sampled in this form during 1957 by a BR delegation which rejected it in favour of the standard B-B, the WR considered it to be suitable as the basis for its next generation of high-power diesels, and proceeded to work-up an outline specification. In February 1959 brief consideration was given to an alternative proposal, namely the re-equipment of a D600 with larger engines and transmissions, but it soon became apparent that any such machine would be not only overweight but also mechanically compromised. Reasoning that it would be better to use the K-M method of construction with which they were already familiar, Smeddle and his team confined their attention to the German locomotive, which during 1958 had been rebuilt with twelve-cylinder intercooled Maybach MD655 engines and prototype Mekydro K184 transmissions, along with revised auxiliaries, to produce an altogether more muscular machine. Boasting a rated power of 3000bhp, ML3000 (as the rebuild was called) weighed-in at just over a hundred tons in full working order, yet could put some 60,000 lbs of tractive effort to the rail at speeds as low as 12mph. After brief tests on the steeply-graded routes of the Black Forest and the Semmering Pass in Austria, as well as dynamometer car tests on the Ruhr-Salzgitter line, ML3000 proceeded to return nearly 6000 miles a month on heavy mineral trains weighing up to 2400 tons, then repeated the feat on equally taxing east-west passenger trains of up to 600 tons without suffering major failure. In each case, the performance of the newcomer eclipsed those both of the V200s and of the Deutsche Bundesbahn's best modern steam power.

After further demonstrations of ML3000 were given to BTC representatives, specifications and details were sent by K-M to Swindon and by September 1959 this material had become the basis of a Type 4 proposal calling for a C-C machine using twin Maybach engines and Voith transmissions. Technically, there were few reasons why the uprated power equipment could not be housed within the existing D800 bodyshell with its four-wheel bogies, a course which K-M would later follow with the V200. However, in addition to express passenger traffic, the WR wanted to see its new Type 4 capable of working heavy freight trains, an area in which the 'Warships' had proved rather deficient due to their low braking force. The use of three-axle bogies would improve traction by increasing the total area of contact between wheelrim and railhead and, along with the new locomotives' additional weight, would ensure that rather more braking power would be available for partially-fitted or unfitted freight workings whilst at the same time preserving the 19-ton axleloading demanded by the BTC. Under these provisos, construction of Type 4 diesel-hydraulics based on ML3000 was authorised, but on condition that overall design should rest in the hands of the BTC's CME, Mr J.F. Harrison. The WR CME and the Swindon Drawing Office under G.E. Scholes were to concern themselves with matters of detail design and construction.

It was accepted from the outset that the K-M superstructure would need to be compressed to comply with the BR L1 loading gauge, but ultimately the BTC's Central Staff would insist upon so many other modifications that a whole new design would evolve. Given this and the expertise in stressed-skin construction that Swindon had by now amassed, K-M participation in the D1000 project was slight compared to the part that had been played in the construction of the first D800s. Certainly, little technical information was exchanged between the two parties, despite the design of the D1000s occurring concurrently with the development of a 2700bhp B-B for the DB, the V200.1, again derived from the ML3000 prototype. Official BTC reaction at this cooling of relations with Krauss-Maffei seems to have escaped the record, but one cannot help suspecting that there must have been at least an element of covert satisfaction present within the BTC's headquarters at Marylebone Road. It is surely no coincidence that, at the same time, the BTC had been discussing diesel-electric designs of 2700bhp and 19 tons axleload, the results of which would prove an eventual nemesis for the diesel-hydraulic on British Railways.

Once the project was under way it proceeded to move very quickly indeed, as Swindon applied the lessons it had learned from the D800. In October 1959 the BTC placed an order for a production run of 74 examples, to be numbered D1000-73, this without having evaluated a prototype or, for that matter, even having completed detail design, such was

Above: 'Westerns' D1000 and D1002 under construction at Swindon Works in the autumn of 1961. Constructional techniques were similar to those of the D800s, Swindon having by this time amassed a pool of both artisan and drawing office staff that held the greatest collective knowledge of stressed-skin construction available within British Railways, and perhaps the UK railway industry as a whole. *(R.H.G. Simpson)*

Below: Weight diagram for the D1000 class as built. *(National Railway Museum)*

especial concern by the BTC, though official figures released in 1965 still showed a Crewe-built D1000 costing some £136,00, 8% more than diesel-electric D1500s manufactured at the same location.

Structurally, the D1000 design was very similar to the D800 except for its greater length of 65' as compared to 58'. The same arrangement of 6½"-diameter longitudinal steel tubes supporting a lightweight honeycomb frame topped by floorplates was evident and, once again, loading gauge restrictions necessitated these tubes being above bufferbeam level, so requiring extra platework to maintain rigidity. Within this honeycomb lay the four main fuel tanks holding some 816 gallons in total, along with a trio of 272-gallon boiler water tanks. Batteries were again located outboard of the main structure in the interests of easy access. Another similarity to the D800s lay in the body structure which, although of light weight, adopted the double-cantrail form to produce an immensely strong end-product, dispensing with the need for partitions between the cab bulkheads. One positive result of BTC control over the design was the adoption of flat-fronted cabs without nose ends, largely due to the desire to increase levels of noise insulation over those of the D800s, but aided by the fact that nose ends were going out of fashion anyway.

Cab interior design was essentially similar to that of the 'Hymeks', though with the pedestals each side of the driver extended to form one continuous desk, akin to that of the D800s. Once again, brake controls lay to the driver's left and power controls to his right although all gauges were now situated below the cab windows, allowing space for the warning lights to be placed on the desk itself. As the locomotives were twin-engined, the engine rev-counter in each cab indicated only the speed of the adjacent engine although a single member of the class would later be equipped with changeover switches in both cabs, enabling either engine to be monitored. Like that of the D7000s', the cab layout would be enthusiastically received by enginemen and would change little through the locomotives' lifespan.

As with the 'Hymeks', the question of internal space would cause considerable problems with the D1000 design. Theoretically, it would have been desirable to have followed the layout used in ML3000 with the engines over the bogies, but in the event the smaller BR loading gauge precluded this and resulted in the engines having to be located centrally, despite the high loading that this would place upon the locomotive's centre-section. Otherwise, normal practice was followed, with two symmetrical power/transmission/cooling groups located one on each side of the locomotive's centre, staggered in order to allow a through walkway. The nominally-central train-heating boiler had therefore to be displaced both transversely and longitudinally in order to allow a cross-over. The boiler itself was of the horizontal-barrel Spanner Mark III variety, fitted-up to give a steaming rate of 2450 lbs/hour. Fuel supply was from the main tanks whilst feedwater capacity amounted to 980 gallons, the three underfloor tanks being supplemented by a further 170-gallon tank at the base of the boiler itself.

the demand for the new locomotives. One surprise was that although all construction was to be entrusted to BR workshops, Swindon was to build only thirty-five locomotives numbered D1000-34, whilst the remaining thirty-nine, numbered D1035-73, were to be built at Crewe. Although Crewe had not built a diesel-hydraulic locomotive so far, let alone one embodying the complex principles of stressed-skin construction, there was sound reasoning behind this decision. Firstly, Swindon was already preoccupied with the series production of D800s and in any case, a distribution of new work amongst BR workshops was desirable so as to minimise delivery delays and preserve employment. Perhaps more important was Crewe's solid record of delivery on time, coupled with lower production costs than at Swindon. Back in the early years of the century, Churchward, when enquired of by a cost-conscious General Manager as to why Crewe could build three engines for the cost of two made at Swindon, had crustily replied "Because one of mine could pull two of their bloody things backwards" but, as Sir William Stanier was later to discover, Crewe's standards of workmanship were equally high as Swindon's, and often significantly cheaper. Given the high cost of the D800s, this latter factor was viewed with

DH/4102/1

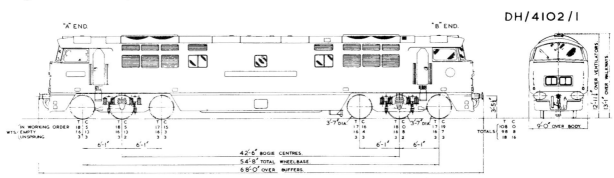

Flanking the boiler on either side were the Maybach MD655 engines, twelve-cylinder units basically similar to the MD650 except for a greater level of turbocharger boost and the application of intercooling, though there were a number of modifications such as a fabricated crankcase and engine frame designed to cope with the increased output. As on the MD870, the intercoolers were located in boxes at the free end of the engine and had their own cooling circuit separate from the main cooling system. Although it necessitated a duplication of components, this provision was vital since the temperature of the main system was thermostatically maintained at around 80°C, which was rather higher than the 65°C required for optimum intercooler efficiency. Also similar to the 'Hymek' was the engine air supply taken direct from paper filters located in the bodyside between the cantrails where ambient air was found to be both cleanest and coolest, and the engine subframes which were fixed to the floor and made contact with the engines themselves through angled pads. Although capable of some 1500bhp at 1500rpm, the MD655s in the D1000s were set to produce 1380bhp at the same speed, this being determined by the input capacity of the chosen transmission units. All 148 engines required for the batch, plus a number of spares, were made by Maybach's UK licensee, Bristol-Siddeley Engines, although as in the case of their MD870 units, it is thought that the first few Ansty-built engines contained a higher proportion of parts shipped ready-made from Germany than subsequent production.

From the output end of each engine (that facing the nearest cab) a short cardan shaft angled upwards to the main transmission block, situated on four resilient mountings above the inner axle of the bogie. Initial thoughts for the D1000 had envisioned interchangeability between two alternative transmission types, namely the Mekydro K184 used in the 'Hymeks' and a new Voith design then still under development, the L308qrV. As design work progressed, it became apparent that the Mekydro transmission blocks would need to be tilted-over on their mountings if loading gauge limitations were to be respected, and although this had been done quite successfully on the DB V200.1s, the WR's engineers were not happy that the greater inclination needed for their own design would not interfere with the lubrication of the K184's gearbox. Early in 1959, therefore, the Mekydro transmission was discarded in favour of the competing Voith design, a move which not only overcame the possible technical difficulties but also helped balance the large Type 3 order for K184s, thus conforming with the BTC's policy of spreading work as evenly as possible amongst British suppliers.

In fact, organisational changes at Voith would cause development of the L308qrV to be halted before work on the first D1000 commenced, leading to the substitution of the same firm's L630rV model. Also of new design, and yet to enter production at Heidenheim, the L630rV followed the familiar triple-converter principles of previous Voith units but, compared to its predecessors, featured numerous improvements and was inevitably larger and more sophisticated. Apart from an increased input capacity, the L630rV offered a 'Crawl Speed Control' for more accurate low-speed control under light load conditions and, conversely, the option of a hydrodynamic brake as an integral part of the transmission assembly, of which only the former found favour with the BTC for the D1000 order. Changeover points between converters were nominally set at 37mph and 55mph though, as before, the exact moment of transition varied according to load. However, the L630rV's final input capacity was not only lower than that expected for the still-born L308qrV, but also less than that of the Mekydro K184, necessitating the derating of the chosen engine type. It was also both heavier and bulkier than the K184. Lastly, being an altogether new model, North British as Voith's UK licensee would have to devote much in the way of time and

Top: Also like the D800s, the 'Westerns' used twin 12-cylinder Maybach engines, though this time of the uprated MD655 variety. Basically similar to the MD650 unit from which it was evolved, the MD655 incorporated intercooling and various other improvements already made in the MD870. Its exclusive use in the D1000 order would serve to make it British Railways' most numerous high-speed diesel engine. *(MTU)*

Bottom: For the D1000 type, the Voith L630rV transmission was chosen so as to spread work amongst suppliers, but this was to create problems when late delivery of the initial batch from Germany delayed completion of locomotives both at Swindon and at Crewe. Although similar in principle to the earlier L306 units, the new transmission was altogether larger and more sophisticated. *(Voith)*

resources to tooling-up if the L630rV was to comply with the BTC's requirement that as much equipment as possible be built in Britain.

The main transmission output shaft was located opposite the input at floor level, but above this and driven from it via a gearbox was a second, auxiliary shaft connected to a Brush dynastarter, with a third shaft from the same point driving the Behr-Serck hydrostatic pump for the cooling fans. Both were situated in the space between the radiator unit and the

Top: The L630rV as located in the 'Western', in the space below the cooling group sometimes branded the 'crematorium' by fitting staff. The engine in its subframe can be seen at the top, with the transmission block in the centre and the Laycock-Knorr air compressor to the left. The output shaft on the left drives the hydrostatic pump for the radiator fans and shutters, whilst that on the right connects transmission and dynastarter. *(Voith)*

Bottom: The 3-axle Krauss-Maffei bogie used under the D1000s was a notably elaborate design by any standards, adding a complex driveline to the already-sophisticated suspension layout of the D800 unit. Readily visible is the high-level distributor gearbox taking the output from the transmission to the axledrive units. *(Author's Collection)*

Right: The appearance of D1000 *Western Enterprise* in its original Desert Sand livery was little short of dramatic by the standards of the day. On 1 February 1962, Inspector J. Beard and Driver F. Cook compare notes on the new machine at Laira depot. *(Colin J. Marsden Collection)*

side doorway, along with a Stones 'Vapor Watchman' oil-fired preheater, the same layout being duplicated at both ends of the locomotive. Although intended to ensure that the engines were never started at undesirably low temperatures when oil might be too viscous to lubricate vital components, preheating of a D1000 from cold taking up to an hour under normal conditions, the units could also be used to prevent frost damage whilst laying-over, the closed radiator shutters acting to forestall heat loss. Given the high power of the locomotive, the customary Behr-Serck cooling units were larger than any used before on a WR diesel-hydraulic, and their situation above the transmission blocks

thus was vital in order to conserve space. Each had a pair of thermostatically-controlled 42$\frac{1}{2}$"-diameter roof fans, driven by individual swash motors fed from the common pump. As in previous locomotives, engine coolant was pumped not only through the main radiators but also heat exchangers carrying lubricating and transmission oils. One innovation was the provision of cross-walkways over the roof fan apertures which also acted as stiffeners, an idea that was later applied to various other BR locomotive types.

Power control was by a Brush system similar to that used in the 'Hymeks', with a pneumatic link between the driver's controller and the governor on the engine itself. This arrangement provided infinitely variable engine speed within preset limits as well as preventing the engine from exceeding a given speed from starting, but in the case of the D1000s failed to reconcile the differing characteristics of engine and transmission, a problem that was not encountered in its diesel-electric applications nor, indeed, on the 'Hymeks'. The difficulty originated in the Voith units' inability to accept the full output of the engines, often betrayed by a tendency to change-up early, the resulting restriction of engine speed serving to reduce effective power outputs further still. This was to prove quite a serious failing when, from an early stage in service, the WR began to subject its D1000s to loadings far in excess of their design specifications. Multiple-working equipment was not fitted, despite the basic layout similarity to the D7000s, as the BTC did not envisage its employment amongst Type 4 locomotives. Air for the control system as well as the brakes and other ancillaries was provided by a Laycock-Knorr compressor, the locomotive itself having straight air brakes operating independently of the train vacuum brakes, which were in turn serviced by a pair of Westinghouse 4VC110 exhausters.

As in the D800s, lack of internal space within the locomotive body posed problems in the location of certain components, and particularly awkwardly-positioned units included the manual controls for resetting the transmission safety trips (prior to their relocation) and those for adjusting the engine fuel settings. Also inaccessible were some of the engine fuel filters which Maybach recommended should be turned at regular intervals, failure to do so often resulting in clogging of the filter element and consequent fuel starvation. If the driver of a recalcitrant 'Western' was of ample build then his problems were increased ten-fold, so tightly packed was the space between the cabs! More seriously, this did complicate maintenance procedures, increasing downtime and occasionally leading to important items being forgotten or otherwise neglected. Whilst speaking of equipment, it is interesting to note that the D1000 design included no provision for electric train heating despite the contemporary experimentation with D870, an omission which symptomised the BTC's failure to tackle the problem of providing train heating in the longer term.

The generally cramped nature of the design reflected not only physical constraints imposed by the BR loading gauge, but also the BTC Chief Civil Engineer's preoccupation with wheel loadings per unit of tyre tread and their possible contribution to track damage. From the CCE's point of view, the D800 had always been excessively highly-loaded in this respect and so a 10% increase in the wheel diameter of the D1000 was demanded, despite the lower axleload of the new Type 4. This not only increased internal congestion but also contributed to the need for a rearranged equipment layout compared with K-M's ML3000. The resiting of the transmission in the BR D1000s required the entire bogie to be turned through 180° so as to maintain the existing driveline arrangements but, apart from this and the larger diameter wheels, the design was initially unchanged. The major differences compared with the D800 unit concerned the provision of a centre axle, which most obviously required a frame outside the centre wheel to carry the secondary suspension, once again consisting of a large inverted leaf spring bearing

on the bogie itself through compensated pairs of helical springs and swing links. Moreover, the radius arm suspension could only be used on the inner and outer axles due to space restrictions, the centre axleboxes being located in ordinary vertical hornblocks, albeit with rubber pads inserted behind the manganese steel axleguide liners. These were intended to give the centre axle the same ride characteristics as the others which were, after all, suspended from rubber-bushed arms. Adopted without any change at all was the horizontal torque reaction member and vertical damper. At the time that the specification was finalised, no trouble had been experienced directly attributable to the unique K-M

design (the WR's problems with its 'Warships' were then only just beginning) and so the suspension arrangement was much like that initially fitted to the D800s. There were some minor improvements, such as the addition of vibration-damping rubber blocks between body and bogie on each side which formed an adjunct to the secondary suspension, along with the inclusion of small centre-pivoted equalising beams between the primary leaf springs.

Driveline arrangements had to be tailored to suit space criteria and were perhaps less than satisfactory from a maintenance point of view. From the output flange of the main transmission block, a cardan shaft led to a Maybach B76 dis-

tributor gearbox between the outer and centre axles, which also acted as a step-up gearbox. As this handled the entire power input to the bogie, some 1100bhp, the precaution was taken of running a cooling circuit between the gearbox and the transmission heat exchanger. From the distributor box, cardans ran in each direction to C33v spur-and-bevel axledrives on the outer and centre axles, whilst another shaft led from the latter to a third C33v unit on the inner axle. The use of spur-and-bevel units on all axles was necessitated by the disposition of the driveline and, on the inner and outer axles, the unused flanges were removed and the resulting holes in the casings plated-over. Another anomaly was the mixture of Hardy-Spicer and Stone-Maybach cardan shafts, unusual for a WR diesel-hydraulic, which resulted from the combination of Voith transmission and Maybach final-drive equipment. During August 1959 Smeddle and his staff had discussed the possibility of disc braking for the new locomotives but, since experience to date did not include vehicles of the D1000's size and output, the eventual design favoured clasp brakes operated through a simple pushrod linkage by four bogie-mounted air cylinders. Sanding was provided on the outer axles, the sandpipes being fed by flexible hoses from sandboxes in the locomotive body. The sanding action itself was pneumatic and was interlocked with the reversing gear so as to provide sanding from the leading end at all times.

As events were to prove, not even the construction of the locomotives would proceed according to plan. Swindon was inundated by work connected with the construction of the D800s and modifications to the D6300s prior to entering service whilst for its part Crewe, although covered by the licensing agreement granted to the BTC by K-M in 1957, had no experience with the stressed-skin method of construction and thus had to be taught those lessons which Swindon had already learned. The situation was further complicated by problems involving the supply of transmission units. As the L630rV unit was completely new, it was decided that the first sixty units should be supplied from Voith's Heidenheim plant whilst NBL readied itself for production of the remaining 103 units in Glasgow. The German-made transmissions, however, were late in delivery with the result that, even with the use of wooden mock-ups to facilitate the laying of pipe and cable runs, locomotives both at Swindon and at Crewe were left in an incomplete state with work being unable to proceed for quite some time. Of the two plants, Swindon was the most badly affected and when supplies finally began to trickle through, it was given first priority. Acutely aware of the potential restriction which might be placed on D1000 production by any interruption in the flow of transmissions from Voith, the WR had begun to investigate alternative sources of supply as early as February 1961, holding talks with BSE regarding the possible use of SRM transmissions in future D1000 orders. When these failed to reach any positive conclusion, Swindon Drawing Office was instructed to redesign the D1000 structure to accomodate the K184, though this too was cancelled in December. In the event, Springburn-made Voith units

Top: At the request of the BTC, D1001 *Western Pathfinder* was finished in maroon with yellow bufferbeams. A spotless D1001 runs around its train at Plymouth North Road on 11 March 1963, having earlier participated in an official photocall at Laira. A 'Warship' and a D6300 are just visible in the background. *(B.J. Miller Collection)*

Middle: As an interim measure, the next few 'Westerns' from both Swindon and Crewe were turned out in standard green, albeit without the grey bodyside stripe. A pristine D1003 *Western Pioneer* is seen heading west through Old Oak Common on 8 June 1962, with an equally immaculate No.7004 *Eastnor Castle* on an eastbound mixed goods to the rear. *(R.H.G. Simpson)*

Below: Development of an idea. The distinctive cab styling adopted for the D1000 was in fact a refinement of the abortive flat-front scheme evolved by the same design consultants for the 'Warships' some years before. This series of sketches illustrates the progression from the Swindon design for the D800, through the first Design Research Unit scheme, to the 'Western' as approved for production. *(Author's Collection)*

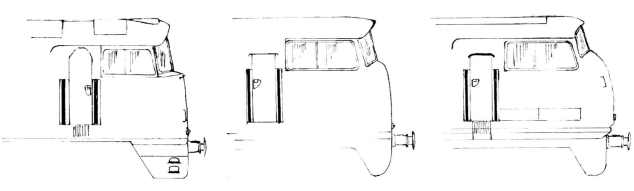

would not begin to be delivered until early 1963, by which time NBL was in chronic financial difficulties. Indeed, the company called in the receivers before the order was completed, and the remainder of the batch was manufactured by a subsidiary operating from within the old North British factory; Voith Engineering (Glasgow) Ltd.

The first locomotive, Swindon-built D1000, took to the rails in December 1961, allocated to Plymouth Laira, and made as great an impact as had D800 before it. Although there was a discernable family resemblance between the DB V200, the D800 and the D1000, the new locomotive was a much larger machine than the D800 and an altogether more impressive-looking beast. The work of Professor Misha Black and J. Beresford-Evans of Design Research Unit, an outside consultancy employed by the BTC to advise on matters of locomotive appearance, the body styling had been based on a much-reworked version of the flat-front scheme proposed for the D800 back in 1956. The three-arc roof and prominent beltline were still there, but the wrapped-round valances of the 'Warship' had given way to a straight-sided skirt whilst the whole bodyside had been given a tumblehome matching the profile of the BR Mark 1 passenger coach. Most striking of all were the cabs, quite sharply truncated without any sort of vestigial nose, but pleasingly profiled with a slight backwards rake that continued downwards in an unbroken line to the bottom of the front skirting, and with a faint but definite vee-shape as seen from above. Split headcode boxes similar to those of the D800s were fitted whilst above the deep cab windscreens the roof terminated in a fashionable peak surmounted by a fibreglass cowl concealing the twin air horns. Despite the extent of the metamorphosis which had taken place between D800 and D1000, much detail work was held in common and the new design succeeded in retaining much of the stance characteristic to the K-M locomotives.

Even the livery was quite unlike anything seen on British Railways before. During the late 1950s, a national programme of increased regional autonomy had been initiated and for its part the WR, disliking the sometimes plain effect of the standard green livery when applied to diesels, cast around for an alternative colour scheme. The first practical result of this was the outshopping of D1000 in an experimental Desert Sand finish with grey roof panels, black cab window surrounds and bogies, and red bufferbeams. One cabsheet on each side carried a light-alloy bas-relief replica of the BR emblem (irreverently referred to as the 'ferret and manglewheel'!) whilst, as if to emphasise the WR's new-found independence, D1000 was named *Western Enterprise* with matching numberplates affixed below the driver's side window on each flank.

From an early stage, it had been decided that the D1000s' front-rank status would entitle the class to be named, but even this would prove to be an eventual source of controversy. The BTC's Locomotive Naming Committee had, after due consideration of several possibilities, recommended that the new locomotives should be named after notable beauty spots lying within WR territory, in a logical progression from traditional Great Western policy. The WR Board, however, wanted to ensure that the parentage of the D1000s should be as well-advertised as possible and at the behest of Keith Grand, Reginald Hanks and Christian Barman in particular it was decided to discount the BTC's suggestion in favour of a series of titles of heroic or stately aspect, all prefixed by the word 'Western'. Even then, there was argument over the style of application, one suggestion being that the name and number should be painted-on in the fashion of some pre-grouping Scottish locomotives. This was soon discounted for reasons of aesthetics and cost of application, traditional metal plates providing a more practical and stylistically-attractive alternative. Prior to painting, some experiments were made with then-fashionable plaque-style plates featuring raised letters but lacking any surround,

though by the time that the locomotive entered service these had been rejected in favour of a more traditional design with a rim. Unlike those fitted to the 'Warships', the new plates were fabricated with light-alloy beading and lettering (to a non-standard 'Grotesque' style) affixed to a steel backplate, marking a partial reversion to traditional Swindon practice. Even back in 1961, British Railways must have realised that these plates would make both attractive mementos and targets for the unscrupulous, for workshop staff were instructed to rivet rather than screw them to the locomotives' bodysides, the heads of those rivets being located in countersunk holes which were then filled flush with the backplate so as to leave no trace of their location!

Not everyone was convinced either by the appearance or the long-term durability of the Desert Sand livery and, for comparative purposes, it was decided that the next few D1000s should be finished in other schemes. At the request of the BTC, which was interested in the possibilities of a unified livery for both locomotives and coaching stock, D1001 *Western Pathfinder* was outshopped in standard maroon with grey roof panels, yellow bufferbeams and a standard coaching-stock cypher in place of the aluminium emblem. Whilst a decision was awaited, D1002-4 were finished in standard green with yellow warning panels, cyphers and red backgrounds to the name- and numberplates, though not the grey bodyside relief, but D1005-8 reverted to the maroon livery of D1001 complete with yellow bufferbeams. The first four Crewe-built locomotives were also finished in green whilst one further livery experiment was undertaken with D1015 *Western Champion* in January 1963. At the suggestion of George Williams and Brian Haresnape of the BTC Design Office, the locomotive was painted in Golden Ochre (to be precise, Stroudley's 'Improved Engine Green' for the London, Brighton & South Coast Railway) with a dark (Cambrian Railways) Bronze Green roof, white window surrounds and black bogies. At the 'B' end a standard yellow warning panel was applied whilst at the 'A' end, one in the shape of a horizontally-elongated 'T' was painted-on but amended to the standard pattern before entry to service. Although an attractive shade in its own right, the Golden Ochre paint looked rather insipid without the LBSCR's elaborate lining-out and was not used on any further 'Westerns' (it had already been applied to a single Brush Type 2 on the Eastern Region where it also failed to find favour). Ultimately, the maroon livery would be chosen, albeit revised with black bufferbeams and standard yellow warning panels.

D1000-8 were first allocated to Plymouth Laira, as were D1035-9 from Crewe, where they joined the 'Warships' in working the heavy West of England trains. In fact, whereas the D800s were working on a simple out-and-back system, the 'Westerns' appeared as part of a complex two-day diagram that took them first to Paddington and then north to Wolverhampton. After servicing at Oxley or Tyseley, they would be deployed on a couple of local passenger turns around Birmingham or possibly a trip to Swindon and back on an overnight parcels working before heading back to London and thence on to Plymouth for maintenance. Before too long, this would be expanded to a three-day diagram similar to the two-day roster except that the locomotive would fit in an additional Paddington-Chester round trip before returning to Plymouth. The type also began to make regular appearances on workings such as the 'Bristol Pullman', the 'Cambrian Coast Express', the 'Devonian' and for a while the 'Pines Express', now diverted off the Somerset & Dorset line and re-routed via Oxford and Reading. Accordingly, enginemen at every major WR depot between Plymouth, London and Chester had to be trained in the handling of the 'Westerns' lest they should need to take charge of one, and would soon be joined by their colleagues in South Wales as the class began to penetrate that area, D1009-11 and D1040-43 having been allocated to Old Oak Common (81A) to work the London-South Wales services.

This caused difficulties at first, as there were simply not enough 'Westerns' in service to go round, let alone be allocated to depots for crew training. Therefore, a certain amount of training had to be done whilst working service trains, a most unsatisfactory process which resulted both in poor driver familiarity and in locomotive failures that could have been avoided. At the time of the 'Westerns' introduction, some enginemen had yet to be persuaded that the transition to diesel traction then taking place was any good thing, and in such an atmosphere of suspicion it was inevitable that minor technical failures were sometimes exaggerated through ignorance or mistrust. A small number of the most senior top-link drivers would never take to the D1000 design and understandably sought to have steam traction allocated to as many of their duties as possible. Fortunately, the next generation of enginemen would recognise the potential as well as the failings of the 'Western', and aim to exploit this to maximum effect. Initial allocations spanned the entire WR with Laira getting fourteen of the type, Bristol Bath Road three, Newton Abbot one, Cardiff Canton twenty-five and Old Oak Common twenty-six by the end of 1963. As deliveries progressed, Crewe Works

showed itself not only to be cheaper in its construction of the type, but also to be building them consistently more rapidly than Swindon and so, in January 1963, D1030-34 of the Swindon order were transferred to Crewe, being completed only a few months after Swindon's final 'Western'. Hence a somewhat confusing situation arose where D1073 was numerically the last of the sequence whilst D1034 was the final example built, but D1029 was actually the last to enter traffic! Completed at Swindon early in 1964, *Western Legionnaire* had been retained by the works' Research and Testing Section and so did not enter revenue-earning service until the July of that year.

The reason behind D1029's retention in this manner lay in the preparation by the new British Railways Board of an official comparison between the two principal varieties of mainline diesel traction. This, the *Report on Diesel-Electric and Diesel-Hydraulic Locomotives on British Railways*, sought to establish the merits and drawbacks of both types of locomotive, contrasting the D7000 'Hymek' against the English Electric D6700 in the Type 3 category, and the D1000 'Western' against the Brush D1500 in the Type 4 range. The WR was well-equipped to implement a study of this kind, having the benefit not only of Swindon's immensely experienced testing section but also of a modern dynamometer car (DW150192) fully equipped with the testing of diesel traction in mind. In the event, however, the programme of controlled road testing on both species of locomotive was restricted to the Type 4 category only and even then not in parallel, D1500 being evaluated some twelve months before D1029. Trials of the latter were marred by the transmissions limiting both engine speed and power over much of the track speed range, with effective power output under maximum load conditions seldom exceeding 2000bhp. Even so, the 'Western' still appeared as significantly more sure-footed than the Brush Type 4, being able to operate under full throttle at low track speeds for prolonged periods without any sign of mechanical distress. Though transmission efficiency fell as a result, the ensuing surplus heat was effortlessly dispersed by the cooling system, allowing a continuous tractive effort in excess of 45,000lbs at 13mph. By contrast, the D1500 could deliver a

Above: The first 'Westerns' to be painted in blue received an experimental Chromatic Blue, sometimes with a matt finish, and retained small yellow warning panels. Though not adopted as standard, this livery still persisted on D1057 *Western Chieftain* on 11 June 1969, when the locomotive was seen passing through Gloucester Central with a train of steel strip from Normanby Park (Scunthorpe) bound for Cardiff. *(Norman E. Preedy)*

Top Left: D1015 *Western Champion* was selected to carry one last experimental livery, in the form of a Golden Ochre finish. Although dirty and lacking its original Bronze Green roof hatches, D1015 is still in largely-original condition on 10 June 1964 as it heads an eastbound freight through Didcot. *(R.H.G Simpson)*

Bottom Left: The 'Westerns' were initially deployed working express trains over the old Great Western route between London and the West Midlands. In the snows of January 1962, an almost-new D1000 at the head of an up Wolverhampton service passes permanent way workers at Hatton Junction. The tracks bearing away to the left lead to Stratford-upon-Avon, Honeybourne and Cheltenham, another once-thriving route now largely gone. *(Norman E. Preedy)*

Below: D1000 was eventually repainted into maroon but retained the light-alloy bas-relief emblems on the cabsides, otherwise fitted only to the LMR 25kV electrics, and is seen in this condition on 25 January 1965 at the head of a westbound parcels train passing Old Oak Common. The emblems were finally removed upon the locomotive's repainting into blue two years later. *(R.H.G Simpson)*

Above: From early 1967, 'Westerns' began to receive the new standard livery of Rail Blue with full yellow ends. The new colours certainly sat better on the 'Westerns' than many of BR's other diesels and are demonstrated to good effect by D1033 *Western Trooper*, seen rumbling across a turbulent River Wye at Chepstow on a sunny 13 May 1976, at the head of the 15.25 Cardiff-Paddington service via Gloucester. *(Graham Scott-Lowe)*

Top Left: After a nine-year absence, regular 'Western' haulage returned to Paddington-Birmingham services from the summer of 1973, albeit on stopping trains via Oxford rather than top-link workings on the direct line through Princes Risborough. On 4 September 1974, No.1037 *Western Empress* passes through pleasant surroundings between Warwick and Leamington Spa with the 12.25 from Birmingham New Street to Paddington. *(Brian Morrison)*

Bottom Left: Despite the advent of the blue livery, maroon 'Westerns' continued to be seen well into the late 'sixties. On a glorious 8 August 1968 a maroon D1038 *Western Sovereign* runs through St Austell with a parcels train bound for the London Midland Region whilst another unidentified 'Western', also in maroon but with full yellow ends, waits in the loop with a Motorail train for Kensington Olympia. *(Roger Siviter)*

continuous tractive effort no better than 30,000lbs at 27mph, although a 10-minute rating of 41,500lbs at 17mph was considered permissible for particularly arduous duties. Thus was laid bare the diesel-electric's most serious shortcoming, namely that the application of full power at low speed under heavy loading carried with it the risk of severe damage to the electrical machinery, and for years the combination of low speeds and high loadings over the South Devon banks would cause diesel-electrics innumerable problems stemming from overheated traction motors.

In nearly every other way, however, it was the diesel-electric that was credited victor, with greater transmission efficiency, better fuel economy and superior availability, all at a lower initial cost. Advocates of the WR policy claimed that the report's allegations of hydraulic transmission failure rates four times greater than those for electric transmissions were more than compensated for by the relative ease and speed of repair, given the physically lighter components. Set against this was the undeniable fact that failure of a hydraulic transmission nearly always meant that the unit would have to be removed from the locomotive for rectification and should an overhauled replacement not be available, then that locomotive would have to stay out of traffic until the offending component had been repaired. Favouritism aside, it was clearly apparent that the 'Western' had demonstrated considerable potential but, more importantly, the Brush Type 4 had succeeded in returning better results in service to date. It was these statistics rather than indications of what might be obtained at some future time that would be presented as justification for the course taken by BRB policies in the years to come.

Even so, the results of these tests surveyed both types in an academic and rather idealistic light, and tended to ignore the fact that life out on the road was very much harder. In late 1963, the WR had been forced to curtail the two- and three-day cyclic diagrams on which the D1000s were employed after concluding that they were incompatible with the locomotives' maintenance requirements, and the very length of time spent investigating troubles of one kind or another served to prompt queries as to the validity of the design, even within the WR itself. Prior to the first D1000s entering service, serious doubts had been cast upon the suitability of the K-M bogie for high-speed running, yet with the time needed to identify the exact cause of the D800s' riding problems and to get approval for a partial redesign of the bogie pivoting gear, corrective modifications could not be made during the course of construction other than to the final five locomotives, D1030-34. As a result, throughout

tive lack of success experienced with the rubber damping blocks between body and bogies, and in due course these were replaced by steel spacers.

Cardan shafts seemed to be a particular weakness with the design, a problem which first became apparent when the seizure of D1000's transmission output bearings precipitated the derailment of a Penzance parcels train only weeks after the locomotive's entry to traffic. Within a short time a fifth of the total fleet was so affected and, applying his considerable and varied talents to the problem, the peerless S.O. 'Sammy' Ell of Swindon Works' Experimental Section eventually deduced that the difficulty lay with the torque reaction arms. Though primarily intended to maintain adhesion under power, they were also meant to cushion angular acceleration of the cardans produced by vertical translation of the wheels, being suspended from the bogie frame by rubber dampers for this purpose. Ell's investigations demonstrated that, far from achieving this, the existing design of torque reaction arm was in fact transmitting the reflex back along the driveline, especially under high loadings at low speed. The resulting forces were being absorbed entirely by the transmission output bearings which, being overloaded in consequence, were very rapidly collapsing and seizing. As in the case of the pivoting gear, the solution was simple but emerged only after a long and expensive investigation, the answer lying in a change to vertical torque reaction members. The original set-up continued to behave satisfactorily on both the D800s and numerous locomotives using the K-M bogie elsewhere, and why only the D1000s should be so afflicted remains a mystery. Further transmission damage resulted from excessive vibration of the cardan shaft to the dynastarter during start-up and shut-down. Use of a softer, rubber-bonded universal joint provided a relatively cheap solution to the problem but, nevertheless, one which took three years to be fully implemented.

There was also a host of engine defects, the BSE-manufactured MD655s suffering from a plague of crankcase cracks and big-end bearing failures. The turbocharger problems already encountered on the MD870s were exacerbated in the 'Westerns' by a complex exhaust layout which gave rise to frequent cases of misalignment after repair. The resulting leakage impaired turbocharger performance and sometimes led to burning of valves and pistons within the engines themselves. Another problem concerned generally high levels of piston ring wear which in turn contributed to crankcase pressurisation and excessive oil consumption, and in the late nineteen-sixties these reached epidemic levels with a consequent increase in reported instances of low oil pressure, excess big-end bearing wear and damaged cylinder liners. An already difficult situation was exacerbated by a re-organisation of activities at Swindon Works, which had resulted in a drop in the output of overhauled engines, and for some while there was actually a shortage of serviceable units. A technical solution was apparently available in the form of special piston rings but, despite the magnitude of the problem, was never tried.

Neither were cooling arrangements immediately successful, despite using familiar equipment. At the design stage it had not been appreciated just how much heat the cooling system of a D1000 could contain and, when shut down after working hard in warm weather, the automatic closing of the radiator shutters could cause a 'Western' to overheat, a thermostatic delay eventually having to be incorporated. Conversely, when standing in cold weather, the automatic operation of the preheaters could not always be relied upon and, despite the closed shutters, coolant temperatures would drop to a point where the engines' own safety mechanisms would initiate a complete shut-down. Standards of thermostat accuracy were little short of abysmal and resulted in a crop of cracked and distorted cylinder heads, a situation which was little helped by severe leakage from water pumps and radiator header tanks, the latter due to the adoption of

Top: On a sunny day during August of 1964, a maroon-painted D1063 *Western Monitor* is seen heading a London-bound train through Kemble, junction for the Cirencester and Tetbury branches. At this time, 'Westerns' were a common sight on trains between London and Cheltenham via Swindon and the Golden Valley route. *(R.H.G Simpson)*

Bottom: Not all 'Western'-powered freight traffic took the form of heavy block workings. On 16 December 1974, No.1012 *Western Firebrand* passes through Brondesbury, on the North London line, with a westbound parcels train. In their closing years, the 'Westerns' became a common sight on cross-London transfers of this sort. *(Kevin Lane)*

1963 priority had to be given to modifying 'Western' bogies with the new swing-link arrangement and, as with the D800s so afflicted, an 80mph speed limit was imposed on the unmodified locomotives. Even after this work was completed, some D1000s continued to display rough-riding characteristics at around the 60mph mark, and particular attention had to be paid to the bogie springing to limit, if not overcome this. Another disappointment was the rela-

inappropriate sealing procedures after repair work. Another source of trouble was the hydrostatic circuit itself, with severe leakage of oil from the pumps caused by excess vibration of the driveshafts, which in turn manifested itself in difficulties with the fan units and radiator shutter mechanisms. Other recurring problems concerned burst or porous hoses and a tendency on the part of the various pipework connections to come loose in service.

As if this was not sufficient, the use of sodium chromate as an engine coolant corrosion inhibitor resulted in certain components being subjected to excessive chemical attack, notably engine piston liners and their rubber sealing rings. This particular problem was shared by virtually every other BR diesel locomotive at one time, regardless of design or manufacture, and was eventually overcome by the use of a completely different inhibitor. Even then, some component specifications had to be revised in order to achieve a reasonable service life. Train-heating boilers were another constant source of worry with all diesel types but especially so with the 'Westerns', often resulting in otherwise serviceable locomotives being sidelined during the winter months. The problem was not helped by inaccurate mounting points which limited interchangeability at depots, or by the catalogue of failings associated with the boilers' electrical control systems. In this regard, the omission of internal bulkheads within the D1000 design was of debatable value, marginally easing access to some components but at the cost of making it vitually impossible to protect the more delicate items against contamination by engine oil and dirt. For some years it was not unusual to see 'Western'-hauled expresses arriving at their destinations double-headed by a 'Hall', 'Grange', or even 'Castle' 4-6-0 pressed into service *en-route* to provide steam heat. In the winter of 1963, with the situation at its worst, all these factors conspired to bring D1000 availability levels below 55%, the lowest for any BR Type 4 with the exception of the Derby/Sulzer 1Co-Co1.

Whilst having few effects upon availability, the bodyshells of the D1000s gave occasional problems, the main of which was caused by the positioning of the main tubular members above bufferbeam level. As a degree of end-load was accordingly transmitted to the upper body, a split in the outer skin would sometimes develop between the cab window recess and the doorway. This in itself was simple enough to weld up but if the job was not done promptly and properly, the whole front end would begin to sag, necessitating costly repairs. More obvious was the frequently shabby state of the locomotives, usually due to peeling of the Prestolith coating between metal and paint which, as time wore on, showed itself to be increasingly prone to damage, resulting in large expanses of bare metal being revealed. Furthermore, the fact that it remained flexible did not make the task of painting any easier as the paint tended to flake, especially after carriage cleaning procedures involving hand-washing with a bucket and brush were replaced by mechanical washing plants where the locomotive hauled its complete rake of coaches through, getting washed itself in the process. The cleaning agent used in these plants was Exmover, a proprietary preparation containing oxalic acid which, whilst being very effective at dissolving baked-on brake dust, when combined with the harsh action of the revolving brushes did little to prolong the life of the locomotives' paintwork. Despite their negative effects on the image of the railway at large, these faults were basically of a cosmetic nature only, and in general the Krauss-Maffei style of construction gave a good account of itself on both the D800 and D1000 classes. One major objection to its use had been its perceived susceptibility to accident damage but whilst several locomotives were involved in serious collisions, Swindon Works never failed to provide a cost-effective repair, and it was not until very late in the diesel-hydraulic era that any locomotives were withdrawn as a direct result of accident damage.

Top: One facet of 'Western' workings often ignored is their early employment on slow, heavy goods workings, a task for which they were better suited than the other diesel-hydraulics due to their greater weight and braking force. D1043 *Western Duke* trundles through Margam on a murky day in June 1971 with a train of unfitted coal empties. *([The Other] Peter J. Robinson)*

Bottom: During the 1970s, construction materials would become an increasingly important source of freight traffic for British Rail as a whole, and the WR in particular. On 27 July 1973, D1063 *Western Monitor* discharges its train of HTV hoppers at Wolverton, on the West Coast Main Line. The train had come from Amey Roadstone's quarry at Tytherington, to give access to which a portion of the former Midland Railway Yate-Thornbury branch had been reopened. *(B.J. Nicolle)*

In many ways, the poor first impression made by the 'Westerns' counted against them for years afterwards. Certainly, when the ex-GWR mainline north of Birmingham became the responsibility of the London Midland Region in 1963, the D1000s were quickly dismissed in favour of D1500 diesel-electrics, though this was at least partly due to the LMR's dislike of diesel-hydraulics on its territory. Some of these were reallocated to Swansea Landore where they facilitated a highly successful programme of accelerated services between London and South Wales, whilst others were transferred to West of England workings instead, where they proved instrumental in implementing the adoption of a schedule under four hours for the Plymouth-Paddington 'Golden Hind' in 1964. At the head of a seven-coach test train on 8 April, D1027 *Western Lancer* had posted the fastest time - under 3´ hours - yet achieved between London and Plymouth, but when the actual service was introduced in the June of that year the loading was restricted to 250 tons.

Above: Despite the transfer of the large South Wales allocation of Class 52s to Laira in 1971, the type remained a common sight west of the Severn Tunnel for several years more. On 25 March 1976, a somewhat grubby No.1058 *Western Nobleman* stands at Bridgend with the 15.00 Paddington-Swansea. By this time, the practise of displaying headcodes had been officially abandoned, and so the indicator panel has been arranged to show the locomotive number. *(Tom Heavyside)*

Top Left: On 30 July 1975, No.1013 *Western Ranger* leaves St Erth yard with a train of milk tanks bound for Acton. The West Country milk traffic was always a popular source of employment for the 'Westerns', and especially so in the last years as they were gradually displaced from passenger duties. *(Brian Morrison)*

Bottom Left: Another important duty for the 'Westerns' was the handling of china clay trains between Cornwall and the Potteries. On 4 October 1976, No.1065 *Western Consort* waits for a fresh crew at Bristol Temple Meads with one such train, the 6V53 Stoke to St Blazey 'Clayliner'. *(B.J. Nicolle)*

320 tons had originally been proposed, but the 'Westerns' were not judged to be sufficiently reliable to be entrusted with express trains this heavy, despite already having been cleared for loads up to 525 tons unassisted over the South Devon banks. Although most of the major modification programmes had already been completed, the availability of the 'Westerns' at that time still failed to meet expectations, and this exerted a corresponding effect upon the sort of duties for which they were rostered. After a brief interlude on the WR's fastest trains between 1962 and 1964, during which they often proved unequal to the demands of top link duties on an everyday basis, the D1000s were redeployed and for much of the later 1960s were returning up to a quarter of their mileage on heavy freight turns.

Admittedly, this was not completely alien territory for the 'Westerns' as, despite their being primarily intended as express passenger locomotives, the design had from an early stage been tailored to suit the requirements of heavy freight movements. As with the D800s however, the D1000s' low weight and braking force were a considerable handicap on unbraked or partially-braked freight consists and resulted in their use on the most demanding duties being relatively restricted. Despite this, they put in some sterling work both on the Somerset quarry trains and on the Scunthorpe-Cardiff steel transfers where, in each case, the locomotives' high power and good torque characteristics were complemented by the continuously-braked rolling stock used, though the high-speed Freightliner workings were air-braked from the outset and continued to remain the province of suitably-equipped D1500s. In contrast to this small number of scheduled services, most 'Westerns' were still being allocated to freight workings by default, principally due to the reluctance of operating staff to diagram for top link passenger duties locomotives widely regarded as unreliable. The result was the frequent employment of D1000s on relatively humble tasks such as vans trains and slow but heavy unfitted mineral workings, though as availability levels began to improve, so did the utilisation of the class on the WR's fastest and most prestigious services, notably in replacing the makeshift pairs of English Electric Type 3s and, subsequently, the ever-less reliable D800 combinations on West of England trains. By 1970, the situation of a few years before had been reversed completely, and it was the 'Westerns' that were assuming responsibility for the bulk of the WR's most important services, whilst the 'Warships' and many D1500s were relegated to more mundane chores.

With the exception of D1004/36/7 which retained their green livery into the late 1960s, all 'Westerns' were eventually repainted into maroon, D1000 *Western Enterprise* retaining its alloy bas-reliefs until maroon gave way to blue in 1967. The first recipient of the blue livery had been D1030 *Western Musketeer* in late 1966, which had carried an experimental scheme of Chromatic Blue with small yellow warning panels and red bufferbeams. It had been joined in this garb by D1017/36/7/43/7/57 (albeit with black bufferbeams) but by March 1967 the decision was taken to discontinue the experiment in favour of the standard Rail Blue with full yellow ends. All members of the class eventually received this livery although some of the last locomotives to carry maroon inevitably received the full yellow ends on top of their existing livery, something which became blatantly obvious when, after only a short time, the yellow paint began to peel! Otherwise, the 'Westerns' physical appearance changed little. In response to service accelerations and rising line speeds, two improved types of windscreen wiper were tried on D1000-class locomotives during the mid-1960s. Following similar trials in the United States, circular action marine-type wipers were fitted to D1006 and D1039 and proved effective in keeping the glass clean but, due to their size and complexity, were judged unsuitable for series use. Four other 'Westerns' were fitted with side-action wipers of experimental design but these too proved unsuccessful, and all six locomotives eventually reverted to standard. Another problem concerned the high temperatures which tended to be produced in the locomotive cabs whilst at work, compounded by the fact that the sliding side windows had to be kept closed at speed if intolerable draughts were to be avoided. In an attempt to improve matters, soon after construction D1004, D1045 and D1052 were fitted with twin ventilators cut into the roof canopy above the windscreens. Subsequently, D1012/28/39/56/71 were modified with a smaller single ventilator fitted on the cab front below the driver's windscreen at each end.

The last major modification to the type came in 1968 when a requirement to work the new Mark 2 coaching stock then entering traffic led to all except D1017-20 being fitted with dual brakes. This was no mean feat considering the cramped interior of the locomotives and necessitated the removal of one of the 272-gallon fuel tanks, its place being taken by a motor-driven Westinghouse compressor. Air reservoirs were placed in the engine room gangway along-side the power units, making it well-nigh impossible to negotiate, others being suspended from the roof or attached to the engines themselves. In the cabs of each converted locomotive, the driver's vacuum brake handle was replaced by a Westinghouse automatic air brake valve which operated directly on air-braked trains, or through a proportional valve when vacuum-braked stock was being hauled. Selection of train air- or vacuum-braking was achieved via a control located within the engine room. The existing Laycock-Knorr locomotive straight air brakes were retained unaltered. At the same time, standard BR AWS (Automatic Warning System) train-control equipment was installed to supplement the WR ATC gear already fitted, AWS rapidly replacing ATC on many parts of the Western Region.

These modifications not only increased the 'Western's working weight from 108 tons to 109 tons but, due to the complexity of the task, also took some considerable time to implement. Ultimately, the rebuild schedule would be over-run by BR's haste to dispense with diesel-hydraulic traction, the first 'Western' withdrawals actually taking place before the final dual-braking conversion (D1023) was completed. Although many of the rebuilt locomotives had very short short working lives in their final form, the programme was unquestionably money well spent, allowing the type to handle not only the new passenger stock but also the burgeoning number of air-braked freight movements at a time when the railway was suffering from a dearth of dual-braked motive power. Under the TOPS system the type became Class 52 but with their short expected lifespan in mind, BR elected not to re-identify the locomotives with the new computerised five-digit numbers. Like the WR's other diesel-hydraulics, the 'Westerns' would retain their original numbers to the very end, although in most cases the redundant 'D'-prefix on the numberplates was painted-over in the background colour.

Below: In February 1963, Maybach sent a proposal to the British Railways Board detailing a 4000bhp diesel-hydraulic based upon the D1000 design but using the same engine and transmission assemblies specified for the 'Hymeks'. The then-current attitude of the BRB towards diesel-hydraulics meant that the proposal was not even acknowledged, let alone acted upon, though it is difficult to see quite what use the WR might have found for a unit of such high power at that time. *(MTU)*

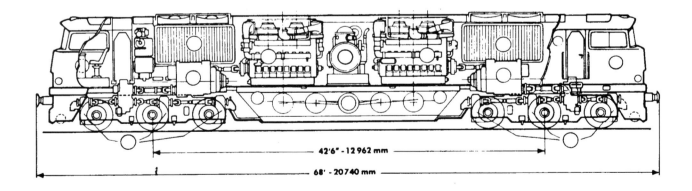

42'6" - 12962 mm

68' - 20740 mm

Chapter 10
THE D9500S

IF the story of the D1000 'Westerns' was one of potential that would not be recognised until too late, then that of the D9500 0-6-0DHs must be of potential that had no opportunity to be recognised. Their arrival on the Western Region came so late that their intended areas of employment had already declined almost totally, and it must remain a matter for conjecture as to whether their very existence was ever justified. As with many of the other WR diesel-hydraulic classes, their genesis owed as much to political factors as to operational ones, and in this case the inability of the WR's strategists to see into the future was to bring down disaster on their heads.

At the time of the WR's first negotiations with Maybach regarding the British production of lightweight diesel-hydraulics, medium-duty locomotives and inter-city multiple-units had featured as strongly as the high-powered V200s. Subsequently, however, largely due to the nature of the WR's immediate requirements, the British manufacture of a V200 variant became paramount in the negotiations and the other matters had faded into the background. Whether the WR's management team actually intended to proceed with the replacement of Class 2 and 3 steam power at that time is no longer clear, the 1955 WR dieselisation policy being largely concerned with the matter of mainline traction. In terms of the lower power classifications there existed a broad concord with the BTC's own plans which foresaw the introduction of diesel railcars and two distinct types of standard shunter, the WR anticipating that greater equipment availability, improved working patterns and the rationalisation of yards and branches would all reduce the need for small locomotives. It was one of the few areas where Paddington and Marylebone Road did initially agree.

As the pace of dieselisation began to accelerate, and the lack of any firm BTC policy on the matter of low-power diesel locomotives proceeded to make itself felt, proposals began to circulate at Swindon for a small diesel-hydraulic suitable for branchline, transfer shunting and light mainline duties. These were mostly based on the Deutsche Bundesbahn V80 design, a single-engined B-B of centre-cab configuration, the basic mechanical units of which were shared with the V200. The mass ordering prognosticated by the fateful 1957 paper *Mainline Diesel Locomotives: Limitation of Variety* acted as a spur to progress and, in August of that year the WR CME, R.A. Smeddle authorised the production of a preliminary diagram for an 800bhp Type 1 based on the V80 design, with the stipulation that axle loadings should be kept as low as possible to give the widest route availability. Work on this was some way advanced when the decision was taken to emulate the DB in uprating the design to 1000bhp and incorporating a steam boiler for passenger service. This made the locomotive a direct competitor to the North British Type 2, and by July 1959 the Swindon proposals had been resolved into a single-cab Type 2 'hood' design using Maybach engines and Mekydro or Voith transmissions. With the WR already committed to fifty-eight of the NBL locomotives and an unspecified quantity of Beyer-Peacock Type 3s, it became increasingly obvious that the proliferation of Type 2s in this manner did not represent

the best use of resources, and the project's resulting loss of impetus culminated in its discontinuance.

At the same time as it had approved the Type 3 order, however, the BTC had for some reason decided that the need did exist for a diesel-hydraulic Type 1, albeit of considerably smaller size, for deployment on shunting and trip freight workings. In March 1960, therefore, Smeddle initiated a design study for a three-axle Type 1 diesel-hydraulic of about 600bhp output and, despite R.C. Bond's dislike of the chosen wheel arrangement, by the middle of April Swindon was awaiting only the approval of the Regional General Manager prior to starting design work. The inspiration behind Smeddle's proposal was the DB's V60 0-6-0DH, an example of which he and his assistant A.C.L. Sly inspected thoroughly on a visit to Germany in June. Upon his return, Smeddle laid out two possible courses of action to the WR Board; either a completely new design could be created to the BTC's outline specifications, or the V60 could be adapted to British requirements and built at Swindon. Some parties at Swindon pressed for a fresh bogie design, but Smeddle favoured the latter method, and the Board agreed with him. It was therefore resolved to study more fully the implications of this decision, especially with respect to the choice of mechanical units, and to investigate the possibilities of obtaining a full set of V60 drawings from Krauss-Maffei at Munich.

As constructed for the DB, the V60 was a competent shunter and light transfer machine that was nonetheless largely derived from pre-war practice. Neither the engine, a six-cylinder Maybach GTO, nor the two-speed Voith transmission were considered suitable for the WR's requirements, and at the end of July talks were held between the WR and Bristol-Siddeley regarding the possible supply of Maybach MD435s instead. Essentially an eight-cylinder version of the MD650s used in the D800s, the MD435 was largely compatible with the larger engines for parts interchange and thus would integrate well with the existing maintenance system. To accompany this, BSE suggested use of its own SRM torque-converter transmission, though several other transmission options were already under consideration at Swindon, including a jackshaft drive which Beyer-Peacock had devised around the Mekydro K104. Smeddle decided to make a jackshaft drive a firm part of the Type 1 specification in September 1960, although he was not altogether happy about the resulting need to raise the cab floor in the middle, and had considered the possibilities of a single cab at one end, in the manner of the English Electric D8000. E.S. Cox counselled him against this alternative, warning that the BTC was experiencing considerable misgivings over operational difficulties then being encountered with the single-cab layout. One tangible result of this was the large order for the unproven, and ultimately unsuccessful D8500 'Clayton' Bo-Bo with its pair of horizontally-mounted Paxman engines, a set of plans for which Cox promised to provide for guidance purposes. To complement these, a firm request for V60 drawings was soon conveyed from Swindon to K-M.

The preservation of the low bonnet lines evident in both the V60 and the D8500 had considerable appeal, and in

Above: The last, least distinguished but undoubtedly most controversial of the WR's diesel-hydraulics were the fifty-six Type 1 0-6-0DHs built at Swindon in 1964/5. Outside the Works upon completion in August 1965, D9549 displays the unconventional application of the standard colours which nevertheless enhanced the appearance of the finished locomotives. Note also the coaching-stock cypher and the 'Grotesque' lettering. *(Colin J. Marsden Collection)*

Below: Weight diagram for D9500-55 *(National Railway Museum)*

January 1961 BSE was asked to investigate the possibilities of fitting the MD435 with the small Napier turbocharger instead of the tall vertical-shaft Maybach unit, though the company warned that this particular design had already proved troublesome in use on other BR diesels. At the same time, negotiations had been proceeding between Swindon and North British in Glasgow on the subject of drivelines, NBL suggesting the Voith L217 transmission in conjunction with a separate reversing gearbox. Predictably, NBL also tried to interest the WR in an engine of its own manufacture, proposing a naturally-aspirated MAN unit, whilst the BTC CME, J.F. Harrison suggested that provision should be made for the new Paxman vee-six derived from the units installed in D830. Once terms of reference for the project were agreed with Harrison, the WR sought tenders for the supply of mechanical equipment, inviting quotes for MAN, Maybach and Paxman engines, Voith transmissions and a final drive of NBL's choice. Although not included in the formal tender, Smeddle further specified that the finished

design should be capable of accepting a Mekydro transmission and Gmeinder final drive unit at some future date if so desired. In addition, BSE provided costings for a 640bhp Maybach MD330 supplied in-unit with an SRM transmission, though this proposal was rejected. The final decision was made in September 1961, and recommended the use of Paxman engines in conjunction with a transmission and final drive supplied by NBL.

Though the Swindon Type 1's detail specification was thus all but fixed, the WR had begun to entertain second thoughts. Firstly, it then had on trial the Yorkshire Engine Company's *Taurus*, an 0-8-0 heavy shunter with twin Rolls-Royce diesels and hydraulic transmission, which a greatly-impressed Smeddle instructed his draughtsmen to use as the basis for a future Swindon/Yorkshire Type 1. A few months later, most probably at the BTC's behest, work commenced on outlining a diesel-electric version of the existing three-axle design, whilst consideration was also given to the prospect of a more powerful bogie concept based on a fusion of DB V80 and 'Clayton' practice. In order to create the best possible design from an operational viewpoint, Smeddle proposed that prototypes of 0-6-0DH, 0-6-0DE and B-B configurations should be built and evaluated in actual service, but was dissuaded by his staff who warned that the BTC was unlikely to approve any major departure from the specification already agreed. Smeddle therefore requested authorisation for the quantity production of the 650bhp 0-6-0DH design, this being granted in May 1962 and then cancelled the very next day! Two months later the project was revived and material ordered sufficient for twenty-six locomotives. At the same time, design work

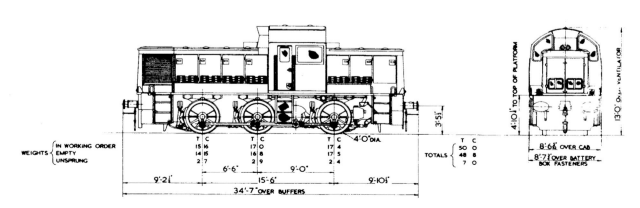

upon the diesel-electric variant was terminated, no ready use being seen for it at that moment in time.

Arguably, much the same could be said about the diesel-hydraulic version, as under the prevailing political climate the only hope for arresting BR's steady economic decline lay in the drastic rationalisation of the railway system. It was inevitable that many goods handling facilities would either be concentrated or discontinued altogether, accompanied by an acceleration of the branchline closures which had been taking place since the mid-1950s. Any move of this kind would exert a devastating effect upon the requirement for small units of motive power, especially upon a railway which still retained large stocks of steam 0-6-0s, and one might reasonably have expected the BRB and the WR to defer construction of the Swindon Type 1s, or even cancel it entirely. Instead of this, the order was expanded to fifty-six units for delivery as soon as possible, and by the time that the publication of the Beeching proposals confirmed the locomotives' superfluity, the process was irreversible. In all probability, the future of Swindon Works at a time when work was getting increasingly scarce weighed more heavily upon the minds of the WR Board than the economic predicament of the BR system in general, and under such circumstances it was quite natural that any proposal entailing the continuance of locomotive construction for a further twelve months or more should have been regarded with favour. Additionally, being diesel-hydraulics, the new Type 1s would doubtless also be maintained there, an important consideration given that nearly all of the WR's growing stud of diesel-electrics were allocated to workshops other than Swindon for heavy repairs. Either way, the results were to prove ignominious.

By the time that work finally got under way Smeddle had retired, but since overall specifications had been agreed with the BRB, detail design of the fifty-six locomotives numbered D9500-55 was allowed to rest in the hands of Innes, the WR's Mechanical Engineer (Design). Although the basic layout remained recognisably that of the K-M V60, the English and German locomotives did not share the same close relationship as existed between the V200 and the D800, the Swindon Type 1's lineage deriving as much from the trusty pannier tank as from any of the larger diesel-hydraulics. Frames were gas-cut from 1'"-thick steel plate in the time-honoured fashion, then rivetted to deep, heavy-section bufferbeams that also acted as a ballast weight. By contrast, internal bracing members were largely of pressed rather than the more traditional forged construction, reflecting the changes made to the Works' capabilities with the cessation of steam locomotive production. The three sets of 4'-diameter spoked wheels were all equipped with Timken roller-bearing axleboxes, suspension being by overhung leaf springs above the axleguides, whilst plain-section coupling rods linked the wheels and the jackshaft assembly.

Superstructure and equipment layout could effectively be divided into three sections, the fore- or 'A'-end bonnet, the cab, and the aft- or 'B'-end bonnet. Unlike any other Type 1 design with the exception of the 'Clayton', the compact power unit and transmission of the D9500 allowed both bonnets to be at a level considerably lower than the cab roof. The resulting large windows gave a good view in both directions, a consideration no less important in shunting operations than on mainline transfer duties. Although nominally central, the cab was in fact placed above the transmission and jackshaft assembly between the second and third axles, and so the 'A'-end bonnet was quite a good bit longer than its 'B'-end counterpart. Mounted immediately at the front end of the locomotive was a Behr-Serck cooling unit, similar to that used in other WR diesel-hydraulics except for its smaller size. Once again, the cooling fan was driven by a high-pressure swash motor fed from a Plessey hydrostatic pump on the free end of the engine. Fan speed was thermostatically controlled by a device lim-

Above: D9500 production viewed from one of the overhead gantry cranes above 'AE' shop, showing to good advantage the arrangement of the different mechanical components within the 0-6-0 chassis. D9501 is nearest the camera, with D9502 directly behind and a third Type 1 on the floor in the foreground, waiting to be wheeled. Other points of interest include engine and transmission units awaiting installation and 'Westerns' D1051 and D1066 undergoing repair. *(Colin J. Marsden Collection)*

iting the oil delivery whilst a further hydraulic circuit determined the position of the opening radiator shutters. Below the cooling unit and between the frames was mounted a 338-gallon fuel tank, along with the associated transfer pump needed to supply the injector pumps, whilst to its rear was a fabricated stand carrying a pair of vacuum exhausters and the heat exchanger for the transmission oil. Last but not least was a lubricating oil priming pump to provide positive lubrication of the engine bearings prior to start-up.

Between this and the cab bulkhead was the Paxman 6YJXL engine, a somewhat puzzling choice given the BTC's decision not to perpetuate the YJXL type in the D800s, though the quality-control problems then emerging in BSE-built Maybach units may have been a contributory factor. The smallest of the YJXL family (eight-, twelve- and sixteen-cylinder units were also available), the 6YJXL was to all intents and purposes a half-sized version of the Paxman engines fitted to D830. The six cylinders shared the same 197mm bore and 216mm stroke with the larger engines but were arranged in a cast iron block of 60° vee-formation. Pistons were of aluminium alloy construction, cooled by oil jets directed from drillings in the fork-and-blade connecting rods. The latter drove a triple-throw forged steel crankshaft of conventional design using shell inserts for both main and big-end bearings, with main bearing caps cross-bolted in the interests of enhanced rigidity. A train of gears from the crankshaft led to the camshaft, housed in a trough between the cylinder banks and actuating the valves via spring-loaded roller-type followers and tubular pushrods. Also operated from the camshaft drive was the engine governor, a centrifugal-weight type with a hydraulic servo mechanism, supplied by Regulateurs Europa.

As with most other vee-six engines, the 6YJXL generated relatively high levels of vibration in the form of both

side-to-side and back-to-front rocking couples. In order to overcome these without the additional complication and expense of the six-plane crank required to produce an even-firing engine, a pair of balancing shafts were incorporated. These shafts, derived from an idea patented by Frederick Lanchester back in 1906, were irregularly weighted and arranged so as to rotate counter to and at a velocity greater than that of the crankshaft. This would succeed in generating forces which would be equal in magnitude yet opposite in timing to the impulses of the reciprocating masses, thus serving to counteract most of the crankshaft's vibrations. The 6YJXL had both a primary balance shaft driven from the free end of the crankshaft, complemented by a Holset viscous damper, and a secondary balancing shaft geared to the flywheel end of the crank. The larger YJXL units were inherently better-balanced than the vee-six, the 8YJXL needing only a secondary shaft, the 16YJXL a second crank-shaft damper and the 12YJXL no compensation at all.

Each cylinder had its own individual cylinder head, cast from aluminium and containing two inlet and two exhaust valves arranged around a central fuel injector. Each pair of valves was surmounted by a bridge piece, allowing a single rocker arm from the pushrod to actuate both valves simultaneously. Removable covers protected the valve gear whilst leaving the injectors unobscured. These were fed by injection pumps located on each side of the engine below the inlet manifolds, shaft-driven from the flywheel end of the crankshaft. A second shaft ran from this point along the longitudinal axis of the engine to drive a water pump for the engine's cooling circuit, which incorporated a tubular heat exchanger for the engine lubricating oil, sited on the left-hand front corner of the engine. It also served a Napier tur-bocharger located astride the vee of the engine adjacent to the exhaust manifolds. Flexible trunking led back from the turbocharger to an exhaust stack mounted on the cab bulk-head, the engine itself being secured to the chassis by four resilient mountings. Overall weight was 6750lbs. Rated at 650bhp at 1500rpm, the 6YJXL was a comparatively simple design and might have been expected to prove trouble-free which regrettably, in the D9500s at least, it did not.

From the engine flywheel a long cardan shaft angled upwards to meet the input flange of the Voith L217u trans-mission block, located above the third axle. Like the other Voith transmissions employed on the WR, the L217u was of

Middle: The first allocations of Swindon Type 1s went to Bristol and Cardiff. A few months after its entry to service, Bath Road's D9502 heads a local pick-up goods past a 'Blue Pullman' beneath the trainshed at Bristol Temple Meads on 14 October 1964. *(G.B. Wise)*

Bottom: The intended role of the D9500s was to replace the pannier tank on shunting and trip freight duties. On 25 January 1965, D9521 exchanges compliments with 0-6-0PT No.4606 engaged on similar transfer work at West London Junction. *(R.H.G Simpson)*

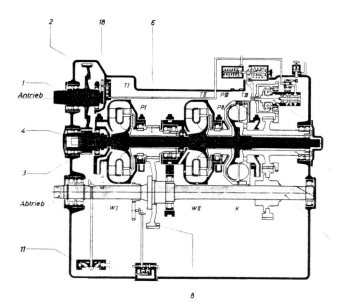

triple-stage design, but differed significantly in that only the two lower stages operated through torque converters. The third and highest stage brought a fluid coupling into play, the characteristic of which was to give a fixed relationship between input and output torques, the absence of any requirement for torque multiplication at high line speeds in the D9500 application allowing the elimination of the third converter. Changeover between the two converters took place at around 15mph, that between the second converter and the fluid coupling at 30mph. Also unlike the larger units, the L217u contained no reversing gears within the main block and, as it was capable of handling the power but not the torque required for a low-speed shunting locomotive, the transmission's output was taken forwards through a cardan shaft to a secondary gearbox mounted low in the frames. This took the form of a triple-reduction reversing final drive gearbox and jackshaft assembly, supplied through Voith but actually manufactured by Hunslet of Leeds.

By comparison with its forward counterpart, the 'B'-end bonnet was relatively empty with much of the available space occupied by the top of the transmission. From the rear end of this a short cardan shaft led to the dynastarter unit, a pedestal above which carried the Westinghouse air compressor and twin brake reservoirs. With no requirement for a train-heating boiler, the only other equipment carried here was a pair of CO_2 fire bottles. Each bonnet was flanked by hinged doors at sides and ends, along with removable roof hatches and twin air horns mounted on the cab bulkhead. In consideration of the transfer duties that the locomotive was intended to perform, the relatively unusual step was taken of providing it with twin headcode indicator panels at each end. This same mainline capability presented special problems in the design of the cab layout, bearing in mind the need to run in either direction with equal ease. This was dealt with by putting each access door at the 'A' end, thus creating a cross passageway, and putting the control cubicle up against the bulkhead. The control panel itself was positioned longitudinally over the transmission, adjoining 'B' bulkhead, with a separate driver's seat and set of controls on each side providing for convenience whilst shunting as well as the good visibility required for mainline running. The cab was rendered commendably quiet, despite the location of the exhaust stack, by the liberal use of glassfibre insulation pads located behind perforated lining panels.

Top: As well as shunting and trip work, the D9500s were intended for use on light freight trains where a D6300 was too large or heavy, or where the use of a larger locomotive simply could not be justified. On 3 June 1966, D9504 hauls a down goods train over the former Midland Railway line west of Bath, by then restricted to freight-only use. *(C.G. Maggs)*

Bottom: Many of the Type 1s were initially allocated to sheds in South Wales, where light freight and transfer traffic had hitherto been plentiful. That this was soon to change is amply demonstrated by the fact that D9518 and crew have time to sit in the sunshine between duties in the Newport area, sometime during 1966. *(Norman E. Preedy)*

Although the physical attributes of the driver's position were necessarily different, the basic control layout was similar to that of the D1000. Brake reservoir pressure, brake cylinder pressure, train vacuum pipe depression, engine speed and speedometer gauges were all mounted on a binnacle facing the driver, in front of which lay a flat desk carrying the brake handles and auxiliary controls. The power and reversing controls, along with that for the horns, were carried on the vertical face of the desk adjacent to the driving seat. All in all, the main drawback of the cab design was the split-level cab floor necessitated by the disposition of the driveline. Driving control was through an electro-pneumatic system similar to that used in the 'Hymek' and 'Western' designs, permitting infinitely-variable engine speed, but was not specified to include any multiple-working apparatus. For a pure shunting locomotive this was of little moment but, given the D9500s' expected use on much heavier mainline transfer movements, would ultimately prove a rather shortsighted omission. Braking followed the usual pattern of locomotive straight air brakes and vacuum train brakes, whilst sanding was on the leading and trailing wheelsets, pneumatically-applied from frame-mounted sandboxes.

Once again, the external appearance of the locomotive was the responsibility of an external advisor, in this case Allen Barnes, Bowden Ltd who achieved an uncompromising yet businesslike result. Of essentially angular character, the outline was nevertheless clean-cut and was set off by the unusual livery scheme chosen. Whilst the bonnets were finished in the customary Brunswick Green with black-and-yellow 'wasp stripes' on the ends, and the underframes in black, the cab unit was finished in Sherwood Green and the bufferbeams in an eye-catching and safety-conscious yellow. With the same objective in view all handrails and footsteps were picked-out in white. The D9500s were the only BR Type 1s to carry the coaching-stock cypher and became equally unique in their use of a painted version of the 'Grotesque' numeral script used on the D1000s. The simi-

larity was not an ironic one; at 31,000lbs tractive effort and 50 tons weight, the D9500s were numbered among BR's heftiest and most powerful shunting locomotives. In fact, the Swindon Type 1 occupied a unique position in the motive power line-up, representing the only intermediate stage between the various 350bhp shunters and the much heavier and more powerful D8000, D8200 and D8500 Bo-Bo designs.

D9500 was released to traffic in July 1964 and allocated to Bristol Bath Road depot for trials, with D9501 going to Cardiff Canton. Evidently the results of each were satisfactory for by the end of the year, Bath Road had gained D9502-5 in addition to D9500 whilst Cardiff was host to D9501/10-6/18-20. Worcester had got D9506-9 in August and September whilst during November and December Old Oak Common received D9521-4, the idea being to replace the powerful but rough-riding outside-cylindered 15xx pannier tanks on empty stock and local freight duties in West London. D9517 was outshopped in November 1964 but loaned to the Research and Testing Section for dynamometer car trials, and so did not take up its intended allocation at Canton until May 1965. In that year, delivery of D9525-8 to Bristol Bath Road was completed in January, D9529-52 to Canton in September and D9553-5 to Bristol in October. D9555 was the last of its type built, the last diesel-hydraulic locomotive purchased by British Railways, and the last locomotive to be built at Swindon for use in the British Isles.

In concept, the D9500s were far superior to their steam counterparts in terms of availability, ease of maintenance and crew comfort during operation, as well as having the power and speed advantages over the 350bhp diesel-electric shunters so necessary for trip workings on busy mainlines. Like most of the other hydraulics, they were initially accorded an enthusiastic reception by footplatemen at least, becoming known for some strange reason as 'Teddy Bears' or sometimes 'Yogi Bears' after a popular television cartoon character. Despite this, even as deliveries were still in progress, railwaymen and seasoned observers alike could divine omens hardly propitious to the long-term future of the type. The Cardiff allocation, intended to replace steam where a 'Hymek' or D6700 was too large but a 350bhp shunter too small or slow, soon found itself a victim of a situation whereby motive power requirements were steadily declining due to changes in the volume and nature of traffic. In normal circumstances, the answer to this would simply have been the transfer of the locomotives to replace steam on another part of the system but, in this instance, the intended employment of the locomotives in marshalling yards, on trip freights and on pilot work was disappearing along with the tank engines it had habitually employed. Branchlines were closing at the rate of several every week and those light, short-haul passenger workings that remained were becoming almost exclusively the province of DMUs.

Added to this the Paxman engine, which in its twelve-cylinder version had proved to be reliable and of comparable performance to its German competitors, became a mechanical nightmare when used in six-cylinder form in the D9500s. Cylinder heads warped and cracked, heat exchanger faults resulted in lubricating oil contamination and bearings failed with monotonous regularity. In addition, there was an outbreak of hose failures similar to those which afflicted the larger WR diesel-hydraulic types at about the same time. Also reminiscent of the other hydraulics was the inordinately high failure rate of auxiliary components, often culminating in more serious troubles. Even on the rare occasions when work was found for the locomotives, they were generally unfit to do it and, given the overall low availability of diesels at this time, it was no surprise that the D9500s should quickly be accorded the lowest priority for any diesel repairs.

With their appalling lack of reliability causing mayhem in the intensive traffic of the West London approaches, Old Oak Common finally washed its hands of the D9500s in October 1965 and, after less than a year in the capital, the complete 81A allocation was dispatched to Bristol Bath Road. Here they spent much of their time trundling unremunerative three- and four-wagon trains along decaying country branchlines or powering permanent way workings for weekend track possessions. A number of locomotives from both Bristol and Canton were subsequently transferred to Swansea Landore, eighteen examples in all being allocated there over a number of years. The idea was to modernise the working of the docks system, where diesel shunters had only recently replaced ancient tank engines of pre-grouping origins, but once again the D9500s arrived too late, Swansea's docks having entered a terminal decline that would see most of them closed within a few years. With the New Year of 1966, the D9500s entered upon the last phase of their life on BR, one marked by mass storage and a spate of transfers. Faced with the indisputable fact that it had fifty-six locomotives of doubtful reliability which it had absolutely no use for, the WR prepared for the wholesale run-down and withdrawal of the type; after all, less troublesome diesel-electrics on other regions were already following in steam's graveyard footsteps. So it was that unwanted or unserviceable D9500s made their way to Worcester Works, where they were quietly decommissioned and put into storage. By the end of the year a round dozen were sombrely awaiting an uncertain fate, although a few of the less derelict examples had been found work back in South Wales.

Top: D9522 climbs out of Sharpness with the 13.20 Sharpness-Berkeley Road goods on 1 June 1967. One of a number originally allocated to Old Oak Common but by then based at Bristol Bath Road, D9522 was spending much of its time on workings similar to this, and a month later would be on the move once again, this time west to Swansea Landore. *(C.G. Maggs)*

Bottom: A forlorn D9535 stands out in the open at Cardiff Canton depot on 7 November 1970, having been in store for close on two years. In this case, appearances are deceptive. Whilst the Class 14 was to find a further thirteen years' use with the National Coal Board, the neighbouring 'Hymek' had less than a year to go before withdrawal and scrapping. *(Hugh Ballantyne)*

At the same time, the WR had been frantically trying to work out some kind of settlement less embarrassing than inviting tenders to scrap. Rumours abounded of an abortive attempt to transfer them to the London Midland Region until someone, perhaps bearing in mind the Landore allocation, suggested that the redundant locomotives be used to modernise the dock railways at Kingston-upon-Hull. To the Eastern Region, the phrase 'diesel-hydraulic' meant trouble in itself and mention of the Paxman name brought back further unhappy memories of the engine problems suffered with the D8200 and D8400 Type 1s. On the verge of disposing of these still-unsatisfactory machines, the ER's management quite understandably did not wish to become encumbered with somebody else's cast-offs and it was not surprising that they should resist any suggestion of a D9500 allocation until late in 1966. The

Above: The National Coal Board proved to be the saviour of the unwanted Class 14s, eventually purchasing nineteen to replace steam traction on colliery railways in Northumberland. On 17 July 1986, NCB No.31 (formerly D9531) arrives at Ashington Colliery with an internal working from the nearby Lynemouth Colliery. *(Paul D. Shannon)*

Left: The British Steel Corporation also became interested purchasers of the type for use in the ironstone fields of the East Midlands. On 16 November 1975, BSC Minerals No.55 (ex-D9507) waits for its train to be loaded by excavator at Oakley Quarry, near Corby. *(Kevin Lane)*

Eastern's final capitulation came when pressure to accept at least a small quantity began to emanate from the BRB itself and, as a result, the best twenty unwanted locomotives from across the WR (D9503-5/12/5/6/20/3/5/41-54) were put into working order and transferred to Hull in January 1967, where they were put to work from the sheds at Dairycoates and Alexandra Dock. As in South Wales though, Humberside's docks were in decline and there was simply not enough work to go around. Given a taste of their poor reliability, and their lack of multiple-unit control which necessitated double-manning of pairs at a time of staff shortages on the railway, those in charge at Hull quickly sidelined the exiles from the South-West. Nevertheless, once officially allocated to the ER, it was Doncaster's responsibility to dispose of the unwanted machines and in May 1967 the WR Operating Department somehow managed to get transferred another nine, D9507/10/1/29/32-4/7/9, initially on loan, then a month later becoming part of ER operating stock. Only D9532/3/7/9 seem to have made the journey to Yorkshire, however, the remaining five locomotives staying in store at Worcester.

The beginning of the end came in December 1967. Unable to find work for its own depleted stud, the WR officially withdrew D9522/31 at Cardiff and placed them in

106

Above: In a sylvan setting, BSC Minerals No.25 (ex-D9523) returns a rake of empties to Glendon East Quarry, near Corby, on 30 March 1978. The twin headlamp fitment visible on the leading bonnet was added by the BSC to the majority of its D9500 fleet. *(Kevin Lane)*

store, moving them to Worcester in January 1968 where D9531 forlornly saw out its third birthday. March saw the condemnation of three more stored D9500s, namely D9501 at Canton and D9506/13 at Worcester. The Eastern Region was delighted to follow the Western's example in this respect and on 1 April 1968, in what might well have been an intentional display of ironic humour, divested itself of the troubled type by condemning its entire allocation of twenty-nine locomotives at one fell swoop. This, of course, included the quintet theoretically allocated to Hull but in fact still stored on WR metals. Further casualties did not take long to appear and by the end of the year D9508/9/17/9/26/30 had also succumbed, leaving only eleven to see in 1969 and their TOPS classification of 14. On 26 April 1969, the final curtain came down on D9500/2/21/4/35 at Canton and D9514/8/27/36/8/55 at Landore, all being put into store either at Landore or at Gloucester Horton Road.

By the time that BR was condemning its last D9500s, the first had already been sold for scrap, D9522/31 having been bought by Arnott Young and moved by rail to that concern's Parkgate premises near Rotherham in July 1968. In this yard, and the many others like it throughout the country which, having sated themselves on BR's redundant steam locomotives, were now seeking fresh plunder in the form of the first diesel casualties, Swindon's Type 1s would undoubtedly have met with an untimely end had it not been for the intervention of the National Coal Board. Anxious to replace run-down and outdated steam traction on colliery railways in north-east England, the NCB entered into negotiations with both the breakers and BR (Arnott Young's agreement with BR being to scrap locomotives, not resell them) for the purchase of D9531 and, upon their successful conclusion, moved its new acquisition to Ashington Colliery, Northumberland for service trials. Arnott Young, meanwhile, wasted no time in converting their other purchase into furnace-sized assets and cut up D9522 that August, the unfortunate locomotive thus ending a life of just three and a half years, of which seven months had been spent in storage. Fortunately for those still awaiting their fate on BR, Ashington's initial experience of D9531 proved favourable and the NCB purchased D9500/2/8/11/4/7/8/21/7/8/36/45 to join it, some quickly being redeployed to the nearby Lynemouth Colliery. D9504/25/40 found a home at the Board's Philadelphia, County Durham installation whilst Bardon Colliery, Tyne and Wear got D9535/55. The British Steel Corporation was also attracted to the design as a steam replacement and over a period of time D9503/7/10/2/5/6/20/2/9/32-3/37/9/41/2/4/7-9/51-4 would be moved to various ironstone quarries in Lincolnshire and Northamptonshire. The Associated Portland Cement Manufacturing Company (APCM) purchased D9505/34 for use at its limestone quarries at Hope, Derbyshire, and D9526 to shunt the Blue Circle works at Westbury, Wiltshire. British Petroleum acquired D9524 for use at the Grangemouth refinery in Scotland, Gulf Oil D9530 for use at its Pembrokeshire terminal and BP-ShellMex D9538 for use at the Shellhaven complex in Essex. Inevitably, some also passed to breakers, namely D9501 to Booth's of Rotherham, D9506/13 to Arnott Young and D9505/19 to Cohen's of Kettering, although D9513 too was later resold to the NCB for use at Ashington.

As on BR, the D9500s led mixed careers in private ownership. Mechanical reliability continued to be poor though much improved over that endured by BR, principally due to the use of improved cylinder heads and more reliable ancillaries in conjunction with the regular inspection of known problem areas such as radiators and heat exchangers. Nevertheless, over the years some were cannibalised to keep others in traffic and at least one (D9544) was dismantled without having done any work for its new owners at all. Changes of location and ownership were frequent, most though not all of the NCB and BSC locomotives eventually being concentrated at Ashington and Corby respectively. BP-ShellMex's D9538 was sold to the BSC in 1971, moving first to Ebbw Vale steelworks and thence to Corby, whilst in 1977 Gulf Oil's D9530 passed to the NCB at Maerdy Colliery in South Wales. More surprising was the sale in 1975 of the two locomotives employed by APCM in Derbyshire, which were towed to Harwich for shipment to a new owner in Bruges, Belgium. Not to be outdone, in late 1980 the BSC sold D9515/48/9 for use on the construction of a mineral line in Spain, the trio first being dispatched to Hunslet at Leeds where they were overhauled and regauged to 5'6" before being shipped to Bilbao. At the time of writing, all three were reported to survive intact at a site near Madrid, whilst of the pair shipped to Belgium, D9505 was still in periodic industrial service with a new owner at Moorbeek Waas, near Ghent. The second locomotive exported to Bruges in 1975, D9534 was subsequently re-exported to Italy, where it is thought to have been scrapped.

At home, the majority of D9500s would find their adoption by industry to be a stay of execution rather than a wholesale reprieve. Whilst less arduous duties coupled with more rigorous maintenance routines succeeded in reducing the incidence of major failures compared with BR days, the mechanical fragility of the design was never truly exorcised. Concerns with only one or two locomotives soon resold them when they began to give trouble, the only exception being BP Grangemouth which re-engined a troublesome D9524 with a slow-running 500bhp Dorman diesel and continued to use it in that form until 1981. The larger fleets employed by the BSC and NCB encouraged the implementation of both preventative maintenance and selective modification programmes in a largely-successful attempt to address specific failings. Even so, the BSC became so exasperated with the Paxman engine that it planned to re-engine its entire fleet, ordering three Rolls-Royce diesels as part of the first phase. Shortly after, however, the decision was taken at a higher level to close the Corby operation in its entirety and the re-engining programme was abandoned. Use of D9500s by the BSC ceased very shortly after and, with the exception of those purchased for preservation, the Corby locomotives were cut up on site in mid-1982.

The contraction of the coal industry at the same time had much the same effect upon the once-prolific NCB fleet which, by the mid-1980s, was viewed as non-standard and life expired. Although many colliery railwaymen preferred the 'Paxmans' to the NCB's other diesel locomotives, citing their greater suitability for heavy trip workings in particular, closure of operations elsewhere meant that the Coal Board was amassing a considerable fleet of surplus industrial-pattern diesels. Motivated by the prospect of standardising upon these, the NCB decided to eliminate its remaining ex-BR locomotives and so prohibited not only major expenditure on repairs but also the transfer of redundant D9500s for further work at other sites. Under these circumstances, the eventual termination of rail operations at Ashington effectively wrote *finis* to the 'Teddy Bears' industrial career, the last working survivors being withdrawn in the spring of 1987.

Chapter 11

DIESELISATION AND DEPLOYMENT

ALTHOUGH the adoption of diesel-hydraulic traction was but one facet of the Western Region's modernisation programme, the nature of this particular form of motive power would shape the methodology of its employment just as much as the major economic forces of the time. With falling traffic levels due to the rise in private motoring and the increasing flow of traditional railway goods traffic onto the roads, dieselisation as conceived by Messrs Grand, Hanks and Phillips was aimed not so much at achieving direct economy of operation as harnessing those economies deriving from greater unit availability and increased traffic volumes attracted through service accelerations. This necessitated getting the very best performance possible out of each individual unit of motive power, a consideration that was to form a cornerstone of the initial WR dieselisation policy. The diesel-hydraulic was not the driving force behind modernisation, but rather the WR's evaluation of the best tool with which to achieve its objectives.

Taking all these factors into account a basic strategy was evolved, the logic of which cannot be faulted but, for various reasons discussed in the following chapter, was never to be fully implemented. Out of the complete regional territory three principal areas were defined, each of which was to be the subject of its own local dieselisation programme or Conversion Scheme. Over a period of time. complete dieselisation would be effected in each of these, the schemes progressing in sequence with one starting concurrent with the completion of its immediate predecessor. The fourth and final scheme would entail dieselising those parts of the Western Region not already within one of these three areas. This would allow steam and diesel traction to be separated from each other, both in the working environment and more importantly for maintenance, where the dirt of the steam running shed could, and did, wreak havoc with the delicate mechanisms of the early diesels. Staff could be familiarised with the new motive power without needing to maintain a comprehensive knowledge of the steam locomotives hitherto indigenous to the area, whilst locomotive diagrams could be revised to take account of the diesels' need for reduced routine servicing time but more lengthy periodic examinations, something which had proved a particular stumbling block in the efficient use of the gas-turbines.

Existing schedules embodied long waits between duties to allow servicing, which modern traction did not require. Over the course of a year these intervals would amount to a substantial amount of service time spent standing idle, but the re-working of complex diagrams to take care of the specific service requirements of only two locomotives had not proved viable. With the large number of diesel-hydraulics on order, this difficulty disappeared providing that each form of traction remained relatively concentrated, yet another point in favour of area conversion. As soon as diesel-hydraulic deliveries were sufficiently numerous, a rapid and total conversion could be applied to the area in question, displaced steam engines either being withdrawn or drafted to some other part of the system in order to work out their remaining years of service.

The subject of the first of these programmes, Conversion Scheme No.1, was the entire WR system west of Newton

Abbot. The reasons for this were severalfold: it was a compact network within which dieselisation strategies could be evaluated quickly and meaningfully; it promised rapid returns on investment by putting the new locomotives to work on the arduous South Devon banks, saving much piloting and double-heading; and the number of locomotives required could be provided within a reasonable timespan by construction both at BR and contractors' workshops. There might also have been a certain element of *deja vu* involved; after all, this was the territory that had been selected for the abortive 1936 electrification and 1947 oil-firing schemes, of which the latter had spawned oil storage tanks at several major WR depots. Motive power requirements would consist of the fifty-eight D6300 Type 2s, seventy Type 4s and smaller numbers of 350bhp diesel-electric shunters and diesel multiple-units. Initially, Conversion Scheme No.1 was centred around the provision of a large modern diesel depot on the site of the old steam shed at Newton Abbot (83A), which would allow the Type 4s allocated there to attain the best possible use on trains between the South-West and the capital. Smaller locomotives and DMUs would also use the depot, working in both directions. Work therefore proceeded on demolishing redundant structures and in their place providing fuelling equipment and servicing facilities in readiness for the new locomotives, D600/1 and D800-2 working out of this depot for their first few weeks of service despite their official allocation to Plymouth Laira.

In the event, there was more to the official allocation of the WR's first Type 4s than met the eye, as before major work had even started at Newton Abbot the decision had been taken to site the principal diesel depot for Conversion Scheme No.1 at Plymouth Laira (83D). A large new structure was erected on wasteland adjacent to the existing steam shed, intended to provide not only for the running maintenance of locomotives but also every other category of work except scheduled overhaul and heavy repair. A five-road maintenance shop boasted tracks set on pedestals above floor level for easy access to underframe equipment, with elevated platforms at solebar height to facilitate work within the locomotive bodies. Also present was an underfloor wheel lathe with special safeguards to ensure that the diam-

Top: Several of the depots required to service the WR's new diesel fleet were adapted from existing facilities so as to save time and expense. On 10 May 1962, four D800 'Warships' undergo routine inspection in the maintenance shed at Newton Abbot, converted from the former steam repair shop. Note the access platforms at solebar height, the rails themselves being supported above floor level so as to allow access to bogie and underframe equipment. *(Colin J. Marsden Collection)*

Bottom: In addition to maintenance and servicing facilities, much additional ancillary equipment was required to keep the fleet running. Typical was the supercession of manual cleaning by the use of automated washing plants such as this photoelectrically-controlled example at the west end of Newton Abbot depot, here seen tending to an unidentified NBL-built D800 'Warship'. *(Colin J. Marsden Collection)*

Top: At a few locations, entire new diesel handling facilities were provided, the first of which was situated at Plymouth Laira. Taken after the whole depot was opened, this view shows the depot with various forms of motive power in evidence, most notably a D600 going through the washer plant and DMUs undergoing routine servicing. To the left can be seen the modern building provided for messing and office functions. *(Colin J. Marsden Collection)*

Bottom: The first WR depot specifically intended to service both diesel-electrics and diesel-hydraulics was Old Oak Common, where extensive workshop facilities already existed. Most notable of these was the massive repair shop or 'factory', which on 15 September 1985 welcomed diesel-hydraulics back to the site for the first time since 1977. D7018 and D1015 *Western Champion* were present for a BR open day, and are seen in the company of No.s 50 007 *Sir Edward Elgar* and 47 500 *Great Western*. *(Colin J. Marsden)*

eters of all connected wheels were kept within the forty thousands of an inch tolerance required if driveline overrun problems were to be avoided, whilst in the yard were washing, sanding and fuelling facilities. Both locomotives and DMUs would eventually be handled, but for some time the multiple units were serviced at the Belmont facility near Millbay Docks, only visiting Laira for more extensive work.

Newton Abbot, meanwhile, became a secondary depot performing minor maintenance upon its own small allocation, the existing 1895 running shed having been adapted accordingly. Additional facilities, including those for limited unit replacement, were provided in part of the old repair shops which, although rebuilt in 1924, were now suitably refurbished for their new charges. Sundry other improvements were made up until the early 1960s, by which time it was recognised that Newton Abbot was never going to become anything more than a relatively unimportant staging-post. In retrospect, Laira should have been selected from the very beginning. As well as being geographically less central, Newton Abbot's importance as a railway centre was to diminish with the run-down of the Heathfield and Moretonhampstead branches, along with the steady diminution of the traffic to and from Kingswear. Its other *raison d'etre*, the provision of pilot locomotives to assist trains on the climb to Dainton, was also to decrease rapidly with the advent of the diesel age. Accordingly, it declined quickly and lost its allocation in May 1973, whilst Laira began to perform maintenance on heavy diesel-electrics from the mid-1970s and so remained the principal WR depot in the West Country, even after the introduction of the Bristol-based HSTs.

With dieselisation of South Devon and Cornwall well in hand, work started on displacing steam from the territory east of Exeter, up through Bristol as far as Worcester in the north and Oxford in the east, but excluding South Wales. This was the ambit of Conversion Scheme No.2, centred upon a new diesel depot at Bristol Bath Road, which would

also have to cater for diesel-electrics handling the southern end of inter-regional workings from the North of England. The old shed at Bath Road was closed to steam from 12 September 1960, work then proceeding on site clearance and the erection of a three-road servicing shed combining fuelling and sanding facilities, along with a separate mechanical washing plant. The existing running shed, a 'Loans Act' building dating from the early 1930s, was partially demolished and converted into a six-road maintenance shed, with elevated platforms and sunken floors in the two bays nearest the Bath Road. Offices and messing facilities were provided in a new block situated between the shed and the roadway itself. As one of the WR's principal motive power depots, 82A already had a large and well-appointed repair shop and this was retained, along with one of the two turntables, as part of the new layout. Work on the new facilities still had to be completed when the first allocation of 'Hymeks', D800s and D1 1Co-Co1s arrived and, for a time, routine diesel maintenance was carried out at the neighbouring St Philip's Marsh depot, which also assumed sole responsibility for WR steam traction in the Bristol area.

Officially opened on 10 July 1961, quite some time before work was actually completed, Bath Road now became a secondary depot, despite its position as focus of No.2 Scheme. As well as sharing responsibility for the London-South West workings with Plymouth Laira, it also provided motive power for the London-South Wales services, those to Crewe via Hereford and Shrewsbury, those

to Birmingham over the old Midland line (hence the Derby/Sulzer Type 4s) and various sundry services, for which a total of some two hundred locomotives would eventually be required. DMUs were housed and maintained in dedicated facilities at St Anne's Park.

The next stage in the process, Conversion Scheme No.3 was something of a hotch-potch, working as it did from both ends of the Western Region. Its main concern was with implementing complete dieselisation within South Wales, but also included the Paddington-Birkenhead line and the route from South Wales to the Midlands via Hereford and Worcester. As discussed in Chapter 9, the dieselisation of the Birkenhead route was to be achieved using 'Westerns' working on a three-day cyclic diagram from Laira, but the rest of the scheme depended upon the provision of two depots in South Wales, one of which would be able to perform major maintenance work. First in operation was the rebuilt facility at Swansea Landore, closed to steam in June 1961 and partially reopened as a diesel depot in February 1963. Intended to provide for the traffic requirements of the coastal plain and the Swansea Valleys as well as a certain amount of mainline work, Landore was made fully operational in May 1963 upon the completion of works that had provided maintenance and servicing sheds as well as fuelling facilities and a mechanical washer. An allocation of ninety locomotives, both diesel-electric and diesel-hydraulic, along with shunters and DMU sets was sufficient to enable the total extinction of WR steam west of Swansea and the closure of a whole group of smaller sheds. Unlike Bath Road, Landore acted as home to local DMU sets, but diesel shunters were maintained at a separate facility at Margam where most of them were employed in yard service.

Much more significant was the decision to provide a major depot and maintenance operation at Cardiff Canton (88A). The creation of such a facility somewhere in South Wales had been taken for granted from the beginning but, with a profusion of suitable sites, the WR waited until 1961 before making any firm locational decision in order to derive the maximum benefit from its experience so far. With the closure to steam of the Canton site in September 1962 and the transfer of its remaining steam engines to Cardiff East Dock, construction work could begin on new servicing and maintenance facilities loosely patterned upon those at Laira. Due to the retention and conversion of some existing structures, servicing and fuelling facilities were offered from October 1963 and heavy maintenance on both diesel-hydraulics and WR-allocated diesel-electrics from early in 1964. Work was completed in September 1964 by which time 88A boasted an allocation of about two hundred locomotives, some of which were shedded at Landore and only visited Canton for heavy maintenance. Facilities included a

Above: Routine fuelling and minor servicing was also carried out at a large number of other locations, where facilities could range from the adequate to the downright primitive. On 16 March 1973, two members of the fitting staff attend to No.7030 outside the old steam shed at Gloucester Horton Road. *(B.J. Nicolle)*

Right: The first round of changes at Swindon Works concerned the implementation of moves necessary in order to allow the building of diesel-hydraulic locomotives at that location. Final assembly was performed on a production-line basis in the main erecting shop, seen here with no less than nine new D800 'Warships' under construction. *(Colin J. Marsden Collection)*

washing plant, fuelling and sanding points, a wheel lathe and heavy lifting gear, Canton assuming responsibility for the heavy maintenance of all WR mainline diesel-electrics, regardless of allocation. 88A also undertook maintenance on the local DMU allocation, though the units operated out of their own depot at Cathays.

If Conversion Scheme No.3 was a hotch-potch, then Conversion Scheme No.4 can only be described as a mopping-up operation consisting of a remit to dieselise all remaining portions of the WR. Oddly enough, the largest area subject to this was the capital itself, though as most mainline services of any consequence were already in the hands of diesels allocated to Laira, Bath Road or Canton, the initial intention had been to downgrade Old Oak Common to the status of a secondary depot only. The burden on existing facilities imposed by WR's increasing complement of diesel-electrics necessitated a reappraisal, the outcome of which was that 81A was to be restructured as an additional maintenance depot, similar in scale to that at Bristol Bath Road. Some facilities already existed, fuel storage and delivery equipment first having been installed for the abortive post-war oil-firing scheme, then adapted and maintained for the two gas-turbines and a growing quantity of diesel-electric shunters. In addition, the existing 1906 shed buildings had been supplemented by a modern office block during the late 1950s, and the desire to retain these later facilities intact would strongly influence any reconstruction work.

Redevelopment of the site began late in 1964, when demolition work commenced on the massive quadruple roundhouse in order to make way for a new servicing shed which came into use in the New Year. Due to the continuing need to service a large allocation of steam locomotives, however, progress was slow until the site's closure to steam that March. Since all the remaining steam facilities were now rapidly removed, attention could be concentrated on the second phase of the project, namely conversion of the enormous repair shop or 'factory' into a fully-equipped

diesel maintenance facility. Although allowing considerable savings in terms of both time and money, the retention of various existing buildings at 81A would cause a number of operational difficulties. Primary amongst these was the question of access to the new lifting shop, home to the heavy lifting equipment so necessary to handle large diesel-electrics, which formerly had been from the shed itself and was now perpendicular to the alignment of the rest of the site. The ultimate solution to this problem was the preser-

vation in working order of the south-west turntable, which also had the added benefit of aiding the passage of locomotives through the servicing side. Old Oak Common became fully operational as a diesel depot in October 1965, although maintenance work tended to be of a medium nature for all except shunters and the depot's own allocation of D6300s. London-area DMUs would not be handled at 81A, but instead had dedicated facilities converted from the former steam sheds at Southall and Reading.

Theoretically, there should have been some allowance for the maintenance of diesel-hydraulics in the West Midlands and indeed, arrangements had been made for this in the third of the Conversion Schemes. The idea had been to adapt existing premises at Wolverhampton Stafford Road so as to provide facilities on a par with those at Laira and Canton, but the proposals lapsed when the secession to the London Midland Region of all WR territory in the Birmingham area saw locomotive and DMU maintenance concentrated at Saltley and Tyseley respectively. The resulting need to turn-around both diesel-hydraulics and diesel-electrics near to Paddington rather than in the West Midlands contributed in part to the decision not to downgrade Old Oak Common to a mere stabling and servicing function. Similarly, it soon became obvious that extra facilities were needed in South Wales and so, upon its closure to steam in October 1965, Newport Ebbw Junction became a maintenance depot. A number of former steam sheds in other areas of the Western Region maintained essential facilities for basic maintenance and refuelling, especially useful in the case of locomotives working away from their home depots for days at a time; Westbury and St Blazey in particular were so important in this regard as virtually to become depots in their own right.

Changes to Swindon Works itself were no less extensive and had to be implemented earlier in order to get the new locomotives into traffic. The strategy of delegating unit-replacement work to depots and allocation of overhaul work on WR diesel-electrics to Crewe and Derby, combined with the closure of the WR's workshops at Caerphilly, Wolverhampton and Worcester, gave Swindon primacy in terms of performing overhaul and damage-rectification work to the diesel-hydraulics, in addition to new construction and major design modifications. The difficulties of adopting an entirely new system were compounded initially by the large volume of continuing steam work and the need to perform all major diesel maintenance until the depot system got into full swing, though the Works' response to the enormous demands made upon it was surely aided by the size and flexibility of its site. Much of the burden would be not in providing new resources, but rather in remoulding and redirecting those already available in order to deal with the new type of work. The traditional emphasis of the Works in dealing with heavy castings, forgings and platework would have to give way to the very different techniques needed for light sheet and tubing, with an

Above: Diesel-hydraulic locomotives overhauled at Swindon usually received only structural and cosmetic attention in the main erecting shops, nearly all mechanical units being removed for attention in other parts of the works complex. In the midst of major repairs during the late 1960s, 'Hymek' D7011 is little more than a bare shell supported on accomodation stands, though with an overhauled engine already fitted. Bogies, transmission and cooling gear will soon follow. *(R.H.G. Simpson)*

Top Right: As well as scheduled repairs, Swindon also undertook accident repairs. In December 1963, a slightly crumpled D1065 *Western Consort* stands outside Swindon shed, awaiting removal to 'A' shop for the rectification of minor collision damage. Behind, a withdrawn 'Hall' 4-6-0 prepares for a more final call to works. *(D.J. Everson)*

Bottom Right: Extensive retraining of many railway staff was required in order to get the best out of the new locomotives. The purpose of this WR CM&EE photograph from June 1962 was to illustrate to breakdown crews the correct method of re-railing a D800 'Warship' using a steam crane, with D844 *Spartan* acting as the model. Note the wooden blocks interposed between the lifting cables and the bodyside to prevent damage to the stressed-skin structure. *(Colin J. Marsden Collection)*

Below: Even once the emphasis had shifted to diesels, it was imperative that Swindon should remain capable of maintaining steam traction for as long as such locomotives were in regular operation on the WR. In June 1965, steam's last full year west of Paddington, D867 *Zenith* and D7051 share part of 'A' shop with 0-6-0PT No.4673 and '2884' 2-8-0 No.3864. It is still hard to comprehend that none of this remains. *(Colin J. Marsden Collection)*

additional requirement for extreme accuracy and constant checking of the stressed-skin structures. Similar standards of accuracy were demanded in the overhaul of engines and transmissions, and would have to be matched by even greater standards of cleanliness if reasonable service lives were to be ensured.

In all, the total number of alterations needing to be carried out at Swindon in order to meet these new demands was estimated to cost close on a million pounds spread over a fifteen-year period. Forging and smithy work was largely eliminated with the completion of the last 9F 2-10-0s in 1960, and various other manufacturing processes were much reduced at the same time. The erecting shops had already been reorganised around a production line created for the D800s in 1958, with sub-assemblies made up in the former smiths' shop being brought together in the main 'A' erecting shop. Both stages made extensive use of purpose-made jigs for accuracy in positioning and welding, which were only part of the volume of new equipment that had to be obtained, along with contour-bending machines, cutting apparatus and presses to produce the complex metal shapes required. A large quantity of electric arc-welding equipment had to be provided (and staff trained in its use) whilst series production of the K-M-style bogies was facilitated by the procurement of several transfer machines, each capable of performing multiple drilling and cutting operations simultaneously. Along with special rotating workstands, the use of these increased productivity immensely. Another major expense was the provision of a testing block adjacent to 'A' shop for the X-ray examination of finished sub-assemblies; as these increased in size and complexity, as in the case of the D1000 bogie, so this facility became increasingly vital in the task of checking the numerous welded joints featured in their construction.

Mechanical units mostly came ready-assembled from the manufacturers and only needed setting-up and installation. Nevertheless, overhaul would be required sooner or later, necessitating the provision of suitable facilities. Furthermore, the WR's goal of performing as much maintenance as possible at the principal running depots dictated that overhauled equipment be tested and correctly set prior to dispatch, in order to minimise the fitting time at the depot and therefore the period for which the afflicted locomotive was out of service. This represented another significant departure from accepted practice and entailed considerable reorganisation. 'B' shop was cleared and refurbished to become the diesel engine repair plant, with individual sections for each type of powerplant, though this facility subsequently moved to the old foundry ('J1' shop), along with a group of specialists handling the repair and recalibration of fuel injection equipment. A similar facility was created to deal with the various types of hydraulic transmission in use on the WR, initially restricted to detailed inspection and periodic servicing but quickly progressing to full overhauls. At this point, so as to derive the maximum benefit from the considerable investment in equipment and staff training, the transmissions operation at Swindon was sub-divided into sections, each consisting of around six men and a technical inspector specialising in one type of transmission only. As with the other repair sections, these were responsible not only for fitting work but also the bench-testing of various sub-assemblies prior to incorporation within the major units. An electrical engineering department was established to take care of the locomotives' electrical gear whilst other sub-departments dealt with engine auxiliaries, driveline components, brake equipment and the ever-delicate train-heating boilers. Simultaneously, the massive task of retraining staff for their new roles and familiarising them with the vast range of new equipment had to be undertaken, and the speed with this was completed was a source of considerable pride to the entire works establishment.

To minimise the risk of a newly-outshopped but never-

theless substandard piece of equipment failing on a locomotive in service, rigorous testing procedures were instituted. With a diesel-electric, the engine and generator set could be subjected to testing and even preliminary running-in by connecting the generator output to a variable-resistance load-bank, but the different characteristics of the diesel-hydraulics demanded the acquisition of several Heenan & Froude dynamometers, which were then installed in a purpose-built test-house on the site of the former boiler de-tubing shop. Installed centrally between two engine beds so as to speed throughput, each dynamometer could handle up to 1920bhp. Similar devices coupled to 'slave' engines were used to test transmission blocks whilst

Above: Swindon's fortunes to a large extent declined with those of the hydraulics. One of the last to receive major attention there was D1063 *Western Monitor*, seen being re-assembled on 28 June 1972. *(Tim Edmonds)*

smaller units were provided to test DMU engines, the testing station being connected to a 20,000-gallon underground reservoir and other cooling plant to absorb the heat generated by the working machinery. Coming into full service in 1965, the plant was estimated to have cost around £500,000 and would prove one of the final extensions to the locomotive works.

The ability to dispatch ready-tested and calibrated units was essential to the well-being of the unit-replacement principle espoused by the WR. The idea behind this was that the main maintenance depots could replace faulty equipment with overhauled spares on their own premises, sending the failed units to Swindon for rectification. The lightweight nature of the diesel-hydraulic components enabled the depots to do just that and, despite the known shorter life expectancy of the high-speed engines, when working well this system could boast locomotive availability levels well above anything other regions could achieve with their main works repair policies. The principal problem was that it rarely did work well. Initially, there was a high incidence of equipment failure and other teething troubles which overloaded the infant system, a situation worsened by the coincidental tightening-up of spares stocks which kept locomotives out of traffic for several weeks at a time. Often, maintenance procedures were inadequate and precipitated the premature failure of already temperamental equipment, lowering availability yet further. In extreme cases locomotives at depots awaiting repair were stripped to virtual hulks to keep their sisters running, culminating in the need to rebuild a locomotive where the adequate provision of minor spares would have sufficed. Even when these failures began to be combated successfully from the end of 1965, the system was still disabled by the decision to curtail the delivery of diesel-hydraulics and fill the gap with diesel-electrics instead. Particularly badly-hit was South Wales which had a maintenance allocation of about three hundred mainline diesel-electrics, all of which had to be taken to Crewe or Derby for heavy or scheduled repairs. Even if Swindon had been responsible for this work, the problem would still have remained as many of the facilities at Laira and Canton were simply incapable of handling the heavy components of the diesel-electrics.

When in 1967 control of Swindon Works was removed from the WR and instead invested in BR's new Workshops Division, the unit-replacement policy for diesel-hydraulics was maintained, although a certain amount of valuable interaction between depots and main works was inevitably lost as a result of the organisational changes. Despite the problems, unit-replacement remained a broadly effective means of maintaining the WR's diesel-hydraulic fleet and changed very little over the years, even after Swindon Works became part of British Rail Engineering Ltd (BREL) in 1970. However, had the WR succeeded in amassing the number of diesel-hydraulics that it had sought, then a further expansion of activities at Swindon would have become necessary in the late 1960s. The early cessation of orders put an end to any such ideas and the resulting flood of standard diesel-electric types onto the WR, all serviced by other BR workshops, effectively sealed Swindon's fate as a major centre for overhauling motive power. Unsurprisingly, this exerted a corrosive effect upon staff morale and as the 1960s drew to a close, the loss of skilled artisans to other industries in the area began to have serious effects upon Swindon's ability to maintain a rapid throughput of equipment. Examples of problems directly attributable to this unhappy situation included a rise in reported Maybach engine failures in the first few weeks after overhaul, as well as cases of locomotives being held at Swindon for up to nine months awaiting the completion of routine repairs.

Despite manifold difficulties, the overall impact of dieselisation on the WR was much more immediate than on other regions, where the simple replacement of steam power by a diesel working to the same schedule was often considered to constitute progress. In keeping with the postwar GWR policy, services were accelerated and increased in frequency, the first to be treated in this way being the 'Bristolian' in 1959. Although it quickly reverted to its previous schedule when the rough-riding problems of the D800s necessitated an 80mph restriction, the 'Bristolian's first weeks of diesel operation provided answers to a number of vital questions posed by the WR's planners in their quest for improvement. The basic concept was further confirmed by trials on the Birmingham services which showed that a D800 could increase contemporary loadings by half again, yet lose no more than a quarter-hour on the existing schedule, and the eventual decision to use the new D1000s instead would mainly reflect the WR's desire to achieve better fuel economy, as well as allowing a greater margin with which to recover any time lost. From the end of 1962, the 'Westerns' greater capabilities would become of paramount importance when these services were accelerated in order to absorb through traffic temporarily displaced from the Euston line, then in the throes of its 25kV electrification, and so preserve lucrative business custom for the railways in the face of fierce competition from fast, reliable motorway coach services between Birmingham and the capital.

By the time that the transfer of these services to the LMR displaced the D1000s to other duties, WR schedules had already been trimmed to a point where start-stop average speeds of 70mph were regularly being attained. Although the 'Westerns' creditable performance on the accelerated South Wales and South West trains were for a time overshadowed by mechanical problems, improvements in availability brought about by the application of service modifications would, in conjunction with the WR deployment of D1500 diesel-electrics and a number of 'Blue Pullman' sets, permit a steady increase in the number of high-speed schedules. Although slightly beyond the capability of the less powerful 'Warships', by the end of 1968 the WR had sufficient numbers of 'Westerns' and Brush Type 4s to allow twenty journeys a day to be made at speeds averaging 70mph or more. Whilst this did represent the pick of the crop, similar standards of improvement were applied across the timetable, with another two hundred services spread between Penzance and Crewe having scheduled average speeds in excess of 60mph. Some of these were due to being diagrammed for haulage by the less powerful D800 and D7000 types, but many more were secondary services over speed-restricted routes featuring numerous station stops, and the attainment of a 60mph average schedule in itself represented a considerable improvement over steam traction. The interest of both professional observers and the travelling public alike, however, was inevitably concentrated upon the fastest and most prestigious services, and these were the ones which the WR chose to emphasise. Even taking into account the problems occasioned by the 'Westerns' early teething troubles, the acceleration of the South Wales services in particular was such that *Modern Railways* would be moved to hail it as one of the most remarkable of any on BR occasioned by the mere substitution of diesel for steam power.

These accelerations had to be hard-fought for, however, and even at the very outset, problems in applying and maintaining accelerated schedules had resulted in the embarrassing situation of some newly-dieselised WR services actually being slower than their steam-hauled rivals on the Southern Region's West of England mainline. Although exacerbated by the early troubles with the D800s, the situation had not been helped by the generally sluggish entry to service of the first diesel-hydraulic orders, the failure of North British in particular to deliver its quota on time being instrumental in both delaying and protracting the implementation of Conversion Scheme No.1. As a result, Cornwall, the initial area of attention, did not bid farewell to steam-hauled services until the spring of 1962, whilst those on the mainline between Exeter and Plymouth continued until the end of the year. By this time, the process of redressing the balance in the WR's favour, which had taken two whole years as well as the loss of important customer goodwill, was itself being threatened by the insidious proliferation of intermediate halts imposed upon many hitherto-express services. Intended to improve stock utilisation and thus reduce the WR's operating deficit, this ill-considered policy was introduced in 1961 and prevailed for eight years, in which time it placed an ever-stronger restraint upon efforts to cut timings across the board. With every passing year, the number of limited-stop services in the regional timetable was reduced yet again, and the WR's achievement in managing to combine this with faster schedules was indeed a significant one. The system was not infallible, however, and some secondary services actually suffered an effective deceleration as the D800 'Warships' responsible for their operation proved incapable of the sort of (very) hard running necessary to recoup time lost by additional station stops. Maintenance of those schedules which had been accelerated was not aided by unduly low levels of locomotive availability, especially amongst the 'Westerns', which actually precipitated the postponement of a new timetable of faster services intended for 1964. Delivery of the final D1000s, having been delayed, came at a time when the WR's most pressing requirement was for Type 3 power on South Wales coal trains, and the necessity of having to 'regear' a number of sorely-needed English Electric D6700s in order to replace recalcitrant 'Westerns' on Paddington-South Wales passenger trains did nothing to endear the big diesel-hydraulics to hard-pressed operating staff.

Whilst faulty and malfunctioning equipment played a major role in lowering standards of locomotive performance, the greatest disruption of the WR's dieselisation programme was caused by the constant shifts then characterising BR policy. Repeated changes of regional boundaries in the Midlands, which brought the first Derby/Sulzer 1Co-Co1s to the WR along with the ex-LMS Birmingham-Bristol line before displacing substantial numbers of D1000 'Westerns' from the Paddington-Birkenhead route, played havoc with the WR's predictions of future haulage requirements and patterns of locomotive deployment. This, along with the decision to curtail diesel-hydraulic deliveries and replace them with diesel-electrics instead, created consider-

Above: Standing in the entrance to the former Long Rock MPD, which provided servicing and fuelling facilities to diesels in the Penzance area after its closure to steam in September 1962, D1013 *Western Ranger* awaits its next duty on 7 July 1976. For the last year or so of its career with BR, D1013 was embellished with white wheel rims and red grounds to the name- and numberplates, modifications which made it undeniably distinctive if not necessarily more attractive. *(Brian Morrison)*

able instability in the WR's motive power situation for most of the mid-1960s, just at the critical time when steam was being eliminated from the region and when a demonstrable continuity of policy would have been most valuable. Although the move undoubtedly succeeded in hastening the final demise of WR steam, it also served to introduce sizeable quantities of equipment having little or nothing in common with existing motive power stocks. The entire maintenance system was dealt a veritable body-blow as a result, with problems not only in obtaining components from Crewe and Derby, but also in handling weighty equipment for which WR depot facilities were not intended.

Under the effect of such great and often contradictory pressures, the WR's dieselisation policy was to degenerate into a pattern of conversion by service rather than by area, and many of the benefits promised by steam's elimination remained largely unrealised during this period. The falling of maintenance standards on both WR diesel-electrics and diesel-hydraulics to a level far below that which had been expected came as no surprise given the circumstances and this, combined with the generally poor availability of diesels on all regions of BR, prompted yet another reversal of official policy, which now sought to cut train loads wherever possible. Locomotive usage then suffered in order to improve timings, these themselves being hindered from 1968 by new rostering arrangements which introduced mandatory crew changes on many of the longer workings. Nevertheless, with WR steam long since gone, the diesel-hydraulic fleet could already be credited with having spearheaded one of the fastest steam-to-diesel conversions yet seen by any major railway system. More importantly, in the face of ever greater competition from the expanding motorway network, it would make an invaluable contribution towards preserving passenger levels, so providing a firm foundation for an even greater level of service in the coming decade.

Chapter 12
ECLIPSE

IN many ways, the political and bureaucratic reaction against the Western Region's diesel-hydraulic orders began even before the first locomotives had been delivered. Chapters 2 and 3 of this volume have sought to show the basic opposition of the BTC to the diesel-hydraulic concept, which in turn was principally a function of its commitment to the heavy, slow-speed machines offered by home industry. Marylebone Road might well have let the WR have its own way with the fourteen Pilot Scheme locomotives, but almost certainly hoped that, when the time came for placing mass orders, a sufficient number of arguments against the diesel-hydraulic case could be found to ensure that the experiment went no further. The over-hasty abandonment of the Pilot Scheme soon put paid to that and several other ideas, and before the anti-hydraulic faction within the BTC's Central Staff was able to slow down the rapidly accelerating sequence of events, it was confronted by a WR which had already gained sanction for 115 diesel-hydraulics and was ardently pressing for yet more.

There can be little doubt that at this point Paddington had gained the upper hand and indeed, things might have continued in this way, culminating in the full realisation of the WR traction policy, had it not been for the gradual attrition of the senior management team responsible for its formulation. First to go was H.H. Phillips, the man who more than anybody had advocated the diesel-hydraulic as the correct form of traction to fulfil WR requirements, who retired on the last day of 1956. WR enthusiasm continued unabated, but there could be no doubt that the scheme had lost its chief protagonist and accordingly, as the years drew on it fell increasingly prey to the interests of the railway construction industry, other BR regions and the BTC itself. As the theoretical owner of all the WR's locomotives, diesel-hydraulic

or otherwise, the attitude of the BTC was crucial. In the spring of 1955 the BTC Chief Mechanical Engineer, Roland C. Bond, had been broadly sympathetic towards the WR's aims and, in the absence of any definitive comparison between diesel-electric and diesel-hydraulic locomotive performance in day-to-day service, had agreed that diesel-hydraulics should account for at least some of the Pilot Scheme orders. In October 1958, however, Bond had been promoted to a position on the General Staff of the BTC, J.F. Harrison succeeding him as CME to the Commission.

Harrison was most certainly no supporter of diesel-hydraulics, a viewpoint which understandably was little altered by the many mechanical afflictions which beset the WR fleet. However, neither did he hold many of BR's existing diesel-electrics in any great regard, instead becoming one of the prime movers in the campaign to produce a new standard diesel-electric design of ample power yet moderate weight to fulfil all future motive power requirements. Like Bond before him, Harrison agreed with the WR's analysis of the critical issues facing the modern railway, but differed from his predecessor in his unequivocal rejection of the diesel-hydraulic as the best tool with which to do the job. The BTC's support for the WR traction policy, given grudgingly from the very start, thus began to evaporate altogether.

Worse was yet to come. The Great Western's attitude prior to nationalisation had done little to endear it to other sectors of the railway industry and what WR supporters saw as a proud independence born of tradition, others saw as arrogance or even snobbery. The BTC Chairman, Sir Brian Robertson, had indeed decreed that regional independence should not be diminished but his sentiments were not reciprocated in many quarters, least of all the Central Staff, where there existed a strong desire to see Paddington at last brought into line by means fair or foul. The WR's position was badly weakened when Keith Grand, the Regional General Manager and a staunch supporter of Phillips' ideas, was promoted off the Western Region to an appointment with the BTC in February 1959, and would be further destabilised when a 1960 survey commissioned by the BTC recommended that no further orders for mainline diesel-hydraulic locomotives be sanctioned. This effectively precipitated the liquidation of North British and Beyer-Peacock, both of which had relied heavily upon such orders for future work.

Although belatedly recognising the economic and operational importance of standardising on proven designs, the 1960 report came too late to redeem a situation that was rapidly going out of control. Almost from the beginning, the Modernisation Plan had proved costlier than expected and, as early as 1957, estimates of total outlay had been revised to £1660 million. Planned economies were slow to materialise and as costs continued to expand, so did criticism of the BTC's policies. In 1960, two separate reports submitted to the Minister of Transport by the House of Commons Select Committee on Nationalised Industries and the independent Stedeford Committee both commented unfavourably upon the BTC's current status, proposing a more commercial approach to the running of the nation's railways. Lord Robertson retired as BTC Chairman in

Below: The first nail in the coffin of the diesel-hydraulics came with the mass allocation of mainline diesel-electrics to WR sheds. On 13 November 1965, English Electric Type 3 D6910, then allocated to Landore, pilots the solitary Paxman-engined 'Warship' D830 *Majestic* on an eastbound freight passing Severn Tunnel Junction on the descent into the tunnel itself. *(G.B. Wise)*

1961, to be succeeded by Dr Richard Beeching, latterly of ICI and himself a member of Stedeford's team. Shortly afterwards, the 1962 Transport Act was to abolish the British Transport Commission in its entirety, its railway interests instead being represented by the British Railways Board, still under the leadership of Dr Beeching. At about the same time J.R. Hammond, former Western Region Chief Civil Engineer and latterly Grand's successor as Regional General Manager, took up a post on the Eastern Region and was himself replaced by Stanley Raymond. With his appointment, the wishes of the BTC to bring the WR into line with national policy were at last consummated, for within a matter of weeks it became apparent that a concerted official effort was being made to eradicate any remnants of the 'Great' from Western. Furthermore, Beeching's regime had led to a none-too-subtle change of tone in terms of policy; his mission was to make the railways pay their own way and as he saw it, that necessitated the condemnation of unprofitable services, outdated working practices and above all, the steam locomotive. Therefore, the race towards full dieselisation that had caused the calamitous abandonment of the Pilot Scheme now resurfaced under the same guise of pursuing profitability. Early deliveries of new motive power had been spread across British Railways as a whole and for the time being this would continue, but with the proviso that the final elimination of steam traction would be phased region-by-region, according to both operational demands and the speed with which initial conversion took place on each. Accordingly, there was much inter-regional rivalry for the honour of being the first to eliminate steam traction and so guarantee the capital required to provide diesel or electric replacements before it was exhausted by other projects.

Raymond, who would eventually succeed Beeching as Chairman of the BRB, was determined that this particular accolade should fall to the Western Region, a policy that brought him into serious conflict with the WR CME, R.A. Smeddle. Despite having served his time under the auspices of the old North Eastern Railway, Smeddle had come to develop deep respect not only for the WR's diesel-hydraulics but also for Swindon's steam locomotives as well. Having masterminded the rebuilding of the 'King' and 'Castle' 4-6-0s with double chimneys and blastpipes, Smeddle intended to retain a small number of the rejuvenated engines in traffic until the full complement of diesel-hydraulics had been received, but in no way did this meet with the approval of the new Regional General Manager. Raymond's remit was to rid the WR of steam and, in his view, such interests were not best served by replacing it with diesel-hydraulics, but rather by introducing diesel-electrics standard with those in use on other regions. It is not really the place of this work to document the decline and fall of WR steam, but reference to the fact that in 1962 four 'Castles' were withdrawn after having been extensively rebuilt and technically updated only the year before serves

Above: First diesel-hydraulics to go under the provisions of the National Traction Plan were the NBL Pilot Scheme locomotives. Withdrawn at the end of 1967, D601 *Ark Royal* sits mouldering in Woodham Brothers' Barry Docks scrapyard on 29 June 1970. Although Woodhams had cut up sister locomotive D600 *Active* that March, the derelict D601 would cling tenuously to life for a further decade. *([The other] Peter J. Robinson)*

Below: A sad end for a historic machine, as D800 *Sir Brian Robertson* visits Gloucester North for the last time, at the rear of a convoy of withdrawn locomotives *en route* to John Cashmore's Newport scrapyard on 13 July 1969. The pioneer 'Warship', looking distinctly the worse for wear after ten months' open storage at Laira, is accompanied by D6314 and D863 *Warrior*, both bound for the same destination behind a Brush Type 4. *(Norman E. Preedy)*

to show how deep was Raymond's intent to implement his decision. Needless to say, the whole affair caused a great deal of friction within the WR and Smeddle retired in September 1962, to be followed by the Regional Chairman, R.F. Hanks, at the end of the year. In fairness to Raymond, the Western Region which he inherited had not been in the best of health, with operating losses exceeding some £30 million. His reforms did much to reduce these but, along with the ramifications of the Beeching Report, engendered considerable adverse publicity and eroded the confidence of passengers and railway staff alike.

With the departure from the WR of all four major management figures who had been involved with the diesel-hydraulic policy from its inception, the way seemed clear for the imposition of the standard diesel-electric locomotive policy, but by this time this was itself coming under criticism from some professional quarters, voiced in journals such as *Diesel Railway Traction* and *The Railway Gazette*. In particular, widespread condemnation of the English

Top: NBL Type 2 No.6338 trundles a short mixed freight from Falmouth Docks to Truro through the station at Penryn on 19 April 1971. This was the last Class 22 seen in service by the photographer, and by the year's end they were all gone. *(G.B. Wise)*

Middle: A distinctly work-worn D827 *Kelly* pulls out of Gillingham with the 08.50 Exeter-Waterloo service on 29 August 1970. Not long after, the class was displaced from the Waterloo route by the Southern Region's own Class 33 diesel-electrics. *(Hugh Ballantyne)*

Bottom: By the end of 1971, all of North British's D800 'Warships' would be gone, their demise hastened by the poor record of the MAN engines in BR service. On 15 October 1971 No.s 844, 858 and 834, along with Swindon-built No. 808, stand withdrawn outside Newton Abbot depot, stripped of nameplates and, no doubt, many other valuable parts. *(Tom Heavyside)*

Electric and Derby/Sulzer Type 4s with their outdated 1Co-Co1 layout and 130/140-ton weight engendered support not only for a modern Type 4 diesel-electric Co-Co design weighing around one hundred tons, but also for the light-weight WR diesel-hydraulics. Itself forced to admit that operational experience had produced little or no real evidence to favour either electric or hydraulic transmission for mainline use, the BRB at last embarked on a course of scientific comparison between the two traction forms, the bulk of which was undertaken between early and mid-1964. Comparing diesel-electrics with diesel-hydraulics in both the Type 3 and Type 4 categories, the results were published in the *Report on Diesel-Electric and Diesel-Hydraulic Locomotives on British Railways* in August 1965.

As recounted in Chapter 9, controlled road tests were carried out on the Type 4 locomotives only, but the report also contained a broad survey of availability levels for both power categories, including the current trends at that time. The bulk of the BRB's argument rested upon the higher initial costs and lower availability records of the two diesel-hydraulic classes as compared with their diesel-electric equivalents, but went on to claim that in the higher power ranges now favoured by BR (2500-2750bhp) the diesel-hydraulic retained few of its previous advantages due to the need to use two engines and transmissions. Given that the study contained no analysis of running costs (it was claimed that this was not possible since none of the types involved had completed a full maintenance cycle), the BRB's reasoning in this regard must have been based on little more than comparison of initial costs combined with the results of the controlled road tests. These, it will be remembered, had been slanted by the mismatch between the 'Western's engines and transmissions which resulted in the hydraulic not being able to realise its full power over a significant portion of the speed range. Doubtless, had similar tests been carried out in the Type 3 category between the D6700 and D7000 types, both single-engined designs, a rather different story might have been told; the BRB and the BTC before it had always tended to see the diesel-hydraulic and the twin-engine format as one and the same thing, which they most certainly were not. The report concluded that, in BR's experience, the advantage lay firmly with the diesel-electric and therefore no further orders for diesel-hydraulics would be placed. It thus became clear both that dieselisation as perceived by Messrs Grand, Hanks, Phillips and Smeddle in 1955 would never come to fruition, and also that the long-term prospects of those diesel-hydraulics already in service on the WR could only be viewed with the gravest concern.

In 1967, less than a decade after their introduction to WR metals, the BRB's decision as to the eventual fate of the diesel-hydraulics was officially made public. The National Traction Plan of that year acknowledged that during and in the years immediately following the Pilot Scheme a great many locomotives had been purchased that in some way or other had failed to meet expectations. Therefore, in the interests of economy it was proposed to reduce BR's current stock of 2976 mainline diesels of twenty-eight types to 2240 of fifteen types by the end of 1974, principally through the elimination of those types that had proved troublesome in service, expensive to maintain, or too few in number to be reasonably termed 'standard'. That, basically, constituted a signed and sealed death warrant for the WR's diesel-hydraulics.

First to succumb to this policy were the D600s, withdrawn *en bloc* on 30 December 1967 along with D6301 and D9522/31. Qualifying for withdrawal under all three categories of the National Traction Plan, the A1A-A1A 'Warships' were no longer sufficiently fleet of foot nor reliable enough for the WR mainline, and too large and heavy for the china clay workings on the branchlines of Cornwall. Although three had been tried on coal trains in South Wales as replacements for the Type 3 diesel-electrics transferred *en-masse* to the Eastern Region in 1967, the experiment had

not been a success and they had soon returned to join their two counterparts at Laira. Given the spares availability problems which had begun to affect MAN-engined locomotives on BR since the liquidation of NBL in 1962, their restricted sphere of operations and their expected demise under the provisions of the National Traction Plan, the WR no longer considered justified the effort required to keep the five D600s in traffic. Remaining in store at Plymouth until July 1968, they were then sold to private breakers in South Wales and hauled to their final resting places in two separate movements at the end of that month. It was probably the same combination of factors which spelt the end for D6301; one of the Pilot Scheme batch of six and mechanically different from the production run of Type 2s, it had very limited multiple-working possibilities and ended its employment with BR largely restricted to Cornwall. After some months in storage at Laira, it too was sold to a firm of South Wales scrap merchants where it would earn the doubtful honour of being the very first WR diesel-hydraulic to be dismantled. As recounted in Chapter 10, the two D9500s were withdrawn due to the lack of any useful work for them to do, three years or so after their introduction.

1968 saw the extermination of the remaining hydraulics delivered under the auspices of the Pilot Scheme. D6300/2-5, non-standard in terms of engine, transmission and control apparatus, were all withdrawn on 26 May and stored at Laira. The first three D800s were also non-standard in terms of transmissions and control systems and accordingly, D801 *Vanguard* was withdrawn in August to be followed by D800 *Sir Brian Robertson* and D802 *Formidable* early in October. The Type 2s were all sold for scrap to Cashmore's of Newport and after being stripped of re-useable parts at Laira, D800 followed them in July 1969. After a protracted period in store, D801/2 were dragged back to Swindon where they were stripped and broken-up at the end of 1970. By the end of the year, a further twenty-one of the NBL Class 22s had been withdrawn from service, one (D6357) only six years into its intended fifteen-year working life. Little of this mattered to the BRB; in its view the greatest possible economy could be achieved through the disposal of non-standard types and in a number of ways its logic was unshakeable. Few on the WR mourned the passing of the NBL locomotives.

As well as the annihilation of the remaining D6300s, 1969 was expected to see significant withdrawals of 'Warships', a

Above: As spares steadily became less easy to obtain, the state of many of the WR's hydraulics became pretty grim. In atrocious external condition, No.7052 comes off the Westbury line at Salisbury with a Severn Tunnel Junction-Eastleigh freight working on 2 August 1971. *(G.F. Gillham)*

Below: No.6319 was the last Class 22 overhauled, being released from Swindon Works in March 1971, but this did not save the locomotive from being condemned just six months later. Seen semi-derelict at Bristol Marsh Junction on 30 November 1972, the locomotive was to become the subject of a private preservation initiative but, after movement to Swindon, was dismantled in error. *(Graham Scott-Lowe)*

strategy which relied upon the transfer from the London Midland Region of some twenty-five Derby/Sulzer Type 4s of Class 46, along with some thirty-one Brush Type 2s of Class 31 from the Eastern Region, to work out of Bristol Bath Road and Old Oak Common depots respectively. Although thirteen Class 46s arrived in March, the rest following over the next few weeks along with five similar locomotives from ER depots, the Eastern Region proved reluctant to release its Class 31s. In order to avoid a locomotive shortage, the WR had little choice but to keep the 'Warships' in service though the solitary 12YJXL-engined D830 *Majestic*, already in store at Newton Abbot, was con-

Top: Several withdrawn 'Warships' were given a short new lease of life by locomotive shortages during 1972, being reinstated and put to work on trains supplying roadstone for the M25 motorway construction project. Minus nameplates, No.829 (formerly *Magpie*) rolls a Westbury-Merstham train through Basingstoke on 29 July 1972. *(John Faulkner)*

Bottom: Ousted by diesel-electrics, the last Class 42 'Warships' succumbed to withdrawal at the end of 1972. In May 1973, the stripped hulk of No.820 *Grenville* rests off its bogies in Swindon Works yard, prior to final cutting-up. *(B.J. Nicolle)*

Top Right: A sunny 26 April 1973 saw No.7000 heading a mixed freight through the Sonning Cutting towards London. The pioneer 'Hymek' was then in its twelfth and final year of BR service, and would be withdrawn from traffic that July. *(G.F. Gillham)*

Bottom Right: To supplant both 'Warships' and 'Hymeks', several Class 31 locomotives were imported from the Eastern Region, but many crews considered them manifestly inferior to the machines they were intended to replace. In the company of Class 52s No.s 1053 *Western Patriarch* and 1054 *Western Governor*, No.31 230 awaits its next duty at Paddington on 21 July 1975. *(Graham Scott-Lowe)*

a result, they tended to get passed over for use on passenger duties, instead ending up on freight workings where the demands of the job were less and any failure not so likely to precipitate major traffic delays. To this would now be added a major difficulty in obtaining vital engine parts; when NBL had entered receivership in 1962, Voith Engineering (Glasgow) Ltd, the subsidiary set up to manufacture and repair hydraulic transmissions in part of the old Springburn plant, had also assumed responsibility for the provision of spares for NBL-supplied MAN engines. In 1970, however, the British assembly of Voith equipment ceased and when the operation was moved to London as a purely sales and service function, the links with MAN were severed. As a result, locomotives often spent periods of six months and more out of traffic whilst by-now obsolescent spares were sourced direct from the manufacturer in Germany. The Maybach-engined Class 42s, by contrast, continued to have their parts requirements satisfied via the old Armstrong-Siddeley plant at Ansty, albeit no longer under the auspices of BSE, that organisation having been absorbed by Rolls-Royce Ltd in October 1966.

The delayed arrival of replacement diesel-electrics resulted in 1970 passing without the withdrawal of a single WR hydraulic, but the breed's sphere of operations was tightened considerably. Though there were a number of notable exceptions to the rule, the main policy became one of containing the diesel-hydraulics on the WR west of Bristol and to this end, Old Oak Common lost its complete 'Warship' allocation in October 1970, Class 42s going to Laira and Class 43s to Newton Abbot. Late in 1970, however, six Derby/Sulzer Class 25 Type 2s arrived on the WR from the London Midland Region, followed in October 1971 by a further batch of Type 2s and a trickle of Class 47 Co-Cos (formerly the D1500 type). This allowed the maturing of the first part of the National Traction Plan as it applied to the WR, namely the eradication of all MAN-engined locomotives from revenue-earning service. The slaughter began with D6307 in March 1971 and ended with the withdrawal of D6338/9 in December, the intervening period having seen all the remaining Class 43s retired as well. That summer had also seen operating responsibility for the Waterloo-Exeter services revert to the Southern Region, which quickly substituted its own Class 33 Type 3 Bo-Bos for the 'Warships', and this more than anything marked the beginning of the end for the D800s. Displaced from many of their remaining passenger turns by the influx of Class 46s from the London Midland and Eastern Regions, and largely confined to freight workings between Plymouth and Bristol, the 'Warship' fleet was being finally run-down. By the end of the year, only nineteen would be left in service. Other victims of the 1971 diesel-hydraulic pogrom were the first 'Hymek' casualties, D7006/81 going in September to be followed in October by D7058-60/6-8/82/3.

Withdrawals continued practically unabated through 1972 despite increasing traffic levels, symptomatic of the WR's determination to complete the phasing-out of diesel-hydraulic traction by September 1973. January 1972 alone saw the withdrawal of some thirty 'Hymeks'. Nevertheless, replacement of mid-range motive power was proceeding neither so smoothly nor so quickly as either the WR or the BRB might have liked, resulting in the reinstatement of a number of stored 'Hymeks' and a stay of execution for the remaining 'Warships'. The only suitable motive power then available for shuttle workings of stone traffic between Merehead, Gatwick and Merstham to supply the M23 and M25 motorway construction projects, several Class 42s, some returned to traffic from store and all in a pretty disreputable condition, were put to work on the service and kept it going until the November of that year when Class 47s were finally made available to replace them. With virtually no work to do, the remaining operating members of the class made sporadic appearances on passenger and freight

demned at the end of March so as to allow the elimination of stocks of Paxman engine spares. Five other 'Warships' would be withdrawn over the next month, namely D840/2/8/58/63, and whilst D842/8 were quickly reinstated a further fifteen or so locomotives (mainly of Class 43) remained in store at Old Oak Common, Newton Abbot and Laira.

The choice of Class 43 to bear the brunt of these early withdrawals was by no means illogical. For some years, the MAN/Voith machines had been cursed with inordinately high failure rates that the WR seemed unable to assuage. As

workings until their final withdrawal in December 1972. On New Year's Eve of that year, some ninety-six diesel-hydraulics remained on the Western Region's stock books; the seventy-four Class 52 'Westerns' supplemented by twenty-two 'Hymeks' in various states of repair. Nine calendar months were left in which to replace them, but the entire conversion scheme was by now badly adrift of schedule.

For the surviving Class 35 'Hymeks', life went on much as normal, though with long periods spent out of traffic as BR directives instructing depot staff to carry out no more than minimum maintenance began to bite. With diesel-electrics in South Wales, Devon and Cornwall dominating all but the long-haul services in those areas, the Thames Valley became the last stronghold of the 'Hymeks', with occasional forays as far as Birmingham, Hereford and Weymouth. More usually, their lot consisted of the lighter stone workings to and from the Somerset quarries, mixed freight, parcels and empty stock duties between Bristol and London, and trip freights between the various marshalling yards around London itself. Allocations were kept both at Bath Road and Old Oak Common but maintenance, when it was given, was largely carried out at Old Oak Common. As the months passed, 'Hymek' workings off the WR became increasingly less frequent, possibly due to fear of breakdown, and by the middle of 1973 they were becoming an uncommon sight west of Swindon, Bristol's last Class 35s having gone in May. The 'Westerns', still intact as a class at this point, had all been allocated to Plymouth Laira in order to ease the maintenance situation, the large South Wales contingent having been transferred to Devon in 1971. At last free of the protracted teething troubles of their formative years, the D1000s were now putting up some very fine performances indeed on the WR's most demanding duties, especially after the dual-braking programme enabled them to work the new Mark 2 coaching stock. Though increasingly assigned to heavy stone and tanker trains, the Class 52s were still well able to take a heavily laden express and run it to time, and now with the knowledge that mechanical failure was a much less likely possibility than it had been in the dark days of the mid-1960s.

Sadly, this was not sufficient to imbue the type with a charmed status, and it would be the lot of several to be withdrawn after sustaining relatively minor damage, the cost of rectifying which could not be justified in view of the locomotives' limited future. Despite this, the first two 'Westerns' to be written-off the stock books were the subject of BR's 'Planned Withdrawal' policy, both D1019 *Western Challenger* and D1032 *Western Marksman* being condemned at Laira on 6 May 1973. D1019, found wanting a replacement engine, was one of four 'Westerns' not to have been included in the dual-braking programme and, given the operational restrictions imposed by vacuum-only train braking, was an obvious candidate for early withdrawal; within three months, the other three unmodified locomotives would also be taken out of service. More surprising was the decision to withdraw the dual-fitted D1032 upon failing a routine examination but, over the next few months, both locomotives would be stripped of most reusable com-

Top: The last months of the Class 35s saw them deployed mainly on light duties. On 8 March 1975, eight days before withdrawal, No.7018 passes West Ealing with a down permanent way train. *(Kevin Lane)*

Middle: On 9 April 1974, various remnants of No.1020 stand in front of the stripped-out bodyshell of No.1002 in the scrap lines at Swindon Works. No.1020 was one of the few Class 52s to be omitted from the dual-braking programme, and thus became a candidate for early withdrawal. *(B.J. Nicolle)*

Bottom: 17 March 1975, and an unidentified 'Hymek' meets its end at Swindon. Already shorn of bogies, power equipment and both cabs, the sorry relic is scant hours away from complete oblivion. *(Graham Scott-Lowe)*

ponents whilst at Laira then, after a period of storage at Bristol St Philip's Marsh, hauled back to Swindon for final disposal. D7000, the pioneer 'Hymek' succumbed to an electrical fire in July and several other dual-braked 'Westerns' were condemned whilst awaiting repair, but as the year wore on it became obvious that there was little hope of meeting the scheduled withdrawal date for WR diesel-hydraulic traction, despite the official 'Hymek Swansong' railtour organised by BR on 22 September. Indeed, at the end of that month there were still nine Class 35s and sixty-six Class 52s in regular service whilst the last diesel-hydraulic to be given a heavy overhaul by BR, D1023 *Western Fusilier* had just been released from Swindon. This, of course, requires a certain amount of explanation.

The replacement of the WR diesel-hydraulics had been delayed by the reluctance of other regions to forego suitable diesel-electrics, but under ordinary circumstances it would have been possible to have made good this delay by the end of 1973. The superceding of the 'Westerns' relied upon the importation of fifty English Electric Class 50 Co-Cos of 2700bhp from the London Midland Region. These locomotives, ordered in 1967 to speed-up services on the non-electrified portion of the Euston-Glasgow mainline by working as 5400bhp multiple-units, had been displaced from their original employment by the completion of the West Coast electrification and the intention was to transfer them to the WR to replace the Class 52s. Poor locomotive availabilities across the board resulted in the Class 50s being needed on the LMR for longer than envisaged and by the end of 1973 only three (D400-2) were on the WR, operating out of Bristol Bath Road. Transfer of the rest would be a slow process and with generally low levels of availability precluding further reductions in fleet strength, the WR had to halt the withdrawals both of 'Westerns' and of the few remaining 'Hymeks' except where absolutely necessary.

By the end of January 1974 another Class 50 had arrived on the WR and two Class 52s condemned, D1002 and D1007. *Western Talisman* was the locomotive involved in the high-speed derailment of the 17.18 Paddington-Oxford express at West Ealing on 19 December 1973, caused by an unsecured battery-box door on the locomotive itself. D1007 ended up on its side and although damage was not particularly severe in absolute terms, the locomotive was quickly pronounced as being beyond economic repair; its service record over the preceding few weeks had hardly been a dis-

Above: Months from withdrawal, D1009 *Western Invader* heads an express away from Exeter St Davids, passing over the level crossing and under the distinctive Exeter Middle signal box on its way to London on 13 August 1976. *(David Birt)*

Below: The final replacement of diesel-hydraulic traction on the WR relied upon the transfer from the London Midland Region of the fifty Class 50 diesel-electrics. An unidentified member of the class pauses in Taunton station with a westbound train on 6 September 1976, being overtaken by No.1010 *Western Campaigner* at the head of a down express. *(J.C. Hillmer)*

tinguished one and in these circumstances, major repairs of any kind were simply beyond consideration. To compensate for the loss of D1007, D1022 *Western Sentinel* was retrieved from storage at St Philip's Marsh, repaired at Laira and put back into traffic. The WR's careful housekeeping continued in February with the arrival of another Class 50, No.411, allowing the withdrawal of an accident-damaged D1000 *Western Enterprise*. Four more Class 50s arrived in March, and by May some thirty-five were in stock, suffi-

cient to put a new timetable of accelerated schedules into operation. The big diesel-electrics were an immediate improvement over a 'Western' insofar as they had a higher line speed and electric train-heating, meaning that they could operate the air-conditioning plants on the latest Mark 2d coaching stock. However, as with the locomotives they were intended to replace, Class 50 performance standards frequently left much to be desired, with availability levels already well below the predicted 11,000 miles per casualty and soon to drop even further as sustained high-speed running began to produce an outbreak of traction motor failures. In good form the Class 50 was a fine locomotive and a match for the 'Western', but since so few actually were in fine form, the WR had no choice but to retain the earlier locomotives, many in a state more befitting the end of steam than the modern railway which BR was so desperate to promote. By this time, much maintenance was being done simply by stripping the hulks of withdrawn locomotives for serviceable parts and, as their fellows were called to Swindon for final dismantling, the last remaining Class 35s began to wane, the final trio consisting of D7017/8/29 being withdrawn from Old Oak Common in March 1975. Class 52 ranks continued to decline and maintenance standards declined with them, the high levels of commitment shown by maintenance staff not always being equal to the profound scarcity of some replacement parts, and more than one ailing 'Western' would reach its destination with only one engine serviceable. For this reason, the decision was taken in 1975 to restrict the type to freight duties only, encouraged by the fact that worsening service problems had led to several locomotives having their train-heating boilers declared unfit for use and subsequently isolated. In practice, such was the lack of motive power that a good, serviceable locomotive could not be refused for a steam-heat passenger duty just because it was a Class 52; this is not to say that a considerable degree of pride in the type did not play its part. Despite this, an undeniable sign of the times was the Swindon Works Open

Day of 13 September 1975, when BR extended to visitors the invitation to 'Scrap your own Western'. The centre of attraction were withdrawn Class 52s D1003/6/31/5/50 which were parked outside the works buildings for souvenir hunters to pillage for whatever took their fancy. A 'supporting cast' of two 'Hymeks', D7000/55 also featured in this rather bizarre spectacle. All seven participants were little more than hulks, already having been stripped of virtually all reuseable components but whilst the gesture was undoubtedly appreciated in some quarters, many BR and BREL staff considered the entire episode to constitute a serious lapse of good taste. Certainly, the effect was to advertise the destruction of these still modern locomotives, which did little to enhance BR's lacklustre public image.

Such was the uncertainty over the motive power situation that, on more than one occasion, the withdrawal of the entire 'Western' fleet was announced, only to be rescinded a

short while later, but the realisation that the end could not be far away came with the arrival on the WR of the final Class 50, No.50 029 in February 1976, and was confirmed later that year by the termination of Swindon's overhaul programme for Class 52 spares. Despite this severance of a vital lifeline, the period as a whole was characterised by a number of elaborate railtours involving the type, several of them outside WR territory. Considering its enthusiasm to rid the system of diesel-hydraulics, BR was most accomodating in this regard and the crowning glory was surely the 'Western Talisman' tour of 20 November 1976, when the Western Locomotive Association took D1023 *Western Fusilier* from King's Cross to York and back, all this in the heart of 'Deltic' country! Although Class 52s had previously worked the occasional freight onto Eastern Region metals, by late 1976 the ER had enforced the G39 ruling concerning locomotive visibility and so D1023 became the only one of its kind to carry the headcode box marker lights in BR service.

Seven 'Westerns', D1010/3/22/3/41/8/58 were still in ser-

vice on New Year's Day 1977, but by the end of January both D1022 and D1058 had succumbed, *Western Sentinel* the victim of derailment damage and *Western Nobleman* with a fire-damaged electrical system. D1041 *Western Prince* lasted until 23 February when a dynastarter failed, leaving D1010/3/23/48 in traffic until the final withdrawal of the type on 26 February 1977. On the final day of service, BR deployed all four on the commemorative 'Western Tribute' railtour from Paddington to Swansea via Swindon, thence to Bristol and as far west as Plymouth, returning to Paddington via the Berks & Hants line. D1023 and D1013 were allocated to work the train throughout, whilst D1010 and D1048 stood by first at Bath Road, then at Laira against the eventuality of one of the train locomotives failing. In the event neither of the reserve locomotives was needed and D1023 would have the honour of heading the WR's last 'Western'-hauled train into Paddington. It was the end of the 'Westerns', the end of the WR's 1955 vision of the future and for many, the end of an entire era.

Chapter 13

EXPERIENCE ABROAD

HAVING examined the reasons behind the introduction of diesel-hydraulic traction on the Western Region, the locomotives themselves and the eventual decision by the British Railways Board to withdraw them from service as quickly as possible, it remains to draw some kind of conclusion about the entire episode. To assist objectivity in this regard, it is profitable to make a comparative study of experience with diesel-hydraulic traction on a number of other systems. Of these, one in particular is of special importance, namely the career on the Deutsche Bundesbahn of the V200-class locomotives, the progenitors of the WR's own diesel-hydraulics.

In the immediate post-war years Germany's railway system was in a very battered state indeed, having been subjected to the triple ravages of Allied bombing, lack of maintenance and political division. Furthermore, many of the remaining serviceable locomotives had been commandeered by the victors for use in the former occupied territories, especially those in the Soviet zone. Through the winter of 1945/6 the railways were afflicted by a desperate shortage of motive power that was only partially assuaged by the loan of British and American military locomotives to the civilian authorities, and which persisted through into early 1947. The need for a thorough reorganisation became paramount as relations between the Russians and the rest of the former allies continued to deteriorate and restrictions on the movement of people and goods in and out of the Soviet zone steadily multiplied. In 1948 the Allied sectors of Germany became the new German Federal Republic and those parts of the old Deutsche Reichsbahn that lay within the Federal Republic's territory became the state-owned Deutsche Bundesbahn. In the Soviet sector, the old Reichsbahn continued under military control and in due course became the state railway system of the communist-controlled German Democratic Republic. In logistical terms, this split a single, homogeneous network based around an east-west axis into two separate systems suffering from a dearth of heavy-duty mainlines with which to carry the now largely north-south traffic. It was a situation that was to prevail for over forty years, and formed a difficult background against which to attempt wholesale reconstruction.

Rather than merely putting the old system to rights, the DB elected from the start to to direct renovation work into creating a modern railway and, like BR in 1955, opted for a gradual replacement of steam by diesel and electric motive power. As well as refining the steam locomotive to a very high level, the prewar Reichsbahn had also carried out a number of electrification projects and this form of traction was perhaps more greatly entrenched in Germany than in any other European country. It was therefore entirely natural that widespread mainline electrification should become the principal objective of the DB's planners, though it was evident from the outset that the attainment of this goal would take some considerable while. In order to bridge the gap between the new electric services and those still worked by steam, it was therefore decided to institute a partial dieselisation scheme at the same time. Some of the impetus for this decision undoubtedly derived from contemporary developments both in the United States and elsewhere, but the concept of the diesel locomotive was by no means alien to German railway engineers and operators.

Before the war, Germany had been the centre of much pioneering work in the development of diesel traction, resulting in the production of some of the first practical mainline diesels. Although a few were operated domestically, notably a 1-C-1 diesel-hydraulic built by Krauss-Maffei which covered some 82,000 miles in traffic between 1934 and 1952, most German-built diesel locomotives of this era were exported. Typical of these was a 4400bhp diesel-electric of the articulated 2-Do-1+1-Do-2 format built by Henschel for the Romanian State Railways in 1937 which, given the fact that it predated General Motors' celebrated FT set No.103 by some two years, must surely rank as the world's first true self-contained multi-purpose mainline diesel. Although further developments were largely halted upon the outbreak of war, this particular machine did inspire a quartet of articulated Do+Do heavy freight locomotives equipped with a pair of 940bhp MAN diesels and Siemens-Schuckert electrical gear, numbered D311 01-4 and built by Krupp in 1941/2. Utilised mainly on munitions trains by the Wehrmacht, D311 02-4 survived the war to be taken into stock as the DB's first large diesels, were renumbered V188 001-3 and continued in freight traffic for many years, making an important contribution to postwar reconstruction. The last to go was V188 002 in the summer of 1972, still in largely original condition though having lost its MAN engines in favour of Maybach units during the late 1950s.

Despite the worthy performance of the V188s, the heavy diesel-electric was not to be the direction chosen by the DB for its modernisation. The years of conflict had seen a huge amount of experience gained in the operation of vehicles using high-speed engines and non-electric transmissions, and the available technology seemed to offer considerable potential for a wide variety of high-power applications. In view of this, the DB's mechanical engineering department in Munich decided that there were important advantages to be gained in opting for lightweight diesel-hydraulics using high-speed engines connected to the wheels via torque converters and mechanical drivelines. Ultimately responsible for this change of direction was Kurt Lampe, whose management of diesel development for the DB between 1948 and 1954 would first bear fruit in the form of the V80, a prototype 800bhp B-B centre-cab locomotive. A joint project between the DB, Krauss-Maffei and Maschinenbau AG Kiel, development of the V80 was simplified by the extensive use of components intended for use in the DB's first postwar diesel railcars. Ten of these lightweight (64-ton) locomotives would be built for light passenger and freight traffic and would allow both the DB and the German locomotive construction industry to gain valuable experience in the field of modern diesel-hydraulic traction. With information gained from this and other sources, Lampe and his Bundesbahn Zentralamt were able to formulate plans for a complete range of mainline diesel locomotives and inter-city DMUs, all based around a common range of interchangeable components. Part of this was a requirement for five prototype 2000bhp B-B diesel-hydraulics, able to operate

anything from a stopping goods train to an east-west express, but principally intended to facilitate the acceleration of the most important passenger services prior to eventual electrification. The DB's chosen classification for the design was V200.

These five locomotives, V200 001-5, were built by the Krauss-Maffei organisation and put into DB traffic in March 1954, working in the Frankfurt am Main area. Although needing to conform to the basic specifications laid down by the DB, most of the design work was left in the hands of K-M which, being allowed by the loading gauge to place both engines and transmissions over the bogies, opted for the characteristic stressed-skin structure. Various parts were subcontracted by K-M to other concerns, principally Henschel, Jung, Krupp, MF Esslingen and Maschinenbau AG Kiel. As with the V80 series, use of a standardised range of mechanical components was envisaged, with engines from Maybach, MAN and Daimler-Benz, transmissions from Maybach and J.M. Voith, cooling equipment from Kuhlerfabrik Behr, cardan shafts from Gelenkwellenbau, and train-heating boilers from MAN, Hagenuk and Körting. In actual fact, all five prototypes were initially equipped with Daimler-Benz or Maybach engines and Maybach-Mekydro transmissions.

After proving the diesel's conclusive superiority in tests against a pair of Class 01 Pacifics on regular passenger trains from Frankfurt to Bebra, Würzburg, Heidelberg and Nuremberg, the five V200s were put to work on a variety of mainline traffic in the Frankfurt area, accumulating impres-

Above: Despite the widespread use of electric transmission in the 1930s, the West German railways chose hydraulic transmission for their first high-power diesels of the post-war period. V200 001 is seen when new in March 1954; when the locomotive was first built, it lacked the stainless steel embellishers, but these were added in time for its entry into service. *(Krauss-Maffei)*

sive mileages in the process. By the close of 1954 an average of 10,000 miles per locomotive per month was being obtained and by the end of 1955, annual mileages for the quintet stood at above 620,000 miles, representing a monthly increase over the previous year of some eleven percent. 1956 saw a further increase with a total of 765,000 miles being amassed that year. Delighted with the results, the DB placed orders for a further eighty-one V200s, delivery commencing that September. V200 006-25 were built under licence by Maschinenbau AG Kiel and delivered between September 1956 and November 1957, whilst V200 026-86 came from Krauss-Maffei between September 1956 and August 1959. Costs to the DB represented about £88,000 per locomotive. As their numbers increased, the V200s were rostered on a regular basis for the fastest and heaviest of those passenger services not yet electrified and by the winter of 1957/8 were handling some of the DB's most prestigious express trains, such as the 'Rheingold', the 'Gambrinus' and the 'Blauer Enzian'.

As could be expected, the production machines dis-

Top: The production series of V200s under construction inside Krauss-Maffei's München-Allach works. It is instructive to compare this with the earlier illustration of D800s being built at Swindon. *(Krauss-Maffei)*

Bottom: V200 026 leaves the Krauss-Maffei erecting shop on 10 September 1956. The first of a series equipped when new with Daimler-Benz engines and Voith transmissions, the locomotive also displays other differences from the initial batch, especially around the front end. *(Krauss-Maffei)*

played slight differences from their pre-production sisters, although many were cosmetic in nature. The major mechanical differences were the inclusion of Behr cooling units with hydrostatic fans in place of the previous arrangement where the fans were driven by electric motors working through Voith viscous couplings. Also driven from the same source was a hydrostatic air pump replacing the electric compressors of the initial batch. Some production locomotives retained the original design of Voith transmission unit but eventually specifications were amended to include the revised LT306r which improved standardisation between the V200s and the DB's various inter-city DMU types. The three forms of power unit used, although of differing designs and capacities, all produced roughly similar outputs and were made interchangeable through the use of common connections and mountings. The Maybach MD650 was the same unit used on the BR D800s and should need no introduction, save to say that in later years when Maybach and Daimler-Benz merged their diesel engine interests under the MTU umbrella, the design was reclassified as the 12V538TA10. The MAN L12V18/21B unit was also that used by BR and should be similarly familiar; in fact, it was found unreliable by the DB and withdrawn from general service some years before the demise of the V200 type. Its inclusion in the V200 specification was largely a result of the earlier 'A' version being used in various inter-city multiple-unit sets, but the new pairing proved to be an unhappy one; as on BR problems were experienced with cylinder heads, valves and valve seats and eventually with the turbochargers as well, possibly from carbonisation. With only five locomotives equipped with MAN engines from new, the curtailment of the type's use in the V200 fleet was covered by spare engines of other makes.

Not used in any of the WR locomotives was the third variety of engines fitted to the V200, the Daimler-Benz MB820Bb. Sometimes referred to as a Mercedes-Benz in line with the manufacturer's cars and trucks, the MB820Bb was a twelve-cylinder vee-formation unit of conventional construction, with a 45° included angle between cylinder banks. A one-piece crankcase was utilised, of cast aluminium in the earliest examples but soon changed to cast iron after problems were experienced with stress cracks. The six-throw forged steel crankshaft was supported by lead-indium plain bearings and featured a Holset viscous damper at its free end to counter torsional vibrations. Connecting rods were of fork-and blade design, as with the Maybach engines, but coupled to pistons which, although of forged light-alloy construction with hardened steel gudgeon pins, lacked any specific oil cooling. In railway traction applications, where full-load conditions were not continuous, Daimler-Benz engineers considered that the cooling effect of the fuel charge would, along with oil splash from the lower cylinder area, keep piston temperatures within permissible limits. Cylinders were of 175mm bore and 205mm stroke, giving a total swept volume of 59.16 litres. A single camshaft running between the cylinder liners and the outer wall of each cylinder bank drove two inlet and two exhaust valves in each of the separate cast iron cylinder heads via pushrods and rockers. This distinctive arrangement reduced valve gear inertia loadings compared with the central block-mounted camshaft of the MAN design, yet was simpler to maintain than the efficient but complex overhead-cam Maybach units. Fuel injection was by a Bosch system with an injection pump for each cylinder bank, complemented by a Brown-Boveri VTR250 turbocharger. Power output was directly comparable with the MAN engine, 1100bhp at 1500rpm, but the Daimler-Benz was substantially lighter than either MAN or Maybach competitors, with a dry weight of just under 8000lbs. In later years, MTU nomenclature referred to the unit as the 12V493TZ10.

All V200s were finished in the same livery of Tuscan Red with black skirting and charcoal-grey cantrails and roof, sweeping down to a vee-shape on the nose end. Colours were separated by polished metal embellishers whilst the locomotives' ownership was proclaimed by raised stainless steel 'DEUTSCHE BUNDESBAHN' lettering on the bodysides, which in more recent years gave way to a transfer of the DB logo. The type was also twice reclassified, first as V200.0 in 1960 and then as Class 220 in 1969, the latter involving renumbering in the series 220 001-86. Lastly, in the late 1970s, some would lose their red and grey livery in favour of the blue and beige Trans-Europ Express colours.

Organisation of the DB during the 1950s focussed upon a number of Bahndienstelle (BDs) or railway departments, each responsible for the operation of a finite area of the DB and thus similar to BR's regions. Within these BDs were a number of Bahnbetriebswerk (Bws) or mainline motive power depots handling servicing, routine maintenance and component exchanges, whilst overhauls, accident repairs and any structural work were handled by a main workshop (Ausbesserungswerk or Aw). The first five locomotives were initially allocated to BD Frankfurt/Main based at Bw Frankfurt Griesheim, and in due course were joined by V200 010/1/3-6/26-8/32/3/37-9/52/6/7/60/1. In 1959 the area's allocation of V200s was achieving mileages of near to 500 miles a day on a 9-day diagram encompassing trains to Bamberg, Bebra, Fulda, Hannover, Heidelberg, Heilbronn, Kassel, Munich, Marktbreit and Würzburg. Bahndienstelle Essen was allocated V200 008,21-3,029,034-6,40-1,58/9/66-84. Based at Bw Hamm, the locomotives took turns on services to Braunschweig, Bremen, Cologne, Dortmund, Hamburg, Helmstedt (the principal rail crossing between East and West Germany), Hildesheim and Oberhausen as well as services to and from Amsterdam as far as Arnhem, which saw each locomotive running an average distance of 600 miles a day. BD Hamburg took V200 006/7/12/17-20/4/5/42-51 working out of Hamburg Altona depot on trains to Eidelstedt, Flensburg, Kiel, Langenfelde, Osnabrück and Westerland, as well as to Odenzaal in the Netherlands, a rota that spread about 5500 miles of work over a twelve-day period. In 1960, a survey of DB motive power showed that the mileages being amassed by V200s at this depot were only exceeded by those of Bw Heidelberg's E10 electrics and Bw Dortmund's VT08 DMUs. BD Karlsruhe was allocated V200 030/1/53-5/62-5/85-6 working out of Bw Villingen, taking in that part of the Black Forest route between Hornburg and Sommerau which climbs some 1400 feet in 15½ miles at an average grade of 1:55. With almost continuous curvature and about half its distance in tunnels, this provided a stern everyday test of the V200s' capabilities.

BD Nuremburg initially took V200 009 at Bw Würzburg but after only a fortnight's service from that depot a change in motive power policy saw it relocated to BD Essen's allocation at Bw Hamm. This was to be the first of many changes in allocation for the V200s, a gradual shift northwards taking place over the years. Bw Würzburg became home to V200s once again in 1962, and between then and 1975 maintained an allocation of about a dozen for the north-south services between Gmünden and Hamburg whilst the route was being electrified. The replacement of steam traction during the course of electrification works provided an important source of employment for V200s in several areas of Germany, an example being the allocation to BD Frankfurt/Main at Bw Limburg/Lahn of eight V200s between 1965 and 1967. For the same reason, BD Mainz maintained a small stud at Bw Kaiserslautern between 1967 and 1973 and BD Hannover a much larger one in that city until 1975. Under the same BD, Bw Braunschweig played host to some twenty locomotives for a year before they were transferred en masse to in May 1976 to Bw Oldenburg. This implemented an earlier decision to concentrate older mainline diesels at one or two depots in order to simplify maintenance, Oldenburg's stud working trains to Bielefeld,

Above: The Daimler-Benz MB820 engine represented an interim stage between the competing MAN and Maybach units in terms of sophistication and power output, but with a dry weight less than either. More reliable than the MAN and cheaper to purchase and maintain than the complex Maybachs, the engines would find considerable favour with the DB, especially for subsequent, more powerful locomotives. *(MTU)*

Below: Much of the V200s' most important work during the 1960s would be in accelerating passenger services in preparation for full electrification. On 4 April 1965, the pylons have already been installed in readiness for the overhead wires at Maubach on the Stuttgart-Nuremburg line as V200 038, one of twenty then allocated to BD Karlsruhe and working out of Bw Villingen, passes with a train for Backnang. *(Nigel Kendall)*

Bremen, Bremerhaven, Cloppenburg, Cuxhaven, Detmold, Emden, Geestemunde, Norddeich Mole, Quackenbruck, Rheine and Wilhelmshaven, amounting to nearly 4000 miles over a fifteen-day period. Bw Lübeck (BD Hamburg) also received an augmented allocation of V200s at this time, having maintained a number of the type since 1972 for trains to Ahrensburg, Bad Oldesloe, Bremerhaven, Buxtehude, Cuxhaven, Hamburg, Kiel and Stade as well as local services around Lübeck itself. Such duties would cover around 3800 miles over a thirteen-day period and many locomotives were therefore outstationed at various locations, returning to Lübeck at weekends for servicing.

Above: After successful demonstrations of the six-axle ML2200 in 1957, the Yugoslav State Railways placed an order for three very similar locomotives. Brand-new, D66 002 *Kozara* and D66 003 *Sutjeska* await dispatch to their new owner in May 1957. *(Krauss-Maffei)*

Below: As the prospect of sales for further 2200bhp C-C locomotives declined, Krauss-Maffei rebuilt the redundant ML2200 as an experimental 3000bhp unit. Renamed ML3000, the renewed locomotive's impressive performance on test inspired several high-power diesel-hydraulic designs, not least BR's 'Westerns'. *(Krauss-Maffei)*

Availability at this or any other time was significantly better for the V200s than it ever was for the WR's hydraulics. At the same time as the WR was congratulating itself over the average 95,000 miles per annum returned by its Maybach/ Mekydro D800s, the annual mileage totals of most V200s were hovering around the 125,000-mile mark. This was no short-term phenomenon; by the time of their withdrawal, at least twenty-three examples of the class had

accumulated more than 2,500,000 miles in total, nearly doubling the WR's best record. The Germans did have the advantage in this regard of longer distances run between locomotive changes, as well as very intensive services in the more populous areas, but there can be little question that their locomotives were the more reliable. Between 1957 and 1964, availability figures for the V200 type as a whole fluctuated between 87% and 91%, the locomotives requiring depot attention on average once every two months to rectify unsatisfactory or non-functioning equipment. Works attention was given about once a year although, late in their careers, the DB embarked on a policy of giving the V200s regular scheduled maintenance at Aw Bremen in order both to concentrate facilities and to resolve any problems in the ageing machinery before they could reach disruptive proportions.

Although the German locomotives accumulated higher mileages than their British counterparts, they did have the advantage of rarely being subjected to loadings above 75-80% of their intended capacity, as opposed to the prolonged periods at full throttle demanded from the WR's hydraulics. Thus could be explained some of the apparent deficiencies in equipment which had not caused problems in DB service, but most of the WR's problems were wholly due to low standards, both of build quality and, from time to time, maintenance as well. In this respect, the vastly better performance figures obtained from the mechanical components in the German locomotives compared with their British counterparts told their own story. Many transmissions were returning 300-450,000 miles between intermediate overhauls, and even then needed only replacement of various bearings, seals and other minor parts. Major overhauls were carried out at about 750,000 miles and although necessarily more extensive, were still largely restricted to bearings, seals and (on Mekydros) clutch parts. Gearwheels (which were interchangeable between transmissions of the same type) and torque converters usually transcended the overhaul process, many lasting the full twenty-year lives of the transmissions themselves. Engine repair cycles were largely determined by German law which required an intermediate overhaul every three years and a main overhaul every five. On this basis, Maybach MD650 units were giving 20-30,000 hours of service between main overhauls, as did the Friedrichshafen-built engines fitted to BR's first D800s. Crucially, there were far fewer failures between overhauls than on the British licensee-made units, and far fewer major components such as cylinder heads and connecting rods requiring total replacement.

Quite a substantial interest was shown in the V200 design from new by potential export customers. Impressed with steam traction acquired from Germany during and after World War II, officials of the Turkish State Railways (TCDD) expressed an interest in the new B-B. Aware of the possible benefits, K-M arranged for V200 005 to leave Munich in April 1955 bound for Turkey, travelling via Austria, Yugoslavia and Greece. Crossing the Bosphorous at Istanbul by ferry, V200 005 then embarked on an 1800-mile tour of duty in Turkey, working as far as Ankara on the 'Taurus Express'. After arriving at Adana in the southern tip of Turkey via a number of other passenger workings, none of which were less than 400 tons tare, V200 005 exchanged its passenger consists for a goods train, arriving back at Ankara on 1 May. Resuming command of the 'Taurus Express' for the journey back to Istanbul, the locomotive recrossed the Bosphorous and headed for Salonika in Greece, departing there with a 500-ton goods train on 8 May. Arriving in Athens, V200 005 worked a passenger train to Oinay and back, then returned to Salonika on another goods duty. Heading north into Yugoslavia, the hydraulic worked the 530-ton 'Orient Express' from Nis to Beograd, normally the responsibility of two steam locomotives, continuing to Zagreb with an ordinary express train and thence to Ljubljana at the head of the 'Orient-Simplon Express'. Returning through Austria, V200 005 reached Munich on 15 May and re-entered DB service at Frankfurt on 17 May! A tremendous amount of interest and goodwill was generated but, disappointingly for Krauss-Maffei, no firm orders for further V200s at that time.

The trip was by no means a failure, however, having provided useful data on the locomotive's performance in a variety of different climates and conditions. V200 005's performance in Yugoslavia also produced a request in 1956 from that country's state railway system, the JZ, for details

Above: When more powerful locomotives were required at home, Krauss-Maffei adapted the existing V200 design to accomodate Daimler-Benz MB835 engines and Mekydro K184 transmissions, resulting in the 2700bhp V200.1 type. At the head of a train bound for Nuremburg on a sweltering 4 July 1969, No.221 122 accelerates away from Backnang, fifteen miles or so to the east of Stuttgart. *(Nigel Kendall)*

Below: Section and plan views of the DB V200.1 locomotives, generally similar to the V200.0 except in detail. Components are numbered thus: 1, Daimler-Benz MB835 diesel engine; 2, twin-fan Behr cooler group; 3, main fuel tank; 4, fuel gravity tank; 5, Mekydro K184 transmission unit; 6, Maybach C34 axledrive; 7, cardan shaft; 8, air pump; 9, dynastarter; 10 & 11, control cabinets; 12, flange oiling apparatus; 13, driver's desk; 14, handbrake wheel; 15, air compressor; 16, induction coil; 17, train heating boiler; 18, water tank; 19, boiler fuel tank; 20, equipment cabinet; 21, crew locker; 22, driver's seat; 23, heating & demisting system; 24, audible warning system; 25, tool cupboard; 26, apparatus cupboard. *(Krauss-Maffei)*

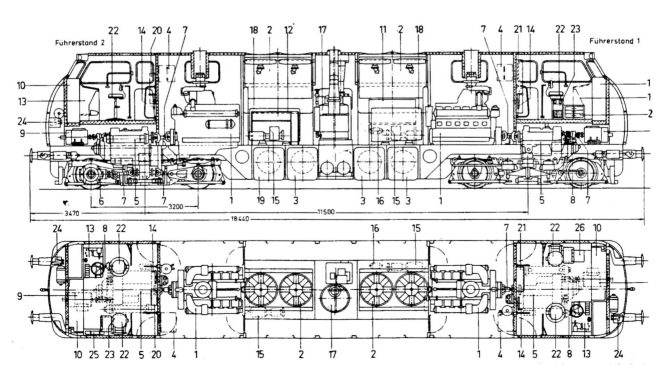

*Above:*The larger engines and transmissions used in the V200.1 design necessitated that the cabs be moved further apart, in turn forcing the use of a slightly squatter profile for the nose ends. This is readily apparent on No.221 145, observed on an eastbound working between Backnang and Oppenweiler on 7 July 1969, as is the replacement of engine room windows by additional radiator grilles. *(Nigel Kendall)*

regarding the feasibility of a V200-type locomotive with a 16-ton axleload to satisfy Yugoslavia's large number of lightly-constructed routes. Even with the use of lightweight construction, such parameters could only be respected through the use of load-spreading three-axle bogies and so, in 1957, K-M built a C-C demonstrator structurally and technically similar to the V200 but for the use of six-wheel bogies and an overall length greater by some six feet. Although the proven Maybach MD650 engines and Mekydro K104 transmissions were retained, a new driveline to the bogies was necessary using three Maybach C33v spur-and-bevel axledrives on each bogie rather than the pair of C32 units on the normal V200 design. The bogies themselves, although following the established K-M principles, were revised in detail, the centre axle in its vertical sliding journals being joined by new radius arms for the inner and outer axles, operating on axle extensions outside the wheelsets rather than between them as before. In consideration of this the bogie frame was also wider, which allowed better access to the final drive components. Some 96 tons in weight in full working order, the locomotive was designated ML2200 (a figure derived from its power rating) and sent to Yugoslavia for evaluation. After trials both there and on the 1:36 grades of the Semmering Pass between Munich and Vienna, the Yugoslavs placed an order for three similar locomotives which were built and delivered in May 1957, bearing the JZ numbers and names D66-001 *Dinara*, D66-002 *Kozara* and D66-003 *Sutjeska*, D66-001 first having been exhibited at the German Industry Fair at Hannover. Compared with the parent ML2200, the principal revisions concerned the provision of an uprated cooling system, and a new type of bogie which reverted to the narrow frames and inside axlebearings of the original V200 design. There were, however, significant alterations to the secondary suspension arrangements though the basic layout was retained, along with the patent K-M swivelling gear, whilst given the generally low line speeds then prevailing in the region, revised final-drive ratios were fitted to give a higher tractive effort at the expense of reduced maximum speed. The Yugoslavs urgently wanted the locomotives in order to be able to speed-up passenger services and although a less than ideal maintenance situation on the JZ at first delayed this, the locomotives eventually settled down to give good service.

The delivery of these locomotives left the ML2200 demonstrator without any real function and after several abortive attempts to sell more of the type, K-M decided to rebuild it as a prototype high-power locomotive as detailed in Chapter 9. The core of the work involved the installation of new Maybach MD655 engines and Mekydro K184 transmissions, but the opportunity was also taken to provide uprated or refined auxiliary equipment where desirable, including new bogies of the latest type. Re-emerging in 1958 the new 3000bhp C-C, renamed ML3000, was demon-

strated to the Austrian State Railway or Österreicher Bundesbahn (ÖBB), the Deutsche Bundesbahn and a party of BTC officials visiting Germany at the time. Serving its purpose well, it inspired high-power K-M-type locomotives both on the DB and on BR, the latter emerging as the D1000 'Western' C-Cs. ML3000 was leased and ultimately sold to the DB, becoming first V300 001 and subsequently 230 001, based at Bw Braunschweig.

The DB locomotive inspired by ML3000 differed from the WR's 'Western' in that it reverted to the basic bodyshell and B-B wheel arrangement of the V200, the lower axleloading and improved adhesion conferred by the C-C layout being of less concern under DB conditions. The principal revisions concerned the power train, the MD655 engines being replaced by twin Daimler-Benz MB835s developing 1350bhp apiece, working through Mekydro K184 transmissions to a Maybach C34 final drive on each axle. To make best use of this increased power, a revised control system was specified which, although of the same all-electric BBC design as before, had fifteen control notches more closely spaced than the seven employed hitherto; BR of course had by this time opted for the greater mechanical simplicity and stepless control offered by electro-pneumatic designs. The 82-ton locomotives that resulted were termed the V200.1 type, the first examples (from a total order for fifty) being delivered by Krauss-Maffei in 1962. They were immediately put to work on heavy passenger trains on the DB's remaining non-electrified routes, where their spirited performances at the head of ten- and thirteen-coach consists enabled schedules to be recast on a par with those of electrified services. Reclassified 221 in the 1969 scheme, they were inevitably demoted with the arrival of more modern power but nevertheless survived in DB service until the late 1980s, working freight traffic in the northern Ruhr area out of Bw Oberhausen.

As if to prove that ML3000 was by no means its last word upon the subject, K-M's design office was soon working on even larger diesel-hydraulics intended, of all places, for that bastion of diesel-electric power; the United States of America. One of the pioneers of dieselisation in the US, the Southern Pacific Railroad had finally eliminated steam from its system in September 1958 and now sought to exploit the potential operating economy of the diesel by running longer and heavier trains than ever before. At that time, however, the most powerful locomotives offered by domestic builders were 2400bhp diesel-electrics, which did not offer a sufficiently ample margin over SP's current power to be of interest. Furthermore, the company was becoming increasingly disillusioned with the frequent electrical system failures that it was suffering with its own diesel-electrics and, looking enviously at the performance of Union Pacific's gas-turbines but fearing their complexity, sought an alternative to both. Surveying the wares of locomotive builders worldwide, Southern Pacific rapidly concluded that the only locomotives to meet all its operating targets were the latest European high-power diesel-hydraulics. Dispatched on a tour of Europe to study diesel-hydraulics at first hand, SP's Director of Research, Frank Kurz would return to SP's San Francisco headquarters to present an analysis remarkably similar to that of the WR in 1955.

Kurz' reasoning was evidently convincing, for in 1959 Southern Pacific's 77th Annual Report disclosed that three high-power mainline hydraulics had been ordered from Krauss-Maffei for test purposes, with "the expectation that substantial savings in maintenance expenses may be realised as compared with conventional diesel-electric locomotives". In fact, since the development costs for the project had promised to be unacceptably high when applied to only three units, SP had solicited the interest of several other railroads in the region and managed to persuade the neighbouring Denver & Rio Grande Western Railroad to order a further three locomotives of identical design. The intention of the D&RGW was to employ the trio in regular freight use over its mainline between Denver, Colorado, and Salt Lake City, Utah, a spectacular yet arduous route that entailed a 9,000-foot crossing of the Rocky Mountains. Electrification of this line had been discussed more than once, most recently in 1947, but had always been discounted due to the high costs and sheer difficulties involved. By exploiting the proven capabilities of diesel-hydraulics in exerting high tractive efforts at low speeds over extended periods, the D&RGW hoped eventually to be able to dispense with the routine piloting and banking of heavy freights on a 54-mile section of the eastbound line over Soldier Summit and a 50-mile stretch at an average 1:50 on the westbound ascent through the Moffat Tunnel. Such a move would return considerable operating economies, hitherto thought unavailable without the benefit of massive capital works and, as on the SP, the diesel-hydraulic order was intended to enable the latest technology to be evaluated under actual operating conditions.

Once overall build specifications had been agreed between K-M, SP and D&RGW, the matter of design work was largely left to K-M's engineers in consultation with Kurz, who had moved to Munich for the duration of the project. Construction of the six locomotives began during 1960, the builders electing to retain the stressed-skin structural principles of the V200, albeit strengthened and altered in a large number of other respects in order to satisfy US operating standards. K-M had originally urged the use of a centre-cab layout, but the Americans had been unhappy about its ability to conform to visibility requirements and instead mandated a single-ended arrangement with an elevated 'turret' cab situated behind a prominent nose. Although the result bore little visual resemblance to the V200, none of that design's rigidity was lost in the transformation, rig tests of the finished structure showing it to be torsionally stiffer than American diesels built on traditional strength frames. Inside were a pair of Maybach MD870 engines, each developing 2000bhp at 1580rpm, governed by a pneumatic control system with automatic barometric adjustment for the high altitudes of the locomotives' intended operating territory. These drove the wheels through Voith L830rU triple-converter transmissions featuring an integral hydrodynamic brake, the first practical application of this to a mainline locomotive. Although the L830rU was new and relatively untried, both Kurz and SP's Manager of

Above: A particular achievement for Krauss-Maffei was the supply of a quantity of 4000bhp C-C diesel-hydraulics to a pair of North American railroads in the early 1960s. The first six locomotives, exemplified by Southern Pacific No.9000, retained the V200's stressed-skin construction though without any external resemblance to the parent design. *(Author's Collection)*

Engineering & Research, Paul Garin, valued the Voith unit's nearly shock-free qualities throughout the operating range and so favoured it over Maybach's rival Mekydro design, despite the latter's earlier use on several lightweight 'Train X' sets employed on the New York Central and New Haven Railroads. Bogies were of the three-axle outside-frame type used on the original ML2200, albeit with 40"-diameter wheels of the American AAR A-40 design so as to allow the use of tyres standard with those of other SP and D&RGW diesels. Overall length was less than an inch short of 66' with a weight in working order of 144 tons and a predicted continuous tractive effort of 78,000lb at 10.5mph.

The first of these machines, termed ML4000 by K-M and claimed to be the most powerful diesel locomotives in the world, was completed in June 1961 as D&RGW No.4001 and was quickly followed by SP No.9000. After being temporarily equipped with German buffing- and drawgear the SP locomotive was submitted to extensive testing, first in the Munich area and then over the Semmering Pass with a dynamometer car in tow, the latter acting also as a demonstration run for senior SP and D&RGW management. Upon completion, the six hydraulics were coupled together and run under their own power to Bremerhaven, from where they were shipped to the United States, arriving in Houston, Texas on 31 October 1961. Southern Pacific forwarded No.s 4001-3 to their new home on the D&RGW and three days later dispatched its own trio, No.s 9000-2, plus dynamometer car, as motive power on a scheduled westbound freight from Houston to Sacramento, California, where they were allocated to the regular freight pool at SP's Roseville depot. There, the three diesel-hydraulics were subjected to dynamometer tests on regular high-speed freight workings of up to 4,000 tons tare over a wide variety of terrain: south over the Los Angeles Division's mainline through the Tehachapi Mountains and Mojave Desert; north on the Pacific Northwest Route through Klamath Falls to Portland, Oregon; and north-east via the 6,300ft ascent of Donner Pass on the Overland Route to Ogden, Utah. Much useful data was amassed by these means, particularly with regard to the quantification of performance levels. These were quickly established to exceed by far anything then on offer from the domestic industry, both in terms of power:weight ratios and the ability to generate very high levels of tractive effort at low speeds for a sustained period of time. Operating staff were also impressed by the locomotives' stopping ability, the hydro-

Above: Subsequent K-M diesel-hydraulics for the United States were of revised design, intended to favour licensed production within the US itself. Some of the greatest changes concerned the locomotive structure, which was now of roadswitcher format riding upon American-pattern equalised bogies. Southern Pacific No.s 9003/4 await entry to service in February 1964. *(Author's Collection)*

Below: Southern Pacific's final new diesel-hydraulics were a trio of Alco DH-643s of 4300bhp apiece. Constructed around paired groups of slow-running Alco diesels and Voith hydraulic transmissions, each of these monsters measured nearly 76' over coupler knuckles and weighed in excess of 178 tons. A greater contrast to the original V200 concept can hardly be imagined. *(Author's Collection)*

dynamic retarder proving able to exert sustained high braking efforts without the wheelslide problems commonly experienced with rheostatic equivalents.

With this initial testing completed, No.s 9000-2 at first continued to be operated as a set, but in due course were rostered in conjunction with representatives of SP's diesel-electric fleet. They also shared the same facilities for service and routine maintenance, although with the benefit of having this overseen by K-M technical staff for the first twelve months, the expertise of which proved invaluable in dealing with a number of service problems. The most notable of these involved the softly-sprung bogies which, whilst riding well, were found to contribute to excessive body sway over poor quality track. The difficulty was soon traced to SP's habit of staggering rail joints, which encouraged the locomotives to lurch first one way and then the other in rapid succession, and a solution was quickly arrived at by modifying the bogies with additional dampers. More problematic was the need for the frequent use of sanding on steep gradients, which resulted in heavy and uneven wear between pairs of wheels and, eventually, troubles with transmission overrun. Given the mountainous nature of much of SP's territory, the root cause of the problem could not be elimi-

nated and so special attention had to be paid to tyre thickness, entailing an increased need for tyre-turning on these locomotives. Operation at high altitudes also revealed a tendency towards pressure drop within the pneumatic control system, resulting in the closing of the throttles on trailing units, whilst the twin-engine format of the hydraulics engendered some difficulty with the engines ingesting each others' exhaust when working in the confines of the many tunnels and snowsheds that characterised SP's mainlines over the Sierra Nevada and Tehachapi mountains. This phenomenon, sometimes referred to as 'short-cycling', starved the rearmost engines of oxygen and resulted in excessive combustion temperatures, causing rapid valve seat recession and occasional piston failures. Lastly, the steeply-sloping windows of the distinctive turret cabs proved especially vulnerable to water leakage during the winter months, to the detriment of both operating staff and control gear.

Despite this, SP at least was sufficiently happy with initial experience to amplify the experiment, placing orders for an additional eighteen units during 1962. Krauss-Maffei would provide fifteen of these, but to a revised design embodying not only those lessons learnt with the first ML4000s but also features aimed at favouring construction under license in the US should quantity orders ever be placed. The stressed-skin structure was thus abandoned in favour of a roadswitcher layout with heavy cast frames and American equalised bogies, whilst the troublesome pneumatic control system gave way to an all-electric Brown-Boveri system compatible for multiple-working with those of American diesels. Numbered 9003-17, the units would enter service during 1964, as would the remaining portion of SP's second diesel-hydraulic order, a trio of Alco DH-643 C-Cs which allied the Voith hydraulic transmission to conventional slow-running heavyweight diesel engines. Similar in concept to the latest K-M design, each locomotive carried two Alco 251-C vee-twelves of 2150bhp apiece which, like many other components, were shared with Alco's 'Century' range of conventional diesel-electrics. Nevertheless, SP No.s 9018-20 still represented a remarkable departure from convention for a mainstream American diesel builder, indicative of Alco's desperate struggle to secure orders in a market increasingly dominated by General Electric and General Motors.

Although these eighteen locomotives represented the intended limit of Southern Pacific's experiments for the time being, the company would nonetheless go on to gain a further three diesel-hydraulics that year. The Denver & Rio Grande Western Railroad, although impressed with the performance of its K-M ML4000s in heavy freight service over the Rockies, was finding that whatever accrued in the way of savings from increased operating economy was rapidly overtaken by the high costs of maintaining three locomotives sharing virtually nothing in common with the rest of the D&RGW diesel fleet. In addition, there had been occurrences of the same sort of combustion problems suffered on the Southern Pacific units but, unlike that of the SP, D&RGW management was no longer prepared to commit itself to expanding its diesel-hydraulic fleet in order to benefit from the resulting economies of scale. Enquiries having

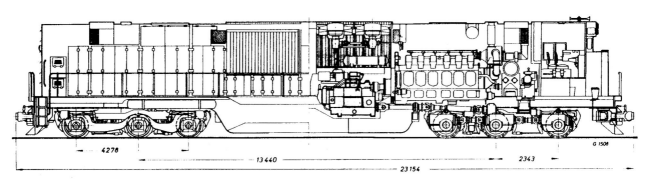

Above: The final variants of the V200 family were the 4000bhp B-B locomotives built for the Spanish RENFE in 1966 and 1967, which represented a synthesis of the V200 and ML4000 designs. No.4001 stands outside Krauss-Maffei's Munich works in November 1966. *(Krauss-Maffei)*

elicited a positive response, the D&RGW units were withdrawn and changed hands to become SP No.s 9021-3, and whilst their D&RGW lettering was soon replaced by SP insignia, they ran for quite some while in their original gold and silver livery before receiving Southern Pacific's grey and red scheme, along with some other minor modifications, at SP's Roseville Shops.

All twenty-four diesel-hydraulics continued in regular SP service until 1968, but in that year SP took the decision to retire the K-M units as and when they fell due for major attention, their Maybach engines having proved prohibitively expensive to operate under US conditions. SP had never really overcome the MD870s' air intake problems at high altitudes and, in addition, had encountered certain difficulties with the bearings. Since no unit-replacement policy had ever been instituted, engine failure meant that the entire locomotive had to be withdrawn from traffic until repaired and, in these circumstances, operating costs of the hydraulics rocketed compared with those of diesel-electrics. The Alcos were better in this regard and, given their parts compatibility with other Alco products in service on the SP, were kept in traffic until 1973. Southern Pacific remained enthusiastic about the principle of hydraulic transmission, describing it as "an excellent piece of equipment which we think would be very practical for US operation", but was adamant that any series production of diesel-hydraulics on its behalf would have to take place in the United States. Whilst Alco was eager and willing to expand diesel-hydraulic production, persistent maintenance problems with the 251-C engines used in a subsequent batch of C-630 diesel-electrics dissuaded SP from placing quantity orders for the DH-643 (or any other Alco) design as it stood. Similar problems on other railroads led to a disastrous decline in orders for Alco locomotives and when the company closed its Schenectady, New York plant in 1969, SP was left with only two potential suppliers, namely GE and GM, neither of which was interested in offering hydraulic transmission on road units.

In addition to the question of supply, Southern Pacific's evaluation of its future needs had itself undergone a funda-mental change. Operational experience with both the hydraulics and the first ultra-high-output diesel-electrics (developed in response to SP's ML4000s) had cast doubts upon the practical value of such powerful locomotives, and whilst small numbers of twin-engined, 5000bhp General Motors DD35s and General Electric U50s were placed in service by both SP and rival Union Pacific, management continued to prefer the greater flexibility inherent in smaller, single-engined units. Such machines were also more welcome on neighbouring railroads when 'run-through' arrangements began to allow the working of long-distance trains from origin to destination without motive power changes, regardless of operating territory. There had also been a general decline in traffic levels since the instigation of the diesel-hydraulic programme and, when the displacement of generators by more compact alternators in the mid-1960s permitted the output of an average single-engined road unit to be raised from 2500bhp to 3000bhp, this new benchmark proved more than adequate to fulfil all of SP's then-current requirements. Since the lower initial costs and greater operational flexibility of such 'new generation' units as General Motors' SD40 and General Electric's U30C were now considered more relevant than the high performance capabilities of the hydraulics, SP's eventual decision to end the experiment was a logical one. Had the domestic industry been more willing to involve itself, Kurz' original vision of a busy mainline schedule dominated by diesel-hydraulic haulage might well have been realised in full. As it was, development of mainline diesel-hydraulics for the United States failed to keep pace with operational changes and eventually, massively over-endowed by contemporary standards, these magnificent machines quite literally priced themselves out of contention.

Top: In later years, both the V200.0 and the V200.1 types were concentrated in Northern Germany for use on a mixture of second-rank passenger and freight duties. No.221 149 stands at Bw Oberhausen in the company of a classmate on 28 February 1988. It is carrying the blue and beige TEE livery which was applied to several of the locomotives in their last years of service. *(Graham Scott-Lowe)*

Middle: In line with a process of continual updating of the motive power stocks, the Deutsche Bundesbahn's last V200.0s were withdrawn in 1984. A down-at-heel No.220 009 was recorded in store at Gmünden on 10 October 1986, along with a Class 601 TEE power car. *(Graham Scott-Lowe)*

Bottom: Two of the original V200s have been retained for preservation in Germany. On 20 April 1987 V200 002, banked by 2-6-2T No.64 289, is seen about to enter Epfendorf station on the privately-run Wutachtalbahn in Southern Germany. After leaving the station, the train will cross a viaduct and then negotiate a long curve before passing over the viaduct in the background, proceeding in the opposite direction, some five minutes later. *(D. Trevor Rowe)*

Even if the publicity accruing from SP's deployment of these locomotives failed to convert rival US railroads, it did succeed in exciting the interest first of the Russians and then of the Chinese who, during the later 1960s, acquired a number of six-axle high-horsepower diesel-hydraulics featuring outputs of up to 4600bhp from both Maybach/Mekydro and Daimler-Benz/Voith power equipment. Although their heavyweight separate-chassis construction strictly takes them beyond the scope of this narrative, they are notable in terms of the technical input which they, along with the ML4000s and a batch of 4000bhp centre-cabs for Turkey, contributed to the last derivative of the V200 design, a 4000bhp B-B for the Spanish RENFE system. These locomotives had to be extensively re-engineered not only in respect of their power equipment but also due to the 5'6" gauge of the Iberian peninsular, though K-M was assisted in this regard by inside-framed bogies and generous overhang of the V200 superstructure. Other exterior changes included standard RENFE buffing- and drawgear and the fitment of a large electric headlight in the roof dome between the cab windscreens. Internally, the locomotives were equipped with twin Maybach MD870 engines of the same rating as the SP locomotives. To handle the increased output twin Mekydro K184B transmission units were specified, representing a significant change from the ordinary K184 in being redesigned to incorporate a second torque converter and a simplified gearbox, some of the stage changes being accomplished by engaging alternate converters as with the Voith system. This ability to empty and fill the converters removed the need to disengage them mechanically whilst changing gear, so allowing further simplification. In view of the high expected train loads, the transmissions were also equipped with hydrodynamic braking as an integral part of the assembly. Used either on its own or in conjunction with the continuous brakes, the hydrodynamic brake proved capable of generating a maximum reverse torque equivalent to around 22,000lb of braking effort at the wheelrim at 11mph.

The first ten locomotives were built by Krauss-Maffei at Munich between November 1966 and January 1967 but, as in the case of previous export orders for the Spanish railways, it had been agreed that subsequent production should be entrusted to a local subcontractor. For the purposes of this particular order, the Spanish participant would be Babcock & Wilcox SA of Bilbao, the first of the twenty remaining locomotives being delivered by that concern in June 1967. Somewhat later, the RENFE awarded K-M a repeat order for two further locomotives to the same design, which was also fulfilled by Babcock & Wilcox SA. These 88-ton locomotives were not only relatively numerous by Spanish standards but also claimed the distinction of being the most powerful diesels in the RENFE fleet. Numbered in the 4000 series, the hydraulics were initially based at the Atocha depot at Madrid, working trains between that city and Barcelona, though diesel haulage gave way to electric traction at Mora de Rubeilos. At first their use was largely restricted to passenger traffic, but they soon displaced steam from goods workings between Madrid and Mora, and subsequently between Madrid and Saragossa. They were also a familiar sight on services to and from Alicante and Cartagena, as well as on Barcelona-Bilbao trains between Mora de Rubeilos and Miranda de Ebro.

Back in West Germany, the first of the Deutsche Bundesbahn's V200s to be withdrawn was an accident-damaged 220 086 from Bw Villingen in October 1973, followed by 220 008 from Bw Lübeck in February 1975. More followed in August 1977 when a firm of Westphalian civil engineers, Heitkamp, having secured a contract with the Saudi Government Railroads Organisation (SGRRO) to transport aggregate over the 350-mile line between Dammam and the construction sites of Riyadh, purchased 220 021 from Bw Lübeck and 220 054 from Bw Oldenburg as suitable motive power. Prepared for their new job at Bw Oldenburg, the locomotives were modified with cab and engine room air conditioning, special engine air filters to keep out the fine aeolian dust particles, extra fuel and water tanks in the space formerly occupied by the train-heating boiler and a 2000-watt searchlight at each end for night working. Once this work was completed they were shipped from Bremen to Dammam by freighter. 220 024/46 from Bw Lübeck and 220 069 from Bw Oldenburg were similarly modified at Aw Nuremburg before being shipped to the Gulf in January 1978, purchases being concluded that August with the sale of 220 006/35 from Bw Lübeck. Despite far-from-ideal maintenance facilities, the locomotives continued to work both ninety-wagon aggregate consists and heavily-laden passenger trains for workers travelling between Riyadh and the construction camps out in the desert until the expiry of the contract early in 1979. Even then, they would be resold not for scrap but rather for use by another contracting firm in the region. Equally surprising was the leasing of 220 013/4/22/31/7/51/ 3/75/6 to the Danish State Railways (DSB) in May 1981 to work trains there until ten locomotives on order from Henschel could be delivered. Moved dead from Flensburg to the DSB depot at Padborg, the locomotives were employed double-headed on both local and inter-city trains from Padborg and Frediricia. Both they and the DB depot staff sent to accompany them returned that October once the new locomotives had entered service.

With the final curtailment of West German mainline steam in the autumn of 1977, the Deutsche Bundesbahn was able to embark on a process of consolidating motive power stocks, particular emphasis being laid upon the best possible utilisation of the large fleet of efficient and powerful electric locomotives. Furthermore, like every other European country, West Germany had seen a shift in passenger traffic from the railways to the roads and even the air, allowing the frequency and consist of some services to be reduced. This of course enabled further reductions in motive power and, naturally enough, the DB focussed upon older locomotive classes. Although still handling some of the most demanding schedules the V200s were, at twenty years of age, elderly by the standards of diesel traction and all had accumulated substantial mileages in service. It was inevitable that a point would soon be reached where maintenance costs would begin to escalate and, recognising this, the DB began to replace them as motive power on the heavier jobs, either with electrics or with younger diesels drafted-in from elsewhere. By the early 1980s, these ageing yet still impressive machines were being concentrated on local freight and passenger work in and around Hamburg, running out their serviceable miles prior to withdrawal. 1983 saw the retirement of most of the V200 allocation at Bw Oldenburg, the survivors being sent to Bw Lübeck for further service. By early 1984 there were only twenty or so left in use and these too were soon replaced, more modern Class 218 dieselhydraulics assuming their duties from the start of the summer timetable. 220 001 was secured privately for preservation whilst 220 002 was retained by the DB itself as part of the collection at the Neuenmarkt-Wirsbirg museum. That one of the K-M hydraulics should join the historic locomotives of the past in this way was undoubtedly the right decision, for the V200 was one of the foundations upon which Germany's present railway system was built. If by the mid-1980s it had no place on the working railway for the surviving veterans of the first generation of diesel traction, at least the DB could retire the type in the knowledge that its considerable potential had been exploited to the full.

Chapter 14
LIFE AFTER DEATH

DESPITE their short and sometimes inglorious life, and their rapid replacement by diesel-electrics in the decade from 1967, the Western Region's diesel-hydraulic locomotives earned themselves a place in railway history as much through the massive enthusiast support demonstrated for them at the end as any other factor. This has been reflected in the relatively large number of locomotives preserved and the following which they still attract, nearly two decades after the demise of diesel-hydraulic power on WR metals.

Not all, however, have earned their proverbial place in the sun and, largely due to their early demise concurrent with that of steam traction, none of the ninety-six locomotives of three types built by North British for the WR have survived. Of the two D600 'Warships' purchased in 1968, Woodham Brothers broke up D600 quite rapidly but D601 *Ark Royal* was to survive in a derelict state at their Barry yard until July 1980. Sadly, a number of rescue bids during the late 1970s were to fail through lack of interest, despite the type's importance as BR's first 2000bhp Pilot Scheme diesel and the generally more enlightened attitude of the preservation movement. One major obstacle was the locomotive's incomplete state, both engines and many other components having been removed and this, coupled with the high scrap value of the aluminium-rich superstructure, rendered the costs of purchase and restoration unviable. D601, along with the last surviving NBL D6100 Bo-Bo and a pair of steam locomotives, would eventually succumb to the temporary and much-publicised resumption of locomotive scrapping operations at Barry. North British's entire series of D800 'Warships' would also meet the torch as

would their Type 2 counterparts. Interest was expressed in one of the smaller locomotives during 1972, but a bureaucratic mix-up saw the locomotive concerned scrapped at Swindon before negotiations could be concluded.

Out of the latter misfortune, however, came the first purchase for preservation of a WR diesel-hydraulic as the prospective Type 2 buyer decided to invest his money and enthusiasm in one of Laira's last operational pair of Class 42 'Warships' instead. D821 *Greyhound* was the chosen machine and was delivered by BR, under its own power, to the Great Western Society's base at Didcot in May 1973. Having formed a nucleus for the infant Diesel Traction Group, *Greyhound* spent several years in store first at Didcot, then subsequently at a gasworks site in Reading, before making the journey back to Swindon Works and a new home by the famous turntable outside 'A' shop. Although still not under cover, the Swindon site had the twin advantages of security and access to the huge reservoir of technical knowledge held by the works staff, and a programme of restoration was carried out on D821 including the installation of a new transmission unit and a partial engine overhaul. With this done, the DTG wished to see its locomotives put to work, so D821 made yet another move, this time to the North Yorkshire Moors Railway, in April 1981. The locomotive was put into regular use on that line for several years, including a period during which it masqueraded as a DB V200, but has more recently moved on to the Severn Valley Railway.

The other member of the final pair, D832 *Onslaught*, came under the aegis of the Railway Technical Centre at Derby for use at the Old Dalby test track as a dead load for developing track materials. Although at one time considered for use as motive power for test trains, D832 was withdrawn for the second time in 1979, subsequently being purchased for preservation and moved to the formative East Lancashire Railway at Bury. Although the locomotive was in basically good condition, the long period of idleness had taken its toll, and among the tasks requiring to be completed before *Onslaught* could be restored to revenue-earning service were a rebuild of one engine and replacement of the other. Many of the required parts came from Swindon Works, which still played home to D818 *Glory*. Initially retained to supply parts for the WR's last 'Warships' and latterly for the RTC's D832, D818 had been put into store at the works and latterly gained a semi-preserved status. Regrettably, after several warnings of its deteriorating condition went unheeded, *Glory* was broken-up by BREL at Swindon in October 1985.

Three 'Hymeks' were preserved *en-bloc* upon withdrawal from Old Oak Common depot early in 1975, namely D7017, D7018 and D7029. D7017 found a new home with the Diesel & Electric Group on the West Somerset Railway where it has proved to be a reliable performer, its only long period of non-availability being during 1982. This was symptomatic of a need for attention to the 'Hymek's electrical control system, a recurrent problem where low levels of activity permit the ingress of moisture, but the locomotive has so far required relatively little in the way of restoration work. The same could not be said for D7029, sold to

Below: A salutary reminder that nothing lasts forever. Considered by BREL beyond economic preservation due to the poor state of its bodywork, D818 *Glory* is dismantled behind the Swindon 'A' shop on 23 October 1985, with No.27 034 awaiting a similar fate in the background. *(B.J. Nicolle)*

the Diesel Traction Group, which had to undergo a complete engine rebuild at that group's Reading site prior to moving to Swindon with D821. Restoration continued apace at Swindon and by 1981 the locomotive was in sufficiently good condition to join the 'Warship' in its move to the North Yorkshire Moors Railway for use on service trains on that line. Although D7029's career on the NYMR was not totally without problems, one difficulty being a spate of recurrent turbocharger failures, the 'Hymek' did put in quite a few seasons' worth of spirited performances between Grosmont and Pickering before migrating south to join D821 at Kidderminster.

D7018 was initially purchased from BR by a private individual who arranged a move to the Great Western Society's depot at Didcot. Like D7029, the locomotive was in a relatively poor mechanical condition and, when the full extent of work needed became apparent, was sold to the D&EG as a source of spares for D7017. Having attracted its own band of devotees, the decision was made to restore D7018 rather than dismantle it, this work including a total engine strip-down and rebuild which was completed during 1985. The locomotive has since seen service alongside D7017 on the West Somerset Railway, a favourite haunt of the class in earlier years. Two further 'Hymeks', D7076/96 were commandeered by the RTC for dead load experiments alongside D832 but by 1980 had passed out of use. Stored for some time at Old Dalby, D7076 was purchased for preservation and moved to Bury in 1983, but D7096 was to tarry a little longer in the wilds of Leicestershire before being sold to a Sheffield scrap merchant and being moved to his premises for dismantling. Extensively robbed of parts, and with a dry weight some fifteen tons below standard, D7096 was not a realistic prospect for restoration but was nevertheless still of interest to preservationists, and eventually nearly all components other than the bodyshell itself were recovered for use on the four surviving 'Hymeks'.

Above: After withdrawal, D832 *Onslaught* saw further service as a dead load at the Railway Technical Centre, Derby, and was purchased from there for preservation. Cosmetically restored, the locomotive made an appearance at the Horwich Works Open Day on 16 August 1980, and was subsequently returned to full working order on the East Lancashire Railway. *(J.C. Hillmer)*

Below: Back on an old stamping ground, 'Hymek' D7017 approaches the West Somerset Railway's station at Blue Anchor with a train from Minehead on 7 September 1986. *(Robert Baker)*

The greatest enthusiast support of all was reserved for the D1000s and this is reflected in the large proportion of the type preserved. As with the 'Kings' before them, workers at Swindon were reluctant to dismantle the 'Westerns', not just from local pride in the design but also a widespread (and sadly prescient) fear that the demise of the diesel-hydraulics presaged the wholesale closure of the BREL operation there. Matters came to a head early in 1975 when, in an attempt to force the return of overhaul work to Swindon, workmen

refused to cut-up D1062 *Western Courier*. For some months the locomotive acted as an unofficial mascot displayed on the Works' turntable and, being in reasonably sound condition, a successful bid for D1062 was made by the Bristol-based Western Locomotive Association. The locomotive was then moved back into the Works itself for some remedial work, including the fitting of newly-overhauled engines, some attention to the electrical system and a full repaint in maroon, much of which was carried out by BR and BREL employees within the WLA membership. Upon completion of this, in May 1977 the locomotive was moved to Newton Abbot to join four other withdrawn 'Westerns' then stored there pending preservation. After a few days, however, D1062 resumed its travels to a new home on the Torbay and Dartmouth Railway, being joined by D1013 *Western Ranger*, also from Newton Abbot, a week later. D1013 had been purchased privately by a WLA member, who then entrusted the locomotive to the care of the Association. Subsequently, both would move to the Severn Valley Railway which has proved to be a long-term home for the pair.

D1013's companions in service on the last day of WR diesel-hydraulic operation would also escape the torch. D1023 *Western Fusilier* was earmarked for the National Collection and, after some preliminary restoration at Swindon, was dispatched to the National Railway Museum at York for public display, although it did subsequently see a period of service on the Torbay and Dartmouth Railway. Also on display at the excellent York museum is a bogie removed from D1023 after the discovery of axle defects, now partially-sectioned and demonstrating admirably the complex suspension and driveline arrangements of the design. D1010/3/41/8 were placed in store at Newton Abbot preparatory to possible purchase, D1010 *Western Campaigner* being bought by the Foster Yeoman quarrying concern. The company had a particular link with the 'Westerns', its first stone train from the Merehead terminal having been hauled by D1035 *Western Yeoman*, and the original intention had been to preserve that machine. Its withdrawal in 1975 as a result of fire damage put an end to that idea, and eventually it was D1010 that would be selected to live on at Merehead in the guise of D1035. Circumstances did not favour the new owners' plans, however, and after a period of storage at Shepton Mallet 'D1035' was subsequently renovated and restored to running order by the D&EG at Didcot, though remaining in Foster Yeoman ownership. D1048 *Western Lady*, again purchased privately, left Newton Abbot for Swindon in June 1978, receiving a bogie change prior to onward movement to the North Yorkshire Moors Railway. Bodily restored at that location and placed in occasional service on NYMR trains, D1048 was put in store at Horwich following a change in ownership in 1980. Resold, it moved to the Bodmin Steam Railway in Cornwall but its planned restoration was hampered by various difficulties, not least of which was a dispute between the owning group and their landlords. As a result D1048 changed hands yet again in late 1993, *Western Lady's* new owner being millionaire and would-be railway mogul Pete Waterman, who apparently intended to renovate it for eventual use on his charter train operation. After fifteen years of storage, however, D1048 was rumoured to be in very poor condition indeed and, given the present state of the charter business, the locomotive's prospects of an early return to traffic remain anything but certain.

Two other late survivors complete the line-up of preserved 'Westerns'. D1041 *Western Prince*, after periods in store first at Newton Abbot, then Swindon and finally at Horwich, found a home on the ELR at Bury alongside D832 and D7076 and by the mid-1980s was the last 'Western' not to have been externally refurbished since withdrawal. This was rectified in 1987 when the locomotive was admitted to the workshops of BREL Crewe for comprehensive body repairs which were completed in February 1988, D1041

Top: D7018 and D1010 rub shoulders at the Great Western Society's Didcot Railway Centre on 24 October 1987. D1010 is masquerading as D1035 *Western Yeoman*, an identity it adopted when purchased by the Foster Yeoman quarrying concern after withdrawal. The green livery then carried was not quite correct in that alloy bas-relief emblems were used rather than the coaching-stock cyphers applied by BR. It is also doubtful as to whether any green 'Westerns' ran in BR service *sans* the yellow warning panels. *(D.H. Tompkins)*

Middle: The first Class 52 to be preserved was D1062 *Western Courier*, secured by the Western Locomotive Association in 1976. Restored to maroon, D1062 pauses at Arley on the Severn Valley Railway with a Bewdley to Bridgnorth service on 31 March 1979. *(D.H. Tompkins)*

Bottom: D9526 came into the hands of the Diesel & Electric Group on the West Somerset Railway via Associated Portland Cement at Westbury, where it had been employed as a works shunter. On 7 September 1986, D9526 basks in the sunshine at Williton, accompanied by the WSR's Park Royal DMU. *(Robert Baker)*

emerging from its birthplace in the original livery of maroon with yellow bufferbeams, thus introducing a further variation in the appearance of the preserved 'Western' contingent. Perhaps the most miraculous story of all is that of D1015 *Western Champion*, rescued by the DTG from the Swindon dump as a partially-stripped and derailment-damaged hulk and which, after extensive restoration, re-emerged in its original Golden Ochre livery during 1982. Along with D7018, *Western Champion* made an appearance at the Old Oak Common Open Day of September 1985, but regrettably suffered a serious failure of the crankshaft main bearings on one of its engines a short while after. Despite this and other difficulties including a flawed axle and an enforced move from the Swindon Works site following the closure of the BREL operation there, restoration has continued apace, latterly at Old Oak Common.

The D9500 0-6-0DHs have also found a place in preservation. Led by APCM's D9526 which passed to the D&EG on the West Somerset Railway in 1980, where it was later joined by an ex-BSC D9551, the floodgates opened and opened until some nineteen different examples were preserved at various locations. Notably, among the last to join the ranks of the preserved were D9500 and D9555 upon their withdrawal at NCB Ashington. For the first time in their lives, the Type 1s are performing the sort of light branchline duties for which they had been intended in the first place and, whilst undoubtedly less economical than a DMU or one of the smaller breeds of diesel shunter, they are that much more versatile whilst remaining cheaper to operate on light trains to sporadic schedules than a steam locomotive or any of the larger types of mainline diesel. As such, they are perhaps the last true working members of the WR fleet, enabling the operation of essential services such as works trains and empty stock movements throughout the year, whereas the larger and more glamorous machines are often activated only on gala days and similar peak periods during the summer.

The shared achievements of the various preservation groups in saving so much is not to be underestimated. Keeping even a D9500 in a reasonable state of repair given the limited facilities offered by most private railways is not something to be taken lightly, and the heavy overhaul of any of the larger varieties of diesel-hydraulic is by rights something which should not be contemplated by any sane indi-

Above: For several years, D1041 *Western Prince* was the only preserved Class 52 not to have been cosmetically restored since withdrawal. This state of affairs was rectified when D1041's owner decided to put the locomotive through BREL's Crewe Works for a full bodywork restoration and repaint. On 4 February 1988 *Western Prince* stands outside the works where it was built some twenty-six years earlier, resplendent in its original maroon livery and without doubt a tribute to the skill of the works staff. *(David Birt)*

vidual lacking recourse to skilled labour, heavy workshop facilities and virtually limitless finances! Locomotives which are, all said and done, highly complex pieces of machinery often have to be stabled and maintained in the open and may see little or no use from the end of the autumn until the beginning of the next spring. Many major components are now unavailable new and only found with difficulty from such sources as scrapyards and secondhand machinery dealers, and running the locomotives always carries the risk of some mishap resulting in the destruction of a perhaps irreplaceable part.

Despite such overwhelming odds, preserved WR diesel-hydraulics are now valued items of motive power on a number of preserved railways, highly in demand by enthusiasts and operators alike, whilst the technical expertise of their dedicated custodians has, on occasion, been instrumental in the restoration of preserved diesel-electrics! Considering their often-sedentary lifestyle, the good order of most preserved WR hydraulics reflects considerable credit upon their keepers, and it is the hope of many that some of the larger machines might eventually be allowed to handle occasional special workings on the mainline. Whilst some of the owning groups are understandably wary about committing their charges to what will undoubtedly be very demanding duties after so many years of virtual retirement, the prospect of a 'Western' or a 'Warship' at work once again on the WR mainline remains something that many people would like to see transpire, this author included. In the meantime, however, it is the private railways that play host to the survivors of the WR's diesel-hydraulic era and, for the informed observer, the summer months still give ample opportunity to hear the song of Maybach and Paxman engines at work in the English countryside.

Chapter 15

CONCLUSIONS

TWENTY years after the close of the WR's diesel-hydraulic era, debate still rages over the rapid changes in BR policy which first sponsored the locomotives' creation and then engineered their early demise. There can be no doubt that the intervening decade saw a fundamental change both in the standing of BR's managers and in their attitude towards the running of Britain's railways, in turn establishing a new order under which the status of the Western's hydraulics was to become ever-more marginal. Despite this, the reality of their impact upon the WR still refutes many of the arguments cited by the BRB to justify their passing. In the eight years between the spring of 1958 and that of 1966, the diesel-hydraulics formed the backbone of a policy that enabled the WR to rid itself totally of steam traction, the first region of BR to be able to do so. Even without the large volume of diesel-electrics used to implement the No.3 Conversion Scheme from 1962 onwards, the end result would still have been the same providing that all the regions had adhered to the original policies of 1958, and would not only have permitted the spreading of investment cost but also the better utilisation of remaining steam power. As it was, a fleet that peaked at 365 locomotives in the mid-1960s and which for the greater part of its existence was at a much lower level managed to amass in excess of 3500 locomotive-years and 175 million locomotive-miles in a period of nineteen years.

Much of the BRB's case as presented in the 1965 *Report on Diesel-Electric and Diesel-Hydraulic Locomotives on British Railways* rested upon the lower costs and enhanced availabilities of the diesel-electrics as compared with diesel-hydraulics. For example, averages for a sample ten-week period in 1964 saw availability figures of 86% for the D1500 compared with 64% for the D1000 in the Type 4 category, whilst the Type 3 category saw the D6700 achieve a figure of 90% compared with the 83% recorded by the D7000. On average, D1500s were accumulating some 11,000 miles between casualties compared with the 8500 miles run by the 'Westerns', with the Type 3 returns standing at 31,000 and 18,000 miles per casualty for the D6700 and the 'Hymek' respectively. Casualty rates were then rising for all but the D6700s. In terms of initial costs, both diesel-hydraulics were more expensive than their diesel-electric counterparts, with a differential of 8.8% between the two Type 4s and 5.6% between the Type 3s. The fact many problems experienced with the hydraulics had been specific to the WR was admitted, the report noting that "when various aspects of under design have been dealt with by modification, it is expected that the differences in reliability will become less", but to the casual observer at least, the report must have appeared as a very substantial justification indeed of the BRB's policies.

Yet in many ways, the report was concerned more with justification than objectivity, and it required very little effort to find considerable shortcomings in its analysis. For a start, the difference in initial costs could easily be explained by the greater proliferation of the two diesel-electric designs compared with the hydraulics, as could the greater total mileages run to date. It was also noticeable that the availability figures for the two diesel-electric classes were compiled from allocations throughout the country, and not just on the

Western Region; other statistics released by BR at around the same time suggested that WR-allocated D1500s were returning availabilities around 5% lower than the class' national average. Neither did the report draw attention to the effects placed on availability by the repair system's capacity to supply skilled labour and spare parts as and when required. The most serious drawback of all, however, was the report's lack of any quantification of the amount of work being performed by each locomotive type between failures, or of the relative cost or seriousness of those failures. Official mileage readings displayed by BR in April 1965 demonstrated that, far from what the report might have led one to expect, the WR diesel-hydraulics were actually returning higher mileages than their diesel-electric counterparts. For the period up to the end of 1964, with their availability record at its (abysmal) worst, the D1000s were returning an average 65,400 miles of haulage per locomotive per annum, which was about 8000 miles per annum more than the Derby/Sulzer 1Co-Co1s, though still some 4000 miles less than the D1500s. Another of the WR's problem children, the D7000 'Hymek', was averaging some 60,000 miles per locomotive despite spending much of its time on short-haul freight work, a figure far exceeding the 50,750 miles per annum average returned by the rival D6700s. The D800s were more impressive still, the same mileage analysis showing the Maybach/Mekydro locomotives to have been posting average mileages of 95,100 miles per locomotive per year, with the MAN/Voith machines somewhat lower at 82,300 miles per locomotive per year. This was sufficient for the aggregate running performance of the class as a whole to be some 7% better than any other BR mainline diesel excepting the Type 5 'Deltics' and the English Electric Type 4s.

Mileage returns for the D600, D6300 and D9500 types were not included, but the information published was still enough to paint a detailed picture picture of diesel-hydraulic performance on the WR's most demanding schedules. As the *Railway Gazette* was subsequently to note, whilst the figures reflected an overall improvement in performance by diesels over steam traction, they in no way supported the policies of the BTC and the BRB in favouring heavy diesel-electrics with slow-speed engines. Although it could be argued that diesel-hydraulic availabilities were continuing to fall whilst those of most diesel-electric designs were tending to rise, it remained an indisputable fact that the majority of the WR's Type 3 and Type 4 diesel-hydraulics were contributing between 16 and 18 service hours per day as opposed to eight hours or so for most diesel-electrics. This meant that routine maintenance of the hydraulics was much less easily accomodated between rostered duties, daily availability thus being affected not only by locomotive failures but also the need to withdraw units from service for planned maintenance. Thus could be explained the dichotomy between the apparently low availabilities of the diesel-hydraulic classes and their ability to return annual mileages far higher then their competitors, the majority of which were quite simply not doing sufficient work to warrant the costs of their acquisition. Only their reduced stand-by charges as compared with steam made the

Top: About to head into the depths of the tunnel itself, No.5925 *Eastcote Hall* leads D601 *Ark Royal* past Dainton Tunnel signalbox with the 6.55 Penzance-Paddington on 7 August 1961. Such close contact between diesel and steam was unavoidable, at least in the early days, but the effluvium of the steam locomotive did little to encourage mechanical reliability on the part of the more delicate diesels. *(Hugh Ballantyne)*

Bottom: D6342 peeps out from under the trainshed at Cheddar with the 10.49 (Saturdays only) Witham-Yatton train on 17 August 1963, the last year in which the line was open for passenger traffic. Although distinctly Brunellian in flavour, the stone-built station with its timber trainshed was in fact the work of Francis Fox of the Bristol & Exeter Railway, and was only one of several notably fine examples of railway architecture erected by the B&ER. *(Hugh Ballantyne)*

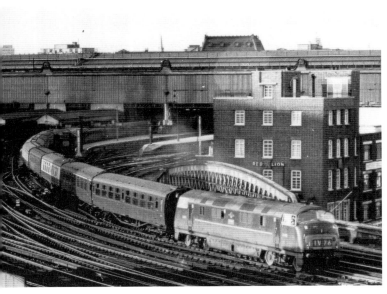

Top: 'Warship' duties on the Waterloo-Exeter route were standardised on Swindon/Maybach locomotives to simplify crew-training and maintenance procedures, though occasional NBL/MAN machines were to be observed acting as substitutes. Such an occasion must have occurred one evening in May 1966 when D855 *Triumph* was seen departing Waterloo with a West of England express. *(Dr L.A. Nixon)*

Bottom: Not all the 'Warships' received the blue livery and D817 *Foxhound* was one of these, retaining maroon livery, albeit modified with all-over yellow ends, until withdrawal in October 1971. Two months before, *Foxhound* was recorded at Salisbury on a westbound working, showing ample evidence of a hard life. The existence of a water column, some four years after the end of Southern Region steam, is noteworthy. *(Kevin Lane)*

dieselisation of BR anything like an economic proposition.

The admittedly greater incidence of diesel-hydraulic locomotive failures also requires some clarification in this respect. Provided that BR's ill-considered stock-limitation policy had not promulgated a shortage of those spares required, the majority of diesel-hydraulic casualties could be remedied within a matter of days at a maintenance depot. By contrast, many diesel-electric failures were of a far more serious nature, involving several weeks' attention at a main works. This was in no way helped by the massive nature of the engines, generators and bogies used on the diesel-electrics, which demanded greater lifting capacities than depots were able to provide, thus necessitating a return to works and further time lost whilst in traffic there and back.

With a large and increasing allocation of standard Type 3 and 4 diesel-electrics, the WR had at least tried to implement a unit-replacement policy for these, based at Cardiff Canton, but was eventually driven to abandon it by the sheer difficulties involved. Ironically, the heavy reliance placed by the comparative report upon the notionally higher availability levels of the D1500 design would be further undermined by the discovery of serious structural fractures in the type's Sulzer 12LDA28C engines during the year of its very publication. The resulting need for an extensive refurbishment programme served to reduce the availabilities of these expensive new locomotives just when they were needed most, though this would never be publically acknowledged. By this time, the structure of both the BRB and the WR was such that the diesel-hydraulic programme was already all but dead and simply awaiting burial.

This, of course, is not to say that the performances put up by the WR's diesel-hydraulic fleet were always above criticism, for quite plainly they were not. All too often though, blame for unreliability was placed on the nature of the engines and transmissions used where in truth other factors were culpable. One sad but inescapable fact is that the root cause of major troubles was almost always traced to license-made units or those of domestic manufacture, often due to the use of inferior materials or workmanship. An example was the use of mild steel for the exhaust manifolds of NBL-assembled MAN engines which rapidly fractured and perforated, leading to turbocharger starvation and a reduction in engine performance. Augsburg-supplied units in D600-1 incorporated manifolds made from a more costly alloy steel which gave no trouble in this regard. Big-end bearing failures were another problem on Glasgow-made MAN engines, often resulting from fractured bearing cap bolts, the same deficiency being responsible for the occasional detached balance weight in engines run at prolonged high speeds. Although NBL revised the design of the big-end bolts in December 1960 to eliminate what it considered to be the cause of the problem, fractures continued to occur, MAN noting that bolts to the original design were continuing to give good service outside the UK. Whilst MAN queried the choice of material for British-made bolts, it is also possible that the breakages were initiated by defective locking plates between the head of the bolt and the bearing cap itself. Whatever its origins, the problem was never fully resolved and bearing bolt fractures plagued the MAN engine right up to the end of its career on BR. The life expectancy of shell inserts on the later B-series units may also have been compromised by that design's strengthened crankshaft, the larger journal diameters of which dictated higher bearing velocities for any given engine speed.

Worrying though they were, these troubles would soon be eclipsed by those arising from the twin maladies of cylinder head overheating and premature valve failure. Indeed, the MAN engine was to become notorious for problems connected with combustion troubles, including valve seat recession, excess piston ring wear and regular instances of complete piston failure. Valvegear wear was also considerable, unsurprisingly given the high inertia loads present in any quick-running diesel engine, and pushrods and rockers had a generally short life. Oddly enough, camshafts in both MAN- and NBL-built units lasted very well indeed though, unhappily, in some engines they were about the only component to do so. Last but by no means least, the design displayed a propensity towards continuous and chronic oil leakage, an unpleasant characteristic which was more often than not aggravated by the pressurisation of crankcase and rocker chambers by combustion gas escaping past worn piston rings. This not only complicated routine maintenance procedures but also contributed to a number of serious engine room fires when stray oil got into electrical equipment.

This catalogue of failings was surprising and unfortunate

given MAN's record of success in the field since producing some of the world's very first diesel engines, but blame cannot be laid wholly at the door of North British. As recounted in Chapter 13, the Deutsche Bundesbahn also experienced persistent problems with their L12V18/21B units which were of course Augsburg-built, with no British components. In contrast, the earlier 'A'-series engines led a fairly untroubled existence both on the DB and British Railways. The eventual consensus of opinion amongst many experts was that the 1957 uprating had proved a costly mistake and that in the L12V18/21B MAN had produced an engine that was too highly-developed for its own wellbeing. On an engine producing more than 17bhp/litre, some of the design's fundamentals looked as if they were being taxed beyond their limits, especially the bottom end which preserved the side-by-side situation of opposing connecting rods long after most rivals had changed over to the vastly superior fork-and-blade layout. There were also the uncooled pistons to which some commentators have attributed the L12V18/21B's combustion troubles, though this conclusion is not supported by the performance record of the equivalent Daimler-Benz product, which also featured uncooled pistons. Save for a compression ratio which is

very slightly higher in the Augsburg unit, there is no apparent difference between the technical composition of the MAN and D-B engines which would explain the need for piston cooling in one but not the other, ceteris paribus. The obvious assumption to be drawn from this is that whilst excessive piston temperatures were undoubtedly a contributory factor in the MAN engines' service problems, especially with regard to piston ring wear, they were by no means the sole cause. The high incidence of valve failures in particular may well indicate problems in this area, possibly arising from inadequate heat dispersal within the heads themselves. Certainly, the quoted exhaust gas temperature of 585° C is very close to the commonly-accepted maximum for engines of conventional construction, the use of four rather than six valves also reducing the scope for heat transfer.

In retrospect, it can be seen that the BTC's purchases of MAN engines were at least partly motivated by political considerations, principally the need to support the ailing North British concern, and was made clear in July 1957 when the Commission, despite admitting that "the possibility of trouble with MAN engines is borne in mind", went ahead and mandated their use in D833-65. The fate of the breed on BR was effectively sealed after a report by the British Internal Combustion Engine Research Association concluded that, despite the relative simplicity of the design, little could be done to improve reliability in service. One engine was fitted with modified cylinder head valve seats which overcame at least some of the problems, but the programme was a WR initiative rather than an official BR one and by the time that the modification had proved successful, the decision had been taken at a higher level to withdraw the MAN-engined classes as soon as possible. Material problems were compounded by the inexperience of BR staff in maintaining and repairing the new units, which in turn gave rise to an inordinate number of engines suffering major failures only a short while after works overhaul, a situation which persisted well into the 1960s. Under such circumstances, it would have been logical for more major repairs to be entrusted to the original suppliers but, unfortunately, the BTC demanded a lengthy warranty on supplier-overhauled engines for a cost no greater than engines overhauled in BR's own workshops without guarantee. Although a few engines were sent north, NBL understandably did nothing to encourage this business.

Neither were the Maybach engines to escape problems in British use, despite an excellent service record in applications across the world. When the first units came to be built (as opposed to assembled) by Bristol-Siddeley, defects arose which seriously compromised availability levels. As related in Chapters 8 and 9, a crop of crankcase cracks on BSE-manufactured MD655 and MD870 units prompted an engineering investigation which in turn revealed the use of poor quality materials and poor welding techniques. Ansty-made engines also proved susceptible to an inordinately high rate of connecting rod failures despite the MD-series' unblemished history to date. Engine strip-downs specifically targeted at locating the source of the failures found that BSE-manufactured rods were showing signs of considerable distress after only 3000 operating hours, whereas German-made engines frequently worked for ten times that period without difficulty. Experimental use of rods made by Maybach at Friedrichshafen in an engine license-made by BSE saw an instant end to the problem, demonstrating beyond doubt that the cause lay not in the design but in BSE's failure to maintain production quality. Engines had little chance of lasting the full period in traffic when they were equipped with such poor quality components, which would first cause big-end troubles and eventually end in total failure, often writing-off the crankcase and crankshaft in the process. In in all fairness to BSE, however, the quality of bought-in components was not always within its grasp. Suppliers frequently misunderstood how highly the engines were stressed and, in order to fulfil their orders more quickly or more easily, substituted off-the-shelf parts and materials which did not comply with the original manufacturers' specifications. Both BSE and NBL were expected to produce their respective types of engine using as much UK-made material as possible, and it must have been frustrating to them when these components failed to match the quality of the German originals, though this was of little comfort to a WR bedevilled by diesel-hydraulic engine failures.

Just such an example concerned BSE's decision to use a cheap British bearing assembly on Ansty-built turbochargers instead of the original German unit. Whilst increasing local content and reducing production costs, the substitution's greatest impact was to increase the rate of turbocharger failures as the bearings began to break up. Other weak points included fracture-prone casings and a drip-feed lubrication system demanding manual priming prior to start-up, a precaution which could be forgotten, with dire results. This last was a shortcoming of the design as originally produced, as were the impellors themselves, which eventually were found to benefit from having their blades wired together for added strength. The Maybach engines' most infamous debility, however, concerned their cylinder heads and there was always some incipient leakage. Normal procedure prior to starting after any length of time out of use was to turn the engines over with decompression valves opened, in order to expel any seepage and so avoid hydraulic locking. However, after a period of standing, MD-series engines would sometimes be found full of coolant, in which case the locomotive could only be considered a failure with a costly strip-down and repair ahead of it before re-entry to traffic. The heads were also subject to cracking and warping with monotonous regularity and, despite lack of trouble with identical components elsewhere, the BRB branded them as "thermally overloaded" and "unsatisfactory", seemingly without bothering to investigate why. In fact, the fault lay not with the engines but with cooling systems that were often incorrectly set-up and which suffered from a plethora of faults with minor but vital ancillaries such as temperature- and pressure-sensing switches which, by failing to operate correctly, could cause thousands of pounds' worth of damage in a matter of minutes. The one-piece Behr-Serck radiator units themselves proved inordinately prone to failure, as they did on contemporary Type 4 diesel-electrics, a fact which might owe something to the inconsistency of BR's water treatment policies, whilst the D1000 class in particular suffered acutely with radiator vapour-locking resulting from badly laid-out pipework.

Below: Over a year after the demise of the Somerset & Dorset line as a through route between Bath and Bournemouth, D7031 leaves Radstock on the former up line on 29 December 1967, bound for Evercreech Junction to pick up a quantity of recovered material. Note the small snowploughs fitted below the locomotive's bufferbeam. On the former down line, D3185 marshals a number of coal wagons from Writhlington Colliery *en route* for Bristol via the ex-GWR North Somerset line. *(Hugh Ballantyne)*

Above: On a sorry remnant of what once was possibly the most beautiful railway in England, D7094 heads out of the 1188-yard Tidenham Tunnel and past the overgrown platform at Netherhope Halt on the erstwhile Wye Valley Railway. Although the line ceased to carry traffic between Monmouth and Chepstow in 1964, its southern extremity remained open as a siding to serve Tintern Quarry, from whence came this train of loaded ballast hoppers on 5 May 1971. *(Norman E. Preedy)*

All three Maybach-engined classes suffered terribly from cooling system defects, an analysis of failures carried out over the winter of 1965/6 highlighting such problems as the cause of a third of all reported casualties. However, engine failures for the Swindon-built D800s with their German-manufactured MD650s accounted for only 2½% of all casualties, a figure equivalent to a third of that returned by BSE-made units in the D1000s and D7000s. The inferences of such statistics were perfectly clear. By 1968, the problems had reached such proportions that Maybach had become concerned for the hitherto-good reputation of the MD-series engines, and published their own summary of diesel-hydraulic traction in the UK in their house magazine '*Maybach Mercedes-Benz Information*'. Advising the reader against the frequent "articles containing polemics against their use", Maybach noted the creditable overall performance of the WR's diesel-hydraulic stable compared with both BR's diesel-electrics and the DB's V200 fleet. Admitting that the performance of the D1000 class had been below par from new, Maybach went on to profess astonishment that, despite availability rates as low as 50-60% which should have indicated something wrong, BR had engaged the type in serious comparison with competing diesel-electric designs and, on the basis of the results, pronounced the concept of the diesel-hydraulic inferior. Coolant-related faults were held to be responsible for at least 58% of all cylinder head failures, and Maybach clearly felt that the BRB's attitude towards the troubles had been a less than constructive one.

Such problems were by no means confined to the hydraulics; many contemporary diesel-electrics suffered similar failures, often with identical componentry, and one manufacturer prominent in the fulfilment of Pilot Scheme orders complained that nearly half of all failures affecting its locomotives were inflicted by minor components bought-in from outside sources. Maybach pointed out that by far the greatest proportion of all reported diesel-hydraulic failures were directly related to ancillary systems such as train-heating boilers (14%) and control equipment (25%). Once again, note was made of the proportionately lower yearly mileages run by most of the diesel-electric classes and the correspondingly greater time available for maintenance, resulting in improved nominal availability figures. By contrast, the scheduled distances run by the hydraulics had been gradually increased until, by 1967, the average daily distance covered by a 'Western' was 500 miles compared to some 300 miles for a WR-allocated D1500. Whilst Maybach's comments were justified, it has to be said that some problems arose from staff unfamiliarity, a situation not helped by the sheer complexity of both Maybach engines and Mekydro transmissions. In later years, the intricate design of the MD-series cylinder head would figure as a major failing in its own right, with problems arising from incorrect setting of the valve clearances and of the camgear actuating the fuel injectors.

Above: Under a stormy sky and the gaze of a solitary onlooker, No.1037 *Western Empress* hammers through Bruton with the 12.15 Exeter-Paddington on 17 March 1975. *(Graham Scott-Lowe)*

As with the MAN and Maybach engines, the Paxman YJXL units used in D830 and in the D9500s had their share of difficulties, most though not all a direct result of failures in ancillary equipment such as cooling units and heat exchangers, especially in the Type 1 0-6-0s. However, the 6YJXL in particular displayed a number of apparently design-related faults, an example of which was a spate of cylinder head problems including warping and cracking of the aluminium castings themselves. Over the years, BR engineers would express reservations over the choice of materials used in a number of Paxman engine designs, and it is true that cast-iron heads were later adopted by subsequent operators, with definite gains in reliability. Other manufacturers, however, used similar aluminium heads without difficulty and it is almost certain that, whilst high failure rates on the D9500s had their roots in poor foundry techniques which resulted in localised hot spots and over-stressing of the castings, the problems were greatly exacerbated by unacceptably low standards of cooling system performance. Another difficulty was the high incidence of crankshaft bearing failures, often attributed to the total surface area of the bearings being inadequate, and bearing area was indeed increased during successive redesigns over the years. In fairness, though, it is also true that any bearing will fail if its lubricating oil supply becomes overheated or contaminated through the sort of cooling system faults so prevalent with the design during its time on BR.

The service record of the six-cylinder engines on the WR was never anywhere near as good as that of the prototype twelve-cylinder units in D830, and it may well be that the (very slight) increase in power rating relative to swept capacity was a deciding factor. It must be remembered that, at the time of the D9500 order being finalised, Paxmans had only limited experience with high-speed, high-output diesel engines for railway traction use, much of which was being provided by the design and installation of the two prototype 12YJXLs in D830. Given both the relative success of this initial venture and the urgency with which British Railways wanted its diesel orders fulfilled, Paxmans appear to have been moved to offer production units to the same basic design, even though a certain amount of final development would inevitably need to be done in day-to-day service, an expedient which is rarely completely satisfactory. The advent of unforeseen mechanical problems dealt a heavy blow to the entire concept of fine-tuning the design under service conditions, something which was further complicated in the case of the YJXL units deployed on the WR by

their relatively restricted numbers and small mileage returns. This was nowhere more apparent than with the troublesome and therefore under-utilised D9500s, which not only hindered operational and statistical analysis of engine performance, but also served to reduce the priority for any retrospective upgrade programme. Eventually, Paxmans got caught in the crossfire between the Western Region and the British Railways Board over the broader debate of diesel-hydraulic against diesel-electric traction and, in the aftermath of the National Traction Plan, the requisite work was never done. Once again, the concept of the high-speed diesel engine became the scapegoat for the short-comings of the operator's own systems. Although in need of further refinement, the fundamental integrity of the YJXL design would become evident when it was selected as a basis from which to develop the 12-cylinder, 2500bhp Valenta engine used in the present-day High Speed Trains.

Unlike the various engine designs, and contrary to popular opinion, once the initial problems were sorted out neither type of transmission gave excessive trouble in service. One such difficulty concerned an early mix-up of transmission oils, caused by the fact that each manufacturer had its own recommendations. Voith specified a relatively thin grade of mineral oil in order to optimise converter performance and whilst the Mekydros would function perfectly well on this, service experience both in Germany and elsewhere caused Maybach to recommend use of a more viscous formula so as to afford some protection to the gearbox bearings under arduous conditions. This was not initially appreciated on the WR and due to differences in language and terminologies some Mekydros were refilled with the wrong oil, resulting in a tangible though not catastrophic reduction in service life. By far the greatest number of problems arose from the failure of auxiliary components such as hoses and thermostats leading to overheating, contamination and sometimes total loss of transmission oil. The usual problem was one of overheating and since electrical sensors intended to detect excess heat often failed to act, quite a number of Voith transmissions suffered damage to, and occasionally destruction of the converter blades. The Voith units habitually ran at a rather higher temperature than their Maybach equivalents, although a couple of Mekydros did overheat to a point where the gearwheels were blued when the electrical safeguards once again failed to act.

Deficiencies in bought-in components were also responsible for a rash of bearing problems in Mekydro units during the mid-1960s, culminating in higher than normal failure rates. Indeed, so bad did this problem become that Swindon, already engaged on a programme of corrective modifications to the K184 units, was swamped with failed Mekydros requiring repair and for a few months in 1965 actually had to suspend routine overhauls of the type altogether. Admittedly, few of these teething troubles should ever have occurred but in time most were overcome, and failure rates fell as a result. Only in later years when spares became almost impossible to obtain did the transmissions once again become a regular service problem, although Voith units always tended to be favoured by the maintenance personnel over the Mekydros due to their comparative simplicity. Common to both designs was a relative intolerance of incorrect or insufficient maintenance although ultimately, as serviceable replacements became ever scarcer, some units soldiered on in service well past their planned overhaul dates to return truly prodigious mileages prior to failure.

In many ways, the least contentious aspect of the BRB's 1965 diesel-electric versus diesel-hydraulic comparison was the revelation that, in most respects, little could be found to indicate any overwhelming superiority on the part of either transmission type. This was a reflection of the huge technical advances which the arrival of the lightweight hydraulics had forced British locomotive constructors to make in order

to remain competitive, even given their favoured status with the BTC. In 1955 the diesel-hydraulic had offered real advantages over the diesel-electric competition and even ten years later, some of these remained. Unchallenged was the hydraulic's ability to generate immense tractive efforts at low speeds, allegations that its adhesion suffers due to having all axles on the same bogie connected instead of being to slip independently being patent nonsense. The diesel-hydraulic layout permits torque transfer to take place and so has a distinct superiority in all but the very worst conditions, this being conclusively demonstrated in the D1000 vs D1500 controlled road tests of 1964; the 'Western's ability to deploy a starting tractive effort equivalent to nearly 28% of its adhesive weight indicated a degree of sure-footedness that was exemplary by any standards. Even with the use of complex wheelslip protection circuitry that reduced power in the event of a slip occurring and so increased its effective level of adhesion, the diesel-electric could not rival the hydraulic's sustained low-speed torque. The deciding factor was the rapid build-up of heat in electric traction motors under such conditions, a difficulty that would only begin to be overcome with a new generation of electrical equipment and electronic control gear. At the time of the delivery of the WR's first diesel-hydraulics, the availability of such equipment in the UK lay a full ten years in the future. In the meantime, damage caused to trackwork through undetected wheelslip would present an ever-increasing headache for British Railways, almost always where high-powered diesel-electric or straight electric traction was in use.

Taken as a whole, the WR diesel-hydraulic fleet was unfortunate in having to contend with more than its fair

share of troubles specific to BR service, which tended to reflect (unfairly) upon the locomotives' conception. The problems stemming from the inconsistent quality of license-built equipment have already been illustrated; in the case of MAN and Maybach engines built in the UK, the failure rate was unacceptably high even given the inevitable deterioration in quality encountered when the production under license of any product is first undertaken by a new manufacturer. The nature of the problem caused by the BTC policy of patronising as many component suppliers as possible went a lot deeper than a simple decline in quality, which could have been targeted and eventually solved. Early on in the locomotives' lifecycles, the WR began to be plagued by the ramifications of poor component interchangeability arising from equipment being procured from multiple sources; all too often, the specifications issued to suppliers had either been insufficiently rigid in the first place, or alternatively had been altered by the manufacturer in the interests of cost reduction without any consultation with the BTC. As a result, nominally identical items from two different suppliers could vary quite markedly and

Above: Leaning into the curve at Bodmin Road, a tired-looking D1065 *Western Consort* pulls a stopping train from Penzance over the last few yards into the station. The photograph was taken on 14 August 1976 and within three months D1065 would be withdrawn from service as the fleet was finally run-down. *(David Birt)*

attempts to mate one to equipment originally fitted to the other would often end in ignominious failure. In order to achieve reasonable repair cycles, the WR was forced to ignore theoretical interchangeability between many components and instead adhere as closely as possible to individual build specifications. Inevitably, both locomotives awaiting equipment and overhauled units waiting to be installed spent time sitting around at Swindon until a suitable partner could be found, when a little more care at the outset would have ensured full compatibility. With the later diesel-hydraulic orders the Western Region largely secured the principle of component interchangeability within each class, but the original conception of having a wide range of locomotives all sharing common equipment was never realised. It must also be said, however, that the WR did not always try so hard as it might have done, especially with locomotives not of its own making; in the case of the later D6300s and the NBL-built D800s, the factors preventing the interchange of engine and transmission types were relatively insignificant, and the failure to address them rather defies explanation.

Another lesson learned the hard way by BR was that design features do not always work well away from their original surroundings. The troubles with the Krauss-Maffei bogie that so perturbed the WR never became apparent on the Continent, despite the design being used under larger and much more powerful locomotives. The critical consideration proved to be the speed of services prevalent on the WR which was much higher than that encountered in Germany. Whilst some technical aspects of the K-M bogie were undoubtedly deficient in this respect, careful observation of the first three D800s under test conditions could quickly have highlighted this fact and suggested possible cures for production locomotives. Instead, in its rush to displace steam, BR purchased *en masse* before assessing the Pilot Scheme machines and so ended up having to modify some 140 sets of K-M bogies. Interestingly enough, similar difficulties arose with the hitherto-excellent Schlieren bogies when used under the 'Blue Pullman' units, confirm-

ing high line speeds as the cause of the problem. Yet troubles arising from the transfer of technology across geographical frontiers were by no means inevitable. In France, Italy, Norway and Japan, all countries with little or no experience of quick-running engines or hydraulic transmission, diesel-hydraulic locomotives mechanically similar to those of the WR were put into intensive service with few difficulties and within a relatively short time had accumulated high mileages. Even in the United States, the early curtailment of diesel-hydraulic activity was mostly due to changing operational requirements coupled with the largely negative reaction of domestic suppliers, though Southern Pacific's failure to embrace unit-replacement maintenance policies undoubtedly did reduce locomotive availability.

Neither were the WR's diesel-hydraulics helped by the gradual erosion of several key stategies underpinning both the Modernisation Plan and the WR's own 1955 proposals. Failure to adhere to a policy of dieselisation by geographical area resulted in the costly damage of diesel machinery by the harmful effluvia of the steam locomotive, whilst the 1961 decision to replace diesel-hydraulic orders with those for diesel-electrics not only complicated the maintenance situation but also ensured that production costs for short runs of diesel-hydraulics were frighteningly high. The tragedy of this was that from the first D600 of 1958 to the last D1000 of 1964, the cost of a complete set of diesel-hydraulic traction equipment for a mainline locomotive remained significantly (circa 8-10%) less than that for a comparable diesel-electric package. The differential in the cost of complete locomotives was accounted for entirely by drawing-office charges and production costs for minor components artificially inflated by the small number of locomotives built. The situation was further complicated by the large number of early design modifications mandated either by BR itself or the various manufacturers and, for a time at the beginning of the nineteen-sixties, hardly a week would go by without a further instruction being issued concerning alterations to locomotives both under construction and in everyday service. The costs of performing this work, and especially of taking locomotives out of traffic in order to allow its completion, remain largely unknown and are probably incalculable.

In this regard, the situation was hardly helped by the large number of independent contractors involved in fulfilling the WR's requirements for diesel-hydraulic locomotives, although this was in turn mandated both by BTC policy and by the WR's incapacity to build all the new locomotives needed at Swindon within a reasonable timescale. Ironically, the eventual failure of some of these contractors to comply with agreed delivery dates would indirectly assist in formulating a case for the elimination of diesel-hydraulics on British Railways. Whilst the WR proposals of 1955 under which these locomotives had been ordered had envisaged modernisation of the railway network as it stood, the subsequent espousal of the Beeching proposals and the resulting diminution of traffic at a stroke removed the need for low-powered line-service locomotives almost completely. The delayed entry of many D6300s and D9500s into WR service thus coincided with the demise of their intended duties and this, along with the displacement of other motive power from mainline duties, would enable the National Traction Plan to eliminate entire classes of locomotives without significant new construction by the simple means of redistributing existing stocks.

Ultimately, however, the failure of the diesel-hydraulics to maintain their position of primacy on the WR must be related to two factors in particular, the first of which was the chronically-shortsighted abandonment of the continuous-braking programme for the wagon fleet. Although intended as an economy measure to help arrest BR's slide into insolvency, the move nevertheless had the immediate effect of rendering the entire diesel-hydraulic fleet obsolete on braking grounds. When 138-ton 'Peak' 1Co-Co1s succumbed to the weight of unbraked trains and were sent slithering helplessly down a gentle gradient with all wheels locked, then a lightweight diesel-hydraulic with its comparatively puny brake force stood little chance. Many of BR's smaller diesel-electrics suffered similar braking deficiencies on loose-coupled movements, culminating in the emergency provision of over a hundred diesel brake tenders intended to provide additional brake force controlled from the locomotive cab. Neither the WR nor any other BR region had given any consideration to the use of dynamic braking systems, quite simply because the promise of a continuously-braked wagon fleet had rendered their provision apparently superfluous, the WR CME, R.A. Smeddle recording in October 1958 that he thought it "senseless to use diesels on loose-coupled freight trains". Had the intention of abandoning the wagon-braking programme been announced earlier, then certainly the D1000 class and perhaps some of the 'Hymeks' as well might have been equipped with transmission units incorporating hydrodynamic braking (see Chapter 13), so easing the situation in this regard. Instead, the 'Westerns' had to wait until the last few years of their lives before having the opportunity to show their true mettle on heavy but fully-braked freight movements.

The second challenge to the hydraulics was even more serious, and was created by the continued development of the diesel-electric. Given BR's enormous demand for diesel locomotives in relation to the aggregate production capacity of its chosen suppliers, it was inevitable that many of the Pilot Scheme designs would be outstripped by technological progress and changing operational requirements before deliveries had even been completed. As diesels had begun to assume the responsibility for British Railways' most important and demanding services at the end of the 1950s, the Western Region had not been alone in feeling the need for more powerful locomotives. The early diesel-electric Type 4s with their 130-ton weights and outputs of 2000-2300bhp compared unfavourably with Class 8 steam power in terms of performance, and their 1Co-Co1 wheel arrangement was proving punishing to the permanent way at high speed. Although the Eastern Region had been successful in securing approval for twenty-two 3300bhp 'Deltics' for its own front-line passenger trains, it had still to replace a large number of Pacifics on less prestigious but nonetheless important and well-patronised express services. The London Midland Region was even worse off, as some years would pass before the electrification scheme would be complete and even then only as far as Liverpool and Manchester. Until that time and for some years after on the section north of Weaver Junction, where the Liverpool line left the main Euston-Glasgow route, the LMR would have to replace its magnificent Stanier Pacifics with Type 4s of little more than half the power. On the grades of Shap and Beattock the superior tractive effort of the diesel was an advantage, but not so much as to compensate for the Type 4s' difficulties in maintaining high-speed schedules elsewhere due to their much lower outputs. Thus could be explained the LMR's favour for the more powerful Sulzer engine, though even this could not supply an entire solution within the framework of the existing Derby Type 4 design. Revised gearing could be made to provide better high-speed performance but at the expense of the low-speed tractive effort required for heavy freight movements, and the BTC had to recognise that the WR had, after all, been correct in its pursuit of locomotives with a high power:weight ratio. The result of this was the evolution of a so-called 'Type 4½' specification, DE/M/5 of April 1960, calling for mainline mixed-traffic locomotives of 2700bhp output with a working weight no more than 115 tons.

By the time that Swindon had formulated the larger D1000 design to deal with the increasing demands upon front-line motive power, domestic suppliers were beginning to respond to DE/M/5 with lightweight diesel-electric designs such as the Brush Type 4, able to produce very similar standards of performance, a little hardier perhaps, more suited to BR tastes and most of all, designed and built in Britain. English Electric was also making considerable progress in this field, first seen in the Type 3 D6700s with their intercooled CSVT engines and coming to maturity in the DP2 prototype of 1962 which combined a 2700bhp-rated sixteen-cylinder version of the CSVT with electronic load regulation, then a technical breakthrough. The increased power:weight ratios of these machines over their predecessors allowed the BRB to use the WR's own arguments against it, the issue being clinched by the diesel-electrics' higher braking force, supposedly greater availability and lower initial cost. By early 1963, with deliveries of D6700s and D1500s replacing orders for 'Hymeks' and 'Westerns' respectively, the serious development of diesel-hydraulic traction for use on British Railways had all but ceased.

It was in the light of these developments that BR undertook the 1965 diesel-electric vs diesel-hydraulic tests, the only true comparative survey of the two modes of traction carried out during the entire 1955-1977 period. Given that the decision to terminate large-scale diesel-hydraulic orders had been promulgated as early as 1960, one can justifiably treat with some scepticism the value of the exercise other than in further justifying the mainstream diesel-electric policy. Nevertheless, there can be no doubt that the tests did present a window of opportunity for the continuation of diesel-hydraulic traction on the WR, at least for the full economic life of those locomotives already in traffic or to which BR was otherwise committed. In the event, the failure of the diesel-hydraulic to display a consistent and overwhelming advantage over BR's latest diesel-electrics, albeit under distinctly adverse circumstances, paved the way for the species' wholesale and premature demise. Admittedly, the various Type 4 1Co-Co1s were as much victims of DE/M/5 as the hydraulics but, with nearly four hundred of them on BR's stock books, their retention on freight and secondary passenger duties made sense at least from a strategic point of view. In the case of the less numerous WR locomotives with their reduced suitability for deployment on slow unbraked goods trains, it was all too easy for a hostile BRB to equate the elimination of diesel-hydraulic power with the promotion of the railways' best interests as a whole.

Having defended the diesel-hydraulic, it must be said that, in retrospect, one can see considerable faults with certain aspects of the WR's 1955 traction policy. In its own way it was eminently practicable, but bore the unmistakeable stamp of Keith Grand's perception of the WR as a complete and distinct operating unit. The WR's studies therefore failed to look at the wider implications of dieselisation on a national basis, taking account only of WR needs and not attempting to examine the ramifications of policy decisions as far as the rest of BR was concerned. From the outset this resulted in a certain amount of operational inflexibility, in that as far as possible WR diesel-hydraulics had to be kept on their own territory so as to avoid maintenance problems in areas where shed staff had not been trained on hydraulics. (This should have been obvious to the Western Region's management, given that problems had already been encountered with WR-allocated BR Standards under repair at other works, Swindon's predilection for 'Westernising' the basic design with GWR-pattern components significantly hampering maintenance away from home.) Some doubts have also been expressed about as to how far the WR's support for the diesel-hydraulics was inspired by its reluctance to become involved with the setting-up of a heavy electrical establishment at Swindon, and it is certainly true that the breed was regarded as a convenient vehicle by which to effect modernisation without the need for major staffing upheavals.

That said, it must be remembered that Swindon did have experience of very heavy-duty electrical transmission before virtually any other part of BR, in the form of the two gas-turbine locomotives, and had decided that it did not like it.

Below: On 1 June 1967, D9517 marshals a quantity of 16-ton coal wagons in the grass-grown sidings at Dursley, terminus of the branch from Coaley on the ex-Midland Bristol-Birmingham main line. As BR's emphasis passed from traditional workings such as this to block trains using modern air-braked wagons, the justification for locomotives like D9517 faded not just from the WR, but from the national network as a whole. *(C.G. Maggs)*

Apart from its great weight and cost, electric transmission was felt to be handicapped by its poor ability to transmit high engine outputs at low track speeds, by its propensity to failure following the inevitable ingress of dirt and moisture, and by the damaging effects of axle-hung traction motors upon the roadbed. Ultimately, however, the WR's prime motivation in its choice of traction was the attainment of a high power:weight ratio, and there is no reason to think that diesel-electric traction would not have been chosen from the outset if it had then been able to equal the 25bhp/ton offered by contemporary diesel-hydraulics. Neither is there any evidence to support the oft-expressed contention that the WR opted for diesel-hydraulics solely due to its limited heavy electrical experience, only to be horrified by the amount of electrical control gear needed by any diesel, regardless of its transmission type. True, there were some initial problems experienced in the fitting-out of D800, but the BBC all-electric system was notably complex by the standards of 1958 and with the help of the manufacturer, the difficulties were very quickly overcome. In overall terms this was nothing more than an example of the teething troubles to be expected with the redirection of any large organisation, and in no way cast doubt upon the WR's reasons for promoting diesel-hydraulic rather than diesel-electric traction. From the beginning it had been realised that new skills and working methods would be required in order to get the best from the new locomotives and in the early years at least, the WR rarely flinched from whatever effort was necessary to acquire these. Only in later years, with the original management team gone and the region subjected to various contradictory pressures from above aimed at eradicating steam as quickly as possible, did the WR's diesel-hydraulic programme begin to display definite signs of having lost its direction.

Many of the failings experienced with the hydraulics were endemic to the system, and would have been encountered regardless of the mode of traction used. Despite having had the benefit of sending a party to study at first hand dieselisation in the United States during the early 1950s, the BTC seems to have learned curiously little from it. The first North American Class 1 railroad to dieselise completely had been the Gulf, Mobile & Ohio in October 1949 but, despite the diesel's burgeoning popularity, by the mid-1950s some of America's largest railroads were still to rid themselves completely of steam traction, offering a graphic demonstration of the profits and pitfalls of dieselisation. Paramount was the need to get maximum utilisation out of the new motive power from the beginning; the diesel's initial costs were far higher than those of comparable steam power and worthwhile savings only materialised through intensive use. This, in turn, was reliant upon diagramming which made the most of the diesel's short servicing and turn-around times, and upon an extremely high level of availability which was basically dependent upon maintenance standards. These could only be guaranteed through the provision of appropriate servicing and repair facilities, divorced from the largely filthy conditions which steam locomotives had to tolerate. Obvious though it might sound, one of the most important steps towards successful dieselisation was that of buying the right locomotives for the job in the first place. As in Britain, commercial locomotive builders were all eager to get a slice of what promised to be a very lucrative pie and competition between them was fierce. The passage of time would demonstrate that not all entrants to the market were equal, but persuasive salesmen and old loyalties would cause not a few railroads to make some very expensive mistakes indeed.

Those American railroads that were most successful in their transition to diesel power were usually those which invested in servicing and maintenance facilities to get the most out of their remaining steam traction whilst dieselising area by area using a small variety of well-proven locomotive types. By contrast, those that saw the steam locomotive as

simply being out of date and replaced it by the diesel without any corresponding attempt at altering working practices to optimise utilisation mostly found that, instead of getting better, their problems got worse in a hurry. By the late 1960s, the American railroad map would be littered with the struggling remains of once-great carriers such as the Chicago, Rock Island & Pacific, the New York Central System and the Pennsylvania Railroad which, by failing to get the maximum use from their new locomotives, were quite literally bankrupted by the enormous costs of dieselisation.

These 'fallen flags' served to demonstrate the dangers of relying upon unproven motive power bought en-masse and then not used to best effect. The warning signs had been apparent to industry analysts from the early 1950s at least, but the BTC then went and repeated the mistake by discarding the provisions of the Pilot Scheme in favour of quantity purchases of nearly every example of diesel motive power offered by British constructors. By doing so, the Commission also taxed British Railways with the long-term burden of a large quantity of locomotives all reaching the end of their useful lives together, potentially requiring yet another massive injection of funds. Had the principles of comprehensively proving a limited number of locomotive types before their general deployment been adhered to, as in the case of the WR with its initial conversion scheme, then the final results of BR's dieselisation could have been rather more positive. As it was, the reality of the situation was that, in general, diesel performance on British Railways into the mid-1970s was usually appalling and availabilities frequently below those of the displaced steam traction. The slightly more delicate mechanisms of the diesel-hydraulics might have made them somewhat more susceptible to the effects of faulty ancillaries and the like, but many observers still feel that they were judged consistently more harshly than were BR's diesel-electrics. To their everlasting credit, no WR diesel-hydraulic class, even the more troublesome

Above: D1041 as many will recall the 'Westerns' in their final days, approaching Sonning Cutting with a train of westbound stone empties on 3 October 1975. Some drivers still relate the consummate ease with which the D1000 class handled these often immensely heavy trains, especially when starting away from rest. With the initial application of power, the 'Westerns' would sink down on their suspension and then, as the small amount of slip in the transmissions' primary converters was taken-up, would rock once or twice on their springs before accelerating smoothly away with a consist that would have stalled any of BR's contemporary diesel-electrics. *(Tom Heavyside)*

NBL types, ever had to be subjected to the costly and embarrassing total refurbishment programmes applied to several contemporary diesel-electric designs soon after their introduction. The epidemic of grave engine problems which afflicted the D1500s has already been mentioned, embarrassing the BRB not only by its emergence contemporaneous with the 1965 diesel-electric vs diesel-hydraulic report but also through the fact that the first documented instances were on machines allocated to the WR! Lightened in order to meet the Brush Type 4 specification, the Sulzer 12LDA28C engines had begun to display serious crankcase fractures, requiring the entire class to be withdrawn one by one whilst the engines were rectified. At the same time, re-timing and re-balancing modifications were necessary to forestall similar difficulties with the earlier 12LDA28B units in the Derby Type 4s.

Only two years later, with this programme still underway, BR was forced to concede that the chronic bedplate fractures now increasingly endemic amongst the Brush Type 2's Mirlees engines were incurable within a traction environment. The only viable solution was to rebuild the entire class of 263 locomotives with English Electric units, the £5 million cost of which would be recouped in part by returning the original engines to Mirlees to be overhauled and sold for marine use. Other diesel-electric designs were plagued with lesser, but still serious problems; even the world-beating 'Deltics' were described as a "maintenance menace" and were tolerated only because they were then the one means open to BR of bringing 'electric' standards of running to the East Coast mainline. Most appalling of all was the fact that, despite conforming to overall BTC specifications, at least half a dozen diesel-electric classes of various designs and manufactures were withdrawn altogether after short and inactive lives, during which they had proved themselves utterly impossible to maintain in regular service. The expense and trouble which resulted over the years makes that incurred by the WR diesel-hydraulics pale into insignificance. Indeed, in 1968 Maybach suggested that the early problems suffered with the D1000s might well have been rectified a lot sooner had BR's technical officers been less preoccupied with getting the principal diesel-electric classes to perform to an acceptable standard. In this contention they were probably correct: maintenance of locomotives in traffic most certainly suffered as staff were transferred to assist in the various refurbishment programmes.

The Western Region, of course, also had its share of hopeless cases, the D9500s being redundant virtually before their construction and the two North British Pilot Scheme batches (D600-4 and D6300-5) being neither sufficiently numerous nor successful to justify the eventual costs of keeping them in traffic. Nevertheless, what should have been a selective weeding-out soon became a case of wholesale clearance, the slightest shortcomings in a diesel-hydraulic serving to justify its extinction. One example concerned the history of engine problems experienced with the NBL-built Types 2 and 4, the correction of which through the use of different prime movers was vetoed by the BRB after similar work on twenty of the Scottish Region's North British D6100 diesel-electrics failed to yield more than mediocre results. Whilst the Board's decision in this particular instance was clearly justified, less easily explicable was its overriding of local initiatives to engineer out some of the MAN engines' more common failings, the call for their wholesale withdrawal coming just as the modifications were returning tangible improvements in reliability. Another clear failing of both BTC and BRB was the complete absence of attention paid to proposals which would have succeeded in increasing the operational flexibility of existing locomotive stocks, not least in the case of the WR hydraulics. The failure of BR to pursue electric train-heating experiments with D870 has already been dwelt-upon; had the gear been fitted, it would have done much to facilitate the subsequent provision of train air-braking equipment by allowing the removal of the troublesome steam generators, thus releasing the internal space required for extra braking reservoirs. Indeed, even if they had lacked provision for any sort of train heating whatsoever, by the end of the 1960s a quantity of dual-braked Maybach-engined D800s could usefully have been employed on Freightliner and similar fast freight duties, but the possibilities were not pursued. By the time that a chronic shortage of mid-range motive power in the mid-1970s awakened BR to the need for maximum operational flexibility, the 'Warships' had long since gone.

The problem of providing electric train-heating on diesel-hydraulics was once again cited as justification for the early demise of the 'Westerns', including those rebuilt for train dual-braking only a short time before. The task would have presented more than a few difficulties but, contrary to the BRB's own claims, they were certainly not insurmountable. Whilst proposals to fit Class 52s with an auxiliary generator powered by a Leyland diesel engine were quickly rejected as being impracticable, similar conversions were

already *de rigueur* for many older diesels on both European and North American systems, and before long the same concept would be used to adapt a number of Scottish Region Type 2s for ETH delivery. An even simpler and mechanically more elegant solution would have been to have fitted the engines with auxiliary generators to supply the ETH circuits, and to have uprated them to their UIC setting of 1500bhp to compensate for the resulting power loss, a suitable model for emulation existing in the conversion of the Eastern Region's 'Deltics' to ETH some years before. The abandonment of proposals to equip D870 for electric heating tended to imply that the D1000s would not be similarly modified, and this assumption was proven true. By the time that the class had overcome its teething troubles, the diesel-electric had been confirmed as BR's motive power of the future. As with the other WR diesel-hydraulic classes, it was not the way but rather the will that was lacking to improve their utilisation.

So was the short-lived Western Region traction policy a bold and far-sighted experiment or merely a poorly-justified attempt at being different? Whilst the somewhat blinkered approach of the WR with regard to such aspects as the compatibility of its own strategies with those adopted by the rest of BR might well serve to vitiate the first evaluation, the available evidence indicates that the latter is most certainly not the case. At the time of the Modernisation Plan, with neither the long-term retention of steam nor the prospect of widespread electrification figuring as available options, the WR's analysis of its needs had indicated that contemporary diesel-electric traction would not prove sufficient to sustain all requirements for the foreseeable future. Under such circumstances, its decision to consider any other traction policy capable of meeting its targets was eminently sensible, and not merely an expression of a vehement desire to be different, as interpreted by the BTC. If some BTC officers found themselves disturbed by the strength of the WR's commitment to its cause, it reflected their own refusal to accept the unique nature of the WR's requirements as much if not more than any determination on the part of those at Paddington to achieve their objectives regardless of cost.

Having witnessed what it believed was a suitable model for emulation in the successful traction policy of the Deutsche Bundesbahn, the crux of the Western Region's objectives was to translate that strategy to its own territory, and an integral part of this was the diesel-hydraulic locomotive. Many still contest that whilst the WR's aims were laudable, its reliance upon the diesel-hydraulic was a mistake, but it should be remembered that over the greater part of the 1960s the D800 'Warships', the WR's first essay in diesel-hydraulic traction, were amassing mileages consistently in excess of half as much again as their predecessors, and at a higher load factor as well, whilst in the process outperforming all but one of their contemporaries on British Railways. In this respect alone, they made a contribution to the modernisation of the Western Region at least equal to that of any other mainline diesel and deserve appropriate recognition by future historians. After protracted initial difficulties, the 'Hymeks' and 'Westerns' too would emerge as some of the WR's most valuable motive power during this decade, and it was unfortunate that they should have their working lives cut short by centralised policies aimed at producing a cheaper railway rather than a better one. In the balance, it is apparent that the WR's use of mainline diesel-hydraulics gave overall results which were no worse and, indeed, frequently superior to anything else seen on British Railways at the time. However, given the species' small numbers, total non-conformity and the political weight carried by the railway construction industry within BRB circles, it was inevitable that the interests of mass-standardisation should eventually find against it.

Appendix One
LOCOMOTIVE DATA

D600 'Warship' A1A-A1A, Type 4

Numbers	D600-4
Builder	North British Locomotive
Company	Glasgow
Engines	*D600-1* Two MAN L12V18/21A of 1000bhp @ 1500rpm
	D602-4 Two MAN L12V18/21S of 1000bhp @ 1500rpm
Transmissions	Two Voith L306r
Length	65'0"
Width	8'8"
Height	12'10"
Wheel Diameter	*Driven* 45"
	Idling 39½"
Fixed Wheelbase	15'0",
Total Wheelbase	50'0", 35'0" between bogie centres
Fuel Capacity	800 gallons
Water Capacity	1000 gallons
Boiler	Spanner Mk 1a
Braking System	*Locomotive:* Air
	Train: Vacuum
Braking Force	88 tons
Tractive Effort	*Starting:* 49,460 lbs (at wheelrim)
	Continuous: 39,600 lbs @ 12.6mph
Gross Weight	117.4 tons
Maximum Speed	90 mph
Minimum Curve	4½ chains dead slow
WR Route Code	Red
TOPS Class	41

The following names were carried:

D600	Active
D601	Ark Royal
D602	Bulldog
D603	Conquest
D604	Cossack

The locomotives were built under NBL Order No.L76, BTC (Swindon) Lot No.425. NBL works numbers were in the series 27660-27664.

D6300 B-B, Type 2

Numbers	D6300-57
Builder	North British Locomotive
Company	Glasgow
Engine	*D6300-5* MAN L12V18/21S of 1000bhp @ 1500rpm
	D6306-57 MAN L12V18/21B of 1100bhp @ 1500rpm
Transmission	*D6300-5* Voith L306r
	D6306-57 Voith LT306r
Length	46'8"
Width	8'8"
Height	12'10"
Wheel Diameter	45"
Fixed Wheelbase	8'6"
Total Wheelbase	31'6", 23'0" between centres

Fuel Capacity	450 gallons	
Water Capacity	500 gallons	
Boiler	D6300-5	Spanner Mk 1a
	D6306-25	Clayton RO-100
	D6326-57	Stone-Vapor OK4610
Braking System	*Locomotive:* Air	
	Train: Vacuum	
Braking Force	*D6300-5*	52.8 tons
	D6306-57	48.1 tons
Tractive effort (at wheelrim)		
	D6300-5	**Starting:** 45,000 lbs
		Continuous: 23,900 lbs @ 10.4 mph
	D6306-57	**Starting:** 43,500 lbs
		Continuous: 30,000 lbs @ 8 mph
Gross Weight	*D6300-5*	68 tons
	D6306-57	65 tons
Maximum Speed	75 mph	
Minimum Curve	4½ chains dead slow	
WR Route Code	Blue	
TOPS Class	22	

D6300-5 were built under NBL Order No.L77, BTC (Swindon) Lot No.426, and carried NBL works numbers 27665-27670.

D6306-57 were built under NBL Order No.L97, BTC (Swindon) Lot No.440, and carried NBL works numbers 27879-27930.

D800 'Warship' B-B, Type 4

Numbers	D800-70	
Builders	*D800-32*	BR Swindon
	D833-65	North British Locomotive Company, Glasgow
	D866-70	BR Swindon
Engines	*D800-2*	Two Maybach MD650 of 1050bhp @ 1500rpm
	D803-29	Two Maybach MD650 of 1135bhp @ 1500rpm
	D830	Two Paxman 12YJXL of 1135bhp @ 1500rpm
	D831-2	Two Maybach MD650 of 1135bhp @ 1500rpm
	D833-65	Two MAN L12V18/21B of 1100bhp @ 1500rpm
	D866-70	Two Maybach MD650 of 1135bhp @ 1500rpm
Transmissions	*D800-32*	Two Mekydro K104
	D833-65	Two Voith Lt306r
	D866-70	Two Mekydro K104
Length	60'0"	
Width	8'10"	
Height	13'0"	
Wheel Diameter	39½"	
Fixed Wheelbase	10'6"	
Total Wheelbase	48'3", 37'9" between centres	
Fuel Capacity	800 gallons	
Water Capacity	940 gallons	

Boiler	D800-12	Spanner Mk 1a	
	D813-7	Stone-Vapor OK4625	
	D818	Spanner Mk IIIa	
	D819-32	Stone-Vapor OK4625	
	D833-70	Spanner Mk 1a	

Braking System Locomotive: Air
Train: Vacuum

Braking Force 55 tons

Tractive Effort (at wheelrim)

D800-2	**Starting:** 48,600 lbs
	Continuous: 43,800 lbs @ 11.8 mph
D803-29	**Starting:** 48,600 lbs
	Continuous: 48,700lbs @ 11.8 mph
D830	**Starting:** 47,780 lbs
	Continuous: 48,700 lbs @ 11.8 mph
D831-2	**Starting:** 48,600 lbs
	Continuous: 48,700lbs @ 11.8 mph
D833-65	**Starting:** 49,030 lbs
	Continuous: 37,000 lbs @ 14 mph
D866-70	**Starting:** 48,600 lbs
	Continuous: 48,700lbs @ 11.8 mph

Gross Weight	D800-29	78.6 tons
	D830	77.8 tons
	D831-2	78.6 tons
	D833-65	80.8 tons
	D866-70	78.6 tons

Maximum Speed	90 mph
Minimum Curve	4^{1}/$_{2}$ chains dead slow
WR Route Code	Red

TOPS Class	D800-32	42
	D833-65	43
	D866-70	42

The following names were carried:

D800	Sir Brian Robertson	**D801**	Vanguard
D802	Formidable	**D803**	Albion
D804	Avenger	**D805**	Benbow
D806	Cambrian	**D807**	Caradoc
D808	Centaur	**D809**	Champion
D810	Cockade	**D811**	Daring
D812	The Royal Navy Reserve 1859-1959		
D813	Diadem	**D814**	Dragon
D815	Druid	**D816**	Eclipse
D817	Foxhound	**D818**	Glory
D819	Goliath	**D820**	Grenville
D821	Greyhound	**D822**	Hercules
D823	Hermes	**D824**	Highflyer
D825	Intrepid	**D826**	Jupiter
D827	Kelly	**D828**	Magnificent
D829	Magpie	**D830**	Majestic
D831	Monarch	**D832**	Onslaught
D833	Panther	**D834**	Pathfinder
D835	Pegasus	**D836**	Powerful
D837	Ramilles	**D838**	Rapid
D839	Relentless	**D840**	Resistance
D841	Roebuck	**D842**	Royal Oak
D843	Sharpshooter	**D844**	Spartan
D845	Sprightly	**D846**	Steadfast
D847	Strongbow	**D848**	Sultan
D849	Superb	**D850**	Swift
D851	Temeraire	**D852**	Tenacious
D853	Thruster	**D854**	Tiger
D855	Triumph	**D856**	Trojan
D857	Undaunted	**D858**	Valorous
D859	Vanquisher	**D860**	Victorious

D861	Vigilant	**D862**	Viking
D863	Warrior	**D864**	Zambesi
D865	Zealous	**D866**	Zebra
D867	Zenith	**D868**	Zephyr
D869	Zest	**D870**	Zulu

Four locomotives, D800/12/64/5 were renamed prior to entering service and therefore never carried their original allocations which were:

D800	Vanguard
D812	Despatch
D864	Zealous
D865	Zenith

In the case of D800/64/5 the displaced plates were applied to subsequent locomotives. Despatch, however, was not re-allocated and the unused plates would be rediscovered at Swindon Works after many years in store.
D800-2 were built under BTC (Swindon) Lot No.428, D803-32 under Lot No.437 and D866-70 under Lot No.448. In line with BR practice, none were accorded individual works numbers.
D833-65 were built under NBL Order No.L100, BTC (Swindon) Lot No.443, and were allotted NBL works numbers in the series 27962-27994.

D7000 B-B, Type 3

Numbers	D7000-100
Builder	Beyer-Peacock (Gorton) Ltd, Manchester
Engine	Maybach MD870 of 1740bhp @ 1500rpm
Transmission	Mekydro K184
Length	51'8"
Width	8'10"
Height	12'10"
Wheel Diameter	45"
Fixed Wheelbase	10'6"
Total Wheelbase	36'0", 25'6" between centres
Fuel Capacity	800 gallons
Water Capacity	800 gallons
Boiler	D7000-44 Stone-Vapor OK4616
	D7045-100 Spanner Mk IIIa

Braking System Locomotive: Air
Train: Vacuum

Braking Force 55 tons

Tractive Effort (at wheelrim)
Starting: 46,600 lbs
Continuous: 33,950 lbs @ 12.5 mph

Gross Weight	75.4 tons
Maximum Speed	90 mph
Minimum Curve	4 chains dead slow
WR Route Code	Red
TOPS Class	35

The D7000s were allotted Beyer-Peacock works numbers in two batches, D7000-44 carrying 7894-7938 whilst D7045-100 received 7949-8004. However, due to B-P and BTC orders beginning and ending at different points, construction took place in no less than six nominally separate batches, viz:

Loco Numbers	BTC (Swindon) Lot No.	B-P Order Number
D7000-4	449	1711
D7005-14	449	1712
D7015-44	449	1713
D7045-69	455	1714
D7070-94	455	1715
D7095-100	457	1715

D1000 'Western' C-C, Type 4

Numbers	D1000-73	
Builders	D1000-29	BR Swindon
	D1030-73	BR Crewe

Engines	Two Maybach MD655 of 1380bhp @ 1500rpm
Transmissions	Two Voith L630rV
Length	68'0"
Width	9'0"
Height	13'1"
Wheel Diameter	45"
Fixed Wheelbase	12'2"
Total Wheelbase	54'8", 42'6" between centres
Fuel Capacity	800 gallons, 714 gallons on locomotives with train air brakes
Water Capacity	980 gallons, 800 gallons on locomotives with train air brakes
Boiler	Spanner Mk IIIa
Braking System	*Locomotive:* Air
	Train: Vacuum, D1000-16/21-73 eventually converted to train dual-braking
Braking Force	82 tons

Tractive Effort (at wheelrim)

Starting: 72,000 lbs

Continuous: 45,200 @ 14.5 mph

Gross Weight	108 tons, 109 tons after dual-braking
Maximum Speed	90 mph
Minimum Curve	4$\frac{1}{2}$ chains dead slow
WR Route Code	Red
TOPS Class	52

The following names were carried:

D1000	Western Enterprise	D1001	Western Pathfinder
D1002	Western Explorer	D1003	Western Pioneer
D1004	Western Crusader	D1005	Western Venturer
D1006	Western Stalwart	D1007	Western Talisman
D1008	Western Harrier	D1009	Western Invader
D1010	Western Campaigner	D1011	Western Thunderer
D1012	Western Firebrand	D1013	Western Ranger
D1014	Western Leviathan	D1015	Western Champion
D1016	Western Gladiator	D1017	Western Warrior
D1018	Western Buccaneer	D1019	Western Challenger
D1020	Western Hero	D1021	Western Cavalier
D1022	Western Sentinel	D1023	Western Fusilier
D1024	Western Huntsman	D1025	Western Guardsman
D1026	Western Centurion	D1027	Western Lancer
D1028	Western Hussar	D1029	Western Legionnaire
D1030	Western Musketeer	D1031	Western Rifleman
D1032	Western Marksman	D1033	Western Trooper
D1034	Western Dragoon	D1035	Western Yeoman
D1036	Western Emperor	D1037	Western Empress
D1038	Western Sovereign	D1039	Western King
D1040	Western Queen	D1041	Western Prince
D1042	Western Princess	D1043	Western Duke
D1044	Western Duchess	D1045	Western Viscount
D1046	Western Marquis	D1047	Western Lord
D1048	Western Lady	D1049	Western Monarch
D1050	Western Ruler	D1051	Western Ambassador
D1052	Western Viceroy	D1053	Western Patriarch
D1054	Western Governor	D1055	Western Advocate
D1056	Western Sultan	D1057	Western Chieftain
D1058	Western Nobleman	D1059	Western Empire
D1060	Western Dominion	D1061	Western Envoy
D1062	Western Courier	D1063	Western Monitor
D1064	Western Regent	D1065	Western Consort
D1066	Western Prefect	D1067	Western Druid
D1068	Western Reliance	D1069	Western Vanguard
D1070	Western Gauntlet	D1071	Western Renown
D1072	Western Glory	D1073	Western Bulwark

D1029 was originally fitted with nameplates reading Western Legionaire. Revised plates carrying the correct spelling were fitted sometime during 1967, possibly using the original components but with the additional letter 'let-in'. Locomotives built at Swindon were covered by BTC (Swindon) Lot No.450 and those at Crewe by BTC (Crewe) Order No.DE286. In line with BR practice, none were accorded individual works numbers. D1030-34 were originally covered by the Swindon order but transferred to Crewe prior to construction.

Some sources indicate that an additional ten locomotives were at one stage intended to be built at Crewe. This may refer to a project discussed at Swindon in December 1961, the proposal being that the locomotives should use 12-cylinder Paxman engines similar to those fitted to D830. Diesel-hydraulic orders ceased before it could be put into effect.

D9500 0-6-0DH, Type 1

Numbers	D9500-55
Builder	BR Swindon
Engine	Paxman 6YJXL of 650bhp @ 1500rpm
	Transmission Voith L217u in conjunction with triple reduction Hunslet reversing jack shaft gearbox
Length	34'7"
Width	8'7"
Height	13'0"
Wheel Diameter	48"
Wheelbase	15'6"
Fuel Capacity	338 gallons
Braking System	*Locomotive:* Air
	Train: Vacuum
Braking Force	43 tons
Tractive Effort	*Starting:* 30,910 lbs (at wheelrim)
	Continuous: 26,690 lbs @ 5.6 mph
Gross Weight	50 tons
Maximum Speed	40 mph
Minimum Curve	4$\frac{1}{2}$ chains dead slow
WR Route Coding	Yellow
TOPS Class	14

The locomotives were built under BTC (Swindon) Lot No.473. No individual works numbers were allocated.

Appendix Two
LIVERIES

D600

As built, body throughout Locomotive Green, BR Specification No.30. Roof panels grey to BSS 2660-9-100. 4"-wide Light Grey waistline to BSS 2660-5-058. Bufferbeam and buffer-stocks red to BSS 2660-0-005. Bogies, wheels, underframe, battery boxes and drawgear black to BSS 2660-9-103. 6" white lettering. Nameplate ground 'Kemitone' Signal Red. BR locomotive emblem. From 1962 onwards, yellow panel on nose end to BSS 2660-0-003.

Late 1966 onwards, D600/2 only. Body and roof panels BR Blue Specification No.53. Bogies, bufferbeams, underframes and battery boxes black to BSS 2660-9-103. Lettering and BR logo in white. Nameplate ground black. D600 with full yellow end to BSS 2660-0-003, large logos on cabsides. D602 with yellow warning panel to BSS 26600-003 (though slightly wider than normal for this class and with non-radiussed corners), small logo above numberplate.

D6300

As built, body and roof panels BR Locomotive Green to BR Specification No.30. Central roof area on some locomotives grey to BSS 2660-9-100. Beltline Light Grey to BSS 2660-5-058. Bufferbeam and bufferstocks red to BSS 2660-0-005. Bogies, wheels, underframe, fuel tanks etc black to BSS 2660-9-103. 6" white lettering. BR locomotive emblem. 1962 onwards, yellow panel on nose end to BSS 2660-0-003.

Late 1966 onwards, body and roof BR Blue Specification No.53. Bufferbeam and stocks, bogies, underframe and drawgear black to BSS 2660-9-103; some early repaints with bogies and underframe in Carriage Umber to BSS 2660-3-039, but eventually changed to black. Yellow panel on nose end to BSS 2660-0-003. 6" letters in white with central logo. From March 1967 onwards, full yellow ends to BSS 26600-003 (originally including roof dome but subsequently terminated at top of windscreen pillars) with lettering in white corporate typeface and logo on each cabsheet.

D800

As built, body throughout in BR Locomotive Green Specification No.30. Roof hatches on some locomotives grey to BSS 2660-9-100. 4"-wide Light Grey waistline to BSS 2660-558. Bufferbeams and stocks red to BSS 26600-005. Bogies and wheels black to BSS 26609-103. 6" white lettering (possibly Light Grey to BSS 2660-5-58 on early locomotives), BR locomotive emblem. Nameplate ground 'Kemitone' Signal Red. D845/58 with yellow headcode box doors to BSS 2660-0-003 and roof domes in white to BSS 2660, 1961-2 only. From 1962 onwards all locomotives with yellow panel on nose ends to BSS 2660-0-003; D800 withdrawn in this livery. From March 1967 onwards D808/10 given full yellow ends to BSS 26600-003.

Late 1964 onwards, D801/5/6/9/11/2/5/7/213/8/9/32/ 4/37-40/2/4/8/55/61/2/5/9/70. Bodyshell Locomotive Maroon throughout. Roof hatches between bulkheads Mid-Grey to BSS 2660-9-097 or black to BSS 2660-9-103. Bufferbeams, stocks, wheels and bogies black to BSS 2660-9-103. Yellow panels on nose to BSS 2660-0-003. 6" white lettering, BR coaching stock cypher above nameplate. Nameplate ground black. D801/40/8 withdrawn in this livery. From March 1967 full yellow ends to

BSS 2660-0003; D809/15/7/38 withdrawn in this livery.

Late 1966 onwards, all locomotives other than D800/1/9/15/7/-38/40/8. Body throughout BR Blue Specification No.53. Some early repaints in matt finish, though 'eggshell' finish eventually standardised. Bogies, wheels, bufferbeams and stocks black to BSS 2660-9-103. Small yellow panel to BSS 2660-0-003 on some locomotives but full yellow ends to BSS 2660-0-003 adopted as standard from March 1967. 6" lettering and logo in white. Black ground to nameplates. Skirts, bufferbeams, bogies and wheels on D864 in Carriage Umber to BSS 2660-3-039; this shade possibly used for bogies and wheels only on some other early repaints, soon reverting to black.

D7000

As built, main part of body BR Locomotive Green to BR Specification No.30. Wide skirt band in green-yellow to BSS 2660-5062. Roof panels Mid-Grey to BSS 2660-9100. Cab window and door surround in white to BSS 2660. Bufferbeams and stocks red to BSS 2660-0-005. Bufferbeam lip black to BSS 2660-9-103 on D7000 only. Underframe, bogies, wheels and tanks black to BSS 26609-103. 6" raised cast numerals in burnished metal finish or painted white to BSS 2660, BR locomotive emblem. From 1962 onwards, yellow nose panel to BSS 2660-0003. From March 1967 onwards, selected locomotives with full yellow ends, cab window and door surrounds to BSS 2660-0003.

December 1966 onwards, loco body and roof BR Blue to BR Specification No.53. Black bufferbeams, stocks, wheels, bogies and tanks to BSS 2660-9-103. 6" cast numerals in burnished metal finish or painted white to BSS 2660, central BR logo. D7004/7/51 with blue window surrounds and black bufferbeam lip; subsequent repaints with white cab window surrounds to BSS 2660 (as for green livery) and blue bufferbeam lip. Full yellow ends and window surrounds to BSS 2660-0-003 adopted from March 1967.

D1000

As built. Loco body in Desert Sand to BSS 2660-3-036 throughout. Roof hatches between bulkheads grey to BSS 2660-9-101. Bufferbeams and stocks red to BSS 2660-0005. Bogies, wheels, drawgear and cab window surrounds black to BSS 2660-9-103. Grounds to name- and numberplates 'Kemitone' Signal Red. Alloy bas-relief emblems on fireman's side of each cab. Yellow end warning panels to BSS 2660-0-003 by 1964.

D1001/5-9/39-42

As built. Loco body in Locomotive Maroon throughout. Roof hatches between bulkheads, bogies, wheels and drawgear black to BSS 2660-9-103. Bufferbeams and stocks yellow to BSS 2660-0003. D1001 only with white cab window surrounds to BSS 2660. Subsequent locomotives with light grey cab window surrounds. Name and numberplate grounds black. BR coaching stock cypher on fireman's side of each cab.

(N.B. The exact formulation of the paint applied to the early D1000s is uncertain, and some of the first Swindon locomotives might have been finished in Coaching Stock Maroon instead of Locomotive Maroon. There was no significant colour variation between the two, Locomotive Maroon simply being a

harder-wearing variety created to withstand the harsh conditions endured on those London Midland Region 'Princess Royal' and 'Princess Coronation' Pacifics restored to Maroon from December 1957 onwards)

D1002-4/35-8

As built. Loco body in BR Locomotive Green to BR Specification No.30 throughout. Roof hatches between bulkheads Mid-Grey to BSS 2660-9-097. Bufferbeams and stocks red to BSS 2660-0-005. Bogies, wheels and drawgear black to BSS 2660-9103. Name- and numberplate grounds 'Kemitone' Signal Red. BR coaching stock cypher on fireman's side of each cab. Yellow end panels to BSS 2660-0-003 (these were adopted at about the time that the first green 'Westerns' entered service and it is debatable whether any D1000s were released to traffic in green without yellow panels).

D1015

As built. Loco body in Golden Ochre (LBSCR 'Improved Engine Green') throughout. Roof hatches between bulkheads in Cambrian Bronze Green. Bufferbeams in Golden Ochre. Bufferstocks, drawgear, bogies and wheels in black to BSS 2660-9-103. Cab window surrounds white to BSS 2660. Experimental 'T'-shaped yellow warning panel to BSS 26600-003 on 'A' end prior to entering service. 'B'-end panel and 'A'-end panel after entry to service of normal design to BSS 2660-0-003 but revised with radiussed lower corners and bottom edge some 3" or so above bufferbeam. Name- and numberplate with black grounds. BR coaching stock cypher on fireman's side of each cab. Bufferstocks and roof hatches between bulkheads repainted in Golden Ochre by June 1964. Cab window surrounds possibly black or dark grey for a while during this period, but definitely repainted Golden Ochre by 30 January 1965 (the locomotive having been specially prepared to work the returning empty stock of Sir Winston Churchill's funeral train that day). Repainted maroon by the end of the year.

D1010-4/6-34/43-73

As built, D1000-3/59/15/35/8-42 as repainted by March 1967. Loco body in Locomotive Maroon throughout. Roof hatches between bulkheads, bogies, wheels, bufferbeams and stocks black to BSS 2660-9-103. Cab window surrounds light grey or white (D1000/1 only). Yellow warning panels to BSS 2660-0-003. Name- and numberplates with black grounds. BR coaching stock cypher or alloy bas-relief emblem (D1000 only) on fireman's side of each cab. From March 1967, full yellow ends and cab window surrounds to BSS 2660-0003 applied to selected locomotives.

D1017/30/6/7/43/7/57

Repainted between late 1966 and early 1967. Loco body in Experimental Chromatic Blue throughout. Yellow warning panels to BSS 2660-0-003. Bufferbeams and stocks (except on D1030), bogies and wheels black to BSS 2660-9-103.

Bufferbeams and stocks on D1030 red to BSS 2660-0-005. Black grounds to name- and numberplates. White BR logo on fireman's side of each cab.

(N.B. The exact specification of D1000s painted in this scheme differed between locomotives, with particular variations concerning the size of BR logos, some of which were handpainted rather than transfers, and the finish of the paintwork itself. Documented variations range from full gloss with small logos on D1030 to full matt with large logos on D1037/57.)

All locomotives repainted after March 1967. Loco body in BR Blue to BR Specification No.53 throughout. Bogies, wheels, bufferbeams and stocks black to BSS 2660-9103; some early repaints with bogies and wheels in Carriage Umber to BSS 2660-3-039, eventually restored to black. Cab front and window surrounds yellow to BSS 2660-0005. Black grounds to name- and numberplates. White BR logo on fireman's side of each cab (including D1000). Yellow battery box door catches to BSS 2660-0-003 on all surviving locomotives from December 1973 (this was specified as early as March 1967 but, progressively having fallen into disuse, was revived as a direct consequence of the West Ealing derailment). D1013 with red grounds to name- and numberplates from 1975. D1023 with headcode box marker lights to BR Specification G39 from November 1976.

D9500

Bonnet side and roof panels, exhaust stack, running plates and tool boxes BR Locomotive Green to BR Specification No.30. Cab sides and ends Sherwood Green, cab roof grey to BSS 2660-9-100. Wheels, underframes and drawgear black to BSS 2660-9-103. Bufferbeams and stocks yellow to BSS 2660-0-003. Bonnet ends black and yellow warning chevrons. Handrails and footsteps in white to BSS 2660. Lettering painted in white 'Grotesque' typeface on cabsides, surmounted by BR coaching stock cypher.

The above is a compendium of livery styles observed on the WR diesel-hydraulic fleet between 1958 and 1977. Whilst it includes significant variations from standard and the experimental schemes applied to the D1000 class between 1961 and 1967, it does not take account of early and incorrect applications of the BR Blue livery (as distinct from Experimental Chromatic Blue) on D800 and D7000 types in particular, minor variations in lettering or schemes carried only in industrial use and/or in preservation. D800 is known to have carried 'Speed Whiskers' on the ends prior to completion, but these had disappeared by the time that the locomotive had been finished in green so are not recorded. Similarly, a D1000-class locomotive is reputed to have been finished in Gloss Black prior to entering service, but no documentary or photographic evidence to support this conjecture has yet been produced. Given its aversion to the black and silver livery imposed upon its gas-turbines, it seems strange to say the least if the WR then went and experimented with the idea of a black 'Western'. More plausible, if still unlikely, is the possibility that a locomotive was temporarily finished in the Cambrian Bronze Green used on the roof hatches of D1015, a particularly deep hue that could and did appear black under shaded conditions.

CASE HISTORIES

	Date to Traffic	First Allocation	Allocation as of Nov.1966	Last Allocation	Date Withdrawn	Final Disposal
D600 Class						
D600	1/58	Swindon	Laira	Laira	12/67	WB 3/70
D601	3/58	Laira	Landore	Laira	12/67	WB 6/80
D602	11/58	Laira	Landore	Laira	12/67	CN 12/68
D603	11/58	Laira	Laira	Laira	12/67	CN 12/68
D604	1/59	Laira	Landore	Laira	12/67	CN 9/68
D6300 Class						
D6300	1/59	Swindon	Laira	Laira	5/68	CN 1/69
D6301	1/59	Swindon	Laira	Laira	12/67	CS 5/68
D6302	1/59	Swindon	Laira	Laira	5/68	CN 11/68
D6303	5/59	Laira	Laira	Laira	5/68	CN 1/69
D6304	6/59	Laira	Laira	Laira	5/68	CN 12/68
D6305	1/60	Laira	Laira	Laira	5/68	CN 11/68
D6306	10/59	Laira	Laira	Laira	12/68	CN 6/69
D6307	10/59	Laira	Laira	Laira	3/71	ZL 12/71
D6308	1/60	Laira	Laira	Laira	9/71	ZL 6/72
D6309	1/60	Laira	Laira	Laira	5/71	ZL 12/71
D6310	1/60	Laira	Laira	Bristol	3/71	ZL 5/72
D6311	1/60	Laira	Laira	Laira	9/68	CN 5/69
D6312	1/60	Laira	Laira	Laira	5/71	ZL 1/72
D6313	2/60	Laira	Laira	Laira	8/68	CN 12/68
D6314	2/60	Laira	N A	Laira	4/69	CN 8/69
D6315	2/60	Laira	N A	Laira	5/71	ZL 1/72
D6316	3/60	Laira	N A	Bristol	3/68	CN 1/69
D6317	3/60	Laira	N A	Laira	9/68	CN 6/69
D6318	3/60	Laira	N A	Laira	5/71	ZL 3/72
D6319	4/60	Laira	N A	Laira	9/71	ZL 12/72
D6320	3/60	Laira	N A	Bristol	5/71	ZL 6/72
D6321	4/60	Laira	N A	Bristol	8/68	CN 7/69
D6322	4/60	Laira	N A	Laira	10/71	ZL 5/72
D6323	4/60	Laira	N A	Laira	5/71	ZL 8/72
D6324	6/60	Laira	Laira	Bristol	5/71	ZL 6/72
D6325	6/60	Laira	N A	Bristol	10/68	CN 6/69
D6326	6/60	Laira	Old Oak	Laira	10/71	ZL 3/72
D6327	6/60	Laira	Old Oak	Bristol	5/71	ZL 7/72
D6328	6/60	Laira	Old Oak	Laira	7/71	ZL 5/72
D6329	6/60	Laira	N A	Bristol	11/68	CN 6/69
D6330	6/60	Laira	Bristol	Laira	10/71	ZL 6/72
D6331	7/60	Laira	Bristol	Bristol	3/71	ZL 3/72
D6332	7/60	Laira	Old Oak	Old Oak	5/71	ZL 12/71
D6333	8/60	Laira	Bristol	Laira	1/72	ZL 8/72
D6334	12/60	Laira	Bristol	Laira	10/71	ZL 4/72
D6335	2/61	Laira	Old Oak	Old Oak	9/68	CN 5/69
D6336	7/61	N A	Bristol	Laira	1/72	ZL 6/72
D6337	3/62	N A	Bristol	Laira	10/71	ZL 6/72
D6338	3/62	Laira	Bristol	Laira	1/72	ZL 2/72
D6339	4/62	Laira	N A	Laira	1/72	ZL 5/72
D6340	4/62	Laira	Old Oak	Laira	5/71	ZL 4/72
D6341	5/62	Laira	Old Oak	Old Oak	11/68	CN 6/69
D6242	5/62	Laira	Old Oak	Bristol	12/68	CN 6/69
D6343	5/62	Laira	Old Oak	Laira	10/71	ZL 1/72
D6344	5/62	Laira	Old Oak	Old Oak	9/68	CN 5/69
D6345	5/62	Laira	Old Oak	Old Oak	9/68	CN 6/69
D6346	6/62	Laira	Old Oak	Old Oak	4/69	CN 8/69
D6347	6/62	Bristol	Old Oak	Old Oak	3/68	BN 11/68
D6348	6/62	Laira	Old Oak	Laira	7/71	ZL 4/72
D6349	6/62	Laira	Old Oak	Bristol	9/68	ZL 10/71
D6350	6/62	Laira	Old Oak	Old Oak	8/68	CN 7/69
D6351	6/62	Laira	Old Oak	Old Oak	11/68	CN 7/69
D6352	7/62	Laira	Old Oak	Bristol	5/71	ZL 11/71
D6353	7/62	Laira	Old Oak	Old Oak	9/68	CN 7/69
D6354	8/62	Laira	Old Oak	Bristol	5/71	ZL 2/72
D6355	8/62	Bristol	Old Oak	Old Oak	9/68	CN 7/69
D6356	9/62	Bristol	Old Oak	Laira	10/71	ZL 1/72
D6357	11/62	Bristol	Old Oak	Old Oak	12/68	CN 7/69
D800 Class						
D800	7/58	Swindon	Laira	Laira	10/68	CN 7/69
D801	11/58	Laira	Laira	Laira	8/68	ZL 10/70
D802	12/58	Laira	Laira	Laira	10/68	ZL 11/70
D803	3/59	Laira	Laira	N A	1/72	ZL 10/72
D804	4/59	Laira	Laira	Laira	10/71	ZL 4/72
D805	5/59	Laira	Laira	Laira	10/72	ZL 6/73
D806	6/59	Laira	Laira	Laira	11/72	ZL 5/75
D807	6/59	Laira	Laira	Laira	9/72	ZL 11/72
D808	7/59	Laira	Laira	N A	10/71	ZL 2/72
D809	8/59	Laira	Laira	N A	10/71	ZL 10/72
D810	9/59	Laira	Laira	Laira	12/72	ZL 9/73
D811	10/59	Laira	Laira	N A	1/72	ZL 12/72
D812	11/59	Laira	Laira	Laira	12/72	ZL 7/73
D813	12/59	Laira	Laira	N A	1/72	ZL 9/72
D814	1/60	Laira	Laira	Laira	11/72	ZL 2/74
D815	1/60	Laira	Laira	N A	10/71	ZL 10/72
D816	2/60	Laira	Laira	N A	1/72	ZL 9/72
D817	3/60	Laira	Laira	N A	10/71	ZL 2/72
D818	3/60	Laira	Laira	Laira	11/72	ZL 10/85
D819	4/60	Laira	Laira	N A	10/71	ZL 2/72
D820	5/60	Laira	Laira	Laira	11/72	ZL 8/73
D821	5/60	Laira	Laira	Laira	12/72	Note A
D822	6/60	Laira	Laira	Laira	10/71	ZL 2/72
D823	7/60	Laira	Laira	Laira	10/71	ZL 5/72
D824	7/60	Laira	Laira	Laira	12/72	ZL 6/75
D825	8/60	Laira	Laira	Laira	8/72	ZL 12/72
D826	9/60	Laira	Laira	Laira	10/71	ZL 1/72
D827	9/60	Laira	N A	N A	1/72	ZL 10/72
D828	10/60	Laira	N A	Laira	8/71	ZL 4/72
D829	11/60	Laira	N A	Laira	8/71	ZL 4/72
D830	1/61	Laira	N A	N A	1/72	ZL 10/72
D831	1/61	Laira	N A	Laira	10/71	ZL 6/72
D832	2/61	Laira	N A	Laira	12/72	Note B
D833	7/60	Laira	N A	N A	10/71	ZL 1/72
D834	7/60	Laira	N A	N A	10/71	ZL 12/72
D835	8/60	Laira	N A	N A	10/71	ZL 1/72
D836	9/60	Laira	N A	N A	5/71	ZL 3/72
D837	11/60	Laira	N A	N A	5/71	ZL 6/72

	Date to Traffic	First Allocation	Allocation as of Nov.1966	Last Allocation	Date Withdrawn	Final Disposal
D838	9/60	Laira	N A	N A	3/71	ZL 7/72
D839	11/60	Laira	N A	N A	10/71	ZL 7/72
D840	2/61	Laira	N A	Laira	4/69	ZL 10/70
D841	12/60	Laira	N A	N A	10/71	ZL 12/72
D842	12/60	Laira	N A	N A	10/71	ZL 3/72
D843	1/61	Laira	N A	N A	5/71	ZL 3/72
D844	3/61	Laira	N A	N A	10/71	ZL 5/72
D845	4/61	Laira	N A	N A	10/71	ZL 5/72
D846	4/61	Laira	N A	N A	5/71	ZL 11/71
D847	4/61	Laira	N A	N A	3/71	ZL 3/72
D848	4/61	Laira	N A	Old Oak	3/69	ZL 7/70
D849	5/61	Laira	Laira	N A	5/71	ZL 6/72
D850	6/61	Laira	N A	N A	5/71	ZL 3/72
D851	6/61	Laira	N A	N A	5/71	ZL 5/72
D852	7/61	Laira	N A	N A	10/71	ZL 5/72
D853	8/61	Laira	N A	N A	10/71	ZL 6/72
D854	9/61	Laira	N A	N A	10/71	ZL 4/72
D855	9/61	Laira	N A	N A	10/71	ZL 4/72
D856	10/61	Laira	N A	N A	5/71	ZL 12/71
D857	11/61	Laira	N A	N A	10/71	ZL 4/72
D858	12/61	Laira	N A	N A	10/71	ZL 5/72
D859	1/62	Laira	N A	N A	3/71	ZL 6/72
D860	1/62	Laira	N A	N A	3/71	ZL 12/71
D861	3/62	Laira	N A	N A	10/71	ZL 7/72
D862	4/62	Laira	N A	N A	10/71	ZL 4/72
D863	4/62	Laira	N A	N A	3/69	CN 7/69
D864	5/62	Laira	N A	N A	3/71	ZL 11/71
D865	6/62	Laira	N A	N A	5/71	ZL 5/72
D866	3/61	Laira	N A	N A	1/72	ZL 9/72
D867	4/61	Laira	N A	Laira	10/71	ZL 9/72
D868	5/61	Laira	N A	Laira	10/71	ZL 3/72
D869	6/61	Laira	N A	Laira	10/71	ZL 6/72
D870	9/61	Laira	N A	Laira	8/71	ZL 4/72

D7000 Class

	Date to Traffic	First Allocation	Allocation as of Nov.1966	Last Allocation	Date Withdrawn	Final Disposal
D7000	5/61	Bristol	Bristol	Old Oak	7/73	ZL 9/75
D7001	7/61	Bristol	Bristol	Old Oak	3/74	CK 7/75
D7002	7/61	Bristol	Bristol	Bristol	10/71	ZL 6/72
D7003	8/61	Bristol	Bristol	Bristol	1/72	ZL 7/72
D7004	8/61	Bristol	Bristol	Bristol	6/72	ZL 8/72
D7005	9/61	Bristol	Bristol	Bristol	7/72	ZL 10/72
D7006	10/61	Bristol	Bristol	Bristol	9/71	ZL 8/72
D7007	10/61	Bristol	Bristol	Bristol	4/72	ZL 6/72
D7008	10/61	Bristol	Bristol	Bristol	1/72	ZL 9/72
D7009	11/61	Bristol	Bristol	Old Oak	5/73	ZL 9/74
D7010	11/61	Bristol	Bristol	Old Oak	1/72	ZL 11/72
D7011	12/61	Bristol	Bristol	Old Oak	3/75	MG 1/77
D7012	12/61	Bristol	Bristol	Bristol	1/72	ZL 5/72
D7013	12/61	Bristol	Bristol	Bristol	1/72	ZL 10/72
D7014	12/61	Bristol	Bristol	Bristol	1/72	ZL 8/72
D7015	12/61	Bristol	Bristol	Old Oak	6/72	ZL 9/72
D7016	1/62	Bristol	Bristol	Old Oak	7/74	ZL 6/75
D7017	1/62	Bristol	Bristol	Old Oak	3/75	Note C
D7018	1/62	Bristol	Bristol	Old Oak	3/75	Note C
D7019	2/62	Bristol	Bristol	Old Oak	9/72	ZL 10/72
D7020	2/62	Bristol	Bristol	Bristol	2/72	ZL 9/72
D7021	2/62	Bristol	Bristol	Bristol	1/72	ZL 6/72
D7022	2/62	Cardiff	Bristol	Old Oak	3/75	CK 1/77
D7023	2/62	Bristol	Bristol	Old Oak	5/73	ZL 4/75
D7024	3/62	Cardiff	Bristol	Bristol	1/72	ZL 11/72
D7025	3/62	Cardiff	Bristol	Bristol	1/72	ZL 6/72
D7026	3/62	Bristol	Old Oak	Old Oak	10/74	CK 2/77
D7027	4/62	Bristol	Bristol	Old Oak	11/71	ZL 8/72
D7028	4/62	Cardiff	Old Oak	Old Oak	1/75	CK 2/77
D7029	4/62	Cardiff	Bristol	Old Oak	2/75	Note A
D7030	4/62	Cardiff	Bristol	Old Oak	5/73	BM 3/74

	Date to Traffic	First Allocation	Allocation as of Nov.1966	Last Allocation	Date Withdrawn	Final Disposal
D7031	4/62	Cardiff	Bristol	Old Oak	5/73	ZL 9/75
D7032	5/62	Cardiff	Bristol	Old Oak	5/73	ZL 7/75
D7033	5/62	Cardiff	Bristol	Old Oak	1/72	ZL 10/72
D7034	5/62	Cardiff	Bristol	Bristol	1/72	ZL 9/72
D7035	6/62	Cardiff	Old Oak	Old Oak	1/72	ZL 8/72
D7036	6/62	Cardiff	Old Oak	Old Oak	6/72	ZL 10/72
D7037	6/62	Cardiff	Bristol	Old Oak	9/72	ZL 11/72
D7038	6/62	Cardiff	Bristol	Bristol	7/72	ZL 5/73
D7039	6/62	Cardiff	Bristol	Bristol	6/72	ZL 8/72
D7040	7/62	Bristol	Bristol	Bristol	1/72	ZL 8/72
D7041	7/62	Bristol	Bristol	Bristol	1/72	ZL 9/72
D7042	7/62	Bristol	Bristol	Bristol	1/72	ZL 7/72
D7043	7/62	Bristol	Bristol	Bristol	1/72	ZL 8/72
D7044	8/62	Bristol	Bristol	Old Oak	5/73	BM 3/74
D7045	8/62	Bristol	Bristol	Bristol	11/72	ZL 7/73
D7046	8/62	Bristol	Bristol	Old Oak	1/72	ZL 7/72
D7047	8/62	Bristol	Bristol	Bristol	1/72	ZL 7/72
D7048	9/62	Bristol	Bristol	Old Oak	1/72	ZL 8/72
D7049	10/62	Bristol	Bristol	Old Oak	1/72	ZL 6/72
D7050	10/62	Bristol	Bristol	Bristol	1/72	ZL 6/73
D7051	10/62	Bristol	Bristol	Old Oak	1/72	ZL 6/72
D7052	10/62	Bristol	Bristol	Cardiff	11/72	ZL 5/73
D7053	10/62	Bristol	Bristol	Old Oak	1/72	ZL 7/72
D7054	11/62	Bristol	Bristol	Bristol	11/72	ZL 3/75
D7055	11/62	Bristol	Bristol	Bristol	4/73	ZL 11/75
D7056	11/62	Cardiff	Old Oak	Bristol	1/72	ZL 6/72
D7057	11/62	Cardiff	Old Oak	Bristol	1/72	ZL 9/72
D7058	11/62	Cardiff	Old Oak	Cardiff	10/71	ZL 6/72
D7059	11/62	Cardiff	Old Oak	Cardiff	10/71	ZL 7/72
D7060	12/62	Cardiff	Old Oak	Cardiff	10/71	ZL 10/72
D7061	12/62	Cardiff	Old Oak	Old Oak	1/72	ZL 7/72
D7062	1/63	Cardiff	Old Oak	Cardiff	10/71	ZL 7/72
D7063	12/62	Cardiff	Old Oak	Cardiff	10/71	ZL 10/72
D7064	1/63	Cardiff	Old Oak	Cardiff	10/71	ZL 9/72
D7065	1/63	Cardiff	Old Oak	Cardiff	10/71	ZL 9/73
D7066	1/63	Cardiff	Old Oak	Old Oak	11/71	ZL 8/72
D7067	2/63	Cardiff	Old Oak	Cardiff	10/71	ZL 7/72
D7068	2/63	Cardiff	Cardiff	Bristol	12/72	ZL 4/75
D7069	2/63	Bristol	Cardiff	Cardiff	10/71	ZL 8/72
D7070	3/63	Bristol	Cardiff	Old Oak	9/72	ZL 9/72
D7071	3/63	Bristol	Old Oak	Old Oak	1/72	ZL 9/72
D7072	3/63	Bristol	Old Oak	Cardiff	9/71	ZL 9/72
D7073	3/63	Bristol	Old Oak	Cardiff	12/71	ZL 10/72
D7074	3/63	Bristol	Cardiff	Bristol	12/72	ZL 7/75
D7075	3/63	N A	Cardiff	Bristol	5/73	BM 2/74
D7076	5/63	Old Oak	Old Oak	Bristol	5/73	Note B
D7077	12/63	Bristol	Cardiff	Bristol	7/72	ZL 10/72
D7078	5/63	Old Oak	Cardiff	Cardiff	10/71	ZL 4/72
D7079	12/63	Bristol	Cardiff	Cardiff	10/71	ZL 8/72
D7080	12/63	Cardiff	Cardiff	Bristol	11/72	ZL 5/73
D7081	12/63	Bristol	Cardiff	Cardiff	9/71	ZL 8/72
D7082	6/63	Cardiff	Cardiff	Cardiff	4/72	ZL 10/72
D7083	6/63	Cardiff	Bristol	Cardiff	10/71	ZL 9/72
D7084	6/63	Cardiff	Bristol	Cardiff	10/72	ZL 10/72
D7085	6/63	Cardiff	Cardiff	Old Oak	10/72	ZL 11/72
D7086	7/63	Cardiff	Cardiff	Cardiff	1/72	ZL 9/72
D7087	7/63	Cardiff	Cardiff	Bristol	10/72	ZL 8/73
D7088	7/63	Cardiff	Old Oak	Cardiff	1/72	ZL 10/72
D7089	7/63	Cardiff	Cardiff	Bristol	5/73	TS 2/76
D7090	9/63	Cardiff	Cardiff	Cardiff	6/72	ZL 9/72
D7091	9/63	Cardiff	Cardiff	Cardiff	8/72	ZL 9/72
D7092	12/63	Cardiff	Cardiff	Cardiff	6/72	ZL 8/72
D7093	12/63	Bristol	Cardiff	Old Oak	11/74	CK 2/77
D7094	12/63	Cardiff	Cardiff	Cardiff	11/72	ZL 7/73
D7095	12/63	Cardiff	Cardiff	Cardiff	10/72	ZL 11/72
D7096	12/63	Cardiff	Cardiff	Bristol	12/72	MG 8/85

Date to Traffic	First Allocation	Allocation as of Nov.1966	Last Allocation	Date Withdrawn	Final Disposal
D7097 12/63	Cardiff	Cardiff	Bristol	12/72	ZL 3/75
D7098 1/64	N A	Cardiff	Cardiff	12/72	ZL 3/75
D7099 1/64	N A	Cardiff	Cardiff	10/72	ZL 10/72
D7100 2/64	N A	Cardiff	Bristol	11/72	ZL 12/74

D1000 Class

Date to Traffic	First Allocation	Allocation as of Nov.1966	Last Allocation	Date Withdrawn	Final Disposal
D1000 12/61	Laira	Laira	Laira	2/74	ZL 7/74
D1001 2/62	Laira	Laira	Laira	10/76	ZL 8/77
D1002 3/62	Laira	Bristol	Laira	1/74	ZL 6/74
D1003 4/62	Laira	Laira	Laira	1/75	ZL 8/77
D1004 5/62	Laira	Laira	Laira	8/73	ZL 9/74
D1005 6/62	Laira	Laira	Laira	11/76	ZL 6/77
D1006 6/62	Laira	Bristol	Laira	4/75	ZL 4/77
D1007 8/62	Laira	Laira	Laira	1/74	ZL 2/75
D1008 9/62	Laira	Laira	Laira	10/74	ZL 9/75
D1009 9/62	Old Oak	Laira	Laira	11/76	ZL 11/78
D1010 10/62	Old Oak	Laira	Laira	2/77	Note C
D1011 10/62	Old Oak	Laira	Laira	10/75	ZL 12/78
D1012 11/62	Cardiff	Laira	Laira	11/75	ZL 4/79
D1013 12/62	Cardiff	Laira	Laira	2/77	Note A
D1014 12/62	Cardiff	Laira	Laira	8/74	ZL 2/75
D1015 1/63	Cardiff	Laira	Laira	12/76	Note D
D1016 2/63	Cardiff	Laira	Laira	2/75	ZL 7/77
D1017 3/63	Cardiff	Laira	Laira	8/73	ZL 3/75
D1018 4/63	Old Oak	Laira	Laira	6/73	ZL 3/74
D1019 5/63	Old Oak	Laira	Laira	5/73	ZL 10/74
D1020 5/63	Old Oak	Bristol	Laira	6/73	ZL 4/74
D1021 6/63	Old Oak	Bristol	Laira	8/76	ZL 2/79
D1022 7/63	Old Oak	Laira	Laira	1/77	ZL 12/78
D1023 9/63	Cardiff	Laira	Laira	2/77	Note E
D1024 10/63	Cardiff	Bristol	Laira	11/73	ZL 8/74
D1025 11/63	Cardiff	Bristol	Laira	10/75	ZL 1/79
D1026 12/63	Old Oak	Laira	Laira	10/75	ZL 7/76
D1027 1/64	Laira	Bristol	Laira	11/75	ZL 6/76
D1028 2/64	Bristol	Bristol	Laira	10/76	ZL 6/79
D1029 7/64	Bristol	Bristol	Laira	11/74	ZL 5/75
D1030 12/63	Old Oak	Bristol	Laira	4/76	ZL 9/76
D1031 12/63	Old Oak	Laira	Laira	2/75	ZL 10/76
D1032 12/63	Old Oak	Laira	Laira	5/73	ZL 11/74
D1033 1/64	Old Oak	Laira	Laira	9/76	ZL 4/79
D1034 4/64	Bristol	Laira	Laira	10/75	ZL 1/79
D1035 7/62	Laira	Laira	Laira	1/75	ZL 9/76
D1036 8/62	Laira	Laira	Laira	11/76	ZL 2/77
D1037 8/62	Laira	Laira	Laira	5/76	ZL 2/77
D1038 9/62	Laira	Laira	Laira	10/73	ZL 11/74
D1039 9/62	Laira	Laira	Laira	7/74	ZL 8/74
D1040 9/62	Old Oak	Laira	Laira	2/76	ZL 8/76
D1041 10/62	Old Oak	Bristol	Laira	2/77	Note B
D1042 10/62	Old Oak	Laira	Laira	7/74	ZL 5/75
D1043 10/62	Old Oak	Bristol	Laira	4/76	ZL 2/77
D1044 11/62	Cardiff	Laira	Laira	2/75	ZL 9/75
D1045 12/62	Bristol	Laira	Laira	12/74	ZL 8/75
D1046 12/62	Bristol	Laira	Laira	12/75	ZL 11/76
D1047 2/63	Cardiff	Laira	Laira	2/76	ZL 8/76
D1048 12/62	Cardiff	Laira	Laira	2/77	Note F
D1049 12/62	Cardiff	Laira	Laira	4/76	ZL 1/77
D1050 1/63	Cardiff	Laira	Laira	4/75	ZL 3/76
D1051 1/63	Cardiff	Laira	Laira	9/76	ZL 7/77
D1052 2/63	Cardiff	Laira	Laira	10/75	ZL 4/76
D1053 2/63	Old Oak	Bristol	Laira	11/76	ZL 6/77
D1054 3/63	Cardiff	Laira	Laira	11/76	ZL 5/77
D1055 3/63	Cardiff	Laira	Laira	1/76	ZL 6/76
D1056 3/63	Cardiff	Laira	Laira	12/76	ZL 5/79
D1057 4/63	N A	Laira	Laira	5/76	ZL 6/77
D1058 3/63	Bristol	Laira	Laira	1/77	ZL 6/79
D1059 4/63	Cardiff	Laira	Laira	10/75	ZL 7/76
D1060 4/63	Old Oak	Laira	Laira	11/73	ZL 6/74
D1061 4/63	Old Oak	Laira	Laira	10/74	ZL 8/75
D1062 5/63	Old Oak	Laira	Laira	8/74	Note A
D1063 5/63	Old Oak	Laira	Laira	4/76	ZL 8/77
D1064 5/63	Cardiff	Laira	Laira	12/75	ZL 7/77
D1065 6/63	Old Oak	Laira	Laira	11/76	ZL 8/77
D1066 6/63	Cardiff	Laira	Laira	11/74	ZL 4/75
D1067 7/63	Cardiff	Laira	Laira	1/76	ZL 9/76
D1068 7/63	Old Oak	Laira	Laira	10/76	ZL 8/77
D1069 10/63	Cardiff	Laira	Laira	10/75	ZL 1/77
D1070 10/63	Cardiff	Laira	Laira	12/76	ZL 5/79
D1071 11/63	Old Oak	Bristol	Laira	12/76	ZL 11/78
D1072 11/63	Old Oak	Laira	Laira	11/76	ZL 3/77
D1073 12/63	Old Oak	Laira	Laira	8/74	ZL 7/75

D9500 Class

Date to Traffic	First Allocation	Allocation as of Nov.1966	Last Allocation	Date Withdrawn	Final Disposal
D9500 7/64	Bristol	Bristol	Cardiff	4/69	Note G
D9501 7/64	Cardiff	Bristol	Landore	3/68	CB 12/68
D9502 7/64	Bristol	Bristol	Cardiff	4/69	Note G
D9503 7/64	Bristol	Bristol	Hull	4/68	BSC 9/80
D9504 7/64	Bristol	Bristol	Hull	4/68	Note H
D9505 7/64	Bristol	Bristol	Hull	4/68	Note I
D9506 8/64	Worcester	Cardiff	Cardiff	3/68	AY 3/70
D9507 8/64	Worcester	Cardiff	Hull	4/68	SE 9/82
D9508 8/64	Worcester	Landore	Cardiff	10/68	DS 1/84
D9509 9/64	Worcester	Landore	Cardiff	10/68	CK 2/71
D9510 9/64	Cardiff	Cardiff	Hull	4/68	SE 8/82
D9511 9/64	Cardiff	Landore	Hull	4/68	NCB 7/79
D9512 9/64	Cardiff	Cardiff	Hull	4/68	BSC 2/82
D9513 10/64	Cardiff	Cardiff	Cardiff	3/68	Note J
D9514 10/64	Cardiff	Cardiff	Cardiff	4/69	NCB 6/85
D9515 10/64	Cardiff	Cardiff	Hull	4/68	Note K
D9516 10/64	Cardiff	Landore	Hull	4/68	Note L
D9517 10/64	Cardiff	Bristol	Cardiff	10/68	DS 1/84
D9518 10/64	Cardiff	Cardiff	Cardiff	4/69	Note M
D9519 11/64	Cardiff	Cardiff	Landore	10/68	CK 1/71
D9520 11/64	Cardiff	Cardiff	Hull	4/68	Note M
D9521 11/64	Old Oak	Bristol	Landore	4/69	Note N
D9522 11/64	Old Oak	Bristol	Cardiff	12/67	AY 8/68
D9523 12/64	Old Oak	Bristol	Hull	4/68	Note L
D9524 12/64	Old Oak	Bristol	Landore	4/69	Note O
D9525 1/65	Bristol	Bristol	Hull	4/68	Note H
D9526 1/65	Bristol	Bristol	Cardiff	11/68	Note C
D9527 1/65	Bristol	Bristol	Cardiff	4/69	DS1/84
D9528 1/65	Bristol	Cardiff	Cardiff	9/68	NCB du
D9529 1/65	Cardiff	Landore	Hull	4/68	Note L
D9530 2/65	Cardiff	Cardiff	Cardiff	10/68	NCB du
D9531 2/65	Cardiff	Bristol	Cardiff	12/67	Note B
D9532 2/65	Cardiff	Cardiff	Hull	4/68	BSC 2/82
D9533 2/65	Cardiff	Cardiff	Hull	4/68	SE 9/82
D9534 3/65	Cardiff	Cardiff	Hull	4/68	SB du
D9535 3/65	Cardiff	Bristol	Cardiff	12/68	DS 1/84
D9536 3/65	Cardiff	Landore	Landore	4/69	NCB du
D9537 3/65	Cardiff	Cardiff	Hull	4/68	Note P
D9538 3/65	Cardiff	Cardiff	Landore	4/69	SE 9/82
D9539 4/65	Cardiff	Cardiff	Hull	4/68	Note P
D9540 4/65	Cardiff	Cardiff	Hull	4/68	DS 1/84
D9541 4/65	Cardiff	Cardiff	Hull	4/68	SE 8/82
D9542 5/65	Cardiff	Landore	Hull	4/68	SE 8/82
D9543 5/65	Cardiff	Landore	Hull	4/68	CB 12/68
D9544 5/65	Cardiff	Landore	Hull	4/68	BSC 9/80
D9545 6/65	Landore	Landore	Hull	4/68	NCB 7/79
D9546 6/65	Cardiff	Landore	Hull	4/68	CB 12/68
D9547 7/65	Cardiff	Landore	Hull	4/68	SE 8/82
D9548 7/65	Cardiff	Cardiff	Hull	4/68	Note K
D9549 8/65	Cardiff	Cardiff	Hull	4/68	Note K

	Date to Traffic	First Allocation	Allocation as of Nov. 1966	Last Allocation	Date Withdrawn	Final Disposal
D9550	8/65	Cardiff	Cardiff	Hull	4/68	CB 12/68
D9551	9/65	Cardiff	Cardiff	Hull	4/68	*Note C*
D9552	9/65	Cardiff	Cardiff	Hull	4/68	BSC 9/80
D9553	9/65	Bristol	Bristol	Hull	4/68	*Note P*
D9554	10/65	Bristol	Bristol	Hull	4/68	SE 8/82
D9555	10/65	Bristol	Bristol	Landore	4/69	*Note M*

Notes

Allocation as of November 1966: only a short period elapsed during which the WR's entire mainline diesel-hydraulic fleet was in capital stock, namely between the delivery of D9555 in October 1965 and the withdrawal of D600-4/6301/9522/31 in December 1967. Given that the detailed allocation history of the diesel-hydraulics is too complex to be documented within this volume, it has been decided to select a suitable point in time to illustrate the distribution of the WR fleet at its height. November 1966 has been chosen both as the approximate middle point of this period, as well as the final month that all the D9500s were in WR stock prior to the commencement of transfers to the Eastern Region.

Last Allocation: refers to the last depot at which the locomotive was officially allocated, rather than sites used for storage after withdrawal.

Final Disposal: refers to the ultimate fate or present status of the locomotive concerned. All entries indicate scrapping unless stated otherwise, the dates referring to the actual date of scrapping rather than sale for scrap. The suffix 'du' after a disposal code indicates that the precise date of scrapping remains unknown.

Prior to 1970 or thereabouts, nearly all withdrawn WR diesel locomotives were offered for sale by tender and eventually disposed of to private scrap dealers. After this date, coincident with the formation of British Rail Engineering Ltd, the WR's redundant locomotives were mainly broken-up at Swindon Works. This had two benefits; of preserving employment at a time when little construction work was being directed there, and of simplifying the salvage of engine and transmission components required by those locomotives still in traffic.

Disposals of whole locomotives to private scrap merchants after this date mainly concern locomotives taken into Departmental service after withdrawal and those D9500s sold for further service to industrial concerns. D801/2/48 were dismantled in the traditional manner in Swindon's 'C' Shop, but were almost certainly the only diesel-hydraulics to be so treated. Subsequent withdrawals were stripped in the main erecting shop before being cut-up in the old wood yard and 'Dump' areas, often being broken-down into quite large sections which were then sold on in bulk to commercial scrap dealers, hence sightings of identifiable compo-

nents at other locations on subsequent dates. The onward disposal of scrap material from BREL Swindon in this manner is not recorded.

A full list of codes used is given below:

AY; Arnott Young, Rotherham, Yorkshire
BM; Bird's Commercial Motors, Long Marston, Warwickshire
BN; J. Buttigieg, Newport, Monmouthshire
BSC; Dismantled on site at Corby by the British Steel Corporation
CB; C.F. Booth, Rotherham, Yorkshire
CK; George Cohen, Kettering, Northamptonshire
CN; John Cashmore, Newport, Monmouthshire
CS; George Cohen, Morriston, Swansea
DS; Dismantled on site at NCB Ashington by D. Short
MG; Marple & Gillott, Attercliffe, Sheffield
NCB; Dismantled on site at Ashington by the National Coal Board
SB; Sold for further use to NV Sobemai, Bruges, Belgium, 1975. Resold for use in Italy and since reported scrapped
SE; Dismantled on site at BSC Corby by Shanks & McEwan
TS; T.J Thomson, Stockton-on-Tees
WB; Woodham Brothers, Barry, Glamorgan
ZL; BR (BREL after 1/70) Swindon Works

Notes/Abbreviations

N A Newton Abbot

A) Preserved on the Severn Valley Railway
B) Preserved on the East Lancashire Railway
C) Preserved on the West Somerset Railway
D) Preserved at Old Oak Common Depot
E) Preserved at the National Railway Museum, York
F) Preserved at the Railway Age, Crewe
G) Preserved on the South Yorkshire Railway
H) Preserved on the Kent & East Sussex Railway
I) Exported to NV Sobemai, Bruges, Belgium in May 1975 but later resold. Still extant in seasonal industrial use at Moorbeek-Waas, Ghent, Belgium in 1995
J) Preserved on the Embsay Steam Railway
K) Sold for further use to Bilbao, Spain, in 1981 Reported still intact near Madrid in 1995
L) Preserved on the Nene Valley Railway
M) Preserved at the Rutland Railway Museum
N) Preserved on the Swanage Railway
O) Preserved on the Bo'ness & Kinneil Railway
P) Preserved on the Gloucestershire-Warwickshire Railway

WR Diesel-Hydraulics in Departmental Use

D832

Dead Load for Railway Technical Centre, Derby from January 1973. Based at the RTC's Old Dalby test track from October 1974 until June 1979. Departmental number 97 401 allocated but not taken-up.

(N.B. The official function of this locomotive in RTC service was as a dead load for developing and testing materials used in track construction, but some sources indicate that it may have been used as a mobile generator at Old Dalby for some while. The locomotive's diesel-hydraulic format would not be best-suited to such deployment and indeed, the abortive allocation of Departmental number 97 401 would rather tend to indicate that, for a time at least, the intention was to restore D832 to full operational status as motive power for RTC test trains. The eventual choice was a Class 24 diesel-electric.)

D844

Temporary train-heating plant at Worcester between October and November 1971. Not taken into Departmental stock.

D7055

Train-heating plant at Bristol Marsh Junction between April 1973 and September 1975. Allocated Departmental number DB968004, although this identity was never carried

D7076

Dead Load for Railway Technical Centre, Derby from August 1974. Based at the RTC's Old Dalby test track from October 1974 until circa 1978 when returned to the RTC at Derby. Dumped out of use at Old Dalby in May 1979, withdrawn from RTC service during 1980. No Departmental number.

D7089

Train-heating plant at Laira between November 1974 and February 1976. Allocated Departmental number TDB968005, although this identity never carried.

D7096

Dead Load for Railway Technical Centre, Derby from August 1974. Based at the RTC's Old Dalby test track from October 1974 until circa 1978 when returned to the RTC at Derby. Dumped out of use at Old Dalby in May 1979, withdrawn from RTC service during 1980. No Departmental number.

D1034

Train-heating plant at Laira between October 1975 and September 1976. Not taken into Departmental stock.

Some components from withdrawn WR diesel-hydraulics remained in service of one kind or another long after the locomotive had ceased to exist as an entity in its own right, usually at depots or in Swindon Works. Examples included a pair of 'Hymek' bogies at Old Oak Common repair shops, used as 'slaves' for locomotives whose own bogies were under repair, and the train-heating boiler from a North British Type 2 retained at Newton Abbot as a steam generator for cleaning purposes.

D818 was retained as a source of spares after withdrawal in November 1972, initially for those Class 42s left in service then subsequently for D832 at Old Dalby. Little if anything was removed for D832 and D818 eventually became an unofficial exhibition piece outside BREL Swindon, being repainted by works apprentices on at least two occasions. It was never taken into Departmental stock and therefore not renumbered, its official status being 'In Store'. Quantities of engines and transmissions were also retained at Swindon for some years after the cessation of the diesel-hydraulic programme, though whether these were intended as a source of spares for those locomotives preserved or were merely awaiting sale for scrap is no longer possible to ascertain.

Appendix Five

THE HYBRIDS

As mentioned in Chapter 2, lightweight quick-running diesel engines, hydraulic transmissions and the Krauss-Maffei design of stressed-skin body structure were not mutually inclusive, although their combination did confer advantages which formed the cornerstones of the WR's original plans. Inevitably, some of these concepts were evaluated by the British railway industry and proposed for, and in some cases used in the fulfilment of BR orders. Whilst not actually part of the WR diesel-hydraulic story, the five examples below are most certainly relevant to it and so deserve at least a few words in explanation.

North British Diesel-Electric Bo-Bos, D6100-57.

Ten of these locomotives were delivered under the provisions of the Pilot Scheme as direct counterparts of D6300-5 and intended to share as many components as possible. In particular, the MAN L12V18/21S engines were identical although coupled to GEC electric transmission. Very little else was shared, however, as the design ran on Commonwealth bogies and used a bodyshell which, whilst similar to that of the diesel-hydraulic's, was several feet longer and arguably, all the better-looking for it. The locomotives were initially allocated to Eastern Region sheds in the London area for Great Northern suburban duties and despite some problems with the engine to generator coupling, performed well enough for the BTC to order some forty-eight production examples. The first of these were also allocated to the Eastern Region at Stratford and Ipswich but the last twenty were delivered to Scottish Region sheds at Kittybrewster (Aberdeen) and Edinburgh St Margaret's. The early promise of the design was not to be fulfilled and the type continued to suffer from problems with both the engine-generator coupling and the braking system. These were quickly accompanied by the various failings which the Western Region had found endemic in the NBL-assembled MAN L12V18/21B engines, especially chronic oil leakage which imbued the locomotives with incendiary tendencies when stray oil found its way into the main generator. The Eastern Region soon disposed of its entire stock of D6100s to the Scottish Region, where their deployment on light duties still failed to avert a repetition of those problems experienced on the ER. Despite this, the locomotives were basically well-made and in terms of their general size and capacity ideal for many of the Scottish Region's second-rank duties. Therefore, in an attempt to address at least some of the greatest difficulties, it was decided during the mid-1960s to rebuild twenty D6100s to incorporate various improvements, chief of which was the replacement of the MAN engine with a twelve-cylinder Paxman 'Ventura' engine of 1350bhp, a close relative of the YJXL described in Chapters 6 and 10. The rebuilds were little if any better than the original design and after spending long periods in store, the entire class was withdrawn by the end of 1971. Despite their obvious similarities (and differences) no serious attempt was made to compare the type with its diesel-hydraulic counterpart, either before or after rebuilding.

The 'Blue Pullmans'.

During 1959, Metropolitan-Cammell of Birmingham was awarded a contract to supply British Railways with five diesel-electric multiple-unit Pullman sets, two six-car units for the London Midland Region and three eight-car units for the Western Region. Their justification lay in the need for the railways to compete with developing airline and motorway coach services by offering rapid, luxurious trains aimed at the business sector, and their origins almost certainly in the diesel-hydraulic multiple-unit proposals examined by the WR in 1955. By the time of the BTC's interest, however (itself largely prompted by the vision and enthusiasm of a solitary part-time Member of the Commission, one H.P. Barker), these had been influenced by such varied machinery as the Dutch/Swiss 'Trans-Europ Express' sets and the American 'Train X' formations promoted by Robert Young and Patrick McGinnis on the New York Central and New Haven Railroads respectively. Although the make-up of the two types of 'Blue Pullman' set varied slightly, both shared a common design of power car at each end, containing a NBL-supplied but German-built MAN L12V18/21B engine coupled to GEC electric transmission units of different type to those in the D6100s. Interestingly, only the rear bogies of the driving cars were powered, joined by the leading bogies of the adjacent saloon car, power being transmitted through jumper cables. The LMR Manchester-St Pancras 'Midland Pullman' entered service in July 1960, to be followed in September by the WR's 'Birmingham Pullman', 'Bristol Pullman' and 'South Wales Pullman'. Although some considerable problems were experienced with the riding of the Schlieren bogies, especially those carrying traction motors, the sets were basically a reliable and attractive mode of travel. The engines in particular gave much better results than their counterparts fitted to the NBL locomotives, their German build and conservative rating (1000bhp at 1445rpm) probably being the deciding factor in this respect. Operationally, however, the 'Blue Pullmans' multiple-unit configuration made the sets relatively inflexible and, as a result, caused problems when traffic patterns changed. Their initial deployment was also the cause of a drawn-out dispute between the BTC and the National Union of Railwaymen regarding the status and remuneration of the stewards and catering staff whose responsibility the new services would be. The completion of the LMR electrification as far as Manchester saw both the 'Midland Pullman' and the 'Birmingham Pullman' discontinued from the spring of 1967, the displaced sets being allotted to extra South Wales services although rarely in full use. Though some argued the case for just such a utilisation, the 'Blue Pullmans' were never put to regular use on trains between Paddington and the South-West due to fears of traction motor overheating on the South Devon banks. Although the sets did occasionally work as far as Plymouth on excursion trains, they were always piloted west of Exeter so as to reduce the load on their electrical equipment. Despite their good mechanical record (perhaps the best of all MAN engines on BR), the units' use on the WR continued to decline and the type as a whole was withdrawn in May 1973, a victim of the general contraction of Pullman services on British Rail.

Proposed English Electric Type 3 Diesel-Hydraulic B-B.

English Electric was one of BR's main suppliers of diesel and electric locomotives during the 1950s and 1960s, and it would be the EE 1750bhp Co-Co design that would become BR's standard Type 3 diesel-electric. Prior to its acceptance however, EE had submitted some other designs, included in which were a number of diesel-hydraulics equipped with Mekydro transmission and intended for the Western Region. Whilst these were not pursued by either party, in 1958 EE more seriously proposed a smaller B-B design based around twin

Napier 'Deltic' T9 engines of nine cylinders and 850bhp apiece, each coupled to a Mekydro transmission. Of 1700bhp and 74 tons all-up weight the design would have made quite an impressive performer, but nothing more was to come of the proposal. Sadly, nothing further is known and in correspondence with the author some years ago GEC-Paxman Diesels, current manufacturers of the 'Deltic' engine range, stated that they were no longer able to provide any details. However, a general arrangement drawing *is* reproduced in *The Deltic Locomotives of British Rail* by the late Brian Webb (David and Charles, 1982) for the benefit of those interested in might-have-beens. It shows what appears to be a conventional girder-frame superstructure but, interestingly enough, one which rides on bogies which are either of the the outside-frame K-M type used on that firm's ML2200 demonstrator, or to the Wegmann pattern which BR tried under passenger coaches for a few years. The drawing as reproduced in that text is, unfortunately, incomplete and it is therefore impossible to be categoric in the absence of additional information. The story has an interesting sequel; when during the mid-1960s G.F.Fiennes was in charge of the Western Region, he responded to the problem of implementing service accelerations west of Exeter by requesting permission to test one of the Eastern Region's 3300bhp 'Deltic' Type 5 Co-Cos over the South Devon banks. Not surprisingly, he was refused.

Brush Diesel-Electric Co-Co, D0280 *Falcon.*

As well as being a locomotive manufacturer in its own right, Brush of Loughborough was an important supplier of electrical equipment for diesel locomotives and was heavily involved in equipping the WR's D1000 and D7000 designs. As part of the Hawker-Siddeley combine, Brush also had close links with Bristol-Siddeley Engines, Maybach's UK licensee for diesel engines, and saw the MD-series as a possible answer to the problem of building a high-power diesel-electric with a relatively low overall weight. Encouraged by a bouyant order book, Brush decided to acquire a pair of intercooled MD655s during 1961, to be built into a prototype locomotive conforming to BR's latest Type 4 specification. Weight saving was a major priority in the design and, acting on advice from colleagues in Hawker-Siddeley's aircraft factories, Brush's engineers created a completely new stressed-skin monocoque superstructure for their locomotive. Of Hirondelle Truss design, this had a conventional girder underframe but of much lighter construction than normal, the necessary rigidity being contributed by the integral load-bearing body. The result was arguably stronger than a conventional strength-frame and significantly lighter, although not quite so light as the K-M structures. Within this body were situated the Maybach engines, each coupled to a Brush generator specifically designed for this application. The locomotive rode on cast steel Commonwealth bogies, the three traction motors on each being fed by the engine and generator set above. Outshopped in December 1961, named *Falcon*, and with its makers hopeful of an order for series production, the locomotive was placed on loan to BR and numbered D0280 in that organisation's experimental series. Its first allocation was to the Western Region where it was subjected to various dynamometer car trials and comparisons with the D1000 'Western' which, of course, used similar engines. During these, *Falcon* recorded a very creditable 70,300lbs of tractive effort, although the 2800bhp, 115-ton locomotive was officially rated at 60,000lbs maximum. After only a few months, however, D0280 was transferred to the Eastern Region for use on both freight and passenger trains and although a good performer, the ER had comparatively little work with which to stretch its capabilities. By this time, BR had been sufficiently impressed

by the Brush monocoque superstructure to order a batch of Sulzer-engined diesel-electrics constructed on similar lines, the first of the D1500 type, and so *Falcon* became an evolutionary dead-end. Despite this, its capabilities were such as to secure BR's approval for its continued service under a hire agreement, subject to certain conditions. D0280 was therefore overhauled at Loughborough and returned to the Western Region early in 1965. Working mostly passenger trains, it suffered the normal cooling system problems with its Maybach engines but steadily improved until by 1968 it was returning over 90,000 miles per annum. Even so, there were always maintenance difficulties caused by the fact that the MD655 engines had been adapted to couple up to electrical generators, and so were not directly interchangeable with the units fitted to the D1000s (although many smaller components were). During that year it was decided to withdraw the locomotive from traffic but following negotiations with Brush, BR instead purchased the locomotive for £20,000, overhauled it and equipped it for dual braking. *Falcon* then had the distinction of being the only one of the four experimental mainline diesels of the 1960s to enter BR capital stock. Repainted in BR blue and renumbered 1200 (although still bearing its nameplates), the sole Class 53 was returned to passenger and latterly freight duties, being withdrawn in late 1975 after a traction motor failure, having accumulated over half a million miles in service. Despite not being chosen as a standard design, *Falcon* represented a milestone in its adoption of monocoque construction for diesel-electric locomotives in Britain, and pioneered many of the most successful features of the D1500 which succeeded it in the scheme of things at Loughborough. It also demonstrated that the Maybach diesels were capable of giving good service although oddly enough, their reliability record was much better during the locomotive's sojourn on the Eastern Region than at any other time. Presumably, once back on the WR familiarity bred contempt, and as the care shown towards a special prototype deteriorated to the same level of attention given to the WR diesel-hydraulics, then so did the typical malaises affecting the Maybach engines become evident.

Proposed Type 4 Diesel-Electric Co-Co, BR Crewe.

A fascinating snippet is contained in *Sulzer Diesel Locomotives of British Rail* (David & Charles, 1978) in which the late Brian Webb made reference to a proposal to build some fifty-nine diesel-electric locomotives at Crewe, based on the D1000 design. This occurred around 1960/61 when the BTC, despite its inherent dislike of quick-running engines, had concluded that it was imperative for future Type 4 construction to offer significantly superior power:weight ratios compared with the existing Derby/Sulzer and EE designs. In addition, a Co-Co wheel arrangement was desired due to the various difficulties encountered with the 1Co-Co1 layout, and the D1000's light weight, high power and compact dimensions provided a tantalising example of what could be produced. Nothing further of the proposal is known, but it is most logical to assume that any such locomotive would have used the same type of engine/transmission groups as featured in D0280 *Falcon* within an adaptation of the existing D1000 bodyshell. This would certainly have made economic sense from BR's point of view as it would have allowed Crewe Works to have made further use of the experience and knowledge of techniques subsequently gained from the construction of forty-four D1000s for the WR between 1962 and 1964. However, the Eastern Region in particular objected to the proposal, and it seems to have lapsed once BR reached agreement with Brush for the building under license of D1500s at Crewe.

Appendix Six
SELECTED BIBLIOGRAPHY

As stated in the Introduction, the scope of this book is necessarily a limited one, although a wide range of sources has been consulted by the author in the process of research. Although all are worthy of consultation by the interested student of locomotive design, it would be remiss not to make special mention of the late Brian Reed's *Diesel-Hydraulic Locomotives of the Western Region* (David & Charles, 1975). Having had the benefit of some personal involvement in the episode, Mr Reed's narrative was the first to relate the truth behind the WR's adoption and use of diesel-hydraulic traction, as opposed to the propaganda of those having vested interests in dismissing the venture as a simple function of Swindon's contrariness, and after twenty years it remains the standard work on the subject. The present author willingly acknowledges a considerable debt to the writings of the late Mr Reed for providing the impetus behind the production of the present volume, and the fact that many of the conclusions and opinions expressed within this book, based on extensive independent research, are nonetheless shared with those contained in the earlier work, stands as tribute to Mr Reed's painstaking investigation and incisive analysis.

However, the excellence of this text notwithstanding, there have been some very worthy books and articles on the subject published by other authors over the years, a selection of which appears below. Each item is unreservedly commended to those in search of further information on the WR diesel-hydraulics, their ancestry, and their careers on British Railways:

Haresnape, Brian; **British Rail Fleet Survey 2: Western Region Diesel-Hydraulics;** Ian Allan, 1982

Endacott, Geoff; **'Westerns', 'Warships' and 'Hymeks' At Work;** Ian Allan, 1988

Birt, David; **The Class 52s - A Tribute to the 'Westerns';** Oxford Publishing Company, 1988

Marsden, Colin, and Collins, M.J.; **Modern Railways Pictorial Profile 8: The 'Hymeks';** Ian Allan, 1985

Marsden, Colin, and Faulkner, J.N.; **Modern Railways Pictorial Profile 12: The 'Warships';** Ian Allan, 1986

Bradley, Rodger P.; **Giants of Steam: The Full Story of the North British Locomotive Co. Ltd;** Oxford Publishing Company, 1995

Hills, R.L., and Patrick, D.; **Beyer-Peacock: Locomotive Builders to the World;** Transport Publishing Company, 1982

Report on Diesel-Electric and Diesel-Hydraulic Locomotives on British Railways; Department of the Chief Engineer (Traction and Rolling Stock), British Railways Board, 1965

The Maybach Tunnel Engine in Diesel Railway Traction, March 1954

Mekydro Hydraulic Transmission in Diesel Railway Traction, April 1960

The Present Status of the Mekydro Hydraulic Transmission in Maybach Information No.MM6119, July 1965

Der Einsatz von Dieselhydraulische Streckenlokomotiven in England in Maybach-Mitteilungen, November 1962 (**Diesel-Hydraulic Traction** in England in Maybach Mercedes-Benz Information No.6428, August 1968)

In addition, the following works provide a useful background to dieselisation on British Railways in general, and on the Western Region in particular:

Russell, J.H.; **Great Western Diesel Railcars;** Wild Swan Publications Ltd, 1985

Robertson, Kevin; **The Great Western Railway Gas Turbines; A Myth Exposed;** Alan Sutton, 1989

Freeman-Allen, G; **The Western Since 1948;** Ian Allan, 1979

Heaps, Chris; **Western Region in the 1960s;** Ian Allan, 1981

Griffiths, Denis; **Locomotive Engineers of the GWR;** Patrick Stephens Ltd, 1987

Rogers, Colonel H.C.B.; **Transition from Steam;** Ian Allan, 1980

Bonavia, Michael R.; **British Rail - The First 25 Years;** David & Charles, 1981

Gourvish, T.R.; **British Railways 1948-73 - A Business History;** Cambridge University Press, 1986

Peck, A.S.; **The Great Western at Swindon Works;** Oxford Publishing Company, 1983

Leigh, Chris; **The Western Before Beeching;** Ian Allan, 1990

Tufnell, Robert; **Prototype Locomotives;** David & Charles, 1985

The Modernisation and Re-equipment of British Railways; British Transport Commission, 1955

Diesel Performance on British Railways in The Railway Gazette, 3 September 1965

The range of literature documenting the work of diesel-hydraulics abroad is a very wide one, but in the context of this work the following items are likely to be of especial interest:

Bretschneider, Arno; **Die Baureihe V200.0;** Eisenbahn-Kurier Verlag, 1981

Garmany, John Bonds; **Southern Pacific Dieselization;** Pacific Fast Mail, 1985

Demitrijevic, D; **2200HP Locomotives in Jugoslavia** in Diesel Railway Traction, January 1958

Felgner, Friedrich Wilhelm; **Die Diesellokomotive V200 im Güterzugdienst** in Eisenbahntechnische Rundschau, Issue 9, 1958

Flemming, Dr Friedrich; **Die Neue Grossdiesellokomotive der Deutschen Bundesbahn, Baureihe V200, im Regeldienst** in Eisenbahntechnische Rundschau, Issue 6, 1954

Gaebler, Gustav Adolf; **Diesel Locomotive Traction in Germany** in Diesel Railway Traction, May 1963

Lampe, Kurt; **Die Dieselhydraulische Lokomotive V200.1 der Deutschen Bundesbahn** in Glasers Annalen Issue 5/1963, reprinted in Krauss-Maffei Informationen No.267

Lampe, Kurt; **Die 6-achsige Diesel-Lokomotive Bauart ML3000** in Motortechnische Zeitschrift Issue 6, Volume 21, June 1960

Lampe, Kurt; **Die dieselhydraulischen 4000-PSLokomotiven der Spanischen Staatsbahn (RENFE)** in Glasers Annalen Volume 92, Issues 6 & 10, 1968

Lampe, Kurt, and Pflug, Erhard; **Die 1000-PS Diesel-lokomotive der Deutschen Bundesbahn für leichten Strecken- und schweren rangierdienst** in Glasers Annalen Issue 4, 1952

Lampe, Kurt, and Gössl, Nikolaus; **Die 2000-PSDiesel-lokomotive der Deutschen Bundesbahn** in Eisenbahntechnische Rundschau Issues 6 & 7, 1953

Morgan, David P; **American-Made Diesels: Guilty or Innocent?** in Trains, June 1961

Morgan, David P; **The Semmering Story** in Trains, October 1961

Pflug, Erhard; **Die Betriebliche Bewährung der V200-Diesellokomotiven der Deutschen Bundesbahn** in Glasers Annalen Volu me 82, Issue 4, 1958

Schüttel, F; **Eine Hydraulische Kraftübertragung für hohe Motorliestungen** in Motortechnische Zeitschrift Volume 21, 1960

Spark, Robert; **Diesels of Mixed Parentage in Trains,** January 1961

Powerful Locomotive on Mountain Grades in Diesel Railway Traction, November 1957

Performance of 3000HP Locomotive in Diesel Railway Traction, October 1959

Below: Whilst much legend has been built up around the feats of the locomotives themselves, human involvement was important too. At Penzance station on 23 April 1976, No.1001 *Western Pathfinder* buffers up to the 10.12 relief train to Derby. *(J.C. Hillmer)*

Beyond the above, a vast amount of information can, and for the purposes of this work has been gleaned from the railway press, manufacturers' archival and technical literature, and contemporary publicity material. A further vital source has been the official BTC, BRB and WR records pertaining to the diesel-hydraulic era, a reasonable proportion of which have been preserved in the archives of the National Railway Museum at York and the Public Record Office at Kew. Some material specifically concerned with the production and maintenance of diesel-hydraulic locomotives at Swindon is held in the archives of that town's Great Western Railway Museum though, at the time of going to press, these records were temporarily unavailable for public inspection. The same unfortunately applies to the Western Region photographic archives which, although part of the National Collection, are presently stored at a location remote from the NRM at York. With regard to those locomotives built by private contractors on behalf of the WR, the surviving records of the Beyer-Peacock company are held by the Museum of Science & Industry in Manchester, though sadly these appear to hold little if any information on the construction of the 'Hymeks'. The North British Locomotive Company is better served, with surviving photographic archives and order books being held by the Mitchell Library in Glasgow. The University of Glasgow acts as custodian for many general arrangement drawings appertaining to NBL's later products, whilst the NRM holds a number of files of NBL/WR correspondence regarding the diesel-hydraulics as part of its Brian Webb Collection.

Sources have been cross-referenced as far as possible and responsibility for any errors that remain, along with any unattributed opinions expressed, may be considered to lie with the author alone.

INDEX

Only principal points in the main text are indexed. Due to their constant repetition throughout the text, references to BR, the BRB, the BTC and the WR are not recorded.